# System in Systemic Functional Linguistics

# Key Concepts in Systemic Functional Linguistics

Series Editors
**Gerard O'Grady**, Cardiff University
**Rebekah Wegener**, University of Salzburg
**Tom Bartlett**, University of Glasgow

Books in this series provide monographic treatments of core theoretical concepts within Systemic Functional Linguistics, together with coverage of more recent concerns in Systemic Functional Linguistic theory and important areas of application and trans-disciplinary collaboration.

Each monograph is organized around a description of the historical factors that led to the emergence of the concept within Systemic Functional Linguistics and a detailed theoretical description of the concept within the overall architecture of the theory.

## Published

*Neo-Firthian Approaches to Linguistic Typology*
William B. McGregor

*Systemic Functional Translation Studies: Theoretical Insights and New Directions*
Bo Wang and Yuanyi Ma

*Verbal Art and Systemic Functional Linguistics*
Donna R. Miller

# System in Systemic Functional Linguistics
A System-based Theory of Language

### Christian M.I.M. Matthiessen

SHEFFIELD UK   BRISTOL CT

Published by Equinox Publishing Ltd.
UK: Office 415, The Workstation, 15 Paternoster Row, Sheffield, South Yorkshire S1 2BX
USA: ISD, 70 Enterprise Drive, Bristol, CT 06010

www.equinoxpub.com

First published 2023

© Christian M.I.M. Matthiessen 2023

All rights reserved. No part of this publication may be reproduced or transmitted in any form or by any means, electronic or mechanical, including photocopying, recording or any information storage or retrieval system, without prior permission in writing from the publishers.

British Library Cataloguing-in-Publication Data

A catalogue record for this book is available from the British Library.

ISBN-13   978 1 78179 901 7   (hardback)
          978 1 78179 902 4   (paperback)
          978 1 78179 903 1   (ePDF)
          978 1 80050 260 4   (ePub)

Library of Congress Cataloging-in-Publication Data

Names: Matthiessen, Christian M. I. M., author.
Title: System in systemic functional linguistics : a system-based theory of language / Christian M.I.M. Matthiessen.
Description: Sheffield, South Yorkshire ; Bristol, CT : Equinox Publishing Ltd., 2023. | Series: Key concepts in systemic functional linguistics | Includes bibliographical references and index. | Summary: «This book introduces the notion of system as the foundation of the systemic functional architecture of language, relating the general notion of system in systems thinking (holistic approaches) to the principle that language is organised as a system of systems (the polysystemic principle) and, by another step, to the technical sense of system in SFL as the basic category of paradigmatic patterning - i.e. the organisation of language as a resource for making meaning"-- Provided by publisher.
Identifiers: LCCN 2022008871 (print) | LCCN 2022008872 (ebook) | ISBN 9781781799017 (hardback) | ISBN 9781781799024 (paperback) | ISBN 9781781799031 (pdf) | ISBN 9781800502604 (epub)
Subjects: LCSH: Systemic grammar. | Functionalism (Linguistics)
Classification: LCC P149 .M38 2022 (print) | LCC P149 (ebook) | DDC 415.01/833--dc23/eng/20220307
LC record available at https://lccn.loc.gov/2022008871
LC ebook record available at https://lccn.loc.gov/2022008872

Typeset by S.J.I. Services, New Delhi, India

# Contents

*List of Tables* — vii
*List of Figures* — xi
*Preface* — xix

1 Introduction: Conceptualizing Language Systemically — 1

2 The System in Semogenesis: Emergence of Complexity — 15

3 The System as a Fractal Principle: The System in Relation to Other Dimensions of Organization — 31

4 The System as a Navigational Tool in Language Description and Text Analysis — 143

5 The System in Different Domains of Application — 163

6 The System: Challenges and Possibilities — 200

7 Conclusion — 252

8 Appendix: Systemic Conventions — 263

*Notes* — 269
*References* — 281
*About the Author* — 306
*Index* — 307

# List of Tables

| | | |
|---|---|---|
| Table 1.1 | Examples of systems of choice | 3 |
| Table 1.2 | Intersection of the systems of HEIGHT, BACKNESS and APERTURE (ROUNDING) | 5 |
| Table 1.3 | Different sets of terms for the two axes of organization | 10 |
| Table 1.4 | Examples of semantic, lexicogrammatical and phonological systems | 12 |
| Table 2.1 | Options in moving and meaning (adapted from Halliday 1998a/2004a: 9) | 18 |
| Table 2.2 | An early stage in the development of Nigel's protolanguage, Halliday's (1975a) case study, taken from Halliday (1975a/2004a: 391) | 19 |
| Table 2.3 | The fusion of axis and stratification in protolanguage | 22 |
| Table 2.4 | Reproduction of Halliday's (1993a/2004a: 333) Table 1 | 23 |
| Table 3.1 | Units and system networks in the interpersonal slice through semantics, lexicogrammar and phonology | 34 |
| Table 3.2 | Systemic terms with associated realization statements | 35 |
| Table 3.3 | The semantic system of speech function and the grammatical system of mood type 'intersected' | 38 |
| Table 3.4 | Systemic intersections of subject person and deicticity – a paradigm for yes/no interrogatives | 40 |
| Table 3.5 | The deployment of the phonological system of tone one stratum up, within lexicogrammar, and the 'multiplication' of systemic values (unmarked (neutral) keys in bold) | 41 |
| Table 3.6 | Lexicogrammatical function-rank matrix, adapted from Halliday and Matthiessen's (2014: 87) function-rank matrix | 49 |
| Table 3.7 | Textual, interpersonal and experiential systems of the clause | 52 |
| Table 3.8 | The intersection of the two systems of theme selection in 'non-predicator theme' clauses | 63 |
| Table 3.9 | Paradigm of 'relational' clauses – intersection of the systems of RELATION TYPE and MODE OF RELATION | 70 |
| Table 3.10 | Logico-semantic type as a fractal system – manifestations within different grammatical domains | 77 |

| | | |
|---|---|---|
| Table 3.11 | Manifestations of the 'cause' subtype of 'expansion' (adapted from Halliday and Matthiessen 2014: Table 10.4, p. 673) | 79 |
| Table 3.12 | Examples of systems realized by lexicogrammatical items at different degrees of delicacy, from closed system items to open set items | 83 |
| Table 3.13 | Examples of systemic descriptions of lexis | 84 |
| Table 3.14 | Examples of serving as realizations of Process for different combinations of systemic terms in Figure 3.22 | 85 |
| Table 3.15 | The complementarity of grammatical and lexical patterning along the cline of delicacy in terms of the paradigmatic axis and the syntagmatic axis | 88 |
| Table 3.16 | Semantic and lexicogrammatical systemic correlates – patterns of realization by clause systems | 93 |
| Table 3.17 | Basic speech functions and their (congruent) realizations by mood types | 96 |
| Table 3.18 | Speech functional interactant profiles for Anne's brother and Anne | 97 |
| Table 3.19 | Exchange between siblings, brother and Anne, at home | 97 |
| Table 3.20 | Examples of initiating and responding moves; NV = non-verbal | 100 |
| Table 3.21 | Semantic function-rank matrix with references to a selection of publications presenting descriptions of English semantics | 110 |
| Table 3.22 | Semantics and the cline of instantiation | 112 |
| Table 3.23 | The division of phonological labour in terms of the phonological rank scale in English (from Matthiessen 2021) | 120 |
| Table 3.24 | The stratal neighbours of lexicogrammar, phonology, and semantics, phonetics | 136 |
| Table 3.25 | Contextual parameters – characterization and references to system networks | 139 |
| Table 4.1 | Systemic analysis of passage of a telephonic service encounter text (Clauses [1] through [17]) | 151 |
| Table 4.2 | Absence and presence of 'periphrastic do' in the systemic environments of POLARITY and INDICATIVE TYPE; shaded options had largely disappeared by 1700 | 161 |
| Table 5.1 | Examples of computational modelling of language informed by SFL and computational tools developed by systemic functional linguists | 165 |
| Table 5.2 | Examples of systemic descriptions of semiotic systems other than language | 187 |

| | | |
|---|---|---|
| Table 5.3 | Realization statements (discursive specifications) associated with systemic terms in the system network reproduced in Figure 5.15 – adapted from Kress and van Leeuwen's (2006: 74–75) | 190 |
| Table 5.4 | Realization statements used in description of a cartographic and linguistic system for generating weather forecasts (adapted from Matthiessen, Kobayashi and Zeng 1995) | 193 |
| Table 5.5 | Relationship between content and expression in Martinec's (2004) description of gesture | 197 |
| Table 5.6 | O'Toole's (1994) function-rank matrix for the systemic description of painting | 198 |
| Table 6.1 | Linguistic theories and schools in relation to their focus on axiality, the differentiation of and specification of paradigmatic and syntagmatic patterns | 202 |
| Table 6.2 | Types of indeterminacy (adapted from Halliday and Matthiessen 2006: 549 ff) | 223 |
| Table 6.3 | Ambiguities of high value modal operator 'must' | 228 |
| Table 6.4 | 'Behavioural' clauses as an overlap category, with some properties of 'material' clauses and some of 'mental' ones (adapted from Halliday and Matthiessen 2006: 551) | 230 |
| Table 6.5 | Paradigm showing the intersection of polarity and mood type, with one impossible combination | 242 |
| Table 6.6 | Personal pronouns in English and Indonesian – grammatical items realizing the systemic terms in Figure 6.21 | 244 |
| Table 7.1 | Examples of different theories of axial order | 255 |
| Table 7.2 | Axiality – different sets of terms for the two axes of organization | 257 |
| Table 7.3 | Properties of systems of increasing complexity operating in different phenomenal realms | 260 |
| Table 8.1 | Systems in system networks | 263 |
| Table 8.2 | Realization statements | 266 |

# List of Figures

| | | |
|---|---|---|
| Figure 1.1 | Embodied systems of choice – phonology grounded in articulatory phonetics | 4 |
| Figure 1.2 | The different but related senses of 'system' in SFL | 11 |
| Figure 2.1 | The graphic representation of a system: (i) entry condition ('interactional'), (ii) contrasting terms (or 'options': 'initiation' vs. 'response'), and (iii) a system related in delicacy through its entry condition ('normal (friendly)' vs. 'intensified (impatient)') | 18 |
| Figure 2.2 | Protolanguage – paradigmatic organization of content into systems of options realized syntagmatically within the expression plane | 21 |
| Figure 2.3 | Expansion of the interactional meaning potential from 9 months to 1 year, four and a half months, based on Halliday's (1975a) case study of Nigel | 23 |
| Figure 2.4 | Axiality-stratification differentiated into stratification and axiality | 24 |
| Figure 2.5 | Ontogenesis as systemic growth – expansion of the meaning potential (including of the registerial repertoire) | 28 |
| Figure 2.6 | Ontogenesis and the emergence out of protolanguage of distinct semiotic systems with different expressive 'modalities' alongside post-infancy spoken language | 30 |
| Figure 3.1 | The stratification of language, with the distinction between the two stratal planes, content and expression and the distinction between internal strata ('form') and interface strata ('substance') | 32 |
| Figure 3.2 | Systems all the way – system networks representing semantics, lexicogrammar and phonology, as illustrated by fragments of the interpersonal systems of SPEECH FUNCTION (semantics: move), MOOD (lexicogrammar: clause), whose elaboration in delicacy by systems of key is illustrated for 'declarative' clauses by the system of DECLARATIVE KEY, and TONE (phonology: tone group) | 36 |
| Figure 3.3 | Schematic representation of experiential (TRANSITIVITY), interpersonal (MOOD) and textual (THEME) clause systems in Halliday (1969) | 45 |
| Figure 3.4 | Schematic representation of experiential (TRANSITIVITY), interpersonal (MOOD) and textual (THEME) clause systems in Halliday (1973a/2003: 315) | 46 |

| | | |
|---|---|---|
| Figure 3.5 | Index of systems of the clause presented in Halliday and Matthiessen (2014) – textual (THEME, CONJUNCTION), interpersonal (FREEDOM, MOOD, POLARITY, MODAL ASSESSMENT) and experiential (TRANSITIVITY: AGENCY, PROCESS TYPE, CIRCUMSTANTIATION) | 47 |
| Figure 3.6 | The function-rank matrix as a directory to systems in the overall system network of the clause | 50 |
| Figure 3.7 | Systemic and structural analyses of two clauses (from the dialogue in Table 3.7 above) | 52 |
| Figure 3.8 | Key interpersonal clause systems, with examples (for systemic conventions, see the Appendix in Chapter 8) | 53 |
| Figure 3.9 | The system of POLARITY with systemic probability attached, the term 'negative' being marked in terms of probability and in terms of syntagmatic realization | 56 |
| Figure 3.10 | The specification of realization statements in the environment of terms in systems, and the dispersal throughout the system of mood of realization statements involving Subject | 58 |
| Figure 3.11 | The potential for multiple Themes in English – textual, interpersonal and experiential, or 'topical', Theme | 59 |
| Figure 3.12 | The markedness of the topical Theme in relation to the system of information | 60 |
| Figure 3.13 | Key textual clause systems, with examples | 61 |
| Figure 3.14 | The interpersonal layer of the clause as interface mediating between the textual and experiential layers in a 'declarative' clause (or 'yes/no interrogative' clause or non-relative 'bound' clause) | 64 |
| Figure 3.15 | Paradigm of examples of thematic options – the point of reference is an example with an unmarked Theme, 'the duke gave my aunt that teapot yesterday', shown in the centre of the radial display | 66 |
| Figure 3.16 | Relative frequency of combinations of selections of process types and circumstance types based on 1019 circumstances | 71 |
| Figure 3.17 | The system of TRANSITIVITY – AGENCY and PROCESS TYPE (but not CIRCUMSTANTIATION) | 72 |
| Figure 3.18 | Augmentation of the clause nucleus of Process + Medium differentiated according to types of expansion and projection | 73 |
| Figure 3.19 | Paradigm showing intersection of PROCESS TYPE and AGENCY (and RANGING for 'middle' clauses) | 75 |
| Figure 3.20 | The fractal system of logico-semantic type and taxis (adapted from Matthiessen 1995a: 91) | 78 |

| | | |
|---|---|---|
| Figure 3.21 | The lexicogrammatical cline of delicacy, extending from grammar towards lexis | 81 |
| Figure 3.22 | Part of Hasan's (1987) systemic description of the extension in delicacy of a domain within 'material' clauses | 85 |
| Figure 3.23 | Example of extension in the delicacy of the systemic description of process type by classification of Levin's (1993) verb classes (indicated by § numbers) – 'material' clauses of motion | 87 |
| Figure 3.24 | Examples of collocational patterns involving Process + Range/Attribute in certain phased intensive and attributive relational clauses, represented as a hybrid system network and taxonomy – the taxonomy being a focus for future systemicization | 90 |
| Figure 3.25 | Metafunctional organization of semantics and lexicogrammar – degree of separation/unification | 93 |
| Figure 3.26 | The interpersonal semantic system of SPEECH FUNCTION | 94 |
| Figure 3.27 | System network fragment for questions, adapted from Hasan (1996: 122–123) | 95 |
| Figure 3.28 | Dialogic exchange consisting of an initiating move and a responding move complex | 99 |
| Figure 3.29 | Interpersonal systems as resources for dialogue – semantics and lexicogrammar, adapted from J.R. Martin (1992: 50, Figure 2.12) | 101 |
| Figure 3.30 | The system of NEGOTIATION operating with the unit of exchange as its domain, adapted from J.R. Martin (1992: 49) | 102 |
| Figure 3.31 | Exchange as sequence of move complexes | 103 |
| Figure 3.32 | Logical and interpersonal analysis of a passage from a telephonic service encounter | 104 |
| Figure 3.33 | The system of LOGICO-SEMANTIC (RHETORICAL) RELATIONS open to rhetorical nexuses in the formation of text | 104 |
| Figure 3.34 | The compositional hierarchies within the content plane – semantics and lexicogrammar | 106 |
| Figure 3.35 | Text analysed in terms of rhetorical relations as a logico-semantic complex and in terms of parasemes (Cloran's rhetorical units), sequences and figures, annotated adaptation of Cloran, Stuart-Smith and Young's (2007) RST analysis | 107 |
| Figure 3.36 | Semantic analysis of the 'Sun Damage' text in terms of rhetorical units (called 'parasemes' here), from Cloran, Stuart-Smith and Young (2007) | 108 |
| Figure 3.37 | Halliday's (1973b) description of maternal regulatory semantics, associated with a situation type characterized in terms of field, tenor and mode values | 113 |

Figure 3.38  Phonological systemic term viewed trinocularly  121

Figure 3.39  The English prosody systems of INTONATION at tone group rank and RHYTHM at foot rank  122

Figure 3.40  Catford's (1977: 227) segmentation of articulation of the word 'stand' – interpretable as a visualization of speaking as the unfolding of simultaneous phonological choices in articulatory stricture type, articulatory location, resonance (velic closure), phonation and initiator power  124

Figure 3.41  The Akan syllable as a gateway between prosodic and articulatory phonology  125

Figure 3.42  The inter-rank realizational relations between syllable and phoneme in the phonology of Akan  126

Figure 3.43  Akan phoneme system network  127

Figure 3.44  Halliday's description of the Peking syllable in terms of initial and final posture, and the shift between them (Halliday 1992b: 107); the full version of his description is reproduced below as Figure 3.45  127

Figure 3.45  The system network of the Mandarin syllable, taken from Halliday (1992b: 118): 'Figure 6.6 Network specifying Mandarin (Pekingese) syllables'  129

Figure 3.46  Systemicized version of Catford's (1977: 162) chart of the oral articulation of English consonants  131

Figure 3.47  English consonants against the background of anatomically possible consonants in terms of the oral cavity, based on a combination of Catford's (1977) Figures 43 and 44  132

Figure 3.48  Ladefoged's 'hierarchy of features', from Ladefoged (1988b: 128)  133

Figure 3.49  Sketch of a system network for field of activity, extended in delicacy to the point where it makes contact with systemic functional description of explanations in education (Veel 1997)  140

Figure 4.1  The systemic term 'declarative' as a node in a network of relations – multiply related in terms of (intra-stratal) delicacy in the system network of MOOD, in terms of inter-stratal realization to 'statement' in the semantic system of SPEECH FUNCTION, and in terms of inter-stratal realization to 'tone 1' in the phonological system of TONE  144

Figure 4.2  The interpersonal clauses systems of English, segmented into regions in Matthiessen (1995a: 383)  146

Figure 4.3  Systemic cartography – stratification-instantiation matrix  147

Figure 4.4  Systemic cartography – function rank matrix, system of MOOD and discursive comments  148

| | | |
|---|---|---|
| Figure 4.5 | Systemic text analysis – tracking choices in clauses as a service encounter unfolds in time | 150 |
| Figure 4.6 | Text score showing selections in experiential, interpersonal and textual clause systems for 'major' clauses and selections of 'minor clauses' in passage of a telephonic service encounter (Table 4.1). Darker shades indicate selections of systemic terms | 153 |
| Figure 4.7 | Text profile showing number of selections in experiential, interpersonal and textual clause systems for 'major' clauses and selections of 'minor clauses' in passage of a telephonic service encounter (Table 4.1); the bars to the right of the system network represent the numbers of selections of each systemic term | 154 |
| Figure 4.8 | Relative frequencies of terms in the system of PROCESS TYPE in a registerially varied sample of 10,382 clauses | 155 |
| Figure 4.9 | Relative frequencies of the intersections of terms in the systems of process type and agency (N = 10,586 clauses) | 156 |
| Figure 4.10 | Relative frequencies of terms in the system of PROCESS TYPE in a small sample of texts from different registers (N = 6,490 clauses) | 157 |
| Figure 4.11 | Systemic selections in relation to the cline of instantiation – systemic probabilities, registerial probabilities/relative frequencies, and relative frequencies in texts unfolding through time | 159 |
| Figure 4.12 | The systemic environment of the auxiliary 'do' in 'do-support' defined by the intersection of the systems of POLARITY and INDICATIVE TYPE (MOOD TYPE) | 160 |
| Figure 5.1 | Instantiating a system in the generation of text – traversal of a system network, system by system | 168 |
| Figure 5.2 | Systemic traversal path for the hypotactic conditional clause nexus 'if there weren't trees on the earth, we would all be dead' | 169 |
| Figure 5.3 | A sequential algorithm for traversing system networks, adapted from Matthiessen and Bateman (1991: 106) | 170 |
| Figure 5.4 | The gradual increase in the stratification of the systemic functional metalanguage | 173 |
| Figure 5.5 | Example of Halliday's (2004b) listing of systems represented algebraically (rather than graphically) | 174 |
| Figure 5.6 | The stratification of the systemic functional metalanguage, illustrated by reference to the paradigmatic part of the theory | 175 |
| Figure 5.7 | The system of MODALITY in English (adapted from Halliday and Matthiessen 2014) | 178 |

| | | |
|---|---|---|
| Figure 5.8 | Xuan's (2015) modal analysis of the written output by Chinese high school students learning English over a year of writing | 179 |
| Figure 5.9 | Ten writing tasks given to Chinese high school students studying English over one year sorted according to fields of activity in Xuan's (2015) study | 180 |
| Figure 5.10 | Successive selections in the system of MODALITY in a text regulating a parent-school association | 181 |
| Figure 5.11 | Choices in translation – system of MODALITY in English, system of MODALITY in German | 183 |
| Figure 5.12 | Semantic choices in the construal of Place of Interest in the contextual structure of topographic procedures | 184 |
| Figure 5.13 | The relative frequencies of realizations of request by imperative or declarative clauses in Italian, German and English, based on Lavid (2000: Figure 1, p. 74) | 186 |
| Figure 5.14 | Winograd's (1968) systemic description of a chord in music | 188 |
| Figure 5.15 | Example of the use of a system network to describe an aspect of the depictive system, showing systemic options in the depictive construal of narratives – Kress and van Leeuwen's (2006: 74) 'narrative structures in visual communication' | 189 |
| Figure 5.16 | Example of multisemiotic meaning potential, with partitions for the sub-potential that can be construed by weather maps (as well as by language), adapted from Matthiessen, Kobayashi and Zeng (1995) | 192 |
| Figure 5.17 | System networks for gestures – content plane: indexical experiential gestures at the content plane; expression plane: forearm, hand and finger systems. Composition of system networks from Martinec (2004) | 196 |
| Figure 6.1 | Conception of language as resource – possibilities opened up by modelling it based on paradigmatic organization and systems thinking | 205 |
| Figure 6.2 | A 'mind map' version of English clause systems, (a) visualized as a mind map, and (b) as a radial display | 207–208 |
| Figure 6.3 | Ervin-Tripp's (1969: 95) flow chart representation of an American address system | 211 |
| Figure 6.4 | System network 'translation' of Ervin-Tripp's (1969: 95) flow chart representation of an American address system (Figure 6.3) | 212 |
| Figure 6.5 | Redrawing of the system network in Figure 6.4, now with 'adult'/'non-adult' and 'name known'/'name unknown' as simultaneous systems | 213 |

| | | |
|---|---|---|
| Figure 6.6 | The system of PROCESS TYPE represented typologically and topologically and viewed trinocularly | 218 |
| Figure 6.7 | Fields of activity as regions within semiotic space shading into one another | 219 |
| Figure 6.8 | Field of activity represented typologically and topologically – one possible systemicization of the discursive pie of fortune | 220 |
| Figure 6.9 | Indeterminacy in agnation among fields of activity | 224 |
| Figure 6.10 | The polysemy of 'will' at different strata and ranks creating conditions for ambiguity | 225 |
| Figure 6.11 | Syntagmatic ambiguity – different systemic analyses represented by selection expressions realized by function structures | 227 |
| Figure 6.12 | The intersection of MODALITY TYPE and MODALITY VALUE and different types of indeterminacy | 228 |
| Figure 6.13 | An example of a blend in the system of MODALITY: if 'low' in value, then 'probability' and 'potentiality' might blend | 229 |
| Figure 6.14 | Different possible cuts in primary delicacy in the system of PROCESS TYPE in the systemic description of English | 232 |
| Figure 6.15 | The systems of TENSE in English and ASPECT in Chinese as complementary systems for construing processes unfolding through time | 235 |
| Figure 6.16 | The Chinese aspect system and the English tense system in a multilingual system network – each in its own separate systemic partition | 236 |
| Figure 6.17 | The complementarity of semiotic systems in the making of meaning, illustrated by the complementarity of language and a pictorial system | 237 |
| Figure 6.18 | Semantic domain model based on sample of WER by WHO, with regions also realized by non-linguistic semiotic systems indicated | 238 |
| Figure 6.19 | Verbal text providing interpretation of map and chart through identifying relationship, and further textual elaboration (WHO's Weekly Epidemiological Record, No. 48, 29 November 1996) | 239 |
| Figure 6.20 | The graphic representation of a conditional marking conditions showing that if a clause is 'exclamative', then it is 'positive' (rather than 'negative') in polarity | 241 |
| Figure 6.21 | A fragment of a multilingual system network – the system of personal pronouns in English and Indonesian unified in a multilingual system network. The system network includes three partitions that are specific to Indonesian (represented by <Indonesian>), viz. the systems of INCLUSIVITY, NUMBER, STATUS (and the dependent system of | |

FORMALITY); the other systems of the system network are shared by English and Indonesian (in a common partition, represented by <Indonesian>, <English>)  243

Figure 6.22 Multilingual system network of MOOD – English, Chinese, and Korean, with speech level in Korean (the system of interactant contact) and the gates with the terms 'familiar interrogative' and 'deferential interrogative' as examples of the systemic interaction with the system of mood type  245

Figure 6.23 The system of MOOD: geographic spread of types of realization of polar interrogative in western West Africa (based on WALS)  248

Figure 6.24 Systemic options for the interpersonal clause grammars of languages around the world  249

Figure 6.25 Systemic interpretation of the accessibility hierarchy for relatives  250

Figure 6.26 Systemic elaboration of addressee pronouns, based on the WALS database  250

Figure 7.1 Trinocular view of axial order – seen 'from above': systemic theory, seen 'from below': structural theory, seen 'from roundabout': system-structure theory  253

Figure 8.1 The system of mood with charts representing relative frequencies in text included  265

Figure 8.2 Typology of realization statements  266

# Preface

Around forty-five years ago, I saw system networks for the first time – in Halliday's (1973b) book *Explorations in the Functions of Language*. I was hooked by – or rather caught in – the net. One reason was that I liked the look of system networks, and other visual representations, including the networks of stratificational linguistics. But there was a deeper reason than visual aesthetics. System networks and the theory of axial organization they represented solved a problem that had puzzled me for a few years at the time. This problem was the apparent incommensurability of the European structuralist insight into axiality, the two axes of linguistic organization – the paradigmatic axis and the syntagmatic axis, and the insight from generative semantics as presented by Ellegård (1971) showing that grammatical structure could be constructed semantically. Paradigmatic accounts seemed to be limited to phonology, morphology and lexis (in the guise of Trier's lexical fields and later 'componential' approaches); one reason was of course that Saussure, as presented to us at the time based on his posthumous *Cours*, as compiled by his followers, had banished syntax to *parole* rather than interpreting it as part of *langue* (see e.g. Seuren 1998, 2016). Semantically transparent grammatical structure seemed to fail to bring out paradigmatic organization. But for me, Halliday (1973b) solved the problem: he represented paradigmatic organization by means of system networks, and showed (also in other publications) how semantically transparent grammatical structure (function structure) could be specified in paradigmatic environments by means of realization statements associated with terms in the systems that form a system network. Thus he showed how a good deal of the burden of modelling and describing could be shifted from the syntagmatic axis to the paradigmatic one, and, crucially, how the two could be related by means of (inter-axial) realization.

Thus I came to value the theoretical power of the systemic approach and the potential of system networks. This approach was unique at the time I first encountered it in the 1970s in its foregrounding of the paradigmatic axis, and it is still unique in this respect (as well as in many others). Starting in 1980, I became involved in a series of projects in computational linguistics concerned with the development of text generation systems where the systemic approach in general and the system network representation in particular played a central role – first at the Information Sciences Institute in Marina del Rey, California, then in Sydney (at Sydney University and Macquarie University, also in collaboration with Marilyn Cross), and then at a long commuting distance from Sydney in Tokyo, at the Sugeno Lab of the Brain Science Division of the RIKEN Institute under the leadership by Michio Sugeno. This last project was completed successfully in 2005, so by then I had learned from a quarter of a century of computational engagement with systemic theory, including system networks. This engagement was also an opportunity for me to learn about representational systems that could be used alongside system networks, for example in the modelling of meaning, or even as computationally 'responsible' realizations of them – like the family of frame-based inheritance networks that had been developed out of the free-for-all use of semantic or conceptual networks in the late 1960s and 1970s. Throughout these projects, a central theme was choice – systems of choice; and it turned out to be one of the aspects of system that I had an opportunity to engage with early on (e.g. Matthiessen 1988b) – and it has continued to be a central concern of mine.

Along the way, I also had other significant opportunities to learn from the engagement with system network. Since 1980, I had been involved in the expansion of a systemic functional description of the grammar of English, initially for the application in text generation – and that task has turned into a long-term research programme for me, an interim report being *Lexicogrammatical Cartography: English Systems*, published in 1995 thanks to Fred Peng. In the mid-1980s, I did my first significant work on the systemic functional description of a language other than English – one that had not previously been described systemic functionally by means of system networks. This was Akan, a member of the Kwa branch of the Niger-Congo family. I described the lexicogrammar of Akan by means of system networks, up to a point in delicacy; here I could draw on my experience with systemic functional work on English, of course, but I made sure that the description wasn't just lifted from English and foisted on Akan – and there were certainly challenges that needed solutions specific to Akan, like so-called serial verb constructions (which in those days were much less well-understood and described generally than today). (As I worked on interpreting and describing them, I came to understand the complementarity of the logical and experiential modes of construing experience within the ideational metafunction.) But in a way, it was my systemic description of the phonology of Akan that proved the greatest challenge – for two reasons: the special features of Akan phonology like the system of syllabic tone and the 'duplication' of the vowel system by the variation in tongue root position (± 'advanced tongue root') and the lack of a model of a systemic functional description of the phonology of a language by means of system network (apart from Halliday's description of English prosodic phonology and Firthian pre-systemic descriptions of a range of languages) – long before Tench (1992) had been published. So I had to work this out for myself, which was daunting but also very rewarding. I came to realize that the phonology of a language is a sounding potential and needs to be described as such – which is a central way in which system networks come into the picture.

Taking a step back to review my own experiences with working with system networks in different research contexts and to review the development and uses of system networks over a period of around thirty years, I chose this as my topic when I was asked to give a plenary talk at ISFC in Ghent in August 1994, 'Paradigmatic organization: 30 years of system networks'. I wrote it up as a paper, and submitted it to the editors of a thematic volume drawing on contributions to the congress, but it was rejected as not being related to the theme. So it remained in my virtual drawer of unpublished papers. When I was asked to contribute a book to the 'key concepts' series, I toyed with the idea of updating my manuscript based on the Ghent plenary and including it as part of the book – it is a long paper, so would have formed a substantial part of the book. But instead I decided to start afresh, and this book is the result. Around the same time in the mid-1990s, as mentioned above, I'd also completed what felt like a mammoth project – a map of the lexicogrammatical resources of English based on system networks (Matthiessen 1995a).

By the mid-1990s, I had also been fortunate enough to be part of or lead projects where we extended system networks to give them the representational power to represent more than one language – multilingual system networks (Bateman et al. 1991, 1999; Matthiessen 2018a), which I suggested could also be used in the representation of a particular language to capture registerial differentiation, e.g. to indicate grammatical systems only available in spoken English because they depend on the tone group as a realizational resource (Matthiessen 1993). Around the mid-1990s, I was similarly involved in projects where we used system networks to represent semiotic systems other than language as part of a computational multimodal text generation system (e.g. Cross et al. 1998; Matthiessen et al. 1998).

Starting in the 1990s, I was also lucky to be given the opportunity to supervise a number of PhD projects focussed on the description of a growing range of languages from different families and with different typological characteristics – in rough chronological sequence: French, Japanese, Chinese, Vietnamese, Thai, (Modern Standard) Arabic, Oko, Bajjika and Dagaare. Teruya's (2007) two-volume systemic description of Japanese demonstrated that systemic descriptions of languages other than English can go far beyond the current coverage of English, drawing on reactances to bring out covert categories systemically. Bardi's (2008) systemic functional description of the grammar of (Modern Standard) Arabic allowed me to return to my three years of trying to learn Arabic in the 1970s, and linguistically interesting challenges that had puzzled me since then of how to reconcile the overt categories of the fifteen or so overt derivational verb patterns with more covert systemic patterns within the clausal system of transitivity.

These various PhD research projects enriched my own experience with grappling systemically with different languages and background in functional language typology from my time as a post-graduate student at UCLA. These descriptive projects also helped me in my search for descriptive generalizations and motifs across languages (e.g. Matthiessen 2004) and the description of two languages spoken in West Africa, Oko by Akerejola (2005) and Dagaare by Mwinlaaru (2017) enabled me to get back to languages of that region, resulting in our first report on comparison and typology – Mwinlaaru et al. (2018), a system-based typology of mood systems in African languages, building on Teruya et al. (2007).

Throughout the forty-five years or so since I first saw/spotted/glimpsed/encountered a system network in Halliday (1973a), a pervasive positive prosody has woven its way through my academic life and also through this book – Halliday's pioneering work that I have benefitted from in writing since the 1970s and in conversation and collaboration since 1980. As I mentioned above, what first attracted me to SFL was Halliday's conception of language as system, enhanced by his system network as a mode of representing axial organization. He continues to be a deep well of stratospheric insights and the most extraordinary collaborator and friend one could ever imagine or wish for. As in so many other writing projects, I have kept returning to our conversations over the decades to work things out.

This book is concerned specifically with the **system** part of Systemic Functional Linguistics (SFL) – only one of many angles on SFL. It is designed to complement contributions such as Lise Fontaine, Tom Bartlett and Gerard O'Grady (eds) (2013) *Systemic Functional Linguistics: Exploring Choice*; Matthiessen (1995a) *Lexicogrammatical Cartography*; Halliday (1976) *System and Function in Language*; Martin (2013) *Systemic Functional Grammar: the next step into the theory*. There are other 'windows on', e.g. function, stratification, variation; and the key concept series edited by Tom Bartlett, Gerard O'Grady and Rebekah Wegener will include an extensive series of titles.[1] No doubt system will be part of all of them, as will stratification, function and other 'key concepts'; but each book will provide a different way into SFL. I have tried to keep this in view as I decided what to include in this book – and whether to merely mention a topic or issue or expand on it. Since there will be other volumes dealing with the stratal organization of language in context, with context, semantics, metafunction, and particular metafunctions and other crucial categories and dimensions in SFL, I have held back on going into them in details that might distract us in focussing on 'system'. Similarly, there will be books dealing with particular fields of research and application – Wang and Ma (2021) on translation studies informed and empowered by SFL have already made a very valuable contribution, so I can focus on system, and leave other aspects of such fields of study.

Alongside the key concepts series, there are other recent rich sources of information about SFL. A number of edited volumes in the last decade and a half have provided expert overviews of most aspects of SFL: Hasan, Matthiessen and Webster (2005/7), Halliday and Webster (2009), Bartlett and O'Grady (2017), Thompson et al. (2019), and also volumes dedicated to particular areas such as education and multimodality. In Matthiessen and Teruya (in press), we provide an overview of the rich range of handbooks and edited thematic volumes; we have designed it to serve as a guide to SFL, and I refer to it for more extensive references to the literature. In the current book, I have focussed largely on immediately relevant references rather than provide anything approaching a systematic review – since systematic references are available in the books just mentioned and since the present book is part of a series of introductions to key concepts in SFL.

This book complements J.R. Martin's (2013) book on axial relations in SFL, written as the second step into the theory after the first step taken by Halliday and me in Matthiessen and Halliday (2009). Martin's book is introductory in nature, carefully taking readers through axial relations, enabling them to develop their understanding in stages and also inviting them to learn how to draw system networks.

In my own work so far, this book can be viewed in the company of Matthiessen (1995a), already mentioned, the eight volumes of my collected works edited by Kazuhiro Teruya and his team (Matthiessen in press/forthcoming), a guide to SFL written together with Kazuhiro Teruya (Matthiessen and Teruya in press), a book of interviews with me conducted by Wang Bo, Helen Ma and Isaac Mwinlaaru (Matthiessen et al. 2022), a forthcoming book on logico-semantic systems (my revised version of RST, originally developed by Bill Mann, Sandy Thompson and myself), and a forthcoming book on the architecture of language according to SFL (Matthiessen forthcoming b). And, of course, the work with Michael Halliday, both his Introduction to Functional Grammar (Halliday and Matthiessen, 2014) and our *Construing Experience through Meaning* (Halliday and Matthiessen 2006 [1999]); but also volumes planned and in different stages of completion.

The language of illustration in this book is mostly English, with a few detours into other languages and references to descriptions that bring out the power of system as a recourse in the development of comprehensive descriptions of different languages. However, I use the description of English only as a source of illustration. The book is not designed as an overview of the description of English, so it is not descriptively comprehensive and it does not in general provide arguments in favour of one descriptive interpretation over another – I can only point to relevant considerations and ways of framing descriptions in terms of Halliday's trinocular vision. The description of English lexicogrammar that I draw on is documented and presented in Matthiessen (1995a) and Halliday and Matthiessen (2014); it is in the IFG tradition of the systemic functional description of English (cf. Matthiessen 2007a).

Like love, SFL is a 'many-splendoured thing', and there are many contributions that I have not been able to refer to in this book. The task I was given for this volume is not encyclopaedic in nature – unlike the recent volumes I have mentioned above, including ones that are in the publication pipeline, like Matthiessen and Teruya (in press), and Matthiessen (forthcoming b). The 'key concepts' series that this book is part of allows, it seems to me, for a range of contributions from introductions expanding on short overviews in handbooks to more advanced accounts. I have tried to occupy the middle ground between an introductory volume and a research monograph addressing specialists in the field. It seems to me that this is an appropriate level for the series. Although I haven't seen other contributions yet, I can imagine that collectively we will illuminate an extensive systemic functional territory but from different vantage points – system, stratification, metafunction, instantiation and so on, each calling for a different cartographic projection system.

**Professor Christian M.I.M. Matthiessen**

Distinguished Professor
Department of Linguistics
University of International Business and Economics,
Beijing

Visiting Professor
FUNCAP research group (https://www.ucm.es/funcap/el-grupo)
Dep. of English Studies
Philology College
Universidad Complutense de Madrid

# Chapter 1

# Introduction: Conceptualizing Language Systemically

This book is about the notion of 'system' in Systemic Functional Linguistics, or SFL. SFL is a **system-based theory** of language in context, so 'system' is quite central to the theory. There are a number of distinct but related senses of system, and I will differentiate them in this introductory chapter (cf. Figure 1.2), and discuss them throughout the book. But, as a way in, let me introduce a key sense of 'system' by means of some naturally occurring examples revealing how language users operate with **systems of choice** when they speak.[1] This key sense of system will run through the whole book.

## 1.1 Examples of Systems of Choice Accessed by Users of Language

First let's consider a passage I have transcribed from a 1952 interview with Bertrand Russell. At the point where we pick up, he has been talking about his childhood with his grandparents, and discusses his grandfather's role in public life:

> [1] [Bertrand Russell in 1952 interview]
> ... and he visited Napoleon in Elba. <u>He</u> was – <u>it was</u> **he** who introduced the Reform Bill in 1832, which started England on the road towards democracy. He was Prime Minister during your Mexican War, during the revolutions of 1848. I remember him quite well, but as you can see, he belonged to an age that now seems rather remote.

Once he has mentioned that his grandfather met Napoleon, he continues, giving the reference to him the status of Theme – the orientation to the next message in his turn in the interview: *he* in *he was*. But then he revises, in real time, and produced *it was he* instead. He retains the reference to his grandfather, *he*, as Theme, but decides to use a special strategy to 'highlight' the Theme (see Figure 3.13), saying *it was he* instead of simply *he*, and picking up the reference to his grandfather with *who* in *who introduced the Reform Bill in 1832*. By choosing this strategy, Russell conveys the sense of exclusion, viz. his grandfather rather than other possible candidates.

This is a textual choice – the choice between not highlighting the Theme (*he*) and highlighting it (*it was he*), and the choice is revealed as an option in the grammar of English precisely because Russell revises his plan for the message in real time. When we examine passages of text in this way, we find evidence of all kinds of choice. Here's an example of a rewording in the interpersonal area of the grammar, more specifically the system of MODALITY (Figure 5.7). It comes from an interview with Barak Obama while he was still president, conducted by Jimmy Kimmel, who asks Obama about life in the White House and what he can do in the living of daily life, like having a snack at night:

[2] Jimmy Kimmel interview with Barak Obama
Obama: Yeah, I wouldn't wake somebody up to have a sandwich.
Kimmel: You're allowed to go into the refrigerator on your own.
Obama: I am, I am. There's a refrigerator, and there's silverware.
Kimmel: When was the last time you actually cooked?
Obama: Now, it's been a while.
Kimmel: It's been a while.
Obama: It's been a while; I won't lie about that.
Kimmel: Do you ever drive?
Obama: I *cannot* drive. I mean, I *am able to* drive.
Kimmel: You haven't got a birth certificate?
Obama: In Kenya, we drive on the other side of the road.

Here the choice is between *can* in *I cannot drive* and *am able to* in *I'm able to drive*. Obama must have realized that although he selected an option of 'permission' in the system of MODALITY, the modal operator *can* also has the sense of 'ability', so his wording *I cannot drive* turned out to be ambiguous, meaning either 'I am not allowed to drive' or 'I'm not able to drive' (cf. Section 6.4.4 on ambiguity and other types of indeterminacy). So, to forestall the misinterpretation, he signals a rewording with *I mean*, and then produces the unambiguous *I'm able to drive*. Like speakers in general – especially under conditions such as those of a media interview, Obama is monitoring himself, and detects the potential ambiguity, and then 'displays' the system of choice between 'permission' and 'ability' as he restates what he has just said.

Here's another example from the system of MODALITY, in this case emerging in the negotiation between two interactants during a hearing in the House of Representatives in the US. Alexandria Ocasio-Cortez, AOC, is interviewing – or interrogating – the CEO of Facebook, Mark Zuckerberg:

[3] Hearings
Zuckerberg: ...
AOC: *Could* I run ads targeting Republicans in primaries saying that they voted for the Green New Deal?
Zuckerberg: Sorry, can you repeat that?
AOC: *Would* I *be able to* run advertisements on Facebook targeting Republicans in primaries saying that they voted for the Green New Deal? I mean if you're not fact-checking political advertisements, I'm just trying to understand the bounds here – what's fair game.
Zuckerberg: Congresswoman, I don't know the answer to that off the top of my head.
AOC: You don't know if I'll *be able to* do that.
Zuckerberg: I think probably.

Since Zuckerberg appears not to understand her question *could I run ads ...*, she rewords it for his benefit as *would I be able to run advertisements ...*, thereby 'explicating' the options realized by *could* as *would ... be able to*.

We also find examples of speakers exploring choices in construing some aspect of experience, trying out different options in experiential systems. The following example is a constructed one in the sense that it comes from a drama, but it serves as a relevant illustration:

[4] A Talent for Murder: author trying out different wordings [03:20]
[Murder mystery writer played by Angela Lansbury, dictating to tape-recorder.] Where was I? Oh yeah. It was murder. There was a sharp audible gasp, Gabrielle's eyes **swept** the room ... **swept** ... **sweeping** the room. Uhm, her eyes **fastened on** Maxwell ... **fastened**    Oh my God, **narrowed on**, **held**, **pinned** – Christ, maybe I should retire – Gabrielle's eyes (I'll clean that up later) her eyes **fastened on** Maxwell ....

Here, after construing the activity of Gabrielle looking around the room as a movement configured as

participant: 'Gabrielle's eyes' + process: 'swept' + participant: 'the room'

the writer is searching for an appropriate lexical verb to serve as the process in the configuration

participant: 'Gabrielle's eyes' + process + participant: 'Maxwell'

and being dissatisfied with *fasten on*, she tries out other related options in the lexical field. As with the examples of textual and interpersonal systems, this illustrates clearly that she operates with a system of choice – in this case, choice in how to construe experience, evoking this imaginary experience for her readers.

*Table 1.1* Examples of systems of choice

| metafunction | system | first option | other option(s) |
|---|---|---|---|
| **textual** | THEME | he (was) | it was he (who introduced ...) |
| **interpersonal** | MODALITY | (I) cannot (drive) | (I) am able to (drive) |
| **experiential** | PROCESS TYPE | (Gabrielle's eyes) fastened on (Maxwell) | ... narrowed on/held/pinned/... |

The examples just presented illustrate that whatever people say is the result of choices in systems with a number of options; and **what they actually say is always against the background of what they could have said** – the **shadow versions** of what they said.

People may become aware of such options – most likely semantic and contextual ones, and also lexical ones; and listeners or readers may comment on other people's choices, as in the following example:

[5] Greg Meyers, *A Closer Look*[2] [08:54]
Greg Meyers: And then there's Trump, who's clearly grasping for just anything to revive his sinking poll numbers and who seems to be road-testing a bunch of different attack lines all at once mainly by changing one word and repeating himself.
[cut to excerpt, 8 June, 2020:] Donald Trump: We won't be defunding our police, we won't be dismantling our police, we won't be disbanding our police, we won't be ending our police force.
Greg Meyers (mock surprise): Ohhhh, someone got a thesaurus.

Like Example [4], this example illustrates options within a lexical experiential field; but in this case, the repetition of related or **agnate** options serves as an interpersonal boost of Trump's 'law and order' message.

The examples just given all come from the **content plane** of language. It is also helpful to consider options from the **expression plane**, particularly since they are more restricted and easier to develop a sense of by practising choosing among them.

## 1.2 Articulatory Systems of Choice: Phonetic Yoga

As we speak, we make a myriad of phonological choices that are manifested phonetically as observable prosodic and articulatory patterns – observable in the sense that our listeners attend to them auditorily, but also observable to ourselves both through auditory feedback and our sense of muscular movement. Normally we are of course not aware of these choices; they are as it were **automated**, and take place below our level of consciousness. We attend to meanings in context in the first instance, not to sounds – and not even usually to wordings. But we sometimes become aware of phonological choices, e.g. because of our 'slips of the tongue' – because of instantial articulatory problems. And we can train ourselves to become aware of phonological choices as they are manifested in terms of our control of our articulatory resources, from the diaphragm to the oral cavity. We can do this by learning to practise what we might call **phonetic yoga** – by extending our ability to adopt different articulatory postures.

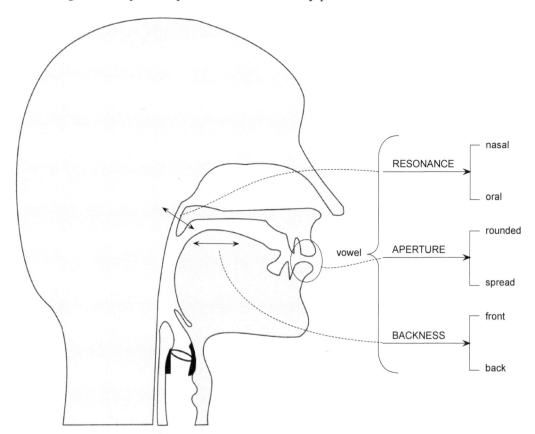

*Figure 1.1* Embodied systems of choice – phonology grounded in articulatory phonetics

Practising phonetic yoga is a good way of becoming familiar with the pervasive **principle of choice** in language. We can identify systems of choice – options corresponding to different articulatory postures. For example, we can explore the articulatory options provided by the systems of RESONANCE, ROUNDING and BACKNESS, as shown schematically in Figure 1.1. Each system can be related to an articulatory region within the oral cavity, each involving a different articulator – the uvula, the tongue and the lips. By moving these, we can realize the terms of the three systems articulatorily. Naturally, the terms will also have to be related to auditory distinctions, and the phonological system of any language is, as it were, phonetically an optimization of articulatory and auditory considerations.[3]

The systems shown in Figure 1.1 can be used to practise opening and closing airflow through the nose, moving the tongue from back to front, and rounding or spreading the lips. Part of the challenge is to vary these systems of choice independently, one at a time. For example, in the pronunciation of English vowels, 'front' always combines with 'spread', as in /i/, and 'back' with rounded', as in /u/; so if English is one's starting point, one would have to learn to produce rounded front vowels like /y/and also spread back vowels like /ɯ/. In other words, just as in e.g. hatha yoga, one has to learn a number of articulatory postures and positions, many of which will transcend those that have been phonologized in a particular language such as Arabic, English or Zulu. In the course of making progress with such exercises, one will get a good sense of articulatory choice as one kind of embodied choice.

By trying out the different combinations of systemic options in the systems of RESONANCE, APERTURE and BACKNESS, we are in fact systematically exploring the **paradigm** that these three systems define. Paradigms were part of the western tradition of linguistics as it was applied to words – noun paradigms defined by e.g. number, gender and case, and verb paradigms defined by e.g. person, number, mode and tense/aspects; and Robins (1959) contrasts WP, word and paradigm, morphology with the approaches oriented towards purely syntagmatic statements in American structuralist morphology in the Bloomfieldian and post-Bloomfieldian tradition (supplementing Hockett 1954). Let me illustrate the way in which intersecting systems of choice define a paradigm by considering the combination of BACKNESS, APERTURE and HEIGHT: see Table 1.2.

*Table 1.2* Intersection of the systems of HEIGHT, BACKNESS and APERTURE (ROUNDING)

| | | BACKNESS | | | | | |
|---|---|---|---|---|---|---|---|
| HEIGHT | | front | | central | | back | |
| close | | i | y | ɨ | ʉ | ɯ | u |
| mid | close-mid | e | ø | ɘ | ɵ | ɤ | o |
| | | | | ə | | | |
| | open-mid | ɛ | œ | ɜ | ɞ | ʌ | ɔ |
| | | æ | | ɐ | | | |
| open | | a | Œ | | | ɑ | ɒ |
| | | spread | rounded | spread | rounded | spread | rounded |
| | | APERTURE | | APERTURE | | APERTURE | |

Here the terms in the system BACKNESS serve as the column headings, the terms in the system HEIGHT serve as the row headings and the terms in the system APERTURE have to be repeated for each of the column headings since it's difficult to display a three-dimensional table in print. But even if we could, we would eventually run out of display potential since there are in fact more than three simultaneous systems of choice; for example, we could add RESONANCE (oral or nasal), VOICING (voiced or unvoiced), TONGUE ROOT POSITION (neutral or advanced), VOICE QUALITY (plain, pharyngealized, etc.). Still, the vowels at the intersections of the three systems in Table 1.2 will serve as a good start for a programme in phonetic yoga. Just as in hatha yoga, one can adopt the postures and positions one by one, e.g. front to back or close to open.

Moving through Table 1.2, one would get a very clear sense of the fact that certain pairs of vowels are very closely related whereas other pairs are more distantly related. This has to do with how many systemic features they share. For example, /i/ and /y/ both lie at the intersection of 'front' and 'close' and they only differ in aperture, /i/ being 'spread' and /y/ being 'rounded'. In contrast, /i/ and /ɒ/ are more distantly related; they differ in terms of all three systems. It is useful to have a term for relatedness, and we will use the term **agnation**, which has been borrowed from Gleason (e.g. 1965) into SFL. The vowels in Table 1.2 are all related or **agnate**, but to different degrees depending on how many of the options in the three systems of BACKNESS, HEIGHT and APERTURE they share. (Since combinations or networks of systems of choice in language are very extensive, it would take a considerable effort to work out how the principle of 'six degrees of separation' applies, but once worked out, it will bring home the bacon.)

## 1.3 The Pervasiveness of Systems of Choice

As illustrated above, systems of choice operate within both the content plane of language and the expression plane. In fact, they are pervasive in the organization of language – and not only in the organization of language but also in the organization of the context in which language operates, its environment of meaning, and in the organization of semiotic systems other than language (Section 3.6). I'll come back to the question of how systems of choice are related to one another; so far, we have only seen that they can be **simultaneous**, as illustrated by the intersections in Table 1.2. There is a more fundamental question to consider first: why should language be organized in terms of systems of choice?

The answer depends on how language is conceptualized in the first place. If, following M.A.K. Halliday, we conceive of language as a resource, more specifically a **resource for making meaning**, we are naturally led to ask, as he was around six decades ago, how this resource is organized. The answer that he developed was this: language is organized as a **meaning potential**, a network of interrelated options in meaning (e.g. Halliday 1973b). This is, in fact, how very young children first experience language, or rather the protolanguage that they construct in interaction with their immediate caregivers (see Chapter 2). This image of language contrasts rather sharply with the one they are very likely to meet later as they enter the institution of formal education. Halliday (2003b

[1977]: 94–95) characterizes the contrast between the two prevailing images of language – language as resource versus language as rule – in terms of a child's experience[4]:

> By the time he is two years old, a child has a considerable awareness of the nature and functions of language. When he starts to talk, he is not only using language; he is also beginning to talk **about** it. He is constructing a folk linguistics, in which (i) saying, and (ii) naming-meaning, denote different aspects of the same symbolic act. And language functions for him both in reflection and in action: as a way of thinking about the world (including about himself), structuring his experience and expressing his own personality, and as a way of acting on the world, organizing the behaviour of others and getting them to provide the goods-and-services he wants. [...]

> Soon, however, the child will go to school; and once he is there, his ideas about language will be superseded by the folk linguistics of the classroom, with its categories and classes, its rules and regulations, its do's and, above all, its don'ts. Here a fundamental ideological change takes place in the child's image of language – and, through this, in his image of reality. Up till now, language has been seen as a resource, a potential for thinking and doing; he has talked about it in verbs, verbs like *call* and *mean, say* and *tell,* and *rhyme.* From now on, language will be not a set of resources but a set of rules. And the rules are categorical – they operate on things; so he must talk about language in nouns, like *word* and *sentence*, and *noun* and *verb*, and *letter.*

> [...]

> So we have enshrined in our folk linguistics these two views, one of language as resource, the other of language as rule. The two co-exist; but since one is a product of our primary socialization, and belongs to the reality that is learnt at our mother's knee, while the other is part of a secondary reality and belongs to the realm of organized knowledge, they impinge on each other scarcely at all. But in our prevailing ideology, the dominant model is that of language as rule (our schools teach the formal grammar of logic, not the functional grammar of rhetoric); and it is only when we come across the writings of those with a different vision of language, like Malinowski, Hjelmslev and Whorf, or alternatively when we make a deliberate effort to change the prevailing image, as some teachers and educators are trying to do, that the notion of language as resource surfaces from our unconscious and we begin to build on the insights that we possess by virtue of this simple fact, observed from the moment of birth (if not before), but so easily forgotten by the philosophers of language, that people talk to each other.

If language is conceived of as resource rather than as rule – as a resource for making meaning, it follows that we need to model it theoretically as a resource rather than as a system of rules. This is where the notion of system of choice turns out to be absolutely central. To bring out the nature of language as a resource for making meaning, we need to model it as a **system of systems** – a system of systems of choice. Here it is almost irrelevant that dominant approaches to language launched in the twentieth century have modelled it as **structure** in the first instance, typically to capture the conception of language as rule. Such approaches simply do not engage with language as a resource for making meaning; they are based on another image of language and are concerned with questions of language that do not relate to its nature as a resource for making meaning.

I will continue to develop the model of language as a system of systems of choice, but let me pause for a moment to consider the distinct but related senses of the term 'system' in English since it turns out that their relatedness will help me pursue the central theme of this book of 'system' as a 'key concept' in SFL.

## 1.4 Distinct but Related Senses of 'System'

The term 'system' in 'Systemic Functional Linguistics' derives from J.R. Firth's 'system-structure' theory. This was Firth's version of the insight explored in European linguistics in the first half of the twentieth century that language is organized along two axes; to make this account terminologically accessible, Halliday (2002 [1963a]: 97) called them the axes of 'chain and choice' in language: technically **structure** in the 'chain' axis and **system** in the 'choice' axis. They are of course generally known as the **syntagmatic axis** and the **paradigmatic axis**; Saussure made the distinction between these two patterns of organization, calling them syntagmatic and associative; Saussure (1916: 170–171) introduced 'rapports syntagmatiques et rapports associatifs', making reference to mental activity:

> Ainsi, dans un état de langue, tout repose sur des rapports ; comment fonctionnent-ils ?
>
> Les rapports et les différences entre termes linguistiques se déroulent dans deux sphères distinctes dont chacune est génératrice d'un certain ordre de valeurs ; l'opposition entre ces deux ordres fait mieux comprendre la nature de chacun d'eux. Ils correspondent à deux formes de notre activité mentale, toutes deux indispensables à la vie de la langue.

[Translated version by Wade Baskin, 122–123:]

> In a language-state everything is based on relations. How do they function?
>
> Relations and differences between linguistic terms fall into two distinct groups, each of which generates a certain class of values. The opposition between the two classes gives a better understanding of the nature of each class. They correspond to two forms of our mental activity, both indispensable to the life of language.

He introduces the syntagm first:

> D'une part, dans le discours, les mots contractent entre eux, en vertu de leur enchainement, des rapports fondés sur le caractère linéaire de la langue, qui exclut la possibilité de prononcer deux éléments à la fois (voir p. 103). Ceux-ci se rangent les uns à la suite des autres sur la chaine de la parole. Ces combinaisons qui ont pour support l'étendue peuvent être appelées *syntagmes.* Le syntagme se compose donc toujours de deux ou plusieurs unités consécutives (par exemple : *re-lire* ; *contre tous* ; *la vie humaine* ; *Dieu est bon* ; *s'il fait beau temps, nous sortirons,* etc.).

[Translated version by Wade Baskin, 123:]

> In discourse, on the one hand, words acquire relations based on the linear nature of language because they are chained together. This rules out the possibility of pronouncing

two elements simultaneously (see p. 70). The elements are arranged in sequence on the chain of speaking [*parole* in the original, CMIMM]. Combinations supported by linearity are *syntagms*. The syntagm is always composed of two or more consecutive units (e.g. French *re-lire* 're-read,' *contre tous* 'against everyone,' *la vie humaine* 'human life,' *Dieu est bon* 'God is good,' *s'il fait beau temps, nous sortirons* 'if the weather is nice, we'll go out,' etc.).

Having introduced the syntagm, he then moves on to *rapports associatifs*:

> D'autre part, en dehors du discours, les mots offrant quelque chose de commun s'associent dans la mémoire, et il se forme ainsi des groupes au sein desquels règnent des rapports très divers. Ainsi le mot *enseignement* fera surgir inconsciemment devant l'esprit une foule d'autres mots *(enseigner, renseigner,* etc., ou bien *armement, changement,* etc., ou bien *éducation, apprentissage)* ; par un coté ou un autre, tous ont quelque chose de commun entre eux.

> On voit que ces coordinations sont d'une tout autre espèce que les premières. Elles n'ont pas pour support l'étendue ; leur siège est dans le cerveau ; elles font partie de ce trésor intérieur qui constitue la langue chez chaque individu. Nous les appellerons *rapports associatifs*.

> Le rapport syntagmatique est *in praesentia* ; il repose sur deux ou plusieurs termes également présents dans une série effective. Au contraire le rapport associatif unit des termes *in absentia* dans une série mnémonique virtuelle.

[Translated version by Wade Baskin, 123:]

> Outside discourse, on the other hand, words acquire relations of a different kind. Those that have something in common are associated in the memory, resulting in groups marked by diverse relations. For instance, the French word *enseignement* 'teaching' will unconsciously call to mind a host of other words (*enseigner* 'teach,' *renseigner* 'acquaint,' etc.; or *armement* 'armament,' *changement* 'amendment,' etc.; or *education* 'education,' *apprentissage* 'apprenticeship,' etc.). All those words are related in some way.

> We see that the co-ordinations formed outside discourse differ strikingly from those formed inside discourse. Those formed out-side discourse are not supported by linearity. Their seat is in the brain; they are a part of the inner storehouse that makes up the language of each speaker. They are *associative relations*.

> The syntagmatic relation is *in praesentia*. It is based on two or more terms that occur in an effective series. Against this, the associative relation unites terms *in absentia* in a potential mnemonic series.

Saussure's term 'associative relations' made sense in view of his reference to memory; but drawing on Saussure's insights, the great Danish structuralist linguist Hjelmslev proposed the term 'paradigmatic' instead, and his term has been generally adopted.[5] However, in his theory of the axial organization of language, Firth introduced the terms **system** and **structure**, which, as already noted, Halliday (1963a) glossed as **choice** and **chain**: see Table 1.3. By the mid-1960s, Halliday (1966a) stated explicitly that the paradigmatic axis was to be given **priority**, with syntagmatic patterns derived from it. I'll return to his transformation of the axial relationship, but first let me dwell on the different but related senses of the term 'system'.

Table 1.3 Different sets of terms for the two axes of organization

| scholars | paradigmatic | syntagmatic |
|---|---|---|
| Saussure | associative (in absentia) | syntagmatic (in praesentia) |
| Hjelmslev | paradigmatic | syntagmatic |
| Firth | system | structure |
| Halliday | system (choice) | structure (chain) |

By adopting the term 'system' in the interpretation of paradigmatic organization, Halliday and other SFL scholars are able to link system in this particular sense to another related sense of system, and by another step to a general sense of system covering both. In his overview of key terms in SFL, Halliday (2009: 232–233) differentiates two senses of 'system', and then he shows how they are related and are ultimately the same notion:

> System (in the sense of $system_1$) is the organizing concept for modelling paradigmatic relations in language. A paradigm is a set of forms which share a common environment, like the set of English finite verbal operators *can/could/may/might/shall/should/will/would/must/ought/need/dare*. Underlying these are several systems of contrasting features ('terms'), such as value: high (*must* ...) / median (*will* ...) / low (*may* ... ); orientation: subjective (*must* ...) / objective (*certainly* ...), and others, together making up the system network of modality; and also features from the system network of tense.
>
> [...]
>
> The term 'system' is extended to be applied to language as a whole (the linguistic system), in the opposition (language as) system / (language as) text. $System_2$ and text are related by instantiation: the text is the observable instance of the underlying systemic potential.
>
> In this sense, system relates to general systems theory. Language can be characterized as a complex dynamic system, one that persists through constant change in interaction with its (eco-social) environment. It belongs to the class of semiotic systems (systems of meaning), in contrast with systems of other kinds, physical, biological and social.
>
> $System_1$ and $system_2$ are in fact the same concept, though operating on a different scale. In both cases the system is the (representation of the) potential that inheres in a given set of phenomena. These systems have all evolved; evolved systems contrast, in turn, with designed systems, which have been brought into being to explain (and sometimes to control) some realm of human experience. A scientific theory is a designed system of this kind.
>
> Usually, 'system' is used to cover system-&-process: the system, together with the processes that derive from (or 'realize') it in real or virtual time.

The different but related senses of 'system' in SFL are set out in Figure 1.2. This figure draws on Halliday's (2009) two diagrams representing his distinction between $system_1$ and $system_2$, but while it incorporates his two diagrams in one, it leaves out some details.[6]

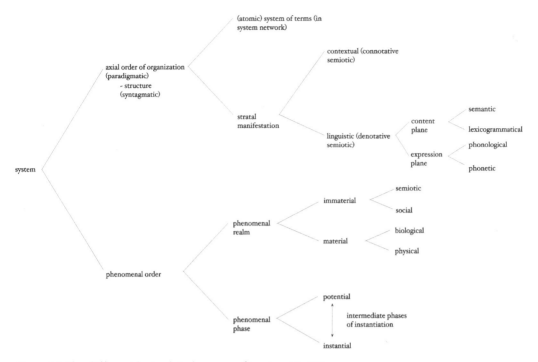

*Figure 1.2* The different but related senses of 'system' in SFL

Referring to Figure 1.2, let me review the general notion of system. We can recognize systems operating within different **phenomenal orders**, shown in the lower half of the figure: (i) In terms of the **phenomenal phase** (the cline of instantiation in SFL), they are all views from the vantage point of the potential pole of the cline, and while they are typically theorized at this location, they can most readily be observed at the instance pole of the cline as instantial patterns of some order – transformed into 'data' by scientific activities of observation and analysis. Here the notion of system is the same across all orders of phenomena – the theoretical model of the relevant potential. (ii) But systems operate in different **phenomenal realms**, and according to the understanding developed within SFL (e.g. Halliday 1996, 2005; Halliday and Matthiessen 2006 [1999]: Chapter 13; Matthiessen 2007b, forthcoming b), there are four phenomenal realms ordered into a **typology of increasing complexity: physical > biological > social > semiotic** systems (which I will return to at the end of the book in Section 7.3). The first two constitute **material** systems (systems constituted in matter, physical and biological), and the next two constitute **immaterial** systems (systems constituted in order and manifested in matter, social and semiotic).

The upper half of Figure 1.2 is concerned with system in the sense of **axial order** of organization along the paradigmatic axis. This includes the 'local' organization of systems as a set of mutually exclusive options 'which share a common environment', as illustrated in Figure 1.1; the options are referred to as the **terms** of the system and the environment as the **entry conditions**. In Figure 1.1, the common environment for three systems is 'vowel' – articulatorily characterizable as relatively free airflow (but shading into semi-vowels and ultimately consonants), and each system with 'vowel' as its entry condition has two terms.

The systemic terms can be phonetic, phonological, lexicogrammatical, semantic and even contextual; they are not things in themselves but simply contrasts or values in the systems that they are part of. Through their entry conditions, such 'atomic' systems form **system networks**. For example, the term 'rounded' in the APERTURE system in phonology, could be the entry condition of another system with two contrasting terms, normal rounding and over-rounding (as in Swedish *hus* /hʉːs/ 'house', contrasting with normal rounding *hund* 'dog').

I will present a variety of systems and system networks throughout the book, but let me give introductory examples from semantics, lexicogrammar and phonology in Table 1.4 (systemic conventions are summarized in the Appendix, Table 8.1). As the table shows, a system consists of an **entry condition**, which may be a simple term (e.g. 'free') or a complex of terms (e.g. 'information' & 'demanding', 'declarative'/'imperative'), and two or more **systemic terms** in contrast (e.g. 'indicative'/'declarative').[7] (See the annotated example in Figure 2.1, to be discussed below.) Terms in systems may have **realization statements** associated with them; they are not illustrated in the table and will be introduced later. The name of a system is not a formal part of it; it is simply a label used to identify it.

*Table 1.4* Examples of semantic, lexicogrammatical and phonological systems

| stratum | name of system | system | | in system network |
|---|---|---|---|---|
| | | entry condition | terms | |
| semantics | COMMODITY TYPE | move | information goods-&-services | Figure 3.2, Figure 3.26 |
| | QUESTION TYPE | information & demanding | polar question elemental question | |
| lexicogrammar | MOOD TYPE | free (clause) | indicative imperative | Figure 3.2 |
| | INDICATIVE TYPE | indicative | declarative interrogative | |
| | MOOD TAGGING | declarative/ imperative | tagged untagged | |
| phonology | APERTURE | vowel | spread rounded | |
| | FALL RANGE | tone 1/tone 13 | wide medium narrow | Figure 3.2, Figure 3.39 |

## 1.5 Summary

In this chapter, I have suggested a way into the exploration of language as system. I began by showing how we can observe systems of choice in naturally occurring texts by attending to occasions where the alternative terms are in evidence because speakers edit their text in real time, for example because while they are monitoring themselves they find a more effective systemic option or they become aware of ambiguities. Next I suggested that we can become participant-observers of systems of choice by practising phonetic yoga – adopting contrasting articulatory postures, varying one system of choice at a time.

Then I changed gears to more theoretical considerations, raising the issue of why language should be organized around choice. The answer is that language is a resource for making meaning, and the best way of theorizing and modelling this resource is to represent it paradigmatically in the first instance, as a network of related systems of choice, while interpreting syntagmatic patterns as secondary in the sense that they are specified by realization statements associated with paradigmatic specifications. The conception of language as a resource for doing something, more specifically for making meaning, is a natural one that children grow up with as they learn how to mean before they enter institutions of formal education where they may meet an image of language as rule – reflected in formal theories of language as rule systems for specifying syntagmatic patterns as structures. I'll pick up the developmental thread in Chapter 2.

Against the background of the presentation of system as system of choice, I then took one step further to identify and examine different but ultimately related senses of 'system' – system of language (including stratal subsystems: the semantic system, the lexicogrammatical system, the phonological system, the phonetic system), system as complementary to text (viewed from different angles along the cline of instantiation), and systems of different phenomenal orders. These related senses of system will occur throughout the book, and are all relevant to a rich, multifaceted understanding of system.

## 1.6 Organization of the Book

The book is organized into seven chapters dealing with different aspects of 'system'; after this introductory chapter, I will offer an overview of the systems that make up the total system of language as a resource – as a meaning potential – in Chapter 3. But first, let's approach system developmentally, noting the gradual increase in systemic complexity and therefore also in power to mean that can be chronicled with system as the window on language development.

The remaining chapters are as follows:

- Chapter 2: The System in Semogenesis: Emergence of Complexity.
- Chapter 3: The System as a Fractal Principle – The System in Relation to Other Dimensions of Organization

- Chapter 4: The System as a Navigational Tool in Language Description and Text Analysis
- Chapter 5: The System in Different Domains of Application
- Chapter 6: The System: Challenges and Possibilities
- Chapter 7: Conclusion

The final chapter is a conclusion in a sense of a step or two back to view the material covered in a wider context; summaries are provided, where appropriate, for individual chapters. I have tried to design the book so that it can be read from (virtual) cover to cover or by dipping into chapters out of sequence.

# Chapter 2

# The System in Semogenesis: Emergence of Complexity

An excellent way of understanding 'system' as it has been used in SFL and the phenomena that it was developed to capture is to observe how its manifestations emerge in the course of **ontogenesis**, from the early phase of young children learning how to mean to the later phase when they have begun to master the mother tongue(s) spoken by members of their immediate meaning group and the wider community that it is part of.

## 2.1 Systems of Moving and Meaning

Starting with Halliday's (1975a) pioneering case study of one young child learning how to mean, a number of systemic functional linguists have undertaken similar case studies tracing the development from children's **protolanguage** into the mother tongue – Painter (1984, 1999), Torr (1997), Walsh (2002), and then development of the mother tongue during the school years – Derewianka (1995, 2003); for overviews of this line of research, see Painter, Derewianka and Torr (2007), Torr (2015) and Williams (2019), and McCabe (2021) brings it all together in a book tracing ontogenesis from early childhood through the school years.

These studies are **longitudinal case studies** (for the significance of this methodological approach also in studies of second/foreign language development, see Ortega and Byrnes 2008), and they have given us considerable insight into the gradual development of language as an increasingly complex and powerful system of making meaning in the lives of individual meaners; they have shed light on the emergence of semiotic and material systems in parallel, of the distillation of system from instances, on the early systemic organization of protolanguage as content-expression pairings ('signs'), the gradual prying apart of these resulting in a differentiation of axis and stratification as separate semiotic dimensions, and the emergence of simultaneous systems engendered by distinct metafunctional modes of meaning. Let me examine the role of system in this gradual developmental process of increasing complexification of language.

As children develop during early childhood, developmental processes take place within the different systemic orders, in a naturally co-ordinated way; they grow biologically, they learn how to behave and interact socially, and they learn how to mean semiotically. Focussing on their semiotic and biological development, Halliday (1998a/2004a) suggests that certain transitions within both the semiotic and the biological realms of phenomena are typically correlated; he characterizes these two developmental processes in terms of meaning (semiotic) and moving (material: biological), and summarizes the transitions as in Table 2.1. Reading this table from left to right, we can see that young children 'grow' more options in both meaning and moving; they expand both their moving and meaning potentials. For example, semiotically, protolanguage emerges with a few systems of options in meaning at the time when young children begin to crawl, thus adding to their movement potential options having to do with shifting vantage point in viewing and interacting with the world around them.

In interaction with their immediate caregivers, children learn how to mean in a sequence of **semiotic phases**. They gain more semiotic power by gradually increasing the 'dimensionality' of their early semiotic system, adding semiotic dimensions. Halliday (2004a: 14) explains how we can arrive at:

> a coherent picture of the child's early semiotic development: how children are steadily increasing the number of 'semogenic vectors', the various parameters that open up the total potential for meaning. First they tease apart the content from the expression; then they separate the system from the instance; then they open up further strata, further levels of organization within the content and within the expression; then they prise apart the distinct functional components inside each stratum. With each step they are opening up a new domain in which to move, so construing a multidimensional semiotic space analogous to the increasing dimensionality of the bodily space in which their material existence is located.

This development thus involves a number of **semiotic dimensions**, or 'semogenic vectors':

- **stratification:** from purely material acts to semiotic acts stratified into two stratal planes, the content plane and the expression plane[1]; then, later, both these planes are further stratified internally (content into semantics and lexicogrammar, and expression into phonology and phonetics);
- **instantiation:** the system is separated from the instance, the system emerging from instances as a distillation or 'memory' of similar repeated instances;
- **functional diversification:** from micro-functions tied to specific contexts (regulatory, interactional, instrumental, personal, and somewhat later heuristic and imaginative) via macro-functions (mathetic and pragmatic) to abstract meta-functions (ideational: logical and experiential, interpersonal and textual) organizing the content plane into simultaneous systems.

In terms of instantiation, the critical issue is when instances become systemic – this is the beginning of protolanguage. Before young children embark on protolanguage, they have engaged in what Catherine Bateson (1979) has called 'protoconversation'; but Halliday (1998a/2004a: 7) points out that his is not yet systemic:

> Representing the newborn child's protoconversation (or 'proto-semiosis') is easy: it just needs a VCR, a video-audio recording of the event. This because the baby's behaviour is not yet **systemic**: apart from the rather clear distinction between the two states, addressing and not addressing, which is a choice of on or off, within the 'addressing' behaviour itself there is no systematic variation in meaning.

Later, when children learn how to sit up, they begin to produce isolated signs (i.e. content-expression pairs); Halliday (1998a/2004a: 10–11) shows that this then leads to the emergence of protolanguage:

> ... [it is] when infants learn to sit up, that their view of the world becomes integrated into a coherent landscape; and it is at this stage that they decide (so to speak!) to mean in earnest – to give full value to the semiotic act, as a distinct and self-sufficient form of activity. At first this takes the form of a few isolated simple signs, with meanings such as 'I'm curious; what's happening?', 'I want that', 'I don't want that', 'play with me' and suchlike – although even here we begin to notice different functional orientations; and the isolates are now clearly emerging as **signs**: that is, as content/expression pairs, such that both the content (the signified) and the expression (the signifier) remain stable over a period of time (even though it may be, in our adult terms, a very short period, sometimes as little as around three to five days).

These signs constitute the first step in stratifying patterns into content and expression; this is a necessary step for the emergence of meaning. They are not merely instantial; they begin to recur. Halliday (1998a/2004a: 11) continues:

> This relative stability of the sign is a necessary condition for enabling such isolates to develop into a **semiotic system**; and this is the next phase – that of the protolanguage. The protolanguage is the child's first semiotic system. In terms of 'meaning and moving', the interlocking development of material and semiotic resources, protolanguage is associated with crawling. When infants learn to crawl (that is, to move themselves unaided from place to place), they are able to see the world in three dimensions, shifting the angle of observation at their will; and this gives an added dimension to their perceptions. It is at this phase that they become able to construe their meaning potential into systems, in this way developing their first real language, in which meaning is created paradigmatically: each utterance has meaning because it is an instance of a systemic choice.

This is then the beginning of 'system' in the sense of a system of terms, a systemic choice – of contrasting options (see Figure 1.2); as Halliday puts it: 'meaning is created paradigmatically: each utterance has meaning because it is an instance of a systemic choice'.

As an illustration, consider an early stage in the protolinguistic phase of the child, Nigel, studied by Halliday (1975a): see Table 2.2. This was Nigel's productive meaning potential at the age of ten and half months. His potential is organized functionally into a set of four **microfunctions**. Each microfunction corresponds to a **context of use**, and it is characterized by a dedicated meaning potential: (1) instrumental – one system, (2) regulatory – one system, (3) interactional – two systems (ordered in delicacy), and (4) personal – four systems (also ordered in delicacy).

The conventions used in the graphic representation of systems of choice here and elsewhere in this book are set out in Figure 2.1. Systems consist of an **entry condition**, either a single term (as in the case of the illustration) or a complex of terms (some combination of conjunction and disjunction of terms), and two or more contrasting **terms** (summarized in the Appendix, Table 8.1). Through entry conditions, systems are **ordered in delicacy**, and form system networks. (More than one system may have the same entry condition, as in Figure 1.1, in which case the systems are simultaneous.)

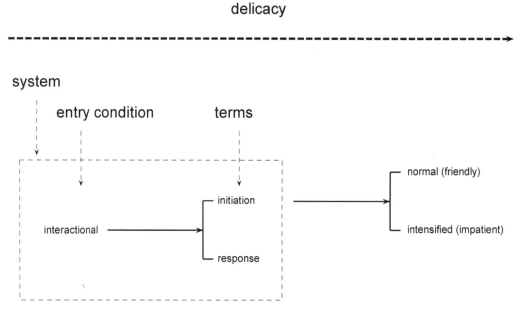

Figure 2.1 The graphic representation of a system: (i) entry condition ('interactional'), (ii) contrasting terms (or 'options': 'initiation' vs. 'response'), and (iii) a system related in delicacy through its entry condition ('normal (friendly)' vs. 'intensified (impatient)')

Table 2.1 Options in moving and meaning (adapted from Halliday 1998a/2004a: 9)

| meaning [semiotic action] | exchange attention | → | yell [directed cry] | → | '!', '?' [express wonder] | → | signs as isolates | → | proto-language [primary semiotic system] | → | language [higher order semiotic system] |
|---|---|---|---|---|---|---|---|---|---|---|---|
| moving [material action] | agitate limbs; cry | → | reach & grasp [directed movement] | → | roll over [shift perspective] | → | sit up [world as landscape] | → | crawl [move vantage-point] | → | walk upright |

*Table 2.2* An early stage in the development of Nigel's protolanguage, Halliday's (1975a) case study, taken from Halliday (1975a/2004a: 391)

| Function | Content systems | | | Expression | | Gloss |
|---|---|---|---|---|---|---|
| | | | | Articulation | Tone | |
| Instrumental | demand, general | | | nã - - - | mid | "give me that" |
| | demand, specific (toy bird) | | | bø | mid | "give me my bird" |
| Regulatory | command, normal | | | ɔ̃ | mid | "do that (again)" |
| | command, intensified | | | m̂nŋ | wide; *ff* | "do that right now!" |
| Interactional | initiation | normal (friendly) | | = ø; dǿ; dɔ́ | narrow mid | "nice to see you (and shall we look at this together?)" |
| | | intensified (impatient) | | ɔnnn | mid | "nice to see you—at last!" |
| | response | | | ɛ; ɔ | low | "yes it's me" |
| Personal | participation | interest | general | = ø | low | "that's interesting" |
| | | | specific (movement) | dɔ́; bø; ø | low | "look, it's moving (? a dog, birds)" |
| | | pleasure | general | a | low | "that's nice" |
| | | | specific (taste) | n̂ŋ | low | "that tastes nice" |
| | withdrawal | | | gʷɣɣ- - - | narrow low | "I'm sleepy" |

*Note:* All above on falling tone; mid = mid fall, narrow low = low fall over narrow interval, etc. At 9 months, Nigel had two such meanings, both expressed as [ø] on narrow mid-low falling tone; one interactional, "let's be together", the other (possibly slightly wider interval) personal "look, it's moving." He also had, however, three meanings expressed gesturally: two instrumental, "I want that," grasping object firmly, and "I don't want that," touching object lightly; and one regulatory, "do that again," touching person or relevant object firmly (e.g. "make that jump in the air again"). The gestures disappeared during NL-1 to NL-2.

In this and subsequent tables, favorite items are indicated by *, and rare or doubtful items by ? Where two or three items are related in both meaning and sound these are shown by =, accompanied by an index number where necessary.

## 2.2 The Emergence of System: Into Protolanguage

Protolanguage is thus organized as a system:

- protolanguage is a semiotic system, albeit a very simple one;
- it emerges when instances have become 'stable' so that they can be interpreted as recurrent instances of terms in systems (which are remembered by the interactants);
- it is organized into such systems, each with its own entry condition and contrasting terms, or options, in meaning;
- collectively, these systems constitute the protolanguage – it is a system of systems.

Protolanguage is characterized by Halliday (2004a: 254) as follows:

> Protolanguage is the form of language that we humans share with what we think of as the 'higher' mammals: mainly primates and cetaceans, but it also appears in our two most favoured pets, cats and dogs, at least when they interact with us. All these are of course different languages; but all have the same formal structure, as systems of simple signs. In the process of his symbolic activity, the child construes meaning into systems; and the

systems are functional in different contexts – I referred to these as **microfunctions** in my analysis. The process is of course dialogic; the others share in construing the meaning potential.

As already noted, protolanguage embodies a distinction between system and instance related by instantiation; Halliday (2004a: 255) clarifies this fundamental point as follows:

> It is in protolanguage, then, that the activity of meaning comes to be construed in the form of a system, such that there is an ongoing dialectic relationship between the system and the instance. The system is the potential for generating instances; and by the same token each new instance perturbs the system. The system is a dynamic open system, metastable in character, that persists only through constantly changing in interaction with its environment; and each new instance constitutes an incursion from the environment, since the material conditions that engender it are never totally identical.

This is what I have characterized as **phenomenal phase** in Figure 1.2 – the cline of instantiation from potential (system) and instance, operating within all types of **phenomenal realm**. As children begin their extended process of mastering the mother tongue of the speech fellowship (speech community) that they grow up in, the cline of instantiation will, as it were, get increasingly extended; they will gradually learn patterns intermediate between potential and instance – codal and registerial varieties. But let's continue to focus on the early part of their semiotic journey.

## 2.3 Axial and Stratal Organization

In protolanguage, the systemic organization of its potential is in principle confined to the content plane: the content plane is organized into a small number of microfunctions, each of which is characterized by its own set of inter-related systems, as illustrated for the personal microfunction in Figure 2.2. The most delicate terms or options in these systems are realized by vocal postures or gestures within the expression plane – in the case of the personal microfunction in this example, only by vocal postures involving articulatory postures and tones. For example, the systemic term 'taste' in the personal content plane system is realized by the vocalization [a] with a low tone in the expression plane. This can be represented as 'taste' ↘ [a] (low tone). The diagonal arrow represents the relation of realization, and it is used as a way of specifying **realization statements** associated with systemic terms. In the case of protolanguage, such realization statements are very simple, consisting only of the specification of the expression plane vocalization or gesture. This can be thought of in Saussurean terms as a pairing of signified and signifier, i.e. 'signified ↘ signifier' – except that the 'signified' is not an isolated atom, but rather a systemic term in a system network. (Full-fledged realization statements of the kind needed in the systemic description of post-infancy adult languages consist of a realization operator plus one or more operands; they are listed in Table 8.2 in the Appendix.)

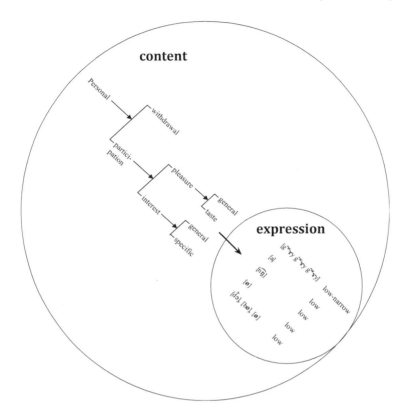

*Figure 2.2* Protolanguage – paradigmatic organization of content into systems of options realized syntagmatically within the expression plane

The vocalizations (or gestures) do not form an independent expression system; they are organized systemically 'from above' in terms of the content plane system. There is no 'double articulation' in protolanguage (in Martinet's, e.g. 1970, sense), but this isn't necessary in view of the limited number of systemic options; at most, protolanguages need somewhere between 120 and 150 distinct expressions – **signifiers**, in the terminology of theories of the sign. The expressions come from a range of sources – Halliday (1998a/2004a: 12):

> As far as the expression is concerned, children will create their protolinguistic signifiers out of anything that is to hand, or to mouth – provided that they can perform it and that those who exchange meanings with them respond. One source I have already referred to is by borrowing from the material domain. Another source is imitation – which can also be a source of confusion for those involved, if it is an imitation of adult speech sounds, because the meaning is not (and cannot be, because the protolanguage is not yet referential) that which the others are disposed to assign to it. Other expressions seem to be just plucked out of the air, so to speak – out of the child's repertory (of sound or gesture) as it happens to be at the time.

So in terms of the semiotic dimensions or 'semogenic vectors', we can say that in protolanguage, the hierarchy of axis and the hierarchy of stratification have not yet been pried apart. In other words, they are not yet separate semiotic dimensions, as shown in Table 2.3; paradigmatic organization = content, expression = vocalizations or gestures.

*Table 2.3* The fusion of axis and stratification in protolanguage

|  | axis: | |
|---|---|---|
| stratification: | paradigmatic | syntagmatic |
| content | microfunctional systems | |
| expression | | vocalizations–gestures |

In interaction with their immediate caregivers, children continue to expand their protolinguistic meaning potentials by adding systems. This expansion characterizes all the microfunctional meaning potential; we can take the interactional meaning potential as an illustration: see Figure 2.3. I have simply compiled Halliday's description of this this meaning potential in snapshots representing six-week periods. At the beginning of this period, the potential consists of two systems, interactional: initiation/response and initiation: normal/intensified. At the end of the period, it consists of nine systems. But the growth does not simply involve an increase in the number of systems – so in systemic options with their associated signifiers as realizations. Something else happens at the end of the period which is very systemically significant: the option of 'personalized' (greetings) now leads to two **simultaneous** systems. One of them is concerned with the identity of the person being greeted, Anna/Mummy/Daddy, and the other with the orientation of the greeting, seeking ('where are you?')/finding ('there you are').

Here Nigel can thus **mean two things at the same time**, one is a precursor to construing the world and the other to enacting a distinction in direction in the exchange, at this stage 'seeking' vs. 'finding'. Interestingly, he achieved this breakthrough by deconstructing aspects of the expression plane; he disassociated articulation and prosody, using the former to denote the person being greeted and the latter to enact the contrast between seeking and finding ('protomood'). This developmental step is of fundamental significance because it opens up the possibility of meaning more than one thing at the same time and concomitantly of splitting the content plane into two content strata, semantics and lexicogrammar. Here is Halliday's (1993a/2004a: 333) succinct account of emergence of the two parallel systems, where he addresses of question of how the young child moves into grammar:

> where is the magic gateway into the grammar? This is again from my own data, when Nigel was 1.3. He was beginning to incorporate names (Mummy, Daddy, Anna) into his protolanguage, but they were not yet referential; they were still microfunctional signs meaning 'play with me', 'I'm giving this to you', and so on. Then, within three consecutive days he constructed the system shown in Table 1 [reproduced here as Table 2.4, CMMIM]. By separating articulatory from prosodic features in the expression, Nigel had deconstructed the sign; in doing so, he had succeeded in varying one dimension of meaning (one system, in the technical sense) while keeping the other one constant, and in the process marked out one of the two meaning systems as referential. Thus, the combination of 'proper name' (Mummy/Daddy/Anna) with mood, or protomood (seeking/finding), provided the magic gateway into this new stratum of lexicogrammar; it enabled him to mean two things at once, so that one of the two meanings became a name. Then (on the trailer principle) he stayed content with that, not following it up until another ten weeks had gone by.

Thus the apparently simple move from systems just being ordered in delicacy (as with engagement: initiation/response) to the emergence of simultaneous systems (as shown in Table 2.4 and the final stage represented in Figure 2.3) is actually a semiotic breakthrough – the 'gateway into grammar'.

*Table 2.4* Reproduction of Halliday's (1993a/2004a: 333) Table 1

|  | Expressed by Prosody | |
|---|---|---|
| expressed by articulation | "Where are you?" (mid level + high level) | "There you are!" (high falling + low level) |
| "Mummy" [ama] | [ā m ā̄] | [à m ā] |
| "Daddy" [dada] | [d ā d ā̄] | [d à d ā] |
| "Anna" [an:a] | [ā n: ā̄] | [à n: ā] |

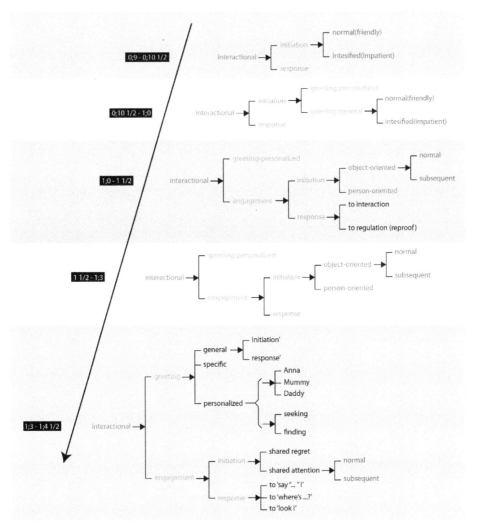

*Figure 2.3* Expansion of the interactional meaning potential from 9 months to 1 year, four and a half months, based on Halliday's (1975a) case study of Nigel

## 2.4 Split of Content System into Semantic System and Lexicogrammatical System

The last stage of the successive stages of the interactional protolinguistic potential shown in Figure 2.3 includes, as we have just seen, a trailer (or 'preview') of the split of the content plane into semantics and lexicogrammar. As noted above, during the protolinguistic phase of ontogenesis, Phase I, the content plane is systemically organized but the expression plane is not – until prosody and articulation are dissociated from one another, as shown in Table 2.4. As young children begin to make the transition from protolanguage to the mother tongue (or tongues) spoken around them, they transform this association of content/systemic and expression/syntagmatic into a system where stratification (content/expression) and axis (paradigmatic/syntagmatic) are **disassociated** from one another. One protolinguistic dimension is differentiated into two linguistic ones, as shown schematically in Figure 2.4.

The split of the content plane into two content strata affect the relationship between language and context (of situation); Halliday (2004a: 303) explains:

> The direct dependence of a speech instance on the perceptual environment disappears the moment he introduces the third level into his system, the lexicogrammatical level of words and structures, since this provides him with an abstract ('formal') level of coding which intervenes between content (the level of reference to the situation) and output. From the time when the child enters the transition to the adult mode, his individual speech acts are no longer constrained by features of the immediate situation.

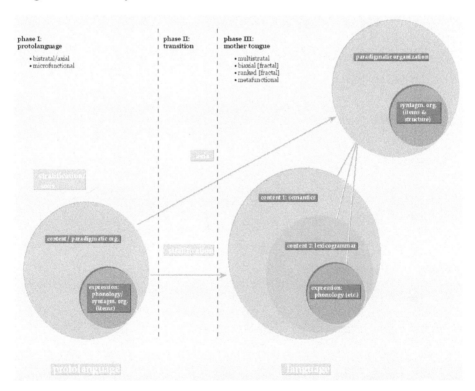

*Figure 2.4* Axiality-stratification differentiated into stratification and axiality

The 'morphing' of protolanguage into language just sketched also involves a re-analysis of the functional organization from a microfunctional one in protolanguage (Phase I), via a macrofunctional one during the transition phase (Phase II) to a metafunctional one in post-infancy adult language (Phase III). The first change, from the microfunctional organization of protolanguage (Phase I) to the macrofunctional organization of the transitional stage (Phase II) is one of generalization. The microfunctions constitute uses of protolanguage, each microfunction being a meaning potential associated invariably with a particular context of use. Towards the end of Phase I, these microfunctions are regulatory ('do as I tell you'), instrumental ('I want'), interactional ('me-&-you'), personal ('here I come'), heuristic, and imaginative. These are changed to generalized types of use in the move to Phase II: interactional, personal, heuristic and imaginative are generalized as the mathetic macrofunction for learning, and regulatory and instrumental as realized as the pragmatic macrofunction for doing. The mathetic and pragmatic macrofunctions are still alternative modes of meaning, just like the protolinguistic microfunctions.

However, the second functional change, from the macrofunctional organization of the transitional meaning potential to the metafunctional one, is one of abstraction. The alternative macrofunctions are transformed into simultaneous metafunctions. As they embark on the mother tongue, children can now begin to simultaneously construe their experience of the world around them and inside them – the ideational metafunction, and enact their roles and relations – the interpersonal metafunction. As Halliday (1985a: xiii) puts it in the passage quoted below: 'using language both to think with and to act with at the same time'. The embryonic transitivity system of the mathetic macrofunction and the embryonic mood system of the pragmatic one have now become simultaneous and thus choices within them are independently variable (though of course with certain combinations more probable than others). In the course of this development, the textual metafunction emerges as an enabling resource for creating ideational and interpersonal meanings as a flow of discourse in context. Unlike the microfunctions, the metafunctions are not associated with fixed contexts of use. Instead, the metafunctions operate within all contexts of use, with variation in the meanings at risk according to the nature of the context. (For more detail, see Matthiessen, forthcoming b, Chapter 2.)

## 2.5 Summary of Ontogenetic Semogenesis

By studying the system from the point of view of ontogenesis, we can see how semiotic acts are differentiated from material acts through stratification into content and expression. Material acts like touching, grabbing, pushing, and sighing are one-level acts; but they can come to serve as the 'material' for semiotic acts, i.e. they can become **natural** expressions of content, as when a sigh is adopted as a natural expression of 'I'm glad to see you', and they come become iconic expressions of content, as when touching an object (without grabbing it and without pulling it towards the self) comes to mean 'give it to me'. Importantly, when the child performs these as semiotic acts, s/he will address the listener by gazing at him or her. Natural and **iconic** expressions pave the way for **arbitrary (conventional)** ones. The important point is that through ontogenetic studies, we can observe how semiotic acts, stratified into content and expression, emerge from single-level material acts under the social conditions of interaction. And we can gain insight into the contrasts between a natural relationship between two strata like the content and expression strata of the protolinguistic sign and a conventional or arbitrary one. As young children begin the transition into the mother tongue spoken around them, the conventional relationship comes to dominate the relationship between content and expression – by then, between lexicogrammar and phonology, and the natural relationship comes to dominate the relationship between the two strata that content is split into, i.e. between semantics and lexicogrammar. As Halliday (1985a: xiii) notes in the preface to the first edition of his *Introduction to Functional Grammar*, a functional theory of grammar is 'designed to bring out' the natural relationship between meaning and wording, i.e. between semantics and lexicogrammar: 'it is a study of wording, but one that interprets the wording by reference to what it means'. He goes on to shed light on the nature of the natural relationship by reference to ontogenesis (xiii–xiv):

> What does it mean, then, to say that grammar is 'naturally' related to meaning? To judge from the way language is built up by children, as language evolved in the human species it began without any grammar at all; it was a two-level system, with meanings coded directly into expressions (sounds and gestures). This at least is how children's 'protolanguage' is organized, the symbolic system they usually construct for themselves before starting on the mother tongue. This is then replaced, in the second year of life by a three-level system in which meanings are first coded into wordings and these wordings then recoded into expressions. There were various reasons why this step had to be taken if the system was to expand; it opened up both the potential for dialogue, the dynamic exchange of meanings with other people, and the potential for combining different kinds of meaning in one utterance – using language both to think with and to act with at the same time.
>
> The existing interface, that between meaning and expression, was already arbitrary, or was becoming so in the later protolinguistic stage: there is no natural connection between the meaning 'I want that, give it to me' and the sound *mamama* or *nanana* often produced by a ten-month-old as its realization. It was necessary for the system to develop this frontier of arbitrariness, otherwise communication would be restricted to the relatively small range of meanings for which natural symbols can be devised. But it was not necessary that the new interface, that between meaning and wording, would should become arbitrary; indeed there was every reason why it should not, since such a system, by the time it got rich enough to be useful, would also become impossible to learn. Thus the lexicogrammar is a natural symbolic system.

When Halliday (1985a) appeared, I remember Sandy Thompson telling me how much she appreciated the notion of the natural relationship between grammar and semantics that Halliday illuminated. It was resonant with developments by her and other West-Coast functionalists. In the same year as Halliday's *Introduction to Functional Grammar*, Haiman (1985a) published his *Natural Syntax*, where explored the iconicity of various syntactic constructions, arguing against the dominant view that syntax was arbitrary. Around that time, there were a number West-Coast Functionalist studies of the iconicity of various grammatical constructions, including Haiman (1985b). (There have, of course, also been arguments against the interpretation of syntax as arbitrary coming from formal approaches to language, notably work building on Richard Montague's foundation, emphasizing the semantic compositionality of syntactic structures and providing representations of the pairing of syntactic and semantic patterns.)

By adopting the ontogenetic perspective, we can also see how the system emerges from patterns that are purely instantial; and particular systems emerge as choices between two or more options – the one of the quotes from Halliday (1998a/2004a: 11) above, 'each utterance has meaning because it is an instance of a systemic choice'. This early protolanguage is organized as a bi-stratal semiotic system of content and expression, and the content plane is organized systemically as systems forming microfunctional meaning potentials that are associated with particular contexts, while the expression plane is simply an inventory of vocal postures or visual gestures ('signifiers') realizing terms ('signifieds') in the systems that make up the microfunctional meaning potentials of the content plane.

(Since Halliday's 1975, pioneering work on ontogenesis, there have been a range of developments outside SFL that support a number of his central insights, conceptually or empirically. Bickerton 1995, uses the term 'protolanguage' in a sense that is different from Halliday's, but ultimately broadly relatable. Aspects of Halliday's 1975, 2004a, account of ontogenesis, and case studies replicating his original study, e.g. Painter 1984, 1999, and Torr 1997, are reinforced by the cognitively oriented account developed by Tomasello, e.g. 2003, 2008, 2019, informed by Vygotsky's work[2]. It would also be very fruitful to interpret the massive empirical ontogenetic data from Deb Roy's Speechhome Project, e.g. Roy et al. 2006; Gorniak and Roy 2007; Gorniak 2005 in systemic functional terms, supplementing their observations concerning material situations with social and semiotic characterizations. Alongside these later parallel developments, it is important to note the dialogic connection with Colwyn Trevarthen's research into ontogeny, e.g. Trevarthen 1974, 1979, 1987, 2009; cf. also Smidt 2017.)

Protolanguage is **multimodal** in the sense that expressions are either vocal postures or visual gestures; but these are **integrated systemically** within the content plane. The protolanguage is one semiotic system, not two parallel ones (one vocal and one gestural). In the same way, post-infancy adult languages integrate articulatory and prosodic 'modalities' within their content plane, i.e. within their lexicogrammars and semantic systems. Thus in English intonation is fully integrated as an expressive resource into the lexicogrammar; it is not a separate semiotic system (see e.g. Halliday 1967; Elmenoufy 1969; Halliday and Greaves 2008; Tench 1990, 1996; Greaves 2007; O'Grady 2010; Bowcher and Debashish 2019).

The protolanguage 'grows' by adding systems, as shown for the interactional microfunction in Figure 2.3. The addition involves further elaboration in delicacy, as when 'initiation' is further differentiated into 'person-oriented' and 'object-oriented'; but at a later stage, the addition will involve the **dissociation of associated variables** to create simultaneous systems (in the last stage of the personalized greeting systems – a systemic expansion within the content plane made possible by the deconstruction of expression into articulation and prosody, as shown in Table 2.4). Toward the end of the protolinguistic phase, new microfunctional meaning potentials emerge (heuristic and imaginative).

Ontogenesis in the sense of learning how to mean during the protolinguistic phase is thus an expansion of the meaning potential, which consists of a number of

28 • *System in Systemic Functional Linguistics*

microfunctional meaning potentials associated with different situation types (contexts of use). This expansion of the meaning potential is **systemic growth**, and can be represented by systems forming system networks. As children move from the protolinguistic phase of learning how to mean, begin to make the transition into the mother tongue, and then move into the final, life-long phase of mastering the mother tongue, we can still track this systemically by setting out successive system networks, as illustrated for the ontogenesis of dialogue by Halliday (1984a). However, the task of tracking their systemic development naturally becomes increasingly challenging in the sense that their meaning potentials become more powerful and thus more complex.

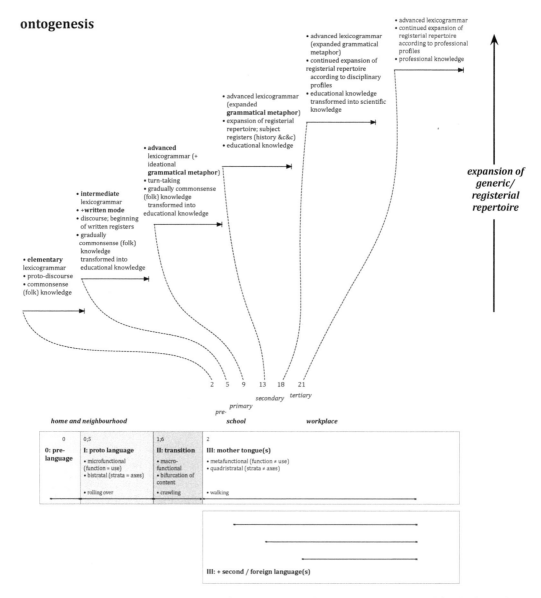

*Figure 2.5* Ontogenesis as systemic growth – expansion of the meaning potential (including of the registerial repertoire)

Even if it is not practically possible to create a comprehensive temporal map of the expansion of the meaning potential throughout ontogenesis, we can identify major phases, as indicated in Figure 2.5. Different parts of this picture have been studied systemic-functionally in considerable detail complementing the early childhood longitudinal case studies mentioned above. These include Derewianka's (1995, 2003) longitudinal case study of one person's gradual mastery of the resources of grammatical metaphor and Christie and Derewianka's (2008) overview of school discourse from primary school up through late secondary school. The early childhood studies and the school-based studies are brought together by McCabe (2021). These studies show very clearly how the meaning potential continues to grow; an important aspect of this expansion is gradual addition to an individual learner's **registerial repertoire**, as s/he moves through the educational system and then into new institutional settings, importantly including workplaces (e.g. Parodi 2010) but also other kinds characteristic of adult life.

One aspect of the development after the protolinguistic phase of ontogenesis is the gradual prying apart from language of semiotic systems with other expression planes – other 'modalities', as shown schematically in Figure 2.6. This aspect of ontogenetic semogenesis needs to be interpreted functionally and systemically in longitudinal case studies, but the general principle is reasonably clear: language develops with a vocal expression plane, and gesture emerges as a separate semiotic system[3] – but one that can be highly coordinated with language as studies of the **complementarity** of lexicogrammars and gestural systems (as post-infancy systems) in different languages have shown (e.g. Lantolf 2010). Language and gesture are both **somatic semiotic systems** in the sense that they have the body as their expression plane (cf. Thibault 2004), and there are a number of other such systems, e.g. facial expression and paralinguistic vocal systems like voice quality. In addition, there are **exosomatic semiotic systems** – systems with expression resources that are detached from the body, like drawing in many cultures (cf. discussions of writing systems as exosomatic forms of memory). So in the semiotic life of children, pictorial semiotic systems may also begin to be learned – though to the extent that they are mastered in terms of pictorial projection systems, this may not be until well into secondary school (say in their 14th year of life; Willats 1997, 2005), and the development of such systems is obviously subject to considerable cultural variation. Well before that time, children will of course have embarked on the process of learning how to write, which includes the expansion of their expressive resources on the expression plane – graphology and graphetics. While the process of writing may be somatic, the product of writing is of course exosomatic (cf. Halliday 1985c).

In the next chapter, I will turn to Phase III – to post-infancy adult language, showing how it has been, and can be, interpreted and described systemically, with examples of semantic, lexicogrammatical, phonological and phonetic system networks.

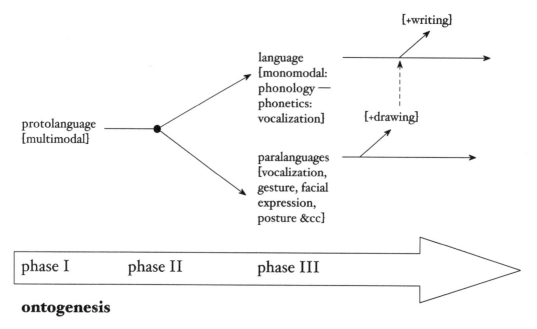

*Figure 2.6* Ontogenesis and the emergence out of protolanguage of distinct semiotic systems with different expressive 'modalities' alongside post-infancy spoken language

# Chapter 3

# The System as a Fractal Principle: The System in Relation to Other Dimensions of Organization

In the previous chapter, I traced 'system' in the ontogenesis of language – its emergence as young children learn how to mean as they construct protolanguages in interaction with members of their immediate meaning group, and then make the transition to the mother tongue (or tongues) spoken by these members. We can now examine the system as a principle of organization in relation to the other dimensions that make up the organization of language in context, starting with the hierarchy of stratification. While the hierarchies of axiality and stratification are fused in protolanguage, they are separated in the transition to the mother tongue (cf. Figure 2.4), so the question arises if the axial organization is the same within all strata.

## 3.1 The System in Relation to the Stratal Organization of Language

It's systems all the way down – rather than turtles. Language is a **system of systems** – semantic, lexicogrammatical, phonological and phonetic (or graphological and graphetic, or the expression plane equivalent in sign languages); and each of these systems is again organized as a system of systems, now specifically in the shape of system networks. In this sense, the organization of systems into system networks is a **fractal**, a fractal principle of organization that is manifested in different stratal environments throughout language; it is manifested as semantic system networks, as lexicogrammatical system networks, as phonological system networks, and as phonetic system networks.

The stratal organization of language is represented diagrammatically in Figure 3.1. Like all semiotic systems, including protolanguage (cf. Figure 2.2 above), language is organized into two stratal planes, the content plane and the expression plane; but unlike protolanguage and other primary semiotic systems, the two stratal planes of language – in the sense of post-infancy adult language – have been split into two strata (cf. Figure Figure 2.4 above). The content plane is stratified into semantics (meaning) and lexicogrammar ([meaning constructed as] wording), and the expression plane is stratified into phonology and phonetics (in the case of spoken language).

The relationship between the two content strata is natural, as is the relationship between the two expression strata. That is, lexicogrammar is natural in relation to semantics; wordings are semantically transparent. Similarly, phonology is natural in relational to phonetics.

The two stratal planes are related by lexicogrammar and phonology; wordings are realized by soundings. These are internal to their planes, and have been characterized as 'form'. The relationship between them is largely conventional, or 'arbitrary'; the realization of wordings by soundings is largely conventional – the Saussurean line of arbitrariness.

Thus while lexicogrammar and phonology are internal to language as 'form', semantics and phonetics interface with what lies beyond language, and have been characterized as 'substance'. The 'form' and 'substance' terminology is well-established in linguistics, but can be misleading if understood as a moulding kind of metaphor, with form moulding substance into different shapes. This invites an understanding of 'form' as something reified in contrast with substance as shapeless. It is much more helpful to think of the four strata in terms of their relative locations in the stratal hierarchy, mapping content beyond language into linguistic content and mapping linguistic expression into expression beyond language.

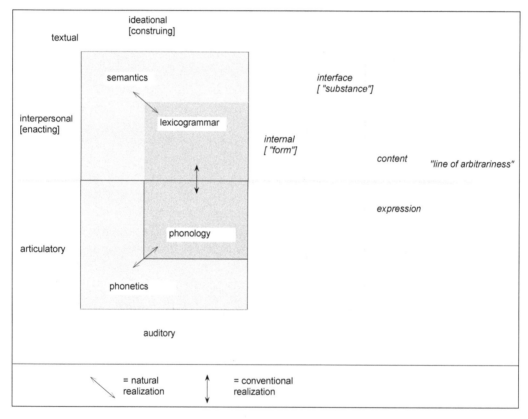

*Figure 3.1* The stratification of language, with the distinction between the two stratal planes, content and expression and the distinction between internal strata ('form') and interface strata ('substance')

The relative location of each stratal system in the hierarchy of stratification determines its overall contribution in the construal of meaning in language – i.e. the semiotic labour that it must perform; and this in turn is reflected in the pressures on the systemic representation. As we shall see, in the history of SFL, more descriptions couched in terms of fully explicit system networks have been produced for the internal stratal systems of lexicogrammar and phonology, with lexicogrammatical system networks being much more numerous than phonological ones. The frontier of descriptive work on the interface ('substance') systems of semantics and phonetics has not been pushed as far yet as for the internal strata. Linguist have also produced semantic system networks, but they have on the whole tended to be less explicit and – very significantly – they have not tended to be designed specifically for the task of interfacing with 'content' outside language. In the case of phonetics, the state of development is more exploratory. The interface strata have also been discussed in reference to the notion of topology as a complement to the notion of typology.

In the remainder of this chapter, I will begin by illustrating the fractal nature of systemic organization in Section 3.2, focussing on semantics, lexicogrammar and phonology and the inter-stratal realizational relations. I will the present accounts of content plane systems (semantics and lexicogrammar) in more detail in Section 3.3 and of expression plane systems (phonology and phonetics) in Section 3.4, noting phenomena of interest like metaphor and issues along the way. In Section 3.5, I will return to the difference between internal and interface systems, and then in Section 3.6, I will explore the use of system network to represent systems external to language, viz. the connotative semiotic system of context and denotative semiotic systems other than language.

## 3.2 Systems All the Way Down

As noted above, according to systemic functional theory, each stratal system of language (Figure 3.1) is organized internally according to the same axial 'template' as a series of system network (with associated realization statements) ordered in terms of the rank scale of its stratum. In theory, the situation could be different: each stratal system of language might be organized according to distinct principles – principles unique to each stratum, and this is of course how many theories of language model it, e.g. with different kinds of rule systems for semantics, syntax, morphology and phonology. This may because they are partial theories – theories of semantics, or of syntax, or of morphology, or of phonology – rather than holistic ones; or because while they cover more than one subsystem, they hold that each one is characterized by a different kind of organization. For example, phonology may be modelled autosegmentally, but grammar may be modelled by means of, say, categorial grammar or Lexical Functional Grammar. In contrast, in Systemic Functional Linguistics, the systemic template is the same for each subsystem; each one is modelled as system networks with realization statements associated with terms in systems.

While this treatment of all strata of language on the same basic model of organization is unusual among linguistic theories, Stratificational Linguistics and SFL are similar with respect to this fundamental theoretical conception of language. Having developed from different starting points in linguistic traditions, the two theories share the conception of language as a vast relational network, an insight illuminated by Louis Hjelmslev in his Glossematics, which has been a source of inspiration in both SFL and Stratificational Linguistics. Starting with the dialogue between Michael Halliday and Sydney Lamb in the 1960s, SFL has remained in contact with Stratificational Linguistics (e.g. Lamb

1966, 1999; Lockwood 1972) and its successor, Relational Network Theory, presented by García, Sullivan and Tsiang (2017). Since Stratificational Linguistics has been developed taking neurocognitive considerations into account, it complements the emphasis on social considerations in SFL. In fact, in terms of networks, Lamb (2013) suggests that relational networks could serve as a mediating form of representation between system networks and neural networks, which could be a representational strategy as we try to relate semiotic systems to biological ones (cf. also Section 5.2.3 on the stratification of metalanguage).

### 3.2.1 Illustration: An Interpersonal Slice through Semantics, Lexicogrammar and Phonology

As an introductory illustration of the manifestation of the systemic principle within the different stratal domains of language, let me start with the interpersonal metafunction and focus on a fragment of the interpersonal resources of English, presenting a stratal slice of semantic, lexicogrammatical and phonological system networks. These system networks provide the resources for interactants to engage in exchanges of meaning in dialogue, adopting speech roles as speakers and assigning complementary roles to their addresses. The system networks have different units as their domains, viz. the semantic unit of move, the grammatical unit of clause and the phonological unit of tone group: see Table 3.1.

*Table 3.1* Units and system networks in the interpersonal slice through semantics, lexicogrammar and phonology

| stratum | unit | system network |
| --- | --- | --- |
| semantics | move | SPEECH FUNCTION |
| lexicogrammar | clause | MOOD |
| phonology | tone group | TONE |

The interpersonal slice through the three strata in Table 3.1 is shown in Figure 3.1 (for overview of the conventions for systems and realization statements, see Table 8.1 and Table 8.2), and covers the following semantic, lexicogrammatical and phonological units and systems:

- **semantics, move:** the options open to a move in dialogue are represented by the system network of SPEECH FUNCTION. It involves three systems at primary delicacy, viz. TURN, ORIENTATION and COMMODITY. The systemic terms in the systems of ORIENTATION and COMMODITY together define the basic speech functions – statement, question, offer and command (which can serve as either 'initiating' or 'responding' moves in the system of TURN). They are of course all elaborated in delicacy, but this elaboration in delicacy is only shown for questions in Figure 3.2, the system of QUESTION TYPE. This is as far as is necessary to go in delicacy for the purposes of illustration – to show the (congruent) realizations by terms in the grammatical system of MOOD TYPE (see immediately below): 'statement' ↘ (is realized by) 'declarative', 'polar questions' ↘ 'yes/no interrogative', 'elemental question' ↘ 'Wh-interrogative', and 'command' ↘ 'imperative'.

- **lexicogrammar, clause:** the options open to a 'free' clause realizing a move in dialogue[1] are represented by the system network of MOOD TYPE: 'indicative'/'imperative' (as illustrated in Table 3.2). The term 'indicative' has associated with it a realization statement specifying the structure common to indicative clauses in general in English: +Mood [i.e. the structure of the clause includes a Mood element], Mood (+Subject; +Finite) [i.e. the Mood element consists of Subject and Finite – their presence is specified but not their relative sequence since the sequence depends on more delicate indicative mood types]. The term 'indicative' is the entry condition of the system INDICATIVE TYPE, 'declarative'/'interrogative'; the term 'declarative' has the realization statement Subject ^ Finite [i.e. Subject precedes Finite] associated with it. The term 'interrogative' leads to the system INTERROGATIVE TYPE, 'yes/no interrogative'/'wh-interrogative', whose terms have associated realization statements: 'yes/no interrogative' ↘ Finite ^ Subject/'wh-interrogative' ↘ +Wh; Wh ^ Finite. The term 'declarative' leads to the system DECLARATIVE KEY, 'neutral'/'marked'; 'neutral' is realized phonologically (i.e. at the stratum immediately below that of lexicogrammar) by 'tone 1' and 'marked' leads to a more delicate distinction among marked declarative keys: 'protesting' ↘ 'tone 2'/'tentative' ↘ 'tone 3'/'reserved' ↘ 'tone 4'/'insistent' ↘ 'tone 5'. The other mood types also lead to key systems, but they are not included in Figure 3.1.

*Table 3.2* Systemic terms with associated realization statements

| mood type | | | realization statement | example |
|---|---|---|---|---|
| indicative | | | +Mood; Mood (+Subject; +Finite) | *he has*/*has he* done his homework |
| | declarative | | Subject ^ Finite | *he has* done his homework |
| | interrogative | yes/no | Finite ^ Subject | *has he* done his homework |
| | | wh- | +Wh; Wh ^ Finite | ***who** has* done his homework; ***what** has he* done |
| imperative | | | | *do his homework* |

- **phonology, tone group:** the options open to a 'simple' tone group realizing a 'free' clause are (at primary delicacy) represented by the system SIMPLE PRIMARY TONE: 'tone 1' ↘ phonetically, a falling tone, ranging from a wide fall to a narrow fall/'tone 2' ↘ phonetically, a rising tone/'tone 3' ↘ phonetically, a level or low rise tone/'tone 4' ↘ phonetically, a fall-rise/'tone 5' ↘ phonetically, a rise-fall. The more delicate options open to the different tones are also grammatically significant, but are not shown in Figure 3.2. Compound tones tend to be selected for textual reasons since they include an additional Tonic element within the tone group realizing information Focus (within New information).

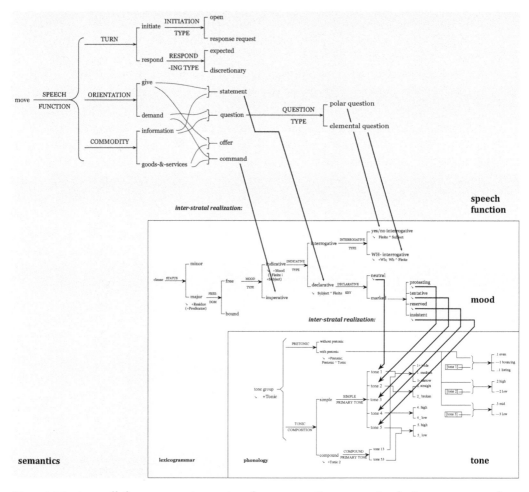

*Figure 3.2* Systems all the way – system networks representing semantics, lexicogrammar and phonology, as illustrated by fragments of the interpersonal systems of SPEECH FUNCTION (semantics: move), MOOD (lexicogrammar: clause), whose elaboration in delicacy by systems of key is illustrated for 'declarative' clauses by the system of DECLARATIVE KEY, and TONE (phonology: tone group)

The descriptive fragments in Figure 3.2 come from three different strata – the two content strata of semantics and lexicogrammar and the higher of the two expression strata in spoken language, phonology. They are all organized as **resources** – resources of meaning, of wording and of sounding; and all three strata of resources are organized in the same way, according to the same **systemic template** – as paradigmatic patterns involving choice represented by system networks. I will elaborate on system networks operating within the different strata of language presently in this chapter, but let me first add some general observations about the 'payoff' created by the systemic patterning within all strata.

## 3.2.2 Content Plane: Double Agnation

Each stratal system network represents paradigmatic patterns – patterns of relatedness or **agnation**. Consequently, agnation can be specified *twice* within the content plane; i.e. agnation in content can be stated in terms of systems of meaning (semantics) and also in terms of systems of wording (lexicogrammar), as illustrated in Table 3.3 below. For example, *shall I do your homework?* is semantically an offer in the system of SPEECH FUNCTION and lexicogrammatically a yes/no interrogative in the system of MOOD TYPE; and *let me do your homework* is semantically an offer and lexicogrammatically an imperative.[2] We might call this the principle of **double agnation** within the content plane, as a complement to André Martinet's principle of double articulation (e.g. Martinet 1970: 7–8).[3]

(With prosodic phonology, there is even the possibility of a third order of agnation since prosodic patterns – intonation patterns in particular – stand in a natural rather than conventional relationship to wording patterns; for example, the basic prosodic phonological contrast between a falling and a rising tone stands in a natural relation to the grammatical contrast between 'declarative' and 'interrogative: yes/no', reflecting the semantic contrasts between 'I'm certain about the polarity' and 'I'm uncertain about the polarity' (cf. Table 3.5).[4] So interpersonal patterns of agnation can be captured thrice across strata, each stratum representing a somewhat different set of generalizations. The same applies to textual patterns of agnation; they can also involve **triple agnation**.)

When we only consider the realizational relationships between semantics and lexicogrammar shown in Figure 3.2, it might seem as if the patterns of agnation are simply stated twice with some variation in systemic contrasts, first within semantics and then within grammar, as shown in Table 3.3 (a). Here the speech functions and the mood types stand in a one-to-one relation, so each can be predicted from the other (they **redound**, in the sense of Halliday 1992a, referring to Lemke's 1985, interpretation). And yet there is an important difference: since the description of the speech functional system has been constructed to tease apart two systemic variables in the form of the systems of ORIENTATION ('giving'/'demanding') and of COMMODITY TYPE ('information'/'goods-&-services'), the description reveals the paradigmatically 'composite' nature of the traditional basic speech functions while at the same time including one, 'offer', that does not correspond to any of the mood types – thus revealing a gap in the content plane: a speech function without a corresponding mood type, unlike the other major speech functions.

When we set out to investigate how offers are realized grammatically, we find that they have various forms of realization, covering the three basic mood types: see Table 3.3 (b). An offer can be realized by a declarative clause (e.g. *I can do your homework*, with the speaker as Subject and a modal operator of 'readiness' as Finite), by an interrogative (e.g. *shall I do your homework*, with the speaker as Subject and a modal operator of 'obligation' as Finite), or by an imperative (e.g. *let me do your homework*, with the speaker as Subject [the special form *let me*, sometimes spelled as *lemme* to reflect the pronunciation)][5]. Even though the speech functional category of 'offer' is dispersed grammatically in its realization, it plays a fundamental role in the system of SPEECH FUNCTION and the strategies for making offers can be described systemically, as Hasan (1987) has demonstrated. The reason why English has not evolved a mood type dedicated to the realization of 'offer' is that offers can be made without the facilitation by language – to an even greater extent than is the case with the speech function of 'command' since with commands language is needed to impose an obligation on the addressee. (And English is not unique in this respect; in general, languages haven't got a mood type dedicated to the realization of offers.)

As we investigate the range of grammatical realizations of the speech function of 'offer', we can take one step further and look for alternative realizations of the three other basic speech functions, as illustrated in Table 3.3 (c). It turns out that alongside the 'standard' patterns of realization shown in Table 3.3 (a), statements, questions and commands all have alternative realizations by different mood types.

*Table 3.3* The semantic system of speech function and the grammatical system of mood type 'intersected'

(a)

|  | SPEECH FUNCTION | | | |
|---|---|---|---|---|
| MOOD TYPE | statement | question | offer | command |
| declarative | √ he has done his homework | | | |
| interrogative | | √ has he done his homework? | | |
| — | | | — | |
| imperative | | | | √ do your homework! |

(b)

|  | SPEECH FUNCTION | | | |
|---|---|---|---|---|
| MOOD TYPE | statement | question | offer | command |
| declarative | √ he has done his homework | | I can do your homework | |
| interrogative | | √ has he done his homework? | shall I do your homework? | |
| imperative | | | let me do your homework! | √ do your homework! |

(c)

|  | SPEECH FUNCTION | | | |
|---|---|---|---|---|
| MOOD TYPE | statement | question | offer | command |
| declarative | √ he has done his homework | [he has done his homework, has he?] | I can do your homework | I want you to do your homework |
| interrogative | I want to know if he has done his homework | √ has he done his homework? | shall I do your homework? | would you do your homework? |
| imperative | | tell me if he has done his homework! | let me do your homework! | √ do your homework! |

There is one cell that I have left empty: the realization of statements by imperative clauses, but we can certainly construct examples such as *believe that he has done his homework!*, *take it from me that he has done his homework!*, *accept that he has done his homework!*

These examples – constructed as illustrations – all involve a 'that' clause representing the propositional aspect of the statement: 'believe'/'take it from me'/'accept' + 'that': proposition. This in fact only the tip of the interpersonal iceberg of negotiation: all speech functions may be realized by a combination of two clauses, one clause representing the proposition or proposal being negotiated, and the other the act of negotiation by means of a verb of saying or sensing serving in that clause. In this way, commands may be realized as if they were statements or questions, questions may be realized as if they were statements or commands, and so on.

The iceberg whose tip we have started to examine is the phenomenon of **incongruence**, more specifically **grammatical metaphor**. Once the content plane has split into two content strata, content$_1$ and content$_2$, i.e. semantics and lexicogrammar, and realizational relations like those illustrated in Table 3.3 (a) have emerged as the 'norm' – that is, realizational relations that are fundamentally one-to-one, then it becomes possible for alternatives to emerge – to develop ontogenetically or to evolve phylogenetically (and even to unfold logogenetically). The 'norm' is the congruent relation realization between a semantic term and a lexicogrammatical one, and the alternatives that emerge are incongruent ones – metaphorical realizations.

Metaphorical realizations always involve an 'as if' feature; for example, the congruent realization of a 'command' is an 'imperative' clause, and the incongruent or metaphoric realizations given in Table 3.3 (c) are realizations of a 'command' by a 'declarative' clause as if it were a 'statement' and by an 'interrogative' clause as if it were a 'question'. The congruent and incongruent realizations are not synonymous; the incongruent ones involve additional features: *I want you to do your homework* is in fact a statement about the speaker's desire as well as a type of command, and *would you do your homework?* is similarly a question about the addressee's willingness as well as a type of command. In this sense, we can say that they are **junctures** of command with statement or question (cf. Halliday and Matthiessen 2006: Chapter 6). In terms of the description of the system of speech function, such incongruent realizations are accounted for by means of more delicate systems – systems providing elaborated options of 'command'. Since we are in the interpersonal metafunction, the further elaboration in delicacy provides additional resources for negotiating the tenor of the relationship between speaker and addressee – in this case, having to do with the degree of imposition on the addressee, which relates to the degree of discretion he or she is afforded in responding, and the degree of 'politeness' (cf. Section 3.2.2.6.2).

As is illustrated by the constructed examples in Table 3.3 (c), incongruent realizations are always more **constrained** systemically than congruent ones. For example, while *would you do your homework* is a yes/no interrogative clause, it is constrained in terms of two systems set out in Table 3.4, viz. (i) SUBJECT PERSON: addressee-subject (i.e. 'you') and (ii) DEICTICITY: modal: modulation: readiness (either 'willingness' *would you* or 'potentiality' [ability] *could you*)[6], both of which are part of the interpersonal clause system network set out in Figure 3.8 further below. Thus in the paradigm for yes/no interrogative clauses involving the systems of DEICTICITY and SUBJECT PERSON, we can locate *would/could you do your homework* at the intersection of 'readiness' and 'addressee' and contrast it with all the other combinations of DEICTICITY and SUBJECT PERSON (see Table 3.4). The term 'addressee' is an interpretation of the traditional notion of 'second person'; but instead of the traditional three-term distinction of first/second/third person, the person system is interpreted as based on speech roles: either 'interactant' ('first and 'second person') – 'speaker' (i.e. 'I')/'addressee' (i.e. 'you')/'speaker-plus' (i.e. speaker plus others, 'we') – or 'non-interactant' ('third person', pronominally 'he', 'she', 'it', 'they'). The term 'readiness' is an option in the system of MODALITY; it covers ability and willingness.

Table 3.4 Systemic intersections of subject person and deicticity – a paradigm for yes/no interrogatives

| | DEICTICITY | | | | | | |
|---|---|---|---|---|---|---|---|
| | temporal | | | modal | | | |
| | | | | modalization | | modulation | |
| SUBJECT PERSON: | past | present | future | probability | usuality | obligation | readiness |
| speaker | *did I do your homework? [yesterday]* | *do I do your homework? [in the evenings]* | *will I do your homework? [tomorrow]* | | | *must I do your homework?* | *would/ could I do your homework?* |
| addressee | *did you do your homework? [yesterday]* | *do you do your homework? [in the evenings]* | *will you do your homework? [tomorrow]* | | | *must you do your homework?* | **would/ could you** *do your homework?* |
| speaker+ | *did we do your homework? [yesterday]* | *do we do your homework? [in the evenings]* | *will we do your homework? [tomorrow]* | | | *must we do your homework?* | *would/ could we do your homework?* |
| non-interactant | *did she do your homework? [yesterday]* | *does she do your homework? [in the evenings]* | *will she do your homework? [tomorrow]* | | | *must she do your homework?* | *would/ could she do your homework?* |

We could examine all the cells in the table, each representing a unique combination of systemic terms from DEICTICITY and SUBJECT PERSON, and determine the most likely co-text and 'uptake' by the addressee in an exchange in a dialogue. The ones in the 'non-interactant' row are likely to be interpreted as congruent realizations of questions – at least in the 'temporal' column; *must she do your homework?* could be interpreted as a challenge to a command, a refusal by proxy. In general, the 'temporal' ones are likely to be congruent realizations of questions; but even here, there may be an implication of a command, for example, *did you do your homework yesterday?* – I know you didn't, so *do your homework now!* At this point, it is very clear that we need to consult naturally occurring dialogic discourse where we know the context (cf. Section 3.2.2.6.2) – we need to analyse a corpus of situated dialogue (in the sense of Gu, e.g. 2002). It will certainly turn out to be the case that one and the same yes/no interrogative clause can be read – or rather heard! – in different ways depending on the tenor of the relationship among the interactants (cf. Halliday's 1975b/2003: 79–80, emphasis on semantics in relation to context in a discussion of Searle and speech act theory: see Section 3.2.2.6).

When we examine the relationship between two adjacent strata of language in context – i.e. context and semantics, semantics and lexicogrammar, lexicogrammar and phonology (or graphology), and phonology (graphology) and phonetics (graphetics), we will find as a general principle that the systemic contrasts at the lower stratum are systemically diversified at the higher stratum. For example, a yes/no interrogative clause is semantically a polar question, but it may also be a command (*would you do your homework?*) or an offer (*shall I do your homework?*) – under certain conditions. In this way, the higher-stratal *valeur* or systemic value is as it were a **systemic multiplication** of the lower-stratal one. This applies, as we have seen, to relationships involving incongruent realizations, but it is a general principle, not one restricted to metaphor.

*Table 3.5* The deployment of the phonological system of tone one stratum up, within lexicogrammar, and the 'multiplication' of systemic values (unmarked (neutral) keys in bold)

| MOOD TYPE: | indicative | declarative | | possibility statement | **statement** | assertion | reservation | contradiction, protest |
|---|---|---|---|---|---|---|---|---|
| | | interrogative | wh- | | elemental **question** | | | (i) tentative question (Wh not tonic) (ii) echo question (Wh tonic) |
| | | | yes/no | uninvolved question | demand question | involved question | assertive question | polar **question** |
| | imperative | <positive> | | invitation | **command**⁸ | insistent command | plea (compromising command) | querying command |
| | | <negative> | | **prohibition** | peremptory prohibition | | | querying prohibition |
| | *generalization of key across mood types* | | | no definite key | definite key | | | |
| | | | | | assurance | | doubt | |
| | | | | | non-reversal of key | reversal of key | | |
| TONE: | | | | tone 3 | tone 1 | tone 5 | tone 4 | tone 2 |

Thus the phonological system of TONE is 'multiplied' lexicogrammatically in terms of a number of key systems (delicate mood systems) operating in the systemic environment of different mood types[7]: instead of one key system corresponding to the tone system, there is one key system for each mood type (and in the case of 'imperative' clauses, with differentiation according to polarity), as illustrated for 'declarative' clauses in Figure 3.1 above. Table 3.5 shows the five primary tones in the last row as realizations of distinct options in KEY for the different basic mood types. Each one of the mood types is elaborated in further delicacy by key systems, as illustrated for 'declarative' clauses above in Figure 3.1.

Rounding off this discussion of 'systems all the way down' from semantics to phonology, let me quote at some length from Halliday (1984a: 10–11):

> In a systemic representation of language, the basic organizing concept is that of choice. A choice has two components: it consists of (1) a set of 'things', of which one must be chosen; and (2) an entry condition – the environment in which the choice is made. The environment of a choice could be thought of as a structural setting or background; but it can equally be represented as the combined outcome of a range of other choices. So meanings are represented as networks of choices. The formal representation of a choice is called (following Firth) a 'system'; hence, a choice network is a system network. The description of a language takes the form of system networks.
>
> All three levels of the linguistic system, semantic, lexicogrammatical, and phonological, are interpreted in this way as system networks. The concept of 'choice', however, has a different significance at each level.
>
> The exchange of meanings is an ongoing process of contextualized choice. An act of meaning in language is a process of semantic choice. Choices at other levels, lexicogrammatical and phonological, tend to be predetermined, because they serve as the realization of choices in the semantic system – although there are 'de-automatized' choices at other levels, for example the choice of parallel grammatical structures, or of syllables that rhyme.

These comments apply to the preview of semantic, lexicogrammatical and phonological systems that I have presented so far (since Halliday's paper was published, we have also made explicit that phonetics is a stratum – the stratum of expression substance). He then goes on to note that semantic choices are related to contextual ones. I will introduce contextual system networks below, but his comments will serve as an excellent preview (Halliday 1984a: 11):

> But semantic choices are also, in the final analysis, the 'realization' of choices at some higher level, somewhere in the semiotic systems of the culture. If they were not, it would scarcely be possible for ordinary spontaneous conversation to have the magical power that it has, the power of constructing and organizing social situations, of providing the foundation for interpersonal relations and the socialization process, of maintaining and giving a history of personal identity, and of creating and modifying the structure of reality. At the same time, it must be borne in mind that once a particular symbolic system comes into being, engendered by the culture, it takes on an independent existence and so engenders meanings of its own, meanings which become part of the culture in their turn; and language is the paradigm example of this process.

He then goes on to make a distinction between semantic acts and non-semantic ones. I will return to this distinction later as I explore the manifestation of system within an ordered typology of systems operating in different semiotic realms. But let me now continue to quote Halliday (1984a: 11):

> Forcing, threatening, and making contact with a person are non-semantic acts, which may or may not be realized semantically through language; ordering, warning, and greeting are semantic acts – which thereby become part of the cultural semiotic and take on social value. In like manner, building a shelter is a non-semantic act, one which happens to be subject to certain natural laws; whereas encoding this process in a transitivity structure is a semantic act – through which a model of transitivity then becomes part of the culture.

As just noted, I will return to this distinction; I will examine the distinction between systems with options in meaning and systems with options in behaviour. In this chapter, I will now discuss lexicogrammatical, semantic and phonological system networks in some more detail. I will then turn to the issue of phonetic system networks, and finally to system networks 'outside' language – contextual system networks 'above' language ('connotative semiotics') and semiotic systems 'alongside' language ('denotative semiotics').

### 3.3 Content Plane System Networks

Content plane system networks are located within the two content strata of language, semantics and lexicogrammar. In the illustration presented in Figure 3.1, the semantic network is the system of SPEECH FUNCTION and the lexicogrammatical network is the system of MOOD. I will start with lexicogrammatical system networks; they have been most extensively developed in descriptions for the greatest range of languages (cf. Teruya et al. 2007), and they can serve as a basis for articulating and illustrating a number of properties relevant to the content plane in general.

#### 3.3.1 Lexicogrammatical System Networks

Systemic descriptions of the lexicogrammars of different languages have been undertaken since the 1960s, and systemic functional linguists have now produced systemic descriptions of a fair number of languages from different families and with different typological characteristics, with new ones being added regularly (see e.g. Caffarel, Martin and Matthiessen 2004; Teruya and Matthiessen 2015; Kashyap 2019). In fact, in addition to having the longest history of description in SFL, the lexicogrammatical stratum is the most comprehensively described for the widest range of languages of all the strata. Consequently, the application of system networks to lexicogrammar has been being tested for a long time, and both positive findings and representational issues are well known, and can provide insights into systemic descriptions of the other strata of language.

The first language to be described systemically was Chinese – by Halliday (1956a, 1959) using his variant of Firth's system-structure theory. But he switched to English as he began using system networks in lexicogrammatical descriptions – as part of the process of 'inventing' this form of representation and giving priority to organization along the paradigmatic axis. The first version came to be known as the 'Bloomington

Grammar' because he worked on it in Bloomington, Indiana (in 1964), and it's presented as a series of system networks for the clauses, and groups/phrases in Halliday (1976).

### 3.3.1.1 Systemic Clustering and the Metafunctional Organization of Lexicogrammar

As he developed the system network description of English, Halliday noticed that systems clustered together into regions with systemic interdependencies while there were far fewer systemic links between the clusters. He explained this phenomenon of **systemic clustering** by developing his theory of the **metafunctional organization** of language. It's not easy to give a clear sense of this clustering since one needs a great deal of space to display the system network of the clause in a comprehensive version up to some point of delicacy, but let me illustrate the clustering effect by means of three schematic representations:

- Halliday's (1969) image of the basic systems of the clause – Figure 3.2,
- Halliday's (1973b: 141) 'summary of principal options in the English clause' – Figure 3.3,
- and an index to the clause systems we present in Halliday and Matthiessen (2014) – Figure 3.4.

While these examples are highly schematic and do not extend very far in delicacy, it is still possible to get a general sense of the systemic clustering Halliday noticed and then explained in terms of his theory of metafunction.

The system networks shown in Figure 3.2 and Figure 3.3 and the system network index provided in Figure 3.4 are all concerned with one domain within the lexicogrammar of English – that of the clause as the highest-ranking unit of the grammar. Just as for the other stratal subsystems of language, it makes sense to start the presentation of the systemic description of lexicogrammar with the clause since it is the highest-ranking unit of the grammar: clauses consist of groups/phrases, groups consist of words, and (in the case of a language like English) words consist of morphemes. And the overall lexicogrammatical 'labour' of any language is divided among the units of the grammar, ordered in terms of the rank scale. For example, within the ideational resources of the lexicogrammar, the task of construing a quantum of change in our experience of the flow of events is parcelled out among clause and group systems, among which nominal groups construe participants and verbal groups processes (circumstances being construed by either adverbial groups or prepositional phrases):

- while the experiential grammar of the clause is concerned with entities as participants in figures (process configurations) (the system of TRANSITIVITY), the experiential grammar of the nominal group provides the resources for characterizing them: construing entities as some kind of thing (THING TYPE), potentially classified taxonomically (CLASSIFICATION), described qualitatively (EPITHESIS) and qualified circumstantially (QUALIFICATION).
- while the experiential grammar of the clause is concerned with goings-on as processes in figures (the system of TRANSITIVITY), the logical grammar of the verbal group provides the resources for construing them as events unfolding in time

relative to a series of other times, typically anchored in the 'now' of speaking (the system of TENSE).

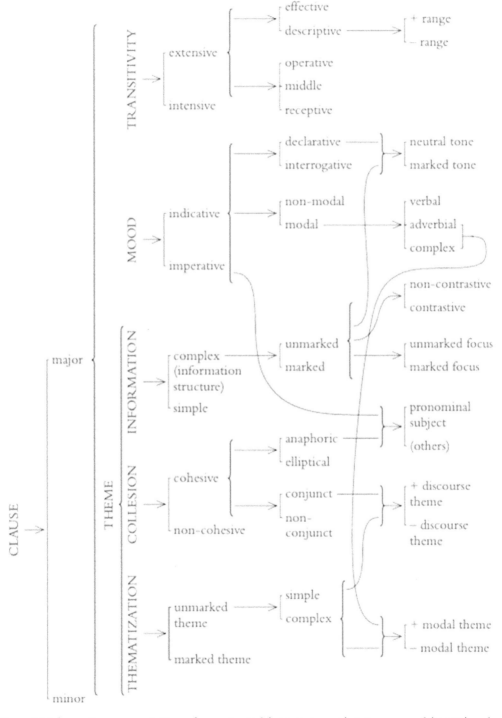

*Figure 3.3* Schematic representation of experiential (TRANSITIVITY), interpersonal (MOOD) and textual (THEME) clause systems in Halliday (1969)

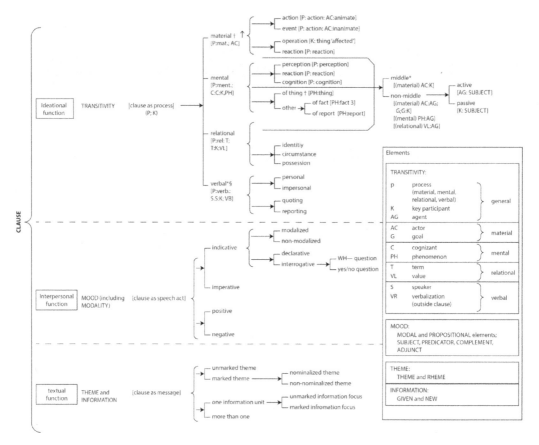

*Figure 3.4* Schematic representation of experiential (TRANSITIVITY), interpersonal (MOOD) and textual (THEME) clause systems in Halliday (1973a/2003: 315)

These are the two highest ranks, those of clause and group/phrase; and the next two ranks also contribute to the overall lexicogrammatical labour, although the division of labour between groups and words varies considerably among the languages of the world. For example:

John: Did you enjoy yourselves last week? –

Mary: Yes, we had an absolutely fabulously supercalifragilisticexpialidocious time at the lake.

Here the word complex *absolutely fabulously supercalifragilisticexpialidocious* serves as Epithet in the nominal group, and at word rank, the adjective serving as the Head of this complex is built up through the logical resources of DERIVATION. In the same way as ideational systems are parcelled out along the rank scale, interpersonal and textual systems are also distributed from clause to group/phrase to word to morpheme. (It is worth noting, however, that the rank scale in a sense constitutes an experiential projection of the resources of the lexicogrammar of a language since it is the experiential metafunction that models our experience configurationally as organic wholes and their parts; cf. Matthiessen 1995a: 88–97.)

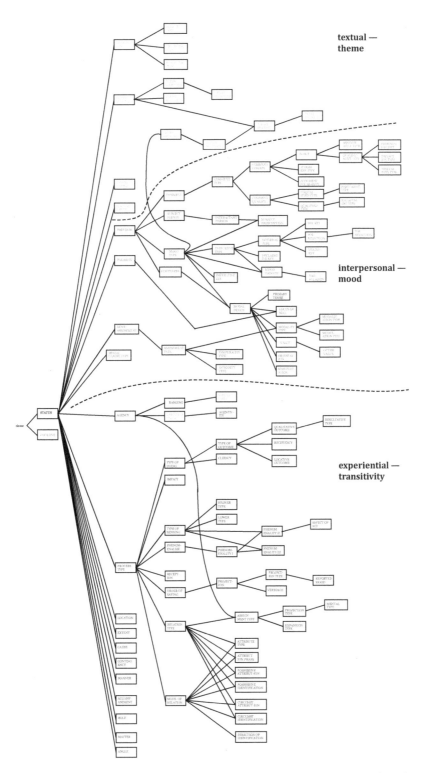

*Figure 3.5* Index of systems of the clause presented in Halliday and Matthiessen (2014) – textual (THEME, CONJUNCTION), interpersonal (FREEDOM, MOOD, POLARITY, MODAL ASSESSMENT) and experiential (TRANSITIVITY: AGENCY, PROCESS TYPE, CIRCUMSTANTIATION)

In summary, the ideational (experiential and logical), interpersonal and textual systems of the lexicogrammar of a language are distributed across units ordered by its rank scale, in English from the clause via the group/phrase and word to the morpheme. To produce a comprehensive map of the lexicogrammar of English or any other language, we can intersect metafunction with rank (and primary class within rank) to define a **function-rank matrix**, as illustrated in Table 3.6. I have adapted this matrix from Halliday and Matthiessen (2014), and it can be viewed alongside the matrices designed for English since Halliday (1970a) and the ones providing overview of other languages, a couple of which are included in Caffarel, Martin and Matthiessen (2004). The three metafunctional guises or roles of the clause in the semantic systems are shown and characterized in Table 3.7 further below.

Function-rank matrices like the one exemplified in Table 3.6 serve as comprehensive maps of all the systems that make up the lexicogrammatical resources of any given language. The systems named in the cells of the matrix cover all of the lexicogrammar, so in this sense the matrix constitutes an exhaustive map of the resources. Naturally, they can all be extended in delicacy; but they are extended in delicacy within the systemic domain named in the matrix, like TRANSITIVITY, MOOD and THEME. (It is thus not the case that new systems suddenly appear at a greater degree of delicacy; systems are always elaborations in delicacy of the systems identified in the matrix at primary delicacy.) The relationship between the systems named in a cell in the matrix and the relevant region of the system network is illustrated for clause rank in Figure 3.6. For example, the system of TRANSITIVITY is located at the intersection of experiential (metafunction) and clause (rank) in the matrix to the left, and it is displayed as a system network to the right – more accurately, as an index into the system network of TRANSITIVITY. For further discussion of such views on linguistic systems and the system as a navigational tool, see Chapter 4 (cf. Figure 4.4).

I noted above that the systems identified in the function-rank matrix are extended in delicacy from the grammatical zone of lexicogrammar to the lexical zone. We can imagine a supplement to the function rank matrix where this extension in delicacy is brought out. This would be a **function-delicacy matrix**, showing how lexicogrammatical systems are distributed in terms of delicacy. This would show variation across the metafunctions in the degree of elaboration in delicacy; moving around the languages of the world, we would probably find that the degree of elaboration in delicacy is ordered metafunctionally, from most elaborated to least elaborated: experiential > interpersonal > textual; and that languages vary typologically in how divide the labour of construing experience between the experiential mode (which tends towards taxonomic differentiation and depth) and the logical mode (which tends towards serial intricacy). Comparing languages, we would most likely find that they vary considerably in where they do the lexicogrammatical work with respect to particular domains such as our experience of space-time and our enactment of assessments of the validity of propositions – more grammatically or more lexically (cf. Halliday and Matthiessen 2006: Chapter 7). And this can certainly change over time within a given language, as studies of grammaticalization have shown. In fact, we would also find variation within a given language during a particular period of time of a registerial nature (cf. the discussion of taxonomic depth varying with degrees of expertise in Wignell, Martin and Eggins 1993, and in Halliday and Matthiessen 2006: Chapter 14).

Table 3.6 Lexicogrammatical function-rank matrix, adapted from Halliday and Matthiessen's (2014: 87) function-rank matrix

| stratum | rank | class | logical | experiential | interpersonal | textual structural | textual cohesive |
|---|---|---|---|---|---|---|---|
| lexicogrammar | clause | | TAXIS & LOGICO-SEMANTIC TYPE | TRANSITIVITY (PROCESS TYPE, AGENCY; CIRCUMSTANTIATION) | MOOD (including KEY); POLARITY, DEICTICITY, MODAL ASSESSMENT; ADDRESS | THEME; VOICE (operative/receptive) | CONJUNCTION; SUBSTITUTION-ELLIPSIS; REFERENCE; LEXICAL COHESION |
| | group/phrase | prepositional phrase | — | MINOR TRANSITIVITY | MINOR MOOD | — | |
| | | nominal group | MODIFICATION | THING TYPE; CLASSIFICATION, EPITHESIS, QUALIFICATION | PERSON; ASSESSMENT (including ATTITUDINAL EPITHESIS); NOMINAL MOOD | DETERMINATION | |
| | | verbal group | TENSE | EVENT TYPE; ASPECT | POLARITY, MODALITY | VOICE (ACTIVE/PASSIVE), CONTRAST | |
| | | adverbial group | MODIFICATION | CIRCUMSTANCE TYPE | COMMENT TYPE | | |
| | | conjunction group | | | | CONJUNCTION TYPE | |
| | word | | DERIVATION | DENOTATION | CONNOTATION | | (LEXICAL COHESION) |
| | information unit | | | — | (KEY) | INFORMATION | |
| phonology | tone group | | TONE SEQUENCE & CONCORD | — | TONE | TONICITY | |

50 • *System in Systemic Functional Linguistics*

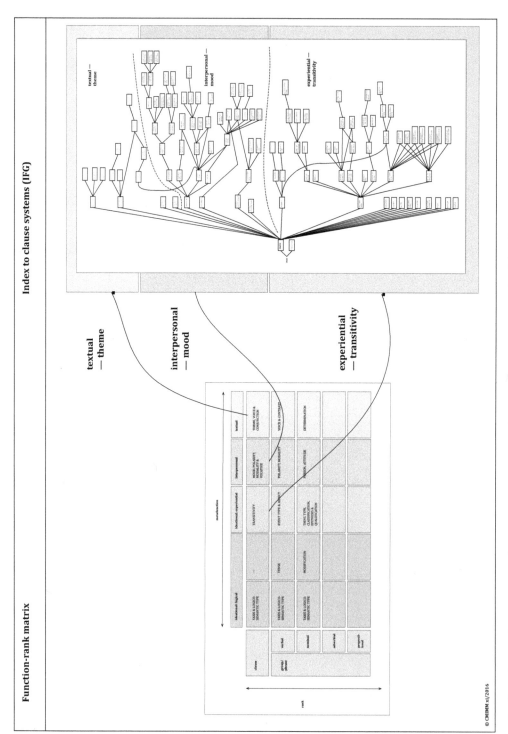

*Figure 3.6* The function-rank matrix as a directory to systems in the overall system network of the clause

### 3.3.1.2 Key Clause Systems

The systems named in the function rank matrix in Table 3.6 are illustrated at clause rank in simplified versions in Figure 3.2 and Figure 3.3 and more elaborated versions of them are presented in Matthiessen (1995a), Halliday and Matthiessen (2014) (cf. the clause systems in the index in Figure 3.5) and various other publications. These publications document the systems of the lexicogrammar of English, and those of a number of other languages are also available (for overviews of systemic functional descriptions of different languages, see e.g. Caffarel, Martin and Matthiessen 2004; Teruya and Matthiessen 2015; Mwinlaaru and Xuan 2016; Kashyap 2019). Here I am using system networks to illustrate points about the systemic organization of language, not to document particular languages. Nevertheless, it will be helpful to present a few key (central) clause system networks to illustrate how systemic descriptions of the resources of lexicogrammar work – what view of the resources of wording they provide us with.

I will continue to use English as the main language of ***illustration*** since it is easy to access systemic descriptions of it at different levels of introduction. The textual, interpersonal and experiential systems of the clause all reflect the role of the clause in the semantic systems – as a **message**, a **move** and a **figure**, respectively, as shown in Table 3.7 (for these the semantic roles of the clause, see also Figure 3.25 below[9]):

- **the clause as a message:** this the clause as a realization of a quantum of **information** in the semantics – a message, contributing to the flow of information (or better: waves of information) in terms of which texts unfold in their contexts of situation; semantically, messages are waves within waves (a hierarchy of periodicity, e.g. Martin 1993);
- **the clause as a move:** this is the clause as a realization of a quantum of **interaction**, a dialogic move, contributing to the ongoing exchange of propositions and proposals between interactants taking part in dialogue (cf. Halliday 1984a);
- **the clause as a figure:** this is the clause as a quantum of change in our **experience** of the flow of events, a configuration of a process, participants directly involved in it and attendant circumstances (a figure; e.g. Halliday and Matthiessen 2006: Chapter 4).

The textual, interpersonal and experiential systems show the paradigmatic organization in English of the semiotic realms of information, interaction and experience. Systemic selections and function structures are illustrated for two clauses in Figure 3.7.

*Table 3.7* Textual, interpersonal and experiential systems of the clause

|  | textual | interpersonal | experiential |
|---|---|---|---|
| clause as (semantic role): | message | move | figure |
|  | a quantum of information in the flow of information | a quantum of interaction in the flow of exchange in dialogue | a quantum of change in our experience of the flow of events ('flux', goings-on) |
| other glosses: |  | clause as exchange, clause as speech act | clause as representation, clause as process |
| key clause systems: | THEME (complemented by INFORMATION of the information unit); VOICE; SUBSTITUTION-&-ELLIPSIS; CONJUNCTION | MOOD; POLARITY, MODAL ASSESSMENT, DEICTICITY, MOOD PERSON | TRANSITIVITY (AGENCY, PROCESS TYPE, CIRCUMSTANTIATION) |
| realized by: | thematic structure: Theme ^ Rheme (Given + New) | modal structure: Mood (Subject, Finite) + Residue | transitivity structure: Process + participant(s) (+ circumstance(s)) |

| selection expression: | *when* | *do* | *you* | *start?* | |
|---|---|---|---|---|---|
| adjunct theme, wh theme; +interpersonal theme; -textual theme | Theme | Rheme | | | |
| wh-interrogative; temporal: present; positive; interactant: addressee; non-assessed | Wh/ Adjunct | Finite | Subject | Predicator | |
|  | Resi- | Mood | | -due | |
| material: transformative & middle: non-ranged | Time | Pro- | Actor/ Medium | -cess | |
|  | adverbial group | verbal group (1) | nominal group | verbal group (2) | |

| selection expression: | *I* | *start* | | *on Tuesday.* |
|---|---|---|---|---|
| subject theme, non-wh theme; -interpersonal theme; -textual theme | Theme | Rheme | | |
| declarative: untagged; temporal: present; positive; non-assessed | Subject | Finite | Predicator | Adjunct |
|  | Mood | | Residue | |
| material: transformative & middle: non-ranged | Actor/Medium | Process | | Time |
|  | nominal group | verbal group | | prepositional phrase |

*Figure 3.7* Systemic and structural analyses of two clauses (from the dialogue in Table 3.7 above)

*3.3.1.2.1 Key Interpersonal Clause Systems*
Having introduced the interpersonal clause system of MOOD as an illustration in Figure 3.1, I will start with the key interpersonal systems of the clause. The key systems are presented in Figure 3.8.

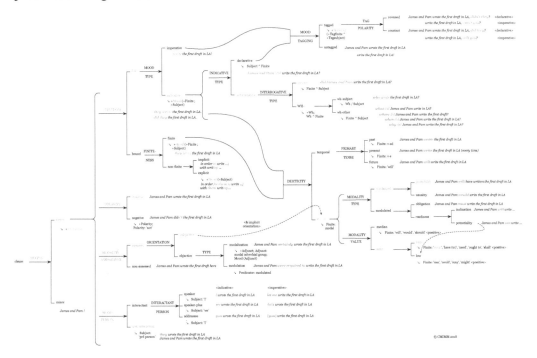

*Figure 3.8* Key interpersonal clause systems, with examples (for systemic conventions, see the Appendix in Chapter 8)

The systems in Figure 3.7 include those shown in Figure 3.1 – the key, or core, systems of the clause as a move in dialogic exchange, viz. STATUS, FREEDOM and MOOD TYPE; but they also include other systems that form part of the resources for exchanging meaning (listed here, with steps in indentation as an indication of degree of delicacy):

> STATUS: major/minor.[10] This system concerns the status of the clause both with respect to the semantics of exchange and with respect to its internal make-up – its range of systems and structural realizations. 'Minor' clauses (or 'clausettes') contribute to opening up and to closing down dialogues, e.g. in the exchange of greetings – in general, they serve to 'punctuate' dialogue; they minor clause options are: greeting (e.g. *Hello. - Hello.*)/call (e.g. *Joseph? - Yes.*)/alarm (e.g. *Fire!*)/exclamation (e.g. *Ouch!*). They have minimal internal structure, typically a single element (potentially expanded in alarms, which can be somewhat intermediate between 'major' and 'minor' clauses. 'Major' clauses can serve to move dialogic exchanges forward, by either initiating new exchanges or responding to ones that have already been initiated. The systems available to 'major' clauses are set out below.
>
> major:
>> FREEDOM: free/bound. Interpersonally, the prototypical clause is 'free': it serves as a move directly contributing to the development of exchanges in dialogue by giving or demanding a commodity, information (propositions) or goods-&-services (proposals),

through the resources provided by the system of MOOD (e.g. *How'd you go at that interview today?*; *There was two ladies interviewing.*). Thus 'free' clauses are characterized by the full range of the interpersonal resources of the clause; they can realize any of the speech functions set out in Table 3.3 above, i.e. statements, questions, offers and commands. In contrast, 'bound' clauses have a reduced interpersonal potential; they contribute to the development of the exchange of meaning only indirectly, either as dependent on other clauses (e.g. *while you're cleaning up* in *While you're cleaning up, I'll take this to the wardrobe mistress.*) or, by another remove from the dialogic mainline of negotiation, as down-ranked (embedded) within a nominal group (e.g. defining relative clauses: *who came to dinner* in *the man [[who came to dinner]]*) or adverbial group (e.g. clauses of comparison: *than most of us could* in *She ran faster [[than most of us could]]*). The least negotiable 'bound' clauses are embedded non-finite ones (which can be said to shade into nominal groups with process nominalizations as Head/Thing).

   free:

      MOOD TYPE: indicative/imperative. This system defines the interpersonal potential of 'free' clauses; it constitutes the grammaticalized version of the basic semantic system of speech function, as indicated in Table 3.3. 'Indicative' clauses provide the resources for exchanging information; 'declarative' clauses realize gifts of information, i.e. statements, and 'interrogative' clauses realize demands for information, i.e. questions. 'Imperative' clauses realize demands for goods-&-services, i.e. commands, when the MOOD PERSON (or 'subject person') is 'addressee', but they can also realize offers (mood person = 'speaker') or suggestions (mood person = 'speaker-plus') – see Table 3.4 above.

      DEICTICITY: temporal/modal. This system specifies the dimension in terms of which the validity of a proposition is argued in relation to the nub of the argument, i.e. the Subject; it has a disjunctive entry condition: either 'indicative' or 'finite'. For 'indicative' clauses, see examples in Table 3.4.

   bound:

      FINITENESS: finite/non-finite. 'Finite' bound clauses are like 'indicative' clauses in that they have a Mood element, consisting of Subject and Finite; in most cases, the order is Subject ^ Finite, as in 'declarative' clauses (the general exception being relative clauses), but there is no systemic contrast in mood. (Bound clauses that are projected, whether finite or non-finite, reflect a projected mood, but this does not embody an interactive dialogic contribution unlike the 'straight' (i.e. non-projected) mood selection of 'free' clauses.)

POLARITY: positive/negative. This system defines the outer poles of validity between positive and negative, the intermediate range between the two being open to 'indicative' clauses through the system of MODALITY (discussed in the context of educational applications in Section 5.3, where the system network is presented in Figure 5.7). The choice is interpersonal in nature: the unmarked term is 'positive', and 'negative' is chosen by speakers if they have reason to believe that their addressees would expect 'positive'.

MODAL ASSESSMENT: non-assessed/assessed. This system is in principle open to all 'major' clauses but it is more restricted in 'bound' clauses than in 'free' ones, and within 'free' clauses it is more restricted in 'imperative' clauses than in 'indicative' ones, and within 'indicative' clauses, it is more restricted in 'interrogative' clauses than in 'declarative' ones. There are two primary domains of assessment, either the proposition being exchanged (e.g. *perhaps surprisingly* in *Perhaps surprisingly, we shall find in their seemingly strictly commercial work many of the themes that are essential to Late Antique speculation and fantasy – to an ecumenic world in a state of prolonged religious crisis*) or the act of exchanging it (e.g. *honestly* in *Are you honestly comparing the USA to the Roman Empire?*).

MOOD PERSON: interactant/non-interactant; interactant: speaker/speaker-plus/addressee. This relates to the nature of the Subject (i.e., semantically, the element being held responsible for the validity of the proposition or proposal realized by the clause – the modally responsible element), but it helps determine the nature of the mood and the pattern of speech functional realizations (see examples in Table 3.4) and its domain of realization can extend across the Mood element in the form of concord ('agreement'). The choice is based on the distinction in speech roles between interactants – first and second person in traditional grammar – and non-interactants – third person. Interactants are further differentiated by the system of interactant person into 'speaker' ('first person singular'), 'speaker-plus' ('first person plural') and 'addressee' ('second person'). The distinction in number between 'singular' and 'plural' applies to the 'non-interactant' option, but is not shown in the system network in Figure 3.7.

These systems are shown together with realization statements and examples in Figure 3.7. The system of ADDRESS is not shown in the system network. It provides the option of identifying the addressee of the clause as a move; if the clauses is 'addressed', it will contain a Vocative function, as in Rhett Butler's *Frankly, my dear, I don't give a damn*, where *my dear* is a nominal group serving as the Vocative, in this example adding an assessment of ironic endearment. This option is in principle open to all major clauses, although it is less likely to be taken up in 'bound' ones, in particular if they are downranked. It corresponds to the 'call' type of minor clauses. (Aspects of the strategies of address are presented in Section 6.2.2 as an illustration of the re-representation of a flow chart by means of a system network.) The system network in the figure also does not include elaborations in delicacy beyond a certain point; importantly, it does not include the delicate mood systems realized by selections in the phonological system of TONE (illustrated in Figure 3.1 by the system of DECLARATIVE KEY).

The system network in Figure 3.8 brings out a number of interpersonal properties of clauses, and also of the systemic organization of lexicogrammar in general:

- It shows the degree of potential allocated for negotiation; quite naturally, it is the greatest for 'free' clauses (and among them, 'declarative' clauses, although this is not reflected in the system network).
- It shows that realization statements are always located in a systemic environment, being associated with terms in systems: syntagmatic specifications are only given at the right point when the systemic information about the presence of functions (e.g. Subject and Finite, both present in 'indicative' clauses), their relative order (e.g. Subject preceding Finite in 'declarative' clauses and Finite preceding Subject in 'yes/no' interrogative ones), so there is no need to change syntagmatic specifications.
- It enables us to show that not all combinations of systemic terms equally probable; for example, in the system of POLARITY, 'positive' has a probability of 0.9 of being

selected but 'negative' has a probability' of 0.1: see Halliday and James (1993). In contrast to this skew system, the system of interrogative type has equiprobable terms, 'wh-' and 'yes/no' are about equally likely to be selected (see Figure 8.1). The probabilistic nature of systems will be discussed in Section 4.3.

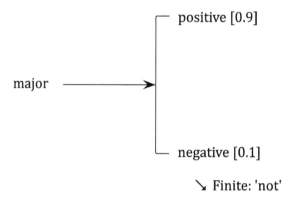

Figure 3.9 The system of POLARITY with systemic probability attached, the term 'negative' being marked in terms of probability and in terms of syntagmatic realization

- It shows the distinction between 'marked' and 'unmarked' systemic terms seen 'from below'; for example, in the system of POLARITY, 'positive' is unmarked in the sense that it has no realization statement associated with it, but 'negative' is marked in the sense that it has a realization associated with it. As just noted, the terms are unmarked and marked also with respect to the probability of instantiation: see Figure 3.9.
- It illustrates the use of disjunctive entry conditions, where the entry condition to a given system consists of a disjunction of terms from two or more less delicate systems; for example, the system MOOD TAGGING, has the entry condition 'declarative'/'imperative' (i.e. either 'declarative' or 'imperative') and the system DEICTICITY has the entry condition 'indicative'/'finite' (i.e. either 'indicative' or 'finite'). This makes it possible to capture generalizations across systemic options that are on alternative paths in the system network; for example, while both 'declarative' and 'interrogative' clauses are 'indicative', and thus have a Mood element, 'declarative' and 'imperative' clauses can be tagged since unlike 'interrogative' ones they don't embody a demand for a verbal response (the response to the typical imperative clause being non-verbal behaviour). The use of disjunctive entry conditions could be taken one step further in the system network in Figure 3.8: we could collect all the instances of the same realization statement, say +Mood (Subject, Finite), that occur more than once in the system network in a system with a single term, a **gate**, and associate the realization statement with that single term, e.g. 'indicative'/'finite': moody clause ↘ +Mood (Subject, Finite).
- It illustrates the use of systemic marking conventions: if 'subjective' is selected, then 'modal' must also be selection; if 'potentiality' is selected, then 'low' must

also be selected. These marking conventions will be discussed in Section 6.4, where I will raise the issue of how to interpret them.

*3.3.1.2.2 Interlude: Realization Statement in Systemic Environments*

Let me elaborate on the point about the location of realization statements since it is a fundamental aspect of the relationship between the paradigmatic and syntagmatic axes and of the primacy given to the paradigmatic axis. The system network represent paradigmatic order – organization along the paradigmatic axis. It is thus entirely free to represent the organization of language as a resource for making meaning. It also provides the environment in which syntagmatic specifications are given. More specifically, terms in systems may have realization statements associated with them; realization statements thus appear in the environment of systemic terms. They specify the various aspects of the function structure of a unit, including the presence of functions (e.g. 'indicative' ↘ + Subject, which means that in an 'indicative' clause Subject is present in its function structure), the ordering relation between two functions (e.g. 'declarative' ↘ Subject ^ Finite, which means that in a 'declarative' clause, Subject precedes Finite), the inclusion of one function as an element of another (e.g. 'indicative' ↘ + Mood (Subject, Finite), which means that in an 'indicative' clause, Mood consists of Subject and Finite), the systemic specification of a function by a systemic term in the unit realizing that function (e.g. 'interactant' ↘ Subject: interactant, which means that in an 'interactant' clause, the Subject is realized by a nominal group with the systemic term 'interactant').

Realization statements thus specify fragments of the function structure of a unit, different aspects of structure being specified by distinct realization statements. Since realization statements specify different aspects of structure, they can be distributed throughout the system network and be placed in the environment of the relevant systemic term, i.e. the term that they actually realize (signal, mark). In other words, realization statements are **paradigmatically sensitive**, not syntagmatically sensitive. For example, the presence of Subject can be specified separately from its ordering in relation to other functions, and from constraints on the unit that realizes it.

The **paradigmatic dispersal of realization statements** specifying different aspects of Subject is shown in Figure 3.10. The systemic terms with which realization statements involving Subject are specified range in delicacy from 'indicative' to 'subject-wh'; and they also appear in simultaneous systems, e.g. 'declarative' ↘ Subject ^ Finite in DECLARATIVE TYPE and 'interactant' ↘ Subject: interactant in SUBJECT PERSON. Thus realization statement appear in exactly the systemic locations where they are motivated, and there is never any need to revise them. For example, the ordering of Subject and Finite is specified as Subject ^ Finite for 'declarative' clauses and as Finite ^ Subject for 'yes/no' interrogatives. And other aspects of Subject are specified in systems not shown in Figure 3.10. For example, conflations of Subject with different participant roles are specified in the system of VOICE (e.g. 'operative' ↘ Subject/Agent; 'medioreceptive' ↘ Subject/Medium; 'benereceptive' ↘ Subject/Beneficiary); and conflations of Subject (as opposed to Complements or Adjuncts) in the system of THEME SELECTION (Figure 3.12).

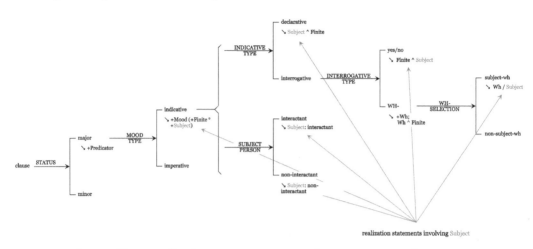

*Figure 3.10* The specification of realization statements in the environment of terms in systems, and the dispersal throughout the system of mood of realization statements involving Subject

Realization statements consist of a realization **operator** and one or more **operands**; they are listed in Table 8.2 in the Appendix. The operators have names that suggest actions – operations; but they can all be interpreted relationally as statements ('declarations') about the function structure of a unit, as shown in the typology in Figure 8.2. Thus while realization statements have also been called 'realization rules', the term **realization statement** is preferable precisely because it does not imply a procedural rule system.

Next in our tour of the systems of the clause, I will turn to textual systems.

*3.3.1.2.2 Key Textual Clause Systems*
Textual systems represent the resources of the clause in its guise as a message – a quantum of information in the flow of information characterizing the unfolding of text; the systems are listed in Table 3.6 and Table 3.7. Apart from the system of CONJUNCTION, the textual systems of the clause provide the strategies for assigning **textual statuses of prominence and non-prominence** to elements of the clause serving within any of the three metafunctional strands of the clause – interpersonal elements serving in the modal structure of the clause as a move (predominantly interpersonal Adjuncts, Vocatives, the Finite element), experiential elements serving in the transitivity structure of the clause as a figure (participants, circumstances or the process), and also textual ones serving in the textual structure of the clause as a message (continuatives, structural conjunctions and conjunctive Adjuncts). The general principle in English[11] is that the Theme extends up to and includes the first experiential element of the clause. This is the experiential, or 'topical', Theme; but there may also be a textual and/or an interpersonal Theme, as illustrated by the example analysed systemically in Figure 3.9, *Nevertheless, unfortunately, many of these strategies utilize harmful organic solvents*. In this example, the writer has chosen to contextualize the clause as a message in relation to its discursive environment, giving the conjunctive Adjunct *nevertheless* thematic status, its interpersonal environment, giving the comment Adjunct *unfortunately* thematic status, and its experiential environment, giving the participant *many of these strategies* thematic status. Thus the Theme is a metafunctional multiple one, providing readers with an

orientation to all three metafunctional environments from which the clause emerges as a message, a quantum of information, in the unfolding text.

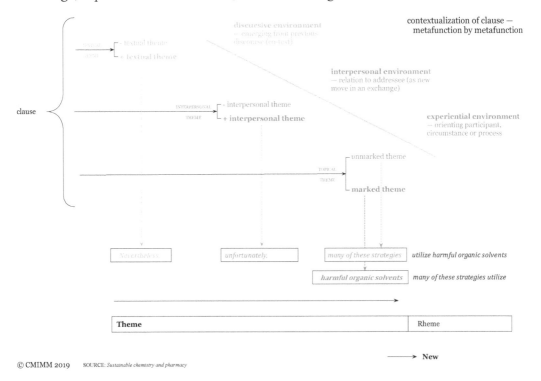

*Figure 3.11* The potential for multiple Themes in English – textual, interpersonal and experiential, or 'topical', Theme

Theme and other textual statuses serve to guide the addressee in his/her processing of the clause as message (e.g. Matthiessen 1992, 1995a,c; Bateman and Matthiessen 1993; Halliday and Matthiessen 2006); prominent and non-prominent statuses are processed in different ways – also actually by speakers in that the textual metafunction also guides speakers in their development of a text one message at a time.[12] The textual systems of the clause concerned with textual statuses are THEME, VOICE and SUBSTITUTION-&-ELLIPSIS. In addition, there is another grammatical unit that operates alongside the clause in spoken English, complementing the clause in the realization of messages. This is the **information unit**, which is the domain of one more system concerned with the textual status of newsworthiness, the system of INFORMATION. The textually prominent status of high newsworthiness is the element of New, complementing the thematically prominent element of Theme and the textually non-prominent element is Given, as explained and illustrated by e.g. Halliday (1967/8), Halliday and Greaves (2008), and Halliday and Matthiessen (2014: Chapter 3).

Here I will focus on the system of THEME as an illustration of a textual system. A version of the system network documented in Halliday and Matthiessen (2014) is presented in Figure 3.13, with examples. The systems of TEXTUAL THEME and INTERPERSONAL THEME are interpreted descriptively as in Figure 3.11 above – as presence or absence of these textual statuses; but the interpretation of the system of (topical) THEME SELECTION is fleshed out in more detail. In the version above in Figure 3.11, the system is characterized simply as 'unmarked theme' and 'marked theme'; but in Figure 3.13 below the different possible candidates are specified in distinct systems. Thus, in the description of the system of theme given in Figure 3.13, there is no choice between 'unmarked' and 'marked' topical Theme; the unmarked status is distributed across different systems and depends on the mood type of the clause. According to this description, the choice of topical Theme is concerned with the modal (interpersonal) functions in the clause, and whether the Theme is unmarked or marked is as it were a side-effect.[13]

In this way, systemic descriptions can make different claims about the grammar, foregrounding different sets of considerations. For example, in the clause *In every major European country the state was increasing its authority* (taken from a historical recount), the circumstantial Adjunct *in every major European country* has been selected as topical Theme, and it turns out that it is marked because the clause is 'declarative' and in 'declarative' clauses about 90% of all topical Themes are Subjects. There are, of course, other aspects of thematic markedness; importantly, marked topical Themes are more likely to be given the status of New in their own information unit than unmarked ones, although this is still possible in the case of unmarked topical Themes. This is illustrated in Figure 3.12: (a) represents the actual example, with a marked topical Theme (Adjunct), which is assigned the status of New in its own information unit; (b) represents an agnate variant of the actual example, with an unmarked topical Theme (Subject), which is assigned the status of Given; and (c) represent another agnate variant of the actual example, again with an unmarked topical Theme (Subject), but here it is assigned the status of New in its own information unit. In versions (a) and (c), the clause is thus chunked into two information units, and the boundary comes after the topical Theme.[14]

(a) marked Theme, two information units

|  | in every major European country | the state | was increasing | its authority |
|---|---|---|---|---|
| clause | Theme | Rheme | | |
| information unit | New | Given | | → New |

(b) unmarked Theme, one information unit

|  | the state | was increasing | its authority | in every major European country |
|---|---|---|---|---|
| clause | Theme | Rheme | | |
| information unit | Given | | | → New |

(c) unmarked Theme, two information units

|  | the state | was increasing | its authority | in every major European country |
|---|---|---|---|---|
| clause | Theme | Rheme | | |
| information unit | New | Given | | → New |

*Figure 3.12* The markedness of the topical Theme in relation to the system of information

Although the candidates are elements of the clause as a figure, i.e. participants, circumstances or the process, they are characterized in terms of the modal functions they serve as Predicator, Adjunct, Subject or Complement, and as Wh-element or not – see further below. This reflects the principle that in English the system of THEME is as it were oriented towards the system of MOOD; specifically, the default or unmarked Theme of a clause depends on the mood type in the system of MOOD. Thus by default, the topical Theme will reveal the mood type of the clause – its interpersonal key signature: the textual starting point of the clause is as it were aligned with its interpersonal overture.

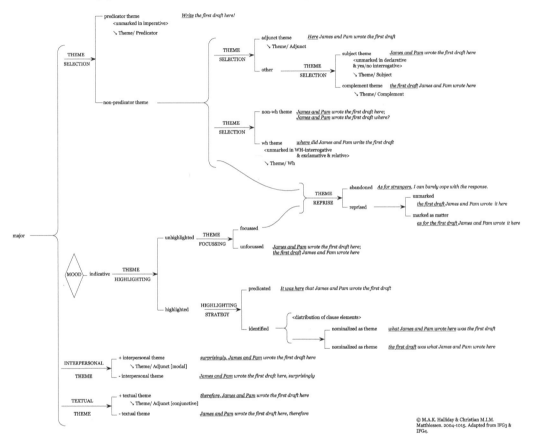

*Figure 3.13* Key textual clause systems, with examples

The examples provided in Figure 3.13 are all agnates of one authentic example, from the following passage of a biography of James Mason, one of Yorkshire's brilliant contributions to the arts and scholarship, like J.B. Priestley, J.R. Firth, M.A.K. Halliday, Robin Fawcett, Malcolm Coulthard and Chris Taylor:

> Christmas 1937 saw Pam, Roy and James on holiday together at Wengen in Switzerland. <u>It was here that James and Pam wrote the first draft of the script for the film</u>, then called Deadwater, which was to become *I Met a Murderer*.

The primary systems in Figure 3.13 all have 'major' (clause) as their entry condition; they are concerned with experiential (topical), interpersonal and textual thematic choices:

THEME SELECTION: predicator theme/non-predicator theme. This system is concerned with which experiential element of the clause to give the status of topical Theme. It is described as a series of binary systems, the first two of which offer a contrast between a particular element and 'other', and the third of which present a contrast between two elements. The first system is predicator theme/non-predicator theme, and the reason for this contrast is that 'non-predicator theme' opens up two choices; while 'predicator theme' is a terminal option, 'non-predicator theme' serves as the entry condition to two systems (set out as a paradigm in Table 3.8):

predicator theme ↘ Theme/Predicator. This is the unmarked topical Theme in 'imperative' clauses, giving the Predicator part of the Process thematic status (but not the Finite), as in *dry the dishes after lunch!* In other mood types, it would be highly marked, e.g. 'declarative' *dry he did the dishes after lunch* (perhaps more likely with the Residue as Theme, which is not covered in the system network: *dry the dishes after lunch he did*).

non-predicator theme

THEME SELECTION: adjunct theme/other (non-adjunct theme)

adjunct theme ↘ Theme/Adjunct. This gives a circumstance serving as Adjunct thematic status, e.g. *after lunch he dried the dishes.*

other (non-adjunct theme)

THEME SELECTION: subject theme ↘ Theme/Subject vs. complement theme ↘ Theme/Complement. This gives a participant serving as either Subject or Complement thematic status, e.g. [subject theme] *he dried the dishes after lunch*/ [complement theme] *the dishes he dried after lunch*. The option 'subject theme' is unmarked in 'declarative' and 'yes/no interrogative' clauses.

THEME SELECTION: wh theme/non-wh theme.

wh- theme ↘ Theme/Wh-. This gives the Wh element of a 'wh-interrogative' or 'relative' clause the status of unmarked topical Theme, e.g. *when did he dry the dishes?*; *the afternoon* [[*when he dried the dishes*]]. In the case of interrogative clauses, the Wh element is also interpersonal Theme and in the case of relative clauses, it is also structural textual Theme (not shown in the system network in Figure 3.13).

THEME HIGHLIGHTING: unhighlighted/highlighted. Whatever the status of the topical Theme as Predicator, Adjunct, Subject or Complement, it may in addition be highlighted by one of two highlighting strategies (both of which co-opt the resources of the identifying relational clause).

unhighlighted.

THEME FOCUSSING: focussed/unfocussed. The 'focussed' option means that the topical Theme is given additional thematic prominence, which is an option that is often selected to achieve a return to an earlier topical Theme. For example: *as for the dishes, he dried them in the afternoon.*

focussed & non-predicator theme

> THEMATIC REPRISE: abandoned/reprised. For example: *as for the dishes, he dried the cutlery in the afternoon* vs. *(as for) the dishes, he dried them in the afternoon.*

highlighted.

> HIGHLIGHTING STRATEGY: predicated/identified. This system concerns the choice between two highlighting strategies, 'predicated' (theme predication, or 'cleft') and 'identified' (thematic equative, or 'pseudo-cleft'): *it was the dishes that he dried in the afternoon* vs. *what he dried in the afternoon was the dishes.*

INTERPERSONAL THEME: +interpersonal theme/-interpersonal theme. This system is the option of giving a purely interpersonal element of the clause the status of Theme (together with the obligatory topical Theme) or not. Modal (interpersonal) Adjuncts are candidates, as are Vocative elements: *happily, he dried the dishes in the afternoon*; *sir, he dried the dishes in the afternoon.* (Note that '+interpersonal theme' can only be selected if a candidate is selected within the interpersonal region of the clause grammar. This applies to modal Adjuncts and to Vocative elements; the Finite element preceding the Subject in a yes/no interrogative clause serves as interpersonal Theme as does the Finite preceding the Predicator when it's present in an 'imperative' clause – unless they are displaced by a marked topical Theme.)

TEXTUAL THEME: +textual theme/-textual theme. This system provides the option of giving a purely textual element of the clause – always a conjunctive Adjunct – the status of textual Theme: *nevertheless, he dried the dishes after lunch.* (Structural conjunctions, both linkers and binders, are obligatorily thematic, as are relative elements, which in English serve as both structural textual Theme and topical Theme[15]; however, cohesive conjunction may be given either thematic or rhematic status in the clause.)

*Table 3.8* The intersection of the two systems of theme selection in 'non-predicator theme' clauses

| modal function: | wh theme | non-wh theme |
| --- | --- | --- |
| Adjunct | Theme/Wh-/Adjunct<br>*When did he dry the dishes?*<br>*the afternoon [[when he dried the dishes]]* | Theme/Adjunct<br>*After lunch he dried the dishes.* |
| Subject | Theme/Wh-/Subject<br>*Who dried the dishes after lunch?*<br>*the person [[who dried the dishes]]* | Theme/Subject<br>*He dried the dishes after lunch.* |
| Complement | Theme/Wh-/Complement<br>*What did he dry after lunch?*<br>*the dishes [[that he dried after lunch]]* | Theme/Complement<br>*The dishes he dried after lunch.* |

The system network in Figure 3.13 brings out a number of textual properties of clauses, and also of the systemic organization of lexicogrammar in general.

- The systems concerned with the selection of topical Theme operate with an **interpersonal 'interface'** to elements of the transitivity structure of the clause: Predicator = Process, Adjunct = a circumstantial element, Subject = a participant and Complement = a participant. In other words, in the description, the experiential transitivity roles of the Process, participants involved in it and attendant circumstances are mediated by the modal functions they serve. This is a property of English, and of many other languages but certainly not all. It is an aspect of how languages around the world have evolved patterns of mapping metafunctions onto one another within the clause, the interpersonal mediation between the textual metafunction and the experiential one being one common pattern.

In English, evidence for the interpersonal 'mediation' between the experiential system of TRANSITIVITY and the textual system of THEME is also provided by the system of VOICE, the basic contrast being between 'operative' ('active') and 'receptive' ('passive'): see Figure 3.14. This system is concerned with the elevation of one of the participants in the clause to the status of Subject, the nub of the argument of the proposition or proposal of the clause. The 'operative' voice is the unmarked option, and for every transitivity type where the system of VOICE is available, one of the participants will be the Subject. The 'receptive' voice is the marked option, and it is realized by the elevation of a participant other than the default one to the status of Subject.

The contrast between 'unmarked' and 'marked' topical Theme in 'declarative' clauses is based on the Subject: the Subject is the unmarked topical Theme – regardless of whether the clause is 'operative' or 'receptive'. Thus in a 'material' clause with Actor + Goal, the Actor will be unmarked topical Theme if it is the Subject in the 'operative' version of the clause, but the Goal will be the unmarked topical Theme if it is the Subject in the 'receptive' version of the clause. For example, in the 'receptive' 'material' clause *the wild places were being destroyed in many parts of the world*, the Goal *the wild places* is the Subject, so it is also the unmarked topical Theme; but in the 'operative' version of the clause, *developers were destroying the wild places in many parts of the world*, it is the Actor that is the Subject, so it serves as the unmarked topical Theme. (Of course, in either version, the circumstantial Adjunct could be given the status of marked topical Theme: *in many parts of the world, developers/the wild places ...*).

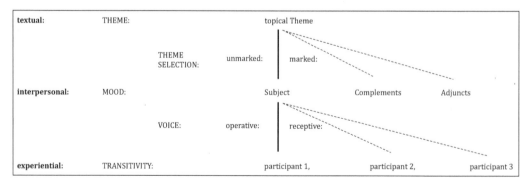

*Figure 3.14* The interpersonal layer of the clause as interface mediating between the textual and experiential layers in a 'declarative' clause (or 'yes/no interrogative' clause or non-relative 'bound' clause)

- If the Predicator is not selected as topical Theme in the system network in Figure 3.13, there are two simultaneous systems of THEME SELECTION. The description is designed to cater for the fact that Wh elements in wh-clauses, either interrogative or relative ones, are unmarked candidates for thematic status.
- Unmarked topical Theme selections reveal the interpersonal key signature of the clause – the mood type; i.e. the interpersonal overture is thematized. In the case of Wh elements in 'wh-interrogative' clauses, they also serve as interpersonal Theme: the query aspect is interpersonal ('tell me!') and the participant or circumstance part is topical Theme. In the case of 'yes/no-interrogative' clauses, the Subject serving as unmarked topical Theme is preceded by the Finite as interpersonal Theme, the point of interrogation being the polarity (positive or negative, i.e. yes or no?), which is typically fused with the Finite.
- The highlighting thematic options are realized syntagmatically by co-opting of experiential resources, specifically 'identifying' clauses (cf. also 'existential' clauses + dependent ones). The textual sense of exclusiveness is due to the identifying structure (*it was the dog that died* – not the man, the cat or some other creature[16]).
- The selection of topical Theme is handled by a series of systems that identify possible candidates, first Predicator, then Adjunct, then Subject or Complement, as shown in Figure 3.13. These systems are simultaneous with the system contrasting 'wh theme' with 'non-wh theme'. A number of these options can serve as unmarked topical Theme depending on the mood type of the clause. This is a descriptive alternative to accounts where there is a system of 'unmarked' vs. 'marked' topical Theme, where the realizations depend on the mood types, as in Figure 3.4 and Figure 3.13 above.
- There is one example of a conjunctive entry condition: the system of THEME REPRISE. has the entry condition 'focussed' and 'non-predicator theme' since the option of a thematic reprise is not open to Predicator as Theme.
- In the system network in Figure 3.13, there is a convention for cross-referencing a term in a system that appears in another system network. This is the diamond with the name of the system inside, MOOD, and the cross-referenced terms to the right, 'indicative'.

Rounding off the discussion of the system of THEME, I include a **radial display** of a paradigm of thematic options: Figure 3.15. At the centre of the display is a 'declarative' clause with an unmarked topical Theme, *the duke gave my aunt that teapot*; since the clause is 'declarative', the unmarked topical Theme is the Subject. Moving outward, the next concentric circle contains examples of 'marked' topical Themes – Adjunct, Complement or the whole Residue. The next two concentric circles illustrate highlighted Themes, first highlighting through identification ('equated') and then through predication ('predicated').

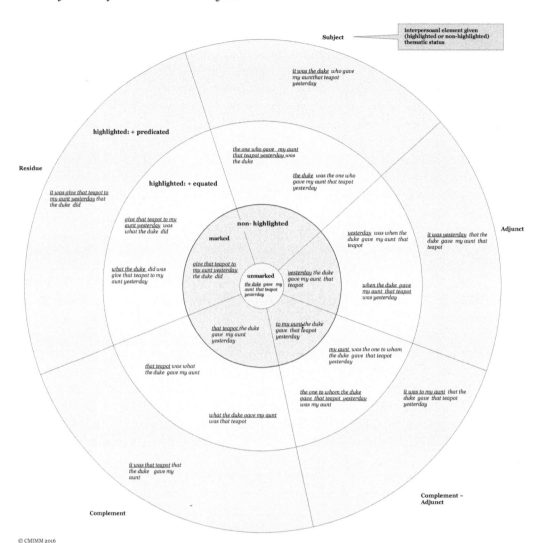

*Figure 3.15* Paradigm of examples of thematic options – the point of reference is an example with an unmarked Theme, 'the duke gave my aunt that teapot yesterday', shown in the centre of the radial display

### 3.3.1.2.4 Key Experiential Clause Systems

Experiential systems represent the resources of the clause in its guise as a **figure** – a quantum of change in our experience of the flow of experience; the systems are listed in Table 3.6 and Table 3.7. (The term 'figure' is used here in the sense of a configuration of a process, one or more participants directly involved in it and indirectly involved or attendant circumstances; cf. Tesnière's 1959, characterization of the clause as a drama.) The experiential systems of the clause make up the system of TRANSITIVITY, which covers nuclear transitivity – PROCESS TYPE and AGENCY, which are represented in the system network in Figure 3.17, and circumstantial transitivity – CIRCUMSTANTIATION.

The system of TRANSITIVITY provides the resources for construing our experience of a quantum of change in the flow of events as a figure, i.e. as a configuration of a process, participants directly involved in it and indirectly involved, or attendant, circumstances. The process plus participants are construed into different domains of experience by means of the system of PROCESS TYPE and into different modes of participation by means of the system of AGENCY. I will start with the system of AGENCY, and then turn to PROCESS TYPE.

The system of AGENCY provides a model of participation in the process based on causation; it is known as the **ergative model** (and contrasts with the **transitive model** recognized by traditional grammarians[17]). According to this model of participation, the process always involves one participant, a participant through which the unfolding of the process through time is manifested. This is the Medium, as in *the door opened, he sneezed, he grieved, he answered, the contribution sufficed* ('was enough'). The configuration of Process + Medium may be construed as having an external cause, the Agent, as in *the wind opened the door*. In this model, there are two more participant roles, Range and Beneficiary. The Range specifies the domain of operation of Process + Medium, as in *she climbed* + *a mountain; she played* + *a game of chess*. The Beneficiary specifies a participant benefitting from a situation represented by Process + Medium + Agent, as in *she built a gazebo* + *for him* (or *she built him a gazebo*). In English, the ergative model generalizes across different process types, and the system of nuclear transitivity embodies the complementarity of the systems of AGENCY and PROCESS TYPE.[18] Before specifying the options in the system of PROCESS TYPE, let me set out the system of AGENCY:

> AGENCY: This system is concerned with the nature of the involvement of participants in the process configuration – more specifically, based on the ergative model: Process + Medium ± Agent. That is, the Process unfolds through the Medium, and there may or may not be an external cause, the Agent.
>
> > middle. 'Middle' clauses construed the combination of Process + Medium as unfolding without an explicitly specified external cause (e.g. *Suddenly the door opened.*).
> >
> > effective ↘ +Agent; Agent: nominal group. 'Effective' clauses construe the configuration of Process + Medium as unfolding through an external cause, the Agent (e.g. *As soon as Julia opened the door, the dog pushed inside*). It is shown here as being present in all 'effective' clauses, but if the clause is 'receptive' and 'non-agentive', the Agent is in fact not present structurally present although it is systemically inherent in the clause (contrast 'middle' *the door opened* with 'effective: receptive: non-agentive' *the door was opened*).

Although the second system of nuclear transitivity is called 'process type', it models not only processes but rather configurations of processes and participants, in particular the participant most tightly bonded with the process, which is known as the Medium – since it is the 'medium' through which the process unfolds in time. So the system of PROCESS TYPE is really concerned with the differentiation of different domains of experience of change based on Process + Medium in the first instance, and augmentations by one to two other participants. Thus Process + Medium form the **clause nucleus** in the configurational modelling of experience. The two systems of PROCESS TYPE and AGENCY both have 'major' as their entry condition and can be described briefly as follows:

> PROCESS TYPE: material/behavioural/mental/verbal/relational/existential. This system construes quanta of change according to six distinct models for different domains of our experience of the flow of events, involving six different combinations of process + at least one participant (Medium) or (in the case of 'relational' clauses), a relationship between two participants (Medium and Range or Medium and Agent)).

**material** ↘ +Actor; Actor: nominal group. 'Material' clauses construe doings-&-happenings, often characterized as actions, activities and events. Their profile of change over time tends to have clear initial and final states, with an outcome that is distinct from the initial state. The Actor is typically, but not necessarily, construed as bringing about the change. The outcome of the change may apply to the entity construed as Actor (non-impacting) or to the Goal (impacting), and may be represented circumstantially by a Role or a Place element or participantally by a resultative Attribute or a Recipient. (In terms of the system of AGENCY, it is always the Medium that registers the change, whether it is Actor or Goal.)

> TYPE OF DOING-&-HAPPENING: This system is concerned with the nature of the outcome of the unfolding of the doing-&-happening through time.
>
>> creative. The process of doing-&-happening is construed as bringing the Medium into existence, e.g. (non-impact, Medium/Actor) *Why does condensation form on the inside of our storm windows in the winter?*; (impact, Medium/Goal) *Specifically, in 1941, DC formed an editorial board.*
>>
>> transformative. The process of doing-&-happening is construed as bringing about a change in the Medium, the limiting case being continuity in the face of possible change, e.g. (impact, Medium/Goal) *Reviews confirm that ample ventilation and double-wall design minimize condensation.*
>
> IMPACT: This system is concerned with the Actor's participation in the Process: does it extend to impact another participant, or not?
>
>> non-impacting (intransitive). The process of doing-&-happening is confined to the Actor (e.g. *The woman hunted in her kitchen, returning with a jumbo box of wooden matches.*), although some aspects of its domain of unfolding may be represented participantally by a Scope participant, which is a participantal representation of the domain over this the process unfold (e.g. *he was walking the streets*, where *the streets* denote the scope or domain of motion). Unlike the Goal (see immediately below), the Scope represents a participant that is not impacted by the Actor's performance of the process.
>>
>> impacting (transitive) ↘ +Goal; Goal: nominal group; Goal/Medium. The process of doing-&-happening extends to impact a participant other than the Actor, viz. the Goal (e.g. *For a long time, humans hunted small game and gathered roots and berries.*).

**behavioural** ↘ +Behaver; Behaver: conscious; Behaver/Medium. 'Behavioural' clauses construe physiological and psychological processes as activity involving one participant, the Behaver, as a conscious being (e.g. *we laugh at our own peril*; *The Rabbit sighed.*). They represent an area of overlap between 'material' clauses and 'mental' ones, also 'verbal' ones (see Section 6.3.4 for overlap as one kind of indeterminacy).

**mental** ↘ +Senser; Senser: conscious; Senser/Medium. 'Mental' clauses construe processes of consciousness, sensing, as inert involving a conscious being as a participant, the Senser, and often also another participant entertained by sensing, the Phenomenon. If the sensing is construed as emanating from the consciousness of the Senser, the Phenomenon serves as Range in the ergative model of the clause, i.e. specifying the domain of sensing (e.g. *wolves might fear hunters*); if it is construed as impinging on the consciousness of the Senser, it is construed as Agent in the ergative model of the clause, i.e. specifying the cause of sensing (e.g. *That calamity might frighten a weaker man but not me*).

**verbal** ↘ +Sayer; Sayer: symbol source. 'Verbal' clauses construe process of saying; the Sayer may be a nominal group denoting a conscious speaker (e.g. *She says he told a group* *of 17 such friends, who'd gathered to meet*), but this is not a necessary constraint in English – it could denote any symbol source (e.g. *The constitution says that there should be a separation of powers.*).

ORDER OF SAYING: This system distinguishes two conceptions of processes of say; they are construed either as activities, close to 'behavioural' and 'material' clauses, or as semiosis, closer to 'relational' clauses. While the former cannot project (report or quote), the latter can.

activity. If the clause is 'middle' in agency (↘ Sayer /Medium), the verbal activity is one of 'talking' (speaking, chatting, conversing, discussing etc.)[19]; and if the clause is 'ranged', the medium of talking may be specified (e.g. *speak Akan*) or the topic (e.g. *talk politics, nonsense*). If the clause is 'effective' in agency (↘ Sayer/Agent), the verbal activity is one of impacting another participant verbally, the Target (↘ +Target; Target/Medium); such processes are positively or negatively loaded (e.g. *Inside the hall, a parade of speakers praised Obama and criticized the Republicans, sometimes harshly.*), so can be used in in the service of the interpersonal system of APPRAISAL (cf. Martin and White 2005) ; for example, contrast (negative:) *The American colonist Benjamin Franklin was praised for his personal industry and frugality* with (negative:) *Most secondary schools are criticised for too much 'chalk and talk', too little independent learning, too little research and investigation and discussion*. The Target is like a verbal analogue of the Goal of a 'material' clause in that it represents a participant that is 'impacted' by the process of saying. The reason is often specified circumstantially (e.g. *The ancient Athenians are often praised for their contributions to the modern world*) or clausally by an enhancing clause (e.g. *Quane praised Singapore for consolidating the number one position.*).

semiosis ↘ +Sayer/Medium. Clauses of 'semiosis' are the core of the lexicogrammatical construal of saying; they are 'middle' and can project the content of saying as a quote or a report within a clause nexus (e.g. report: *Newly declassified documents have revealed that the US military designated WikiLeaks founder Julian Assange an enemy of the state*; quote: *He revealed, 'As a singer, there were times where I was upset standing …'*). This type of verbal clause may be configured with a Receiver, a participant representing the addressee in interaction (e.g. *to me* in *it was revealed to me quickly that some kids just like blue a lot*). The content of saying as semiosis may be named by means of a nominal group serving as Verbiage rather than a projected clause (e.g. *the information* in *The company revealed the information Tuesday*).

**relational**. 'Relational' clauses construe a (prototypically static) relationship between two participants; the relationship is one of being, having or being-at. The nature of the participants depends on the mode of the relationship, attribution or identification (see below). Examples of the intersection of these two systems, RELATION TYPE and MODE OF RELATION, are set out in Table 3.9.

RELATION TYPE: This system concerned with the nature the relation that is construed as holding between the two participants being related – what kind of being-&-having it is. There are three types: 'intensive', which can be characterized pure being, 'possessive, which means generalized possession or 'have' – not only ownership but also part-whole relations and association, and 'circumstantial', which covers the range of enhancing circumstantial relations – 'be at' and other combinations of 'be' plus circumstantial preposition.

MODE OF RELATION: This system is concerned with two modes of being related to, either the relation between a member to a set (or a sub-class to a class) or the relationship between two elements being equated with one another.

attributive ↘ +Carrier; +Attribute; Carrier: nominal group; Attribute: nominal group; Carrier/Medium, Attribute/Range.

identifying ↘ +Token; +Value; Token: nominal group; Value: nominal group

**existential** ↘ +Existent; Existent: nominal group; Existent/Medium. 'Existential' clauses can be interpreted as the limiting case of being – being in the sense of an entity existing or an event occurring. For example: *There will be condensation on the outside of the glass.*

Table 3.9 Paradigm of 'relational' clauses – intersection of the systems of RELATION TYPE and MODE OF RELATION

| RELATION TYPE: | MODE OF RELATION | |
| --- | --- | --- |
| | attributive | identifying |
| identifying | she's a great grammarian | she'd the greatest grammarian of her generation: the greatest grammarian of her generation is her |
| possessive | she has a beautiful property | she owns the beautiful property on the opposite side of the lake: the beautiful property on the other side of the lake is owned by her |
| circumstantial | her property is on the other side of the lake | her property faces this side of the lake: this side of the lake is faced by her property |

This is the briefest of sketches of the system of PROCESS TYPE in the experiential clause grammar of English. This system construes quanta of change into models based on different domains of our experience of goings-on.

In addition to the more nuclear transitivity systems of PROCESS TYPE and AGENCY, the system of transitivity also includes circumstantial **augmentations** of the configuration of process + participants – the system of CIRCUMSTANTIATION (see Figure 3.18). This system can be described as a set of simultaneous systems, grouped according to the logico-semantic types of projection and expansion, mentioned immediately above as a fractal system:

expansion of process + participants
  enhancing augmentation
    PLACE: *Christian missionaries from Europe were active <u>in the southern part of Nigeria</u>*
    TIME: *<u>One summer evening</u>, the Rabbit saw [[two strange beings creep out of the bracken]].*
    DISTANCE: *they can be carried <u>thousands of miles</u> by gentle currents*
    DURATION: *So I've been around the New England coast <u>all my life</u>.*
    FREQUENCY: *I rewrote that <u>thirty times</u>.*
    REASON: *The American colonist Benjamin Franklin was praised <u>for his personal industry and frugality</u>*
    PURPOSE: *I had to sing <u>for my supper</u>*
    CONCESSION: *However, <u>despite these adjustments</u>, significant risk still remains.*
    CONDITION: *... to stabilize the situation <u>in the event of a large-scale humanitarian crisis</u>*
    BEHALF: *Let there be work, bread, water and salt <u>for all</u>.*
    MANNER (QUALITY): *and she and I weren't getting along <u>very well</u>.*
    MANNER (COMPARISON): *that he moved <u>like a cat with rickets</u>.*
    MANNER (MEANS): *we will continue to provide the American people <u>with the number one military in the world</u>*
    MANNER (DEGREE): *I wanted to see white sharks <u>so badly</u> [[that it was worth it]].*

extending augmentation
: ACCOMPANIMENT: *Then, <u>with a friend</u>, I did a column for the Yale Daily News on hunting and fishing.*
elaborating augmentation:
: ROLE: *I didn't last very long <u>as a teacher</u>*

projection of process + participants
: ANGLE: *It knocked out power in the capital's Colonia Guerrero neighborhood, <u>according to Televisa network</u>.*
: MATTER: *Tell me <u>about the Paris Review</u>.*

These systems of CIRCUMSTANTIATION are, as noted, simultaneous with the more nuclear transitivity systems of PROCESS TYPE and AGENCY, but they still interact with them. While there may be absolute interactions such that certain combinations do not occur, so far research has only brought out **quantitative tendencies** (e.g. Matthiessen 1999, 2006a). These tendencies are shown for a small sample of circumstances (N = 1019) in Figure 3.16. For example, circumstances of 'matter' tend to occur in 'verbal' and 'mental' clauses (e.g. *Tell me about the Paris Review*; *'it's written in stone, necessarily,'* Kelly repeated about the deadline; I seriously worry about the one issue that appears to be a mere by-product).

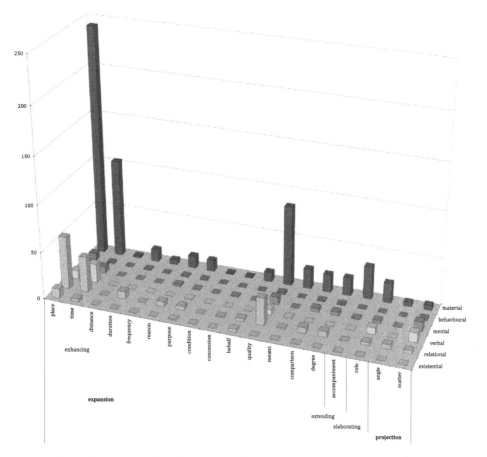

*Figure 3.16* Relative frequency of combinations of selections of process types and circumstance types based on 1019 circumstances

72 • *System in Systemic Functional Linguistics*

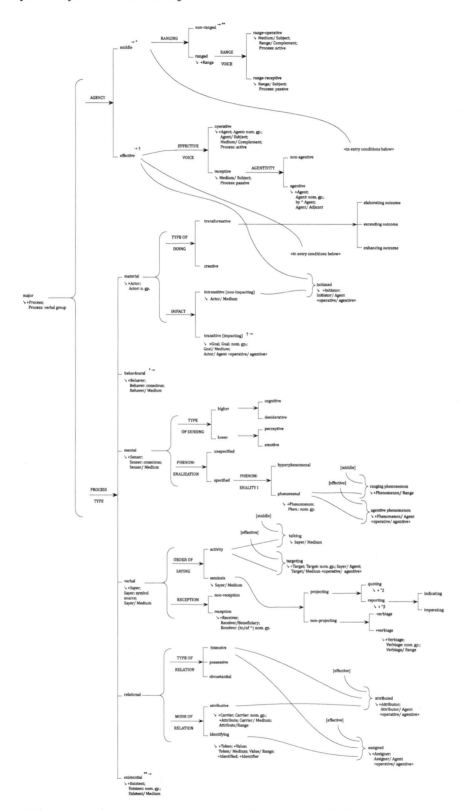

*Figure 3.17* The system of TRANSITIVITY – AGENCY and PROCESS TYPE (but not CIRCUMSTANTIATION)

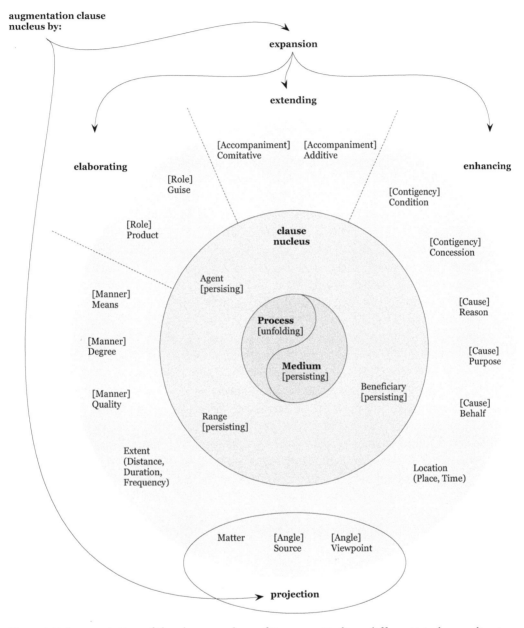

*Figure 3.18* Augmentation of the clause nucleus of Process + Medium differentiated according to types of expansion and projection

The nuclear transitivity system network in Figure 3.17 brings out a number of experiential properties of clauses, and also of the systemic organization of lexicogrammar in general:

- The systems of PROCESS TYPE and AGENCY interact systemically to define the transitivity potential and constraints on that potential. A number of more delicate transitivity systems have conjunctive entry conditions with systemic terms

from both these systems. All process types combine with 'middle', but 'effective' is more constrained (see Figure 4.9 below).
- These two systems embody complementary perspectives on transitivity. Focussing on 'material' clauses, we can identify the **transitive model** of Actor + Process ± Goal, which is a model of extension of the process to impact the Goal (is it confined to the Actor, or does it extend to impact the Goal?) and the **ergative model** of Process + Medium ± Agent, which is a model of external causation (is the configuration of Process + Medium construed as being caused by an external cause, the Agent, or not?).[20] These two models are described as co-existing in the transitivity system, some transitivity patterns being more clearly illuminated by the transitive model, e.g. *he hunted : he hunted the mouse* as Actor (*he*) + Process (*hunted*) ± Goal (*the mouse*), and other patterns being more clearly illuminated by the ergative model, e.g. *the water froze : he froze the water* as Process (*froze*) + Medium (*the water*) ± Agent (*he*).
- The system network illustrates the use of **marking conventions** (Section 6.4). For example, if clauses are 'behavioural' in PROCESS TYPE, they are 'middle' in AGENCY, as indicated by pairing of 'behavioural' * → and 'middle' → *; if clauses are 'impacting' (transitivity) in PROCESS TYPE (in the system of IMPACT), they are 'effective' in AGENCY, as indicated by 'impacting' † → and 'effective' → †; if clauses are 'existential' in PROCESS TYPE, they are 'non-ranged' in AGENCY (in the system of RANGING), as indicated by 'existential' ** → and 'non-ranged' → **.
- The system network illustrates the use of **gates**, i.e. 'defective' systems with a complex entry condition but a single term, e.g. 'effective' & 'non-impacting' (intransitive): 'initiated' ↘ +Initiator; Initiator/Agent; 'effective' & 'activity' (saying as activity): targeting ↘ +Target; Sayer/Agent; Target/Medium. Thus in the system network, curvy lines emanate from 'effective' and 'intransitivity (non-impacting)' and meet as a conjunctive entry condition of the gate represented by 'initiated'. While not shown in the system network Figure 3.17, some of these gates lead to more delicate systems, e.g. 'assigned' is the input to a system differentiating different kinds of assignments of identity (cf. Matthiessen 1995a: 314–318).

The system of PROCESS TYPE is also discussed elsewhere in this book, used as an illustration of **systemic probabilities** distilled from relative frequencies in text (Figure 4.8), including variation in probabilities across registers (Figure 4.10), and of the complementarity of **topology and typology** in relation to trinocularity (Figure 6.6).

Rounding off the presentation of this sketch of the system of TRANSITIVITY, let me present a paradigm of PROCESS TYPE intersected with AGENCY as a **concentric circle diagram**: see Figure 3.19. The diagram shows clearly which combinations are possible in the transitivity system of English; the constraints needed to block combinations that do not occur are represented in the system network in Figure 3.17 above by marking conventions (e.g. if 'existential', then 'non-ranged'). The greatest range of transitivity patterns is available for 'material' clauses, followed by 'relational' ones, and then 'mental' ones. The least extended one is 'existential', followed by 'behavioural'; neither of them combines with 'effective', only with 'middle' (unless the Process is realized by an analytical causative verbal group complex).

*The System as a Fractal Principle* • 75

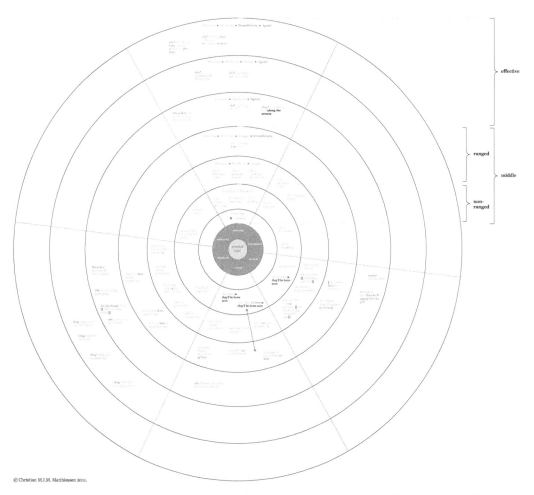

*Figure 3.19* Paradigm showing intersection of PROCESS TYPE and AGENCY (and RANGING for 'middle' clauses)

In the description of the system of circumstantiation (summarized diagrammatically in Figure 3.18), we saw that the transitivity nucleus of the clause (process + participant[s]) can be augmented circumstantially, and that these circumstantial augmentations belong to a small number of general types, as shown in Figure 3.18: either 'projection' (angle or matter) or 'expansion' (circumstances other than angle or matter), and if 'expansion', then the expansion is 'elaborating' (role), 'extending' (accompaniment) or 'enhancing' (space, time, cause, manner and all the remaining types of circumstance). Interestingly, the three types of 'expansion' also show up within nuclear transitivity in the system of RELATION TYPE (shown in Figure 3.17): 'elaborating' corresponds to 'intensive' 'relational' clauses, 'extending' to 'possessive' ones and 'enhancing' to 'circumstantial' ones. Based on patterns of agnation, we can in fact identify the following proportionalities between circumstance type and relation type:

elaborating (e.g. *as a grammarian, she ...*) : intensive (e.g. *she is a grammarian*) ::

extending (e.g. *with her research assistant, she ...*) : possessive (e.g. *she has a research assistant*)::

enhancing (e.g. *in her office, she ...*) : circumstantial (e.g. *she is in her office*)

(It turns out that these proportionalities show up when we examine lexicogrammatical metaphor, which I will return to in Section 3.3.1.4.) But what about the other primary type of circumstance, i.e. 'projection'? It turns out that in the system of RELATION TYPE, it is split between 'intensive' and 'circumstantial', which relates to the way in which the grammar of English construes semiosis (cf. Matthiessen 1991b). But instead of exploring the details of this area of the grammar, I will instead now focus on the general phenomenon that CIRCUMSTANCE TYPE and RELATION TYPE illustrate. They are both manifestations of a general **fractal system** that is manifested within different environments of the lexicogrammar of English. I have introduced the fractal types of 'projection' and 'expansion' just now in the context of the experiential clause system of transitivity; but they are actually manifested most fully in the logical environment of clause complexing, where it can be described as: projection/expansion [elaborating/extending/enhancing] – see Figure 3.20. The description of such systemic fractals is an important aspect of the development of comprehensive descriptions guided by holistic theory.

*3.3.1.3 Systemic Fractals*

As we have seen, there was an early 'pay-off' resulting from the commitment to the development of comprehensive systemic descriptions – descriptions that could serve as a resource for a variety of tasks, centrally including text analysis (cf. Halliday 1964). This was the discovery of the systemic clustering that Halliday explained by developing his theory of metafunction. In addition, the comprehensive descriptive project has led to other discoveries – discoveries due to the potential for **systems thinking** that comprehensive descriptions make possible. Almost certainly the most important discovery is the discovery of **systemic fractals** (e.g. Halliday 1981, 1985a; Matthiessen 1995a; Halliday and Matthiessen 2006; Martin 1995[21]).

Systemic fractals are general systems that are manifested in different lexicogrammatical environments (and actually also in different semantic environments); they are found within each of the metafunctions:

- **ideational:** the logico-semantic distinction between 'expansion' and 'projection', and their subtypes; the tactic distinction between 'parataxis' and 'hypotaxis', and the general principle of logical 'recursive' systems and univariate structures;
- **interpersonal:** the system of ASSESSMENT: the polarity distinction between positive ('purr') and negative ('snarl') assessment; the scalar distinction of low to high degree (value);
- **textual:** the thematic principle – the distinction between thematic and rhematic elements, and complementing it, the information principle – the distinction between given and new information (and focus of new information within the latter).

Table 3.10 Logico-semantic type as a fractal system – manifestations within different grammatical domains

| domain | system | term | projection | expansion | | |
|---|---|---|---|---|---|---|
| | | | | elaborating | extending | enhancing |
| clause nexus | TAXIS | | projection: quoting / reporting | elaborating; restating / clarifying / exemplifying (including non-defining relative clauses) | extending: additive / alternative / contrastive | enhancing; temporal / causal / conditional &c |
| | | parataxis | John said: 'I'm running away' | John didn't wait; he ran away | John ran away, and Fred stayed behind | John was scared, so he ran away |
| | | hypotaxis | John said he was running away | John didn't wait, which surprised everyone | John ran away, whereas Fred stayed behind | Because he was scared, John ran away |
| clause | PROCESS TYPE | material | — | transformative: elaborating outcome | transformative: extending outcome | transformative: enhancing outcome |
| | | relational | — | she painted the house white | she gave him a blender | she pushed him away |
| | | | —[22] | intensive | possessive | circumstantial |
| | | | — | the house was white | he had a blender | he was away |
| | | mental | Phenomenon as name of projection | — | — | — |
| | | | she believed the news | — | — | — |
| | | verbal | Verbiage as name of projection | — | — | — |
| | | | John told her the news | — | — | — |
| | CIRCUMSTANTIATION | | Angle, Matter | Role | Accompaniment | Time, Place, Duration, Distance, Manner (quality, degree, means), Cause (reason), Condition, Concession ... |
| | | | according to John, he ran away; John told her about his escape | as the accused, John ran away | John ran away without Fred | John ran away at midnight; John ran away out of fear; John ran away very fast ... |

The System as a Fractal Principle • 77

78 • *System in Systemic Functional Linguistics*

We have already seen that the logico-semantic distinction between 'projection' and 'expansion' is manifested within different grammatical domains (for more details, see Halliday and Matthiessen 2014: Table 10.7, p. 447, Table 10.3, pp. 670–672, Table 10.6, pp. 680–685). The manifestations of these types are illustrated for the domains of clause nexus and clause in Table 3.10. Within the clause nexus, they are manifested in terms of a tactic relation that links the clauses in the nexus. In the clause, they are manifested within both nuclear transitivity and circumstantiation (cf. Figure 3.18 above). In nuclear transitivity, the manifestation may involve the Process itself (as in relational clauses) or one of the participants, viz. Medium, Range, Agent or Beneficiary. For example, in 'material' clauses the Range (as Scope) involves elaboration (e.g. *he played a bad game of tennis*), extension (e.g. *he received the parcel*), or enhancement (e.g. *he crossed the square*).

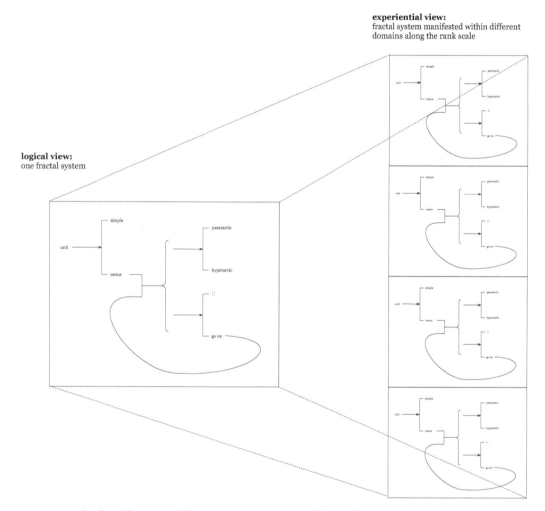

*Figure 3.20* The fractal system of logico-semantic type and taxis (adapted from Matthiessen 1995a: 91)

Similarly, the ideational systems of LOGICO-SEMANTIC TYPE and of TAXIS are manifested throughout the lexicogrammatical system in the formation of nexus of units forming complexes at the different ranks – clause complexes, group/phrase complexes, word complexes and morpheme complexes: see Figure 3.20 (adapted from Matthiessen 1995a; for a recent reference, see Liu and Wang 2021). This figure represents the manifestation of the system of TAXIS throughout the lexicogrammar, and also of the 'recursive' logical system for forming extended complexes. Fractal systems are adapted in their manifestations to the environments that they are manifested in. As far as environments defined by rank are concerned, the general principle is that fractal systems within grammar are manifested most fully at clause rank, but the manifestations at lower ranks are more constrained, i.e. the constraints increase with the move down the rank scale.

### 3.3.1.4 Fractals and Metaphor

Ideational and interpersonal fractal systems open up the possibility of lexicogrammatical **metaphor** because they can be manifested in different lexicogrammatical environments – so alongside the environment that constitutes the congruent realization of some meaning, they are other environments that can provide domains of incongruent realizations. For example, the fractal type of 'expansion' is manifested textually by means of cohesive sequences of clauses marked by conjunctions, logically by means of paratactic or hypotactic combinations of clauses, experientially by means of circumstances or relational processes or by means of qualification within a nominal group. Using a set of examples from IFG (Halliday and Matthiessen 2014: 673), I can illustrate this for the 'cause' subtype of expansion: see Figure 3.5. Since this type of grammatical metaphor has become more frequent in English over the last 500 years, as shown by Halliday (1988), metaphor also contributes to the development of fractal patterns.

*Table 3.11* Manifestations of the 'cause' subtype of 'expansion' (adapted from Halliday and Matthiessen 2014: Table 10.4, p. 673)

| domain | system | metafunction | example |
| --- | --- | --- | --- |
| cohesive clause sequence | CONJUNCTION | textual | *She didn't know the rules. Consequently, she died.* |
| clause complex | TAXIS: parataxis | logical | *She didn't know the rules; so she died.* |
|  | TAXIS: hypotaxis |  | *Because she didn't know the rules, she died.* |
| clause (simple) | MODULATION | logical + experiential | *Her ignorance of the rules caused her to die.* |
|  | CIRCUMSTANTIATION | experiential | *Through ignorance of the roles, she died.* |
|  | PROCESS TYPE: relational |  | *Her death was due to ignorance of the rules.* |
|  |  |  | *Her ignorance of the rules caused her death.* |
|  |  |  | *The cause of her death was her ignorance of the rules.* |
| nominal group | QUALIFICATION |  | *her death through ignorance of the rules* |

Viewed 'from above', from the point of view of semantics, the lexicogrammatical domains set out in Table 3.10 represent different **coding opportunities** – different opportunities to realize patterns of meaning. They are clearly **agnate**, but also clearly not synonymous.[23] An interesting issue is how to represent this type of agnation created by fractal systems and expanded through lexicogrammatical metaphor within the ideational metafunction.

In general, the approach to similar patterns within the interpersonal metafunction has been to extend interpersonal semantic systems in delicacy, as in the case of speech function, or to add simultaneous systems, as in the case of modality, to take account of the expansion in the interpersonal meaning potential created by interpersonal metaphor. For example, the system of MANIFESTATION of orientation in modality, either 'subjective' or 'objective', depends on the metaphorical use of 'mental' and 'relational' clauses for the realization of the option of 'explicit' manifestation: see Figure 5.7 in Chapter 5.

### 3.3.1.5 Towards Lexical Delicacy

The stratum of lexicogrammar is extended systemically (i.e. along the paradigmatic axis) in **delicacy** from the grammatical zone to the lexical zone. This systemic conception of grammar and lexis as a unified resource goes back to Halliday (1961); he presented the possibility of moving from descriptions of grammar towards descriptions of lexis as the 'grammarian's dream'. This conception contrasts sharply with the folk model of two separate books dealing with wording, the grammar book and the dictionary; and it similarly contrast's fundamentally with Bloomfield's (1933: 274) conception with them as separate, the dictionary being the repository of idiosyncratic details:

> Strictly speaking, then, every morpheme of a language is an irregularity, since the speaker can use it only after hearing it used, and the reader of a linguistic description can know of its existence only if it is listed for him. The lexicon is really an appendix of the grammar, a list of basic irregularities. This is all the more evident if meanings are taken into consideration, since the meaning of each morpheme belongs to it by an arbitrary tradition.

Bloomfield's conception was taken over into early generative linguistics and remained the default position until the interest in lexicalism and lexical rules in the early 1970s.

What the folk model and the US structuralist and early generative models arguably have in common is a combination of **syntagmatic orientation and mode of access** – i.e. the resources of wording are accessed from the point of view of the listener/reader (or analyst as listener/reader) rather from the point of view of the speaker/writer, a point of view that Halliday had explored already in the mid-1950s as part of his involvement as a linguist in the early machine translation project directed by Margaret Masterman at Cambridge University (Halliday 1956b). The listener/reader tends to access the resources of wording 'from below', so s/he'll adopt a view that foregrounds access to grammatical and lexical items encountered in texts to be processed for the sake of understanding, translation and so on (for 'views', see Section 7.1): this is the **dictionary view** of not only lexis but actually also of grammar (cf. Matthiessen 1991a, 1995a; Matthiessen and Nesbitt 1996). At the same time, this angle of access as the view of lexis and grammar is reinforced by theories that are syntagmatically oriented since grammatical structure and lexical items ('content words') seem very different in nature and grammatical items ('function words') may be hard to relate to lexical items (at least before studies of grammaticalization began to take off in the late 1980s).

However, if paradigmatic organization and syntagmatic organization are given equal status or particularly if paradigmatic organized is 'promoted' to the status of the primary axis of organization (the axial re-think or systemic turn in SFL; cf. further Section 6.1 and Figure 6.1), it becomes possible to explore the relationship between grammar and lexis in a new light – the light of systemic organization and of system networks as a representation of patterns along the paradigmatic axis. Then delicacy can supplement constituency as a 'tool for thought', and Halliday's (1961) theoretical vision of lexis as most delicate grammar begins to make sense.

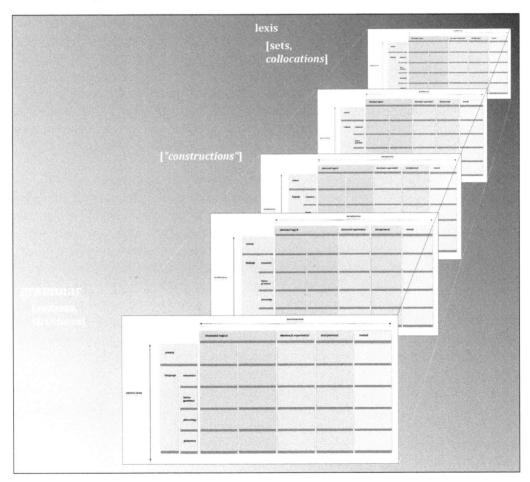

*Figure 3.21* The lexicogrammatical cline of delicacy, extending from grammar towards lexis

If we fast-forward around a decade from Halliday's (1961) vision of lexicogrammar as a unified resource of wording extended systemically along the cline of instantiation from grammar to lexis, we arrive at a picture roughly like the one presented in Figure 3.21. The extension in delicacy from grammar to lexis theoretically involved **all systems identified in the function-rank matrix** – i.e. across the metafunctions and down the ranks from clause to word (or morpheme). Lexical distinctions will be located within systems whose points of origin are grammatical; they do not suddenly appear mid-delicacy unrelated to any grammatical systems. Paradigmatically, the move along the cline of delicacy from grammar is a move from closed systems to open sets; and syntagmatically, it is a move from grammatical structures to lexical collocations: see Halliday and Matthiessen (2014: Chapter 2), with illustrations from Nelson Mandela's presidential inaugural address. Tucker (1996, 1998: Chapter 6) and Neale (2002) present detailed accounts of the use of system networks in the description of lexis.

The systems that (as far as we know) extend in delicacy from grammar to lexis are located within experiential and interpersonal systems in particular:

- experiential systems of the clause (TRANSITIVITY, particularly PROCESS TYPE), of the nominal group (THING TYPE, EPITHESIS [QUALITY TYPE]), verbal group (EVENT TYPE) and of the adverbial group (CIRCUMSTANCE TYPE) are extended in delicacy, having evolved the lexical resources for construing the world as meaning – including the construal of experiential taxonomies;
- interpersonal systems of the clause (MODAL ASSESSMENT), of the nominal group (ATTITUDINAL EPITHESIS, connotative aspects of THING TYPE) and of the adverbial group (COMMENT TYPE) are extended in delicacy, having evolved lexical resources for enacting values in the exchange of meanings negotiated by interactants.

Some experiential and interpersonal systems are highly grammaticalized and do not extend in delicacy towards lexis; the interpersonal system of MODALITY is the most grammaticalized part of the system of MODAL ASSESSMENT and the interpersonal system of PERSON is fully grammaticalized, as is the system of POLARITY (although contrasts in polarity may of course also be lexicalized as with *fail* in *fail to do*, where 'negative' is lexicalized – but also ideotionalized, so the clause remains grammatically positive interpersonally, as in *some schools are failing to give an adequate education to working class children*, which is positive in terms of interpersonal grammar, as shown by the unmarked reversal in tag polarity: *some schools are failing ... aren't they?*). Some systems extend in delicacy to some degree and tend to be more open than prototypical grammatical system, like the experiential system of MINOR PROCESS TYPE, which is concerned with options realized by prepositions.

Logical systems tend to be highly grammaticalized, like the systems of TAXIS and of TENSE in English. The system of LOGICO-SEMANTIC TYPE extends a bit further in delicacy, but terms in this system are realized (in combination with the tactic distinction between hypotaxis and parataxis) by the fairly closed set of structural conjunctions (linkers and binders). The textual system of (cohesive) CONJUNCTION is concerned with the logico-semantic type of expansion and terms are realized by non-structural, cohesive conjunctions, which constitute a more open set than structural conjunctions. Other textual systems are fully grammaticalized, with terms realized by grammatical items, as in the cases of DETERMINATION and SUBSTITUTION. (Systems that are realized by grammatical structures, like the system of THEME, are of course fully grammaticalized.)

When terms in lexicogrammatical systems are realized by items – grammatical or lexical – rather than by structures (or phonological preselections in systems of INTONATION), these items may belong to closed systems, semi-closed systems/semi-open sets or open sets, as illustrated in Table 3.12. I have divided the cline of delicacy into these three degrees of delicacy, but delicacy is of course a continuum.

Table 3.12 Examples of systems realized by lexicogrammatical items at different degrees of delicacy, from closed system items to open set items

| metafunction | system | grammatical | grammatico-lexical | lexical |
|---|---|---|---|---|
| | | closed systems | semi-closed systems/ semi-open sets | open sets |
| logical | TAXIS & LOGICO-SEMANTIC TYPE | structural conjunctions: linkers & binders | verbs of phase, conation and modulation in hypotactic verbal group complexes | |
| | TENSE | grammaticalized verbs: tense auxiliaries | | |
| experiential | PROCESS TYPE | (grammaticalized lexical verbs: *do, happen*) | high frequency verbs: *do, make, take; say, think; be, have* | lexical verbs of 'doing-&-happening', 'behaving', 'sensing', 'saying', 'being-&-having', 'existing' |
| | MINOR PROCESS TYPE | | prepositions serving as minor Process | |
| | THING TYPE | grammaticalized nouns: general nouns (Halliday and Hasan 1976), fact nouns (Halliday and Matthiessen 2014: 536) | 'basic level nouns' (cf. Halliday and Matthiessen 2006: Ch. 14) | lexical nouns within the whole range of different types of entity |
| interpersonal | MODALITY | grammaticalized verbs: modal operators; grammaticalized adverbs: modal adverbs | | |
| | MODAL ASSESSMENT (OTHER THAN MODALITY) | MOOD ASSESSMENT: grammaticalized adverbs (e.g. temporal expectation: *already, still, just, soon*) | COMMENT ASSESSMENT: comment adverbs | (CONNOTATION dispersed throughout lexis) |
| | | | POST-DEIXIS OF PROJECTION: adjectives of modality, evidentiality, attitude | attitudinal lexis |
| textual | VOICE | grammaticalized verbs: voice auxiliaries (*be, get* + v-en) | | |
| | CONJUNCTION | | cohesive conjunctions | |
| | DETERMINATION | determiners, pronouns | | |

One good way of investigating the difference between lexical and grammatical items is to view them phylogenetically in the evolution of languages and to track processes of **grammaticalization**, as when certain lexical verbs of motion gradually move to the grammatical zone of lexicogrammar to serve as grammatical items realizing terms in grammatical systems, like *going to* in English and *aller* in French (cf. Matthiessen 1995a). As lexical items, they are likely to be fairly general (like deictic motion, *go* vs. *come*) but they are part of a lexical field with many close agnates (cf. Figure 3.23); however, as grammatical items, they are no longer part of this open-ended paradigmatic neighbourhood but are agnate with other grammatical items, as in *it's going to rain : it will rain* (and not with lexical agnates from the lexical set that the lexical verb *go* belongs to; we don't expect to find *it's going to rain - it's running to rain - it's trotting to rain - it's strolling to rain - it's sauntering to rain*).

The task of extending the description of grammatical systems in delicacy to 'net in' lexical sets is rather daunting in terms of its scope, and full-fledged system networks are still fairly limited in scope; examples are given in Table 3.13. In the 'system networks' column, I have listed examples with fully developed lexical system networks, and in the column to the right, I have listed examples that are more like classifications of verbs (in different senses) and verb classes by means of the first steps in delicacy of a grammatical system.

*Table 3.13* Examples of systemic descriptions of lexis

| metafunction | system | system networks | classifications sorted according to grammatical systems |
|---|---|---|---|
| experiential | PROCESS TYPE | illustrative: Hasan (1985a), lending & borrowing; Hasan (1987), disposal; discussion of criteria and approaches: Tucker (2014) | Neale (2002, 2006); Matthiessen (2014b) |
| | THING TYPE | illustrative: Halliday and Matthiessen (2006/1999: 198–201), clothing | |
| | QUALITY TYPE | comprehensive: Tucker (1998) | |
| interpersonal | APPRAISAL: ATTITUDE | comprehensive (but without realization statements and taxonomic in nature): Martin and White (2005) [located by them within semantic stratum] | |

In her description of the extension in delicacy of certain domains within the system of process type, Hasan (1987) shows that lexical verbs, or sets of verbs, realize **systemic combinations of terms** in lexicogrammatical systems; these realizations correspond to verb senses since any one verb is likely to have more than one sense. Her description uses the power of system networks fully to involve simultaneous systems (like ACCESS and CHARACTER) and complex entry conditions, as can be seen from the fragment in Figure 3.22. Examples of verbs realizing the Process (or really, the Event of the verbal group serving as the Process) are given in Table 3.14. The column and row headings are systemic terms from the system network in Figure 3.22.

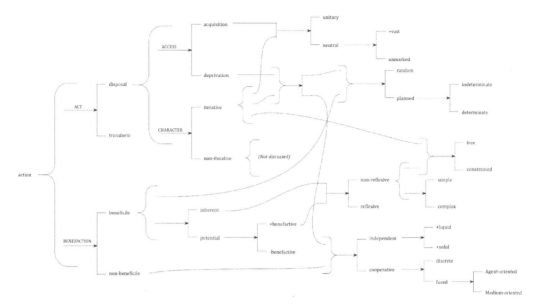

*Figure 3.22* Part of Hasan's (1987) systemic description of the extension in delicacy of a domain within 'material' clauses

*Table 3.14* Examples of serving as realizations of Process for different combinations of systemic terms in Figure 3.22

|  | acquisition |  | deprivation |  |
|---|---|---|---|---|
| non-benefacile |  |  | independent<br>solid *strew*<br>liquid *spill* |  |
|  |  |  | cooperative<br>*share* |  |
| benefacile | *buy* | unitary *gather* | random *scatter* | *give* |
|  |  | neutral<br>unmarked *collect*<br>vast *accumulate* | planned<br>indeterminate *divide*<br>determinate *distribute* |  |
|  | non-iterative | iterative |  | non-iterative |

Neale (2002) provides a comprehensive elaboration in delicacy of the system of PROCESS TYPE based on the description in the 'Cardiff grammar', the version of SFG developed by Robin Fawcett, Gordon Tucker and their team at the University of Cardiff (e.g. Schultz and Fontaine 2019), the central descriptive chapter with presentations of the system network description being her Chapter 8. Compared to Hasan's (1987) illustrative descriptions, Neale's account is arguably more taxonomic in nature. On a parallel track, growing out of the systemic description of TRANSITIVITY in Matthiessen (1995a), I started a research project in the 1990s, one that is still ongoing and partially reported on in Matthiessen (2014b). I intended it as a resource to be used in the development of truly systemic descriptions of the system of PROCESS TYPE; I classified all of Levin's (1993) primary and secondary verb classes according to the description of PROCESS TYPE in Halliday's IFG, also taking account of Matthiessen (1995a) and supplementing Levin's classification with information from my own work in areas that are not foregrounded in her work (e.g. considerations of potential for projection and the nature of the unmarked present tense).

The classification of Levin's verb classes in terms of the system of PROCESS TYPE is illustrated for 'material' clauses of motion in Figure 3.23 (cf. Neale 2002, in particular pp. 244–247). The system network extends up to and includes the system of TRANSFORMATIVE OUTCOME, which is concerned with the nature of the outcome of the unfolding of the process in time as it affects the Medium in the Process + Medium configuration in the first instance (cf. Figure 3.17 above): 'elaborating outcome' – the quality of the Medium, including change in any of its aspects (like composition, texture, state, temperature or colour if concrete), 'extending outcome' – prototypically the possession or aggregation of the Medium (like change in ownership), 'enhancing outcome' – the circumstance of the Medium, prototypically change of location in space, i.e. motion. Under the third type, 'enhancing outcome', I have classified a number of Levin's (1993) verb classes and subclasses having to do with motion; I have presented this classification as a taxonomy spliced into the system network since it has not yet been systemicized[24]. Systemicizing it would mean identifying properties to be represented by simultaneous systems, like the nature of the Medium (e.g. animate vs. inanimate), the manner of motion (quality, means), the place of motion (direction, medium of motion [e.g. on land, in water]); the result of systemicizing these taxonomic distinctions would likely look like Figure 3.22.

Hybrids like the system network with a taxonomy spliced in as a **placeholder** for a systemic description are just that – **hybrids**. They are intended as descriptive stepping stones, but they can still prove useful before fully systemicized system networks have been developed, as is illustrated by the study of the varied deployment of 'material' clauses of motions in different registers where the construal of motion plays an important role such as topographic procedures, recounts of journeys, narratives of journeys and explanations of celestial mechanics (e.g. Matthiessen and Kashyap 2014).

In addition to the descriptions listed in Table 3.13, work on lexis in computational modelling based on SFL can provide insights into the description of lexis (e.g. Cross 1991; Matthiessen 1991a); and work outside SFL involving some kind of 'componential analysis' will also be an important source of information, like the work in ethnoscience on lexical folk taxonomies that began in the 1950s (e.g. Goodenough 1956; Frake 1962) and examples in Leech (1969, 1974). (Here it is important to interpret 'components' paradigmatically as systemic values rather than as constituent parts of senses, as has been done in both interpretative and generative semantics within generative linguistics, and also, arguably, by Anna Wierzbicka, e.g. 1996, in her interesting Leibnizian approach to semantics.)

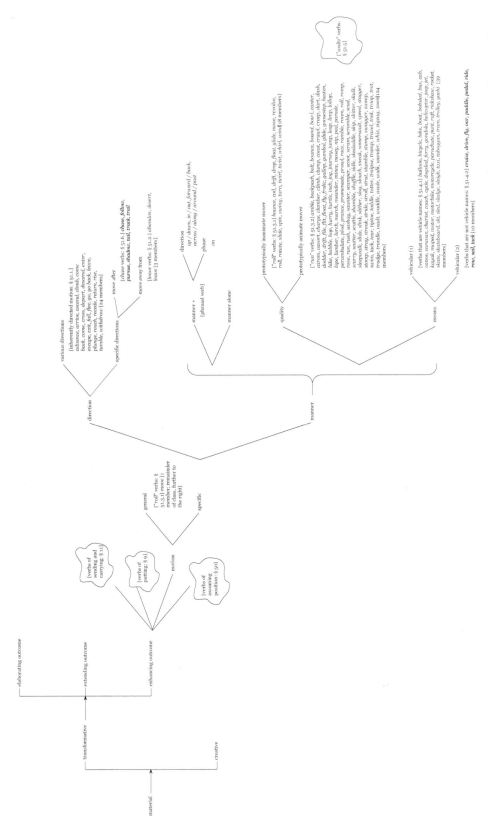

*Figure 3.23* Example of extension in the delicacy of the systemic description of process type by classification of Levin's (1993) verb classes (indicated by § numbers) – 'material' clauses of motion

In the development of system networks that originate in grammar and are elaborated to cover different lexical fields, we need to adopt the standard **trinocular vision** as in all lexicogrammatical description, in terms of all the relevant semiotic dimensions:

- the hierarchy of stratification (with lexicogrammar wedged between semantics and phonology [or graphology]), ensuring that systemic descriptions of lexis can be semantically motivated but are based on grammatical and lexical evidence;
- the rank scale (as the internal organization of lexicogrammar, e.g. in the elaboration of the systems of THING TYPE and of EVENT TYPE, consideration from above in reference to the system network of the clause and considerations from below in reference to the system networks of words of different primary classes);
- the hierarchy of axiality (shunting along the cline of instantiation to calibrate lexical systems in relation to both more delicate lexical ones and less delicate grammatical one, and adopting the view 'from below' in terms of lexical patterns along the syntagmatic axis, both collocations and 'constructions' in the sense of 'construction grammars');
- the cline of instantiation to take account both of frequency of instantiation and (registerial) variation in instantiation according to the nature of context (cf. Wignell, Martins and Eggins 1993, on variation in lexical taxonomies according to degrees of expertise; and see also Halliday and Matthiessen 2006: Chapter 14).

Different aspects of these considerations are discussed by Matthiessen (1991a, 1995a), Wanner (1997), Tucker (1998, 2014) and Neale (2002). Let me just note one consideration here, one that derives from Firth's insight into **collocations**. Firth characterized collocations as the company that words keep, and they can be interpreted as lexical patterning along the syntagmatic axis (cf. Figure 3.24). Thus we can recognize the complementarity of grammatical and lexical patterning along the cline of delicacy and view it both paradigmatically and syntagmatically, as specified in Table 3.15 (see Halliday and Matthiessen 2014: Chapter 2). Intermediate between the grammatical zone and the lexical zone we find grammatico-lexical patterns that have been studied under the heading of 'constructions' in construction-grammatical approaches (including also Lexical Pattern Grammar, a corpus-informed development within the Birmingham School introduced by Hunston and Francis 2000). In SFL, Tucker (2007) explores the systemic interpretation and description of 'phraseology', glossed as 'an amalgam of grammatical and lexical organisation' (p. 952) located 'between grammar and lexis'.

*Table 3.15* The complementarity of grammatical and lexical patterning along the cline of delicacy in terms of the paradigmatic axis and the syntagmatic axis

| axis | grammatical zone | grammatico-lexical zone | lexical zone |
| --- | --- | --- | --- |
| paradigmatic | systems (open) | grammatico-lexical systems | sets (open) |
| syntagmatic | structures | 'constructions', 'phraseology' | collocations |

We have already seen that paradigmatically lexical sets can be approached from the grammatical pole of the cline of instantiation and be described by means of delicate systems, as illustrated in Figure 3.22, from Hasan's (1987) descriptive project, or as an intermediate descriptive stage by means of hybrid system networks and taxonomies, as in Figure 3.23, based on Matthiessen (2014b). Grammatical structures are specified fragment by fragment by means of realization statements associated with terms in systems; in other words, syntagmatic patterning within the grammatical zone of lexicogrammar is specified in paradigmatic environments. But how do we account for collocations systemically; how do we relate collocational combinations of particular items to structural combinations of functions realized by grammatical units, and how do we represent collocational patterns in system networks?

The notion of collocation was discussed at an early stage by Halliday (1966b) and it became a focus of research in the Birmingham School corpus-based research into lexis led by John Sinclair (e.g. Sinclair 1966, 1987, 1991; Renouf and Sinclair 1991), and led to investigations of 'phraseology', 'semantic prosodies' and other properties that can productively be investigated 'from below' in large corpora. Complementing this line of research, Halliday and Hasan (1976) also shed light on collocation as an aspect of LEXICAL COHESION (interpreted semantically by J.R. Martin, 1992, in terms of his description of the system of IDEATION).

Since collocations are syntagmatic patterns of wording viewed from the lexical pole of the cline of delicacy, it makes sense to investigate whether they can be related to syntagmatic patterns of wording from the grammatical pole, i.e. to structures. It is clear that a significant number of collocations can be related to configurations of functions that are tightly bonded within grammatical function structures. Certain collocations involve experiential configurations such as:

- clause:
  - Process + Medium (e.g. *twinkle + star, cut + record, compose + music, pen + letter, stream + video*),
  - Process + Range (e.g. *take + bath, wreak + havoc*),
  - Process + Manner: degree (e.g. *love + deeply, want + badly, understand + completely*),
- nominal group:
  - Thing + Epithet (e.g. *strong + tea, powerful + argument, heavy + traffic*).

Such patterns are illustrated in Matthiessen (1995a), with references to lexical functions such as MAGN in the Russian Meaning Text Model (e.g. Mel'čuk 1986, 2015: Chapter 14); and collocations involving Process + Manner: degree are explored in Matthiessen (2009a). The configuration of Process + Range/Attribute involves the special case of intensive attributive relational clauses of inceptive phase (clauses of 'becoming'), which give rise to a range of collocations illustrated in Figure 3.24. If the representation of inceptive phase is 'specific' rather than 'general' (Process: *become, get*), then the next systemic contrast has to do with assessment; either the Process + Range/Attribute combination is assessed as 'neutral', in which case there are a few patterns with Process: *turn* or *go* + Range/Attribute: 'colour' (*pale; blue, green, red, orange, crimson* &c.), or it is 'loaded'. If 'loaded', it is either 'positive' with the sense of fulfilment, or 'negative' with the sense of deterioration. Interestingly, there are many more negative collocations than positive ones. This is of course an example of a lexicogrammatical domain where experiential denotations are differentiated in terms of interpersonal connotations (which would be picked up in a description of appraisal: Martin and White 2005).

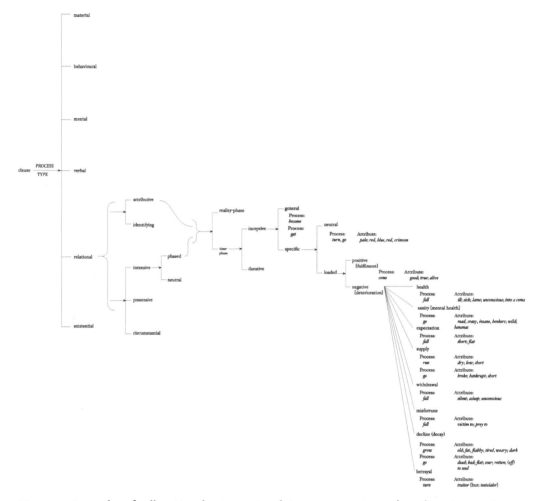

*Figure 3.24* Examples of collocational patterns involving Process + Range/Attribute in certain phased intensive and attributive relational clauses, represented as a hybrid system network and taxonomy – the taxonomy being a focus for future systemicization

The collocations illustrated above can often be related to **lexical metaphors** (cf. Matthiessen 2009a), e.g. *love* in relation to abstract space, with specifications of degree in terms of vertical location in this abstract space of emotion: *love deeply, be in (deep) love, fall out of love*. Lexical metaphors constitute the basis not only for collocations of individual lexical items such as *love* + *deeply* but collocations of classes of lexical items; thus *deeply* as the Head of an adverbial group serving as Manner: degree collocates not only with *love* as the Event of a verbal group serving as Process, but also with a number of other verbs related to the lexical metaphor of emotions as vertical locations an abstract space, e.g. *appreciate/love/cherish/treasure/care/miss/adore/resent/hate/detest/*

*regret* // *concern/sadden/disappoint/trouble/offend/hurt/embarrass/terrify* + *deeply* (cf. also *feel/have deep affection for*), contrasting with lexical metaphor of cognitive coverage of an abstract space, e.g. *know/believe/understand/grasp/misunderstand/realize/remember/forget* // *convince* + *completely/fully* (cf. the collocational sets in Figure 3.24). The collocations are typically manifested across grammatical environments as in the case of *love*: Process (*love*) + Manner: degree (*deeply*), Epithet (*deep*) + Thing (*love*), Epithet [Modifier (*deeply*) + Head (*loving*)] + Thing (*attitude*), Thing (*depth*) + Qualifier (*of love*). Many, perhaps all, of these represent a lexical spread across word classes created by grammatical metaphor.

A more general overview of descriptive challenges inherent in the treatment of 'phraseology' is offered by Tucker (2007). Such descriptive challenges involve 'multi-word' lexical items, including (outside SFL) what Allerton (2002) calls 'stretched verb constructions' (e.g. *take a risk with, put in danger, make an accusation against*); see also Steiner (1985) for discussion. Tucker (2007) proposes and evaluates a few different systemic functional approaches to the interpretation and description of patterns of 'phraseology'[25].

### 3.3.2 Semantic System Networks

Like lexicogrammatical system networks, semantic system networks organize content rather than expression; their domain of operation is the higher of the two content strata, i.e. semantics, and they are realized lexicogrammatically when their semantic domains have lexicogrammatical correlates (i.e. clauses and lower-ranking units on the grammatical rank scale; see further Section 3.2.2.3 on semantic composition). The 'fission' of content into semantics and lexicogrammar makes **double agnation** possible, as noted above (Section 3.1.2). For example, when Alec Guinness writes *My name escapes me*, we can relate it lexicogrammatically to other 'cognitive mental' clauses such as *I forget my name*; but at the same time we can recognize a lexical metaphor where remembering is construed semantically in terms of memory as a container. Similarly, the clause *[Do you] Want me to tell you one of my ideas for murdering my father?* (from Hitchcock's Strangers on a Train) is grammatically a 'yes/no interrogative' clause, at the same time it is semantically an offer (of information).

#### 3.3.2.1 Content Plane: Semantics and Lexicogrammar

As noted above, the two content strata of language, semantics and lexicogrammar stand in a **natural** relationship to one another as opposed to a conventional one, like the relationship between lexicogrammar and phonology (see e.g. Section 2.5, which includes an extended quote from Halliday's, 1985a, characterization of the natural relationship between semantics and lexicogrammar), and this natural relationship has made possible the emergence of metaphor – lexicogrammatical metaphor, as outlined in Section 3.1 above. The systemic organizations of the two content strata share a number of properties, centrally:

- they are both content strata, concerned with the systemic representation of content within the content plane of language (which, critically, involves *valeur* in addition to signification; cf. Hasan 1985b);

- they are both organized metafunctionally, manifesting both the spectrum of the metafunctional modes of meaning and their distinctive modes of expression;
- they are both organized compositionally.

There are also important differences relevant to the representation of the systemic organization of semantics:

- while they are both content strata, they have different stratal neighbours: lexicogrammar is located between two linguistic strata, semantics and phonology (or graphology, or sign), and it is thus an inner form stratum, but semantics is located between one linguistic stratum, lexicogrammar, and extra-linguistic systems (context, other denotative semiotic systems, bio-semiotic systems), so its organization has to be such that it can serve as an interface to these extra-linguistic systems (it is an interlevel, as explained by Halliday 1973b);
- while they are both organized metafunctionally, the metafunctions may be systemically (and structurally) more separate in semantics than in lexicogrammar, which allows for, and is reflected in, incongruent realizations involving lexicogrammatical metaphor (Figure 3.25);
- while they are both organized compositionally, the semantic compositional hierarchy extends upwards beyond the highest-ranking domain of lexicogrammar (the clause and its combination into the clause complex) and the semantic compositional hierarchy may be subject to more diversification across the spectrum of metafunction and more variation across registers (Figure 3.34).

These similarities and differences in systemic organization are inter-related; for example, the metafunctional separation in semantics relative to lexicogrammar is related to the potential for different compositional hierarchies (Section 3.2.2.3). I will start with the internal organization of semantics and save the question of the 'stratal neighbourhood' outside language since it has not been fully foregrounded in systemic functional work on semantic system networks, and I will come back to it after I have reviewed descriptions of semantics represented by means of system networks (Section 3.2.2.6).

*3.3.2.2 Move: The System of Speech Function; Exchange: The System of negotiation*
Metafunctionally, the clause realizes three different semantic units – experientially, a figure (a quantum of change in the flow of events); interpersonally, a move (a quantum of interaction in dialogic exchange); and textually a message (a quantum of information in the flow of text): see Table 3.16 and Figure 3.25. I have already sketched the realizational relationship between the system of SPEECH FUNCTION and the system of MOOD, representing it systemically in Figure 3.2, where the inter-stratal realizational relations are represented by downward pointing arrows from the systemic terms being realized at the next stratum below to the terms realizing them, as in the case of the arrow from 'statement' (semantics) to 'declarative' (lexicogrammar) and of 'protesting' (lexicogrammar) to 'tone 2' (phonology). I will continue with this interpersonal 'slice' through the content system, focussing on the clause as a move.

*Table 3.16* Semantic and lexicogrammatical systemic correlates – patterns of realization by clause systems

|  | semantics | | ↘ | lexicogrammar | |
|---|---|---|---|---|---|
| experiential | figure | FIGURATION | ↘ | clause | TRANSITIVITY |
| interpersonal | move | SPEECH FUNCTION | ↘ | | MOOD |
| textual | message | PERSPECTIVE | ↘ | | THEME |

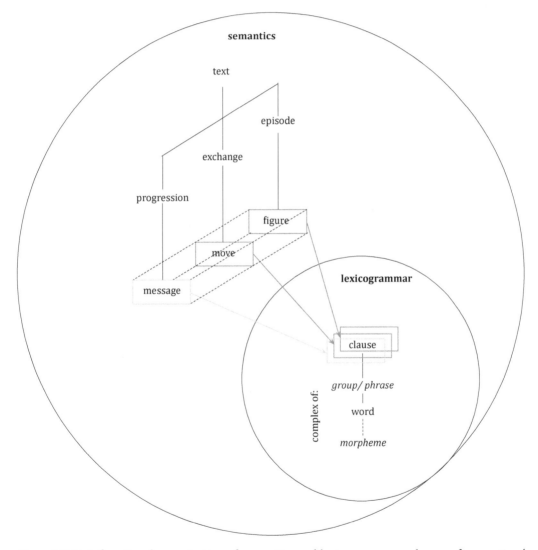

*Figure 3.25* Metafunctional organization of semantics and lexicogrammar – degree of separation/unification

Interpersonally, the clause realizes a move in the semantics. A move is a move in the development of dialogue, either one where a speaker initiates a new exchange of meanings in the dialogue, or responds to one that has already been initiated. The system of SPEECH FUNCTION provides interactants with the resources for initiating exchanges and responding to exchanges that have already been initiated, exchanging either information or goods-&-services, as illustrated in Table 3.3 above. Moves thus enter into dialogic patterns of exchange; exchanges consist of one or more moves, as schematized in Figure 3.25. At the same time as a clause realizes a dialogic move in an exchange, it also realizes a figure and a message, semantically participating in other larger patterns (Figure 3.25).

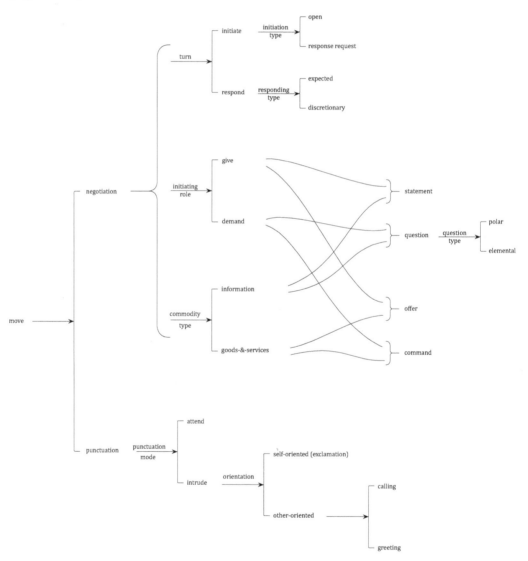

*Figure 3.26* The interpersonal semantic system of SPEECH FUNCTION

The system of SPEECH FUNCTION thus has the move as its domain of operation; the system network is presented up to a few steps in delicacy in Figure 3.26 (see Halliday 1984a; Halliday and Matthiessen 2014: Chapter 4). The systems are all concerned with options in dialogic interaction, enabling speakers to take up a speech role and assign a complementary one to the listener. The primary contrast is between 'negotiation' and 'punctuation' – between what we might call major moves and minor ones. Major moves serve to negotiate the exchange of a commodity, either information or goods-&-services, moving the dialogic exchange forward by the speaker giving or demanding the commodity, while minor moves serve to punctuate dialogue – opening it up by calls or greetings, or closing it down by greetings, or by attending to it ('backchannelling') or reacting (exclamations).

In the system network shown in Figure 3.26, the basic speech functions are interpreted as combinations of terms from the systems INITIATING ROLE (the orientation in the exchange: 'give'/'demand') and COMMODITY TYPE (the nature of what is being exchanged: 'information'/'goods-&-services') following Halliday (1984a); see examples in Table 3.17. Only one of them has been elaborated further in delicacy here, viz. 'question'; this is motivated 'from below' since 'interrogative' clauses in English are either 'yes/no interrogative' or 'wh-interrogative'; but semantically this is, in my systemic sketch here, simply based on the need to take account of the grammatical distinction in mood type between 'yes/no' and 'wh-': all speech functions could and ultimately need to be elaborated in delicacy – also actually to take account of realizational distinctions. Hasan provided an early detailed example of the systemic elaboration of one of the basic speech functions, viz. offer; she circulated a manuscript in 1987 called 'Offers in the making'. It was part of the system network she had developed in the context of her large-scale research project analysing conversations between mothers and young children (Hasan 1989, 2009) – and covered in her coding manual for the project, but it never got published at the time.[26] As an illustration of the elaboration in delicacy of the systemic description of options within the system of speech function, I have adapted Hasan's (1996: 122–123) illustrative description of the system of questions: see Figure 3.27. Her description includes considerations 'from below' – in this case, reflected in the realization statements preselecting systemic features within the interpersonal clause system network of MOOD, like 'declarative' and 'tagged: reversed polarity'. Preselections of grammatical features will include not only those realized structurally within the clause but also those realized phonologically by selections in the system of TONE.

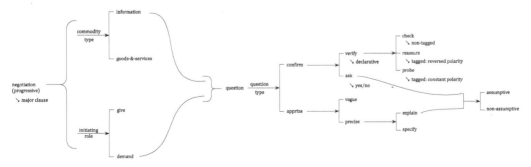

*Figure 3.27* System network fragment for questions, adapted from Hasan (1996: 122–123)

Table 3.17 Basic speech functions and their (congruent) realizations by mood types

| | COMMODITY TYPE | |
|---|---|---|
| INITIATING ROLE | **information** | **goods-&-services** |
| giving | statement | offer |
| | ↘ declarative | ↘ (various) |
| | He built me a gazebo. | Shall I build you a gazebo? Let me build you a gazebo. I can build you a gazebo. |
| demanding | question | command |
| | ↘ interrogative | ↘ imperative |
| | Has he built you a gazebo? What has he built you? | Build me a gazebo! |

As mentioned above, Hasan's semantic systemic description was used in the analysis of interactions between mothers and young children during her large project in the 1980s, and since then the description has also served as the resource in other projects involving the analysis of dialogue. In addition, Andy Fung has developed a version of this systemic description, producing an account of Cantonese, focussing on questions in particular, and applied it to the analysis of medical consultations in an accident and emergency department of a large hospital in Hong Kong (Fung 2015, 2018).

Let me pause for a moment to give an illustration of speech functional selections in a text, a dialogue between Anne and her brother, taken from 'Talking Shop' (Halliday 1978b). They're at home, in a sharing context; Anne's brother initiates the first exchange of the dialogue by asking her about a job interview she has gone to that day: see Table 3.19. I have presented the dialogue in such a way that it is easy to see the successive moves and the speech functional analysis of them.

As can be seen from the analysis, the dialogue between Anne and her brother is largely 'driven' by him in that he initiates exchanges and demands information from her (questions). This can be interpreted as an instance of his enactment of his relationship to her as an interested and supportive brother. His only statement is *That's good*, an assessment of the information she has just given him that she got the job. The interactants speech functional selections accumulate to produce **systemic interactant profiles** (cf. Matthiessen 1995a: 406–410). Such profiles represent the interactants in a dialogue in terms of the systemic selections they make, bringing out similarities, differences and complementarities. Table 3.18 shows the interactant selections system by system. This is just a short passage of dialogue, and profiles can change in the course of dialoguing – that's one aspect of interactants negotiating their roles; but of course long dialogues or even sequences of dialogues can be profiled in this way. For example, when we profile the speech functional selections in medical consultations, we will find that doctors initiate and demand information (or goods-&-services during examination and treatment) and patients respond and give (cf. Thompson 1999; Slade et al. 2015; Fung 2018).

*Table 3.18* Speech functional interactant profiles for Anne's brother and Anne

| system | term | Brother | Anne |
|---|---|---|---|
| TURN | initiate | 5 | 0 |
|  | respond | 1 | 12 |
| INITIATING ROLE | giving | 1 | 12 |
|  | demanding | 5 | 0 |
| COMMODITY TYPE | information | 6 | 12 |
|  | goods-&-services | 0 | 0 |

*Table 3.19* Exchange between siblings, brother and Anne, at home

| Brother | | Anne | |
|---|---|---|---|
| speech functional selection | turn | speech functional selection | turn |
| negotiation: initiate & demand & information | How'd you go at that interview today? | | |
| | | negotiation: respond: expected & give & information | All right. |
| | | negotiation: respond: expected & give & information | There was two ladies interviewing. |
| | | negotiation: respond: expected & give & information | One of them was O.K. |
| | | negotiation: respond: expected & give & information | and the other one was a pro-o-o-oper nasty person. |
| negotiation: initiate & demand & information | What – did they ask you questions and things? | | |
| | | negotiation: respond: expected & give & information | Yea. |
| | | negotiation: respond: expected & give & information | M'report would look good: 80% in English, 65 in Maths and 42% in science. Jeez it looked good. |
| negotiation: initiate & demand & information | Do you reckon you got it? | | |

| Brother | | Anne | |
|---|---|---|---|
| speech functional selection | turn | speech functional selection | turn |
| | | negotiation: respond: discretionary & give & information | I don't know. |
| | | negotiation: respond: discretionary & give & information | Probably, I might have, anyway. |
| negotiation: initiate & demand & information | Well – are they going to ring you up or what. | | |
| | | negotiation: respond: expected & give & information | Yea, they just did. |
| | | negotiation: respond: expected & give & information | I got it. |
| negotiation: respond: expected & give & information | Hm. That's good. | | (Anne laughs.) |
| negotiation: initiate & demand & information | When do you start? | | |
| | | negotiation: respond: expected & give & information | Monday. I've got to go in on Monday. |
| | | negotiation: respond: expected & give & information | I start on Tuesday. |

The dialogue in Table 3.19 is a **co-authored text**, jointly constructed by Anne and her brother – as are dialogues in general. The siblings take turns making their contributions. The brother's first turn, *How'd you go at the interview today?*, consists of a single move; he initiates an exchange with his sister by demanding information from her. The next turn is hers, and she chooses to respond to his move, thereby developing the exchange that he has initiated. Her turn is not just a single move, but a **complex of moves**. She begins responding with a move where she gives the information her brother has demanded, saying *All right* (elliptical version of *it went all right*). She could have stopped at that point since her move was sufficient as a response, but she chooses to elaborate on the move by providing some commentary on the interview. First she provides a general description of the interview situation, *There were two ladies interviewing*, and then she elaborates on this statement by assessing them contrastively, *One of them was O.K. and the other one was a pro-o-o-oper nasty person.*

Anne's **move complex** is analysed as part of this exchange in Figure 3.28. Each move is analysed systemically by means of a simplified version of the speech function system network in Figure 3.26. The selections made by the brother and Anne are shown by systemic features in bold so that one can see the selections as paths through the system network (traversal paths; see Section 5.2.2). As the analysis shows, in her answer to her brother's question, Anne starts with a nuclear move, and she then expands it with three other moves; the four moves together form her answer, but *All right* is the nuclear part of the answer.

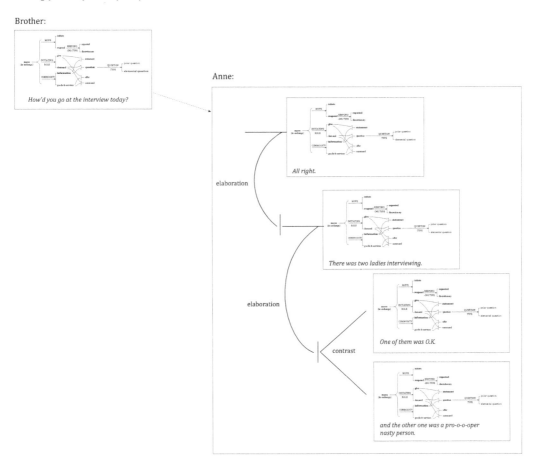

*Figure 3.28* Dialogic exchange consisting of an initiating move and a responding move complex

Figure 3.28 represents Anne's move complex in response to her brother's initiating move by means of logico-semantic, or rhetorical, relations, using a systemicized version of Rhetorical Structure Theory, originally developed by Bill Mann, Sandy Thompson and me starting in the early 1980s: see Matthiessen (forthcoming a). The relations realize selections in the system of LOGICO-SEMANTIC (RHETORICAL) RELATIONS shown in Figure 3.33. In order to develop her first move in response to her brother's question, Anne chooses 'expansion: elaborating' – elaboration & 'nucleus-satellite' & 'external', relating her first move by a rhetorical relation of elaboration to her second move, *There was two ladies interviewing*. She then makes the same choice again, but expands her elaboration through a rhetorical nexus organized as a contrast: 'expansion: extending' – contrast & 'multi-nuclear' & 'external'.

*Table 3.20* Examples of initiating and responding moves; NV = non-verbal

| INITIATING ROLE | COMMODITY TYPE | initiating move | responding move |
|---|---|---|---|
| giving | information | **statement** | **acknowledgement** |
| | | Eve: *I'd like anything Miss Channing played ...* | Margo: *Would you really? How sweet –* |
| | | **statement** | **contradiction** |
| | | Eve: *I thought you'd forgotten about me.* | Karen: *Not at all.* |
| | goods-&-services | **offer** | **acceptance** |
| | | Margo: *Won't you sit down?* | Eve: *Thank you.* |
| | | **offer** | **rejection** |
| | | Karen: *I'm going to take you to Margo...* | Eve: *Oh, no ...* |
| | | Eve: *While you're cleaning up, I'll take this to the wardrobe mistress –* | Margo: *Don't bother. Mrs. Brown'll be along for it in a minute.* |
| demanding | information | **question** | **answer** |
| | | Margo: *Did you see it here in New York?* | Eve: *San Francisco.* |
| | | Karen: *You're not going, are you?* | Eve: *I think I'd better.* |
| | | Karen: *What's your name?* | Eve: *Eve. Eve Harrington.* |
| | | Lloyd: *How was the concert?* | Karen: *Loud.* |
| | goods-&-services | **command** | **undertaking** |
| | | Margo: *Don't get stuck on some glamour puss –* | Bill: *I'll try.* |
| | | **command** | **NV compliance** |
| | | Bill: *Throw that dreary thing away, it bores me –* | Margo: [NV: Margo drops it in the wastebasket, keeps rummaging.] |

I will return to the system in Figure 3.33. Here I just wanted to show how move complexes can be formed by means of the resources provided by this system (for a discussion of clause complexing in exchanges, see Ventola 1988), and to lead up to the question of how exchanges are to be analysed systemically within the interpersonal semantic system. Exchanges **emerge** as patterns as interactants engage in dialogue, co-authoring the texts; they emerge as sequences of moves – minimally one move, but prototypically two, an initiating move followed by a responding move, as illustrated for different combinations of 'giving'/'demanding' and 'information'/'goods-&-services' in Table 3.20. All of the examples are taken from Joseph L. Mankiewicz's screenplay of his film *All About Eve*, so it's possible to examine their dialogic environment – and to view the performances in his film.[27]

Examples exchanges such as those given in Table 3.20 can be analysed as emergent patterns of successive speech functional selections move by move, as I put it above; but a number of systemic functional linguists have posited a semantic rank above that of move – they have treated **exchange** as a **unit**, one rank above that of move, rather than as an emergent pattern of successive moves. This actually goes back to pioneering work within the 'Birmingham School' in the 1970s, specifically Sinclair and Coulthard's (1975) classic study of classroom discourse (modelled on Halliday's 1961, pre-systemic scale-&-category theory). Within SFL, Berry (1981) adopted aspects of their framework, and proposed a systemic approach to account of exchange structure that included exchange as a unit, also drawing on Labov's distinction between primary and secondary knowers and actors (Labov 1972; Labov and Fanshel 1977). This inspired J.R. Martin and his group at Sydney University, and they continued to posit exchange as a unit one rank above that of move and to develop descriptions of the system of NEGOTIATION with the unit of exchange as its domain.

Thus J.R. Martin (1992: 50) distinguishes two semantic ranks in the interpersonal area of the semantics, those of exchange and move; exchange is the domain of the system of NEGOTIATION and move of the system of SPEECH FUNCTION, as shown in Figure 3.29. While the move is realized by the clause, and terms within the system of SPEECH FUNCTION are realized by terms within the system of MOOD, the exchange is a domain or unit without a grammatical analogue, so the system of NEGOTIATION is realized by exchange structure at the semantic stratum but not by any kind of grammatical structure. This is entirely consistent with the relationship between semantics and lexicogrammar presented in Figure 3.25 above.

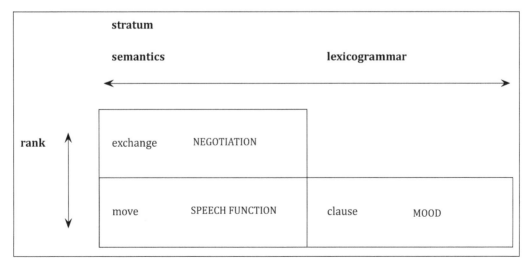

*Figure 3.29* Interpersonal systems as resources for dialogue – semantics and lexicogrammar, adapted from J.R. Martin (1992: 50, Figure 2.12)

The system of NEGOTIATION has the exchange as its domain of operation, and systemic terms are realized by specifications of the structure of an exchange, stated in terms of functions filled by moves at the rank below. J.R. Martin (1992: 49) presents a system network representing the resources of negotiation within an exchange; I have adapted it here as Figure 3.30.[28] There are three simultaneous systems open to an exchange, viz. INITIATOR, EXCHANGE COMMODITY and FOLLOW-UP. In an exchange, the interactants exchange a commodity, either 'information' or 'goods-&-services'. The speaker or the addressee has got (or controls) this commodity, and either the one having the commodity or the one lacking it may initiate the exchange. In addition, there may be a follow up. The exchange structures are specified by means of realization statements associated with systemic terms in Figure 3.30, and illustrative examples are presented to the right of the term they illustrate. Systemic terms in angle brackets appearing above each example (e.g. <information>) are cross references to terms in simultaneous systems.

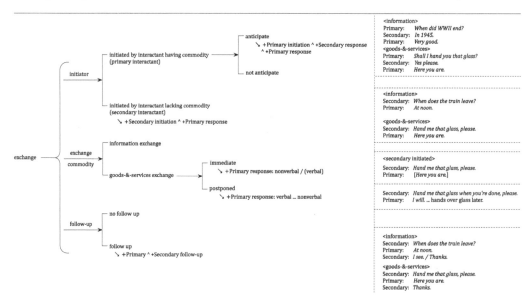

*Figure 3.30* The system of NEGOTIATION operating with the unit of exchange as its domain, adapted from J.R. Martin (1992: 49)

Dialogues unfold as sequences of exchanges; one exchange is followed by another. However, one interesting issue is what the status of the exchange is, and thus of the system of NEGOTIATION. Is the exchange actually a dialogic **unit** above the move on an interpersonal semantic rank scale, or is it simply a **pattern** that emerges as speakers develop dialogue one move at a time? Is the system of NEGOTIATION one that interactants take turns at selecting options within or does it represent the analyst's perspective on exchanges co-constructed by the interactants?

One option would be to build on the notion of **move complex** introduced above, and to interpret exchanges simply as sequences of move complexes, as shown in Figure 3.31 – the limiting case of a move complex being a move simplex. Here each turn is analysed as a move complex, but by another step, we can adopt an intersubjective perspective (cf. Bateman 1985) and explore the possibility of interactants co-authoring such complexes of moves as they develop the exchanges that make up a dialogue (just as they do according to the exchange-rank model[29]). This possibility is illustrated for a telephonic service encounter in Figure 3.32. Here the interactants are represented as constructing the logico-semantic complexing of moves together. For example, when the Server/Operator says *... and the value deal is ... Would you like to try that?*, the Customer/Caller could accepted the offer saying *Yes please*, but instead he rejects it saying *Ah, no thanks*, thereby creating a rhetorical relation of 'antithesis' between the two moves. (Alternatively, it would be possible to explore the relations between the moves in terms of speech-functional relations rather than logico-semantic relations. For example, instead of positing 'antithesis' in the analysis of the service encounter, we could posit 'rejection' in relation to the Server's offer. Discourse analysts have recognized similarities between speech functions and logico-semantic relations; to give another example, the relation between question and answer can be related to 'solutionhood' (problem-solution): see e.g. Grimes 1975, and Longacre 1976, 1996.)

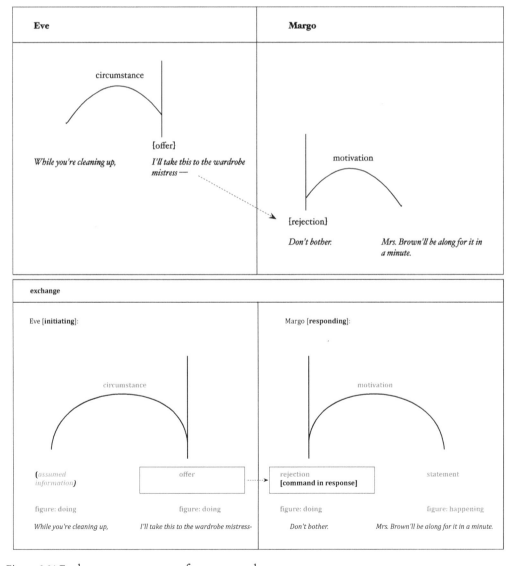

*Figure 3.31* Exchange as sequence of move complexes

104 • *System in Systemic Functional Linguistics*

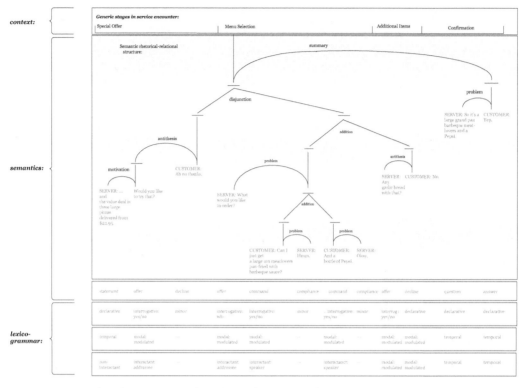

*Figure 3.32* Logical and interpersonal analysis of a passage from a telephonic service encounter

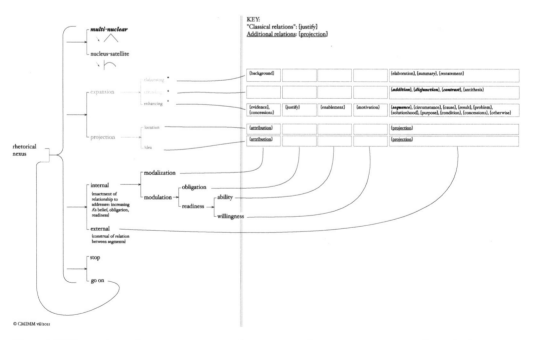

*Figure 3.33* The system of LOGICO-SEMANTIC (RHETORICAL) RELATIONS open to rhetorical nexuses in the formation of text

In the work by Ruqaiya Hasan and her research group – also in Sydney but at Macquarie University, they did not posit exchange as a unit located one rank above the rank of move; instead, as already indicated, they worked with systemic descriptions at the rank of move (or 'message' in their terms). Around that time – the second half on the 1980s and into the 1990s, there was an interesting debate about the contrast between synoptic and dynamic perspectives on both systemic and structural patterns, and drawing on insights from computational linguistics, Mick O'Donnell also contributed (O'Donnell 1990; O'Donnell and Sefton 1995).[30] Further contributions from the foundational period to the study of the interpersonal semantics of dialogue include Bateman (1985), Ventola (1987) and Fawcett (1989).

*3.3.2.3 Semantic Composition*

The comparison above of approaches to the interpretation and representation of exchanges in dialogue provides an interpersonal window on the general question of **composition** within the semantic stratum (cf. Figure 3.34). In the lower of the two content strata, lexicogrammar, there is a clearly established **rank-based** organization; systems have units as their domains that are ordered according to the rank scale, as in English: clause > group/phrase > word > morpheme.[31] But the interpretation of the nature of composition within semantics is less clear. We can identify two sources of variation in the theoretical interpretation and representation of semantic composition – the composition of text:

- metafunctional mode of composition:
  - logical mode of composition: text as logico-semantic (rhetorical) complex
  - experiential mode of composition: ranked units forming a rank-based constituency hierarchy, e.g. text > parasame > sequence > message/move/figure > element
  - interpersonal mode of composition: prosodies of variable extent
  - textual mode of composition: waves within waves of different kinds of textual prominence
- registerial variation in composition according to ecological adaptation – according to the varied demands across contexts in terms of different settings of field, tenor and mode values

As always, considerations must be **balanced trinocularly** – 'from below', from the vantage point of lexicogrammar; 'from above', from the vantage point of context; and 'from roundabout', from the vantage point of semantics itself.

Let's start with the view from below: Figure 3.34. From the point of view of lexicogrammar, it is clear the semantic composition extends beyond the most extensive domain of grammatical systemic and structural patterning – i.e. beyond the clause and combinations of clauses into the clause complex (e.g. Halliday 1978a: 129). A clause corresponds to – realizes – a message (textual), a move (interpersonal) and a figure (experiential), as already shown in Figure 3.25. In the congruent case, these metafunctionally distinct semantic units are the same in the sense that they are mapped onto one another: message = move = figure.

Clauses may combine tactically into clause complexes, and clause complexes realize semantic sequences; again, in the congruent case, sequences of messages = sequences of moves = sequences of figures. Clause complexes constitute the most extensive grammatical domain of systemic and structural organization; they can be networked and they are organized in terms of tactic structure (univariate structure; cf. Halliday 1965, 1979). Beyond them, the lexicogrammar only provides cohesive 'clues'. However, semantics is not limited to the grammatical scale of ranking units and their complexes; semantic composition transcends the sequence realized by the clause complex, as shown in Figure 3.34.

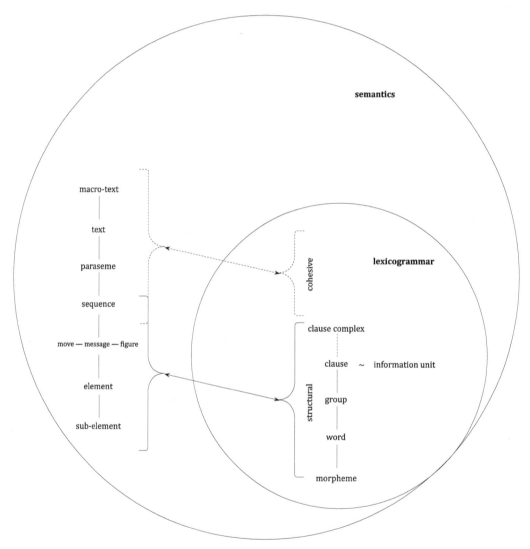

*Figure 3.34* The compositional hierarchies within the content plane – semantics and lexicogrammar

What is located above the sequence in semantic composition? Cloran (e.g. 1994, 2010) has suggested that texts consist of rhetorical units, and Hasan (e.g. Hasan et al. 2007: Section 5.1) has supported her account (cf. also Cloran, Stuart-Smith and Young 2007; Bartlett 2016).[32] In Figure 3.35, I have replaced this with the term **paraseme**, sometimes used by Halliday, since this label is more clearly indicative of the particular *rank* of the unit (all semantic units are arguable 'rhetorical'). Immediately above parasemes, we can posit the text[33]; and we can also recognize that texts often form complexes of texts, what we can call **macro-texts** (cf. Martin's, e.g. 1994, category of macro-genre).

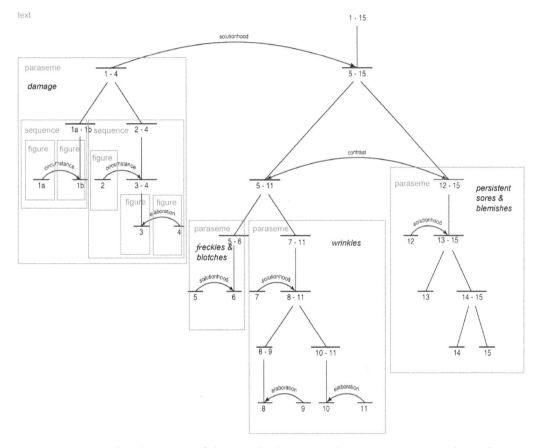

*Figure 3.35* Text analysed in terms of rhetorical relations as a logico-semantic complex and in terms of parasemes (Cloran's rhetorical units), sequences and figures, annotated adaptation of Cloran, Stuart-Smith and Young's (2007) RST analysis

As an alternative to a rank-based constituency mode of the semantic composition of text, we can also interpret text as logico-semantic or rhetorical-relational **complexes**, as already suggested (cf. Figure 3.32). In this interpretation, internal nesting of complexes corresponds to constituency. In principle, a text analysed as consisting of a number of parasemes corresponds to the global logico-semantic relational organization of the text, and the composition of parasemes into sequences corresponds to further internal nesting. These two alternative analyses of text can be illustrated by reference to a persuasive text, *Sun Damage*, analysed by Cloran, Stuart-Smith and Young (2007) in terms of constituent parasemes (Rhetorical Unit Analysis [RUA]), complexing (Rhetorical

Structure Theory [RST] analysis) and phasal analysis, as originally developed by Michael Gregory (e.g. Gregory 2002; Stillar 1991; Malcolm 2010). I will focus on the first two here in order to bring into contrast approaches to composition drawing on rank-based constituency, which arguably derives from experiential considerations, and approaches based on logical complexing (for the logogenetic view of text reflected I phasal analysis, see Section 4.3). The RST analysis presented by Cloran, Stuart-Smith and Young (2007) is shown in Figure 3.35. I have superimposed a constituency analysis based on parasemes (rhetorical units) [shown in Figure 3.36], sequences and figures. In this double analysis, the whole text is analysed as a rhetorical-relational complex, globally organized as a nucleus-satellite solutionhood rhetorical nexus; the satellite corresponds to one paraseme and the nucleus, which is expanded as a multi-nucleus contrast nexus, corresponds to three parasemes. From the point of view of the rhetorical-relational analysis, the parasemes vary in complexity from a single solutionhood nexus (the second paraseme) to a nexus with internal nesting involving four relations (the first paraseme).

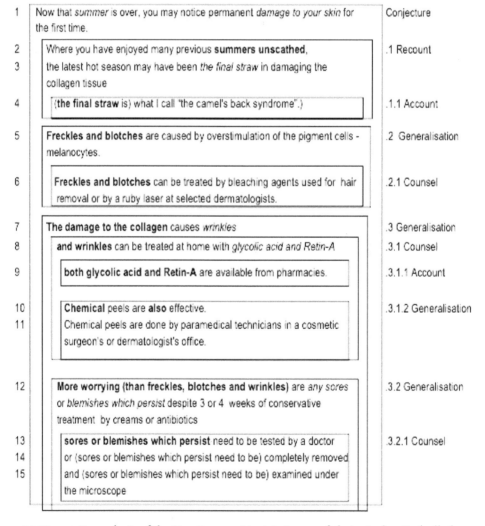

*Figure 3.36* Semantic analysis of the 'Sun Damage' text in terms of rhetorical units (called 'parasemes' here), from Cloran, Stuart-Smith and Young (2007)

The analysis of the *Sun Damage* texts serves only as illustration of the two different modes of composition identified above – the logical mode of complexing and the experiential mode of rank-based constituency. But by viewing the two analyses together in Figure 3.35, one can get a reasonable sense of the complementary insights into the composition of text provided by the two modes. Naturally, one fundamental question is whether we need both or whether one can be 'derived' from the other or turns out simply not to be needed. The best way of addressing this question would be a reasonably large-scale research project carrying out systematic analysis of an extensive corpus of texts sampled from a reasonably wide range of registers.

At the same time, we also need to consider the other metafunctional modes of organization – the interpersonal organization of text as **prosodic patterns** and the textual organization of texts **undulating patterns** – as **waves** consisting of peaks of textual prominence and troughs of non-prominence.

Exploring the syntagmatic organization of text in metafunctional terms, Martin (1996c: 60) emphasized the multi-functional modes of organization of text (cf. Halliday 1979, 1981):

> In this paper we have followed up suggestions by Halliday about modes of meaning, types of structure, and some ways in which a text is like a clause. The main lesson is that *a text is not a tree*; no form of constituency representation, however elaborate, can respect the complementary particulate, prosodic and periodic structuring principles by which ideational, interpersonal and textual meanings are construed.

He suggests (p. 64) that constituency representation is 'a kind of metafunctional compromise, in which modes of meaning and complementary types of structure tend to be neutralised'. This makes sense both in relation to the discussion above about complementary compositional principles and in relation to insights produced by research in the last two decades or so into the syntagmatic organization of semiotic systems other than language. One interesting issue is, obviously, what the implications are for the paradigmatic organization of the different metafunctional modes of meaning. I have already suggested what the system for logico-semantic complexing looks like – Figure 3.33; so the issue is more specifically concerned with the nature of interpersonal systems engendering prosodies and textual systems engendering waves.

### 3.3.2.4 Semantic Function-Rank Matrix as an Interim Report

Just as we can survey the systems that make up the resources of lexicogrammar by means of a **function-rank matrix** (see Table 3.6), we can provide an overview of the systems that constitute the resources of semantics by means of a function-rank matrix. However, such a matrix must at present be more tentative since, while there is general agreement about the distribution of the meaning potential of semantics across metafunctions, the account of semantic composition is, as I have suggested above, still being explored, with no consensus as yet about the best model. For example, are dialogic exchanges to be interpreted as sequences of moves or as a ranking unit above the unit of move; and more generally, how is composition to be conceptualized metafunctionally – as one compositional hierarchy like the rank scale of lexicogrammar or as metafunctionally distinct patterns.

Table 3.21 Semantic function-rank matrix with references to a selection of publications presenting descriptions of English semantics

| rank – domain | | general | ideational | | interpersonal | textual |
|---|---|---|---|---|---|---|
| general | metafunctionally specific | | logical | experiential | | |
| general | | *name in Halliday and Matthiessen's (1999/2006) account of the meaning base:* | ideation base | | interaction base | text base |
| text | | J.R. Martin (1992); Martin and Rose (2008) [written language] | logico-semantic organization: Matthiessen (forthcoming b); CONJUNCTION: Martin (1992) | | macro-proposal: J.R. Martin (1992); APPRAISAL: Martin and White (2005) | macro/hyper-Theme ^ New: Martin (1993b) |
| exchange | | | | | NEGOTIATION: Berry (1981); Martin (1992: 46 ff); Ventola (1987); Eggins and Slade (1997/2005), also with systemic descriptions of SPEECH FUNCTION | |
| sequence | | | ideation base: SEQUENCE: Halliday and Matthiessen (1999/2006: Ch. 3) | | | |
| | figure; move; message | | | ideation base: FIGURATION: Halliday and Matthiessen (1999/2006: Ch. 4) IDEATION: Martin (1992a) | SPEECH FUNCTION: Halliday (1984); Hasan (1987, 1996)[34] | |
| element | | | | ideation base: Halliday and Matthiessen (1999/2006: Ch. 5) | | IDENTIFICATION: J.R. Martin (1992) |

In Table 3.21, I have used a compositional hierarchy that is rank-like, but for clarity, I have separated general units and metafunctionally specific ones. The cells are the 'semiotic addresses' of semantic systems that have been identified and described systemically in the SFL literature. There are a number of different proposals for the same domain, which are either alternative or complementary in nature, as in

- the approach to exchange patterns already noted,
- the treatment of logico-semantic relations in text, and
- the interpretation of the experiential resources of figures.

I have not included parasemes, or 'rhetorical units', since we haven't as yet got a body of systemic descriptions based on system networks at this rank. The model of semantic composition based on the system of logico-semantic (or rhetorical) relations complements the rank-based compositional account, as shown above (cf. Figure 3.33).

### 3.3.2.5 Semantics and the Cline of Instantiation

As the higher of the two content strata of language (for discussion concerned with its stratal location, see Section 3.2.2.6 immediately below), semantics interfaces with context, and it is directly exposed to contextual demands 'from above' on language. These demands can be viewed relative to the cline of instantiation, as shown in Table 3.6. At the potential pole of the cline, we find the overall **meaning potential**, interfacing with the **context of culture** of a given community; and the instance pole, we find acts of meaning unfolding as **text** in **contexts of situation**. Intermediate between these two poles, we find sub-potentials of the overall meaning potential or, if we approach the mid-range between the instance pole, we find recurrent acts of meaning forming text types. All three **phases** of semantics along the cline of instantiation have been explored in the systemic functional literature, as illustrated in the table.

Accounts of the instance pole – of texts unfolding in contexts of situation – presuppose descriptions higher up the cline of instantiation. But how far up do we need to move in order to locate such descriptions? The analysis of the dialogue between Anne and her brother set out in Table 3.19 above references the system of SPEECH FUNCTION, which is located at the potential pole of the cline of instantiation; in other words, it is specified as selections from a key system of the interpersonal part of the overall meaning potential. In practical terms, this is possible because systemic functional linguists have developed comprehensive descriptions of this system; but that is not the case for all areas of the overall meaning potential.

The task of producing a systemic description of the whole meaning potential of any language is a huge one, so it makes sense to look for ways of constraining it that are not artificial but rather motivated by the nature of language. One natural way of reducing the initial complexity of the task is to describe sub-potentials of the overall meaning potentials – sub-potentials located further down the cline of instantiation. Such sub-potentials cover the 'meanings at risk' in a given type of context (cf. Halliday 1978a) – broadly defined in terms of institutions or more narrowly defined in terms of the situation types that make up institutions.[35] In other words, such sub-potentials are

**registers**, i.e. functional varieties of language. Thus as we describe semantics systemically, we can target registers, for example, by describing one register at a time. This turns out to be independently motivated for other reasons as well, not only as a complexity reducing method. If we describe a given register, we can orient the description towards the **strategic** nature of the register in its contextual environment.

One pioneering example of such a register-specific semantic system is Halliday's (1973b) systemic description of what we might call maternal regulatory semantics – the semantic strategies used by a mother needing to control her young son, more specifically in order to prevent him from playing on a dangerous building site: see Figure 3.37. This description brings out the primary strategies open to her in the regulatory context: she can warn or threaten her son. Warning and threatening are speech functions, but they are more delicately specified than the general speech functions of statement, question, offer and command discussed above (see Figure 3.26) and they involve only a limited range of these general speech functions. I will pick up the discussion of such register-specific semantic systems in the next subsection (or 'situation type specific systems', if we view the from above, from the vantage point of context).

Having discussed issues that come up in work on the internal organization of semantics, I will now turn to the status of semantics as an interlevel or interface between the content plane of language and what lies beyond language (Halliday 1973b).

*Table 3.22* Semantics and the cline of instantiation

|  | **potential** | **sub-potential** | **instance** |
|---|---|---|---|
| phase of instantiation: | meaning potential | meaning sub-potential | acts of meaning |
| scope of system: | semantic system | register-specific systems | texts |
| examples of references: | Halliday (1984a): SPEECH FUNCTION system | Halliday (1973b): regulatory semantics; Patten (1988) | [Halliday (1977): text as semantic choice] |

### 3.3.2.6 Semantics as an Interlevel – The Interface to Extra-Linguistic Content

#### 3.3.2.6.1 The Nature of Semantics

So far, I have discussed the internal organization of the semantic system, focussing on the systems that have been presented in the systemic functional literature – most of which have been proposed as descriptive resources to be used primarily in text analysis. I have noted lexicogrammatical realizations of semantic features, thus looking down from semantics. However, as noted in connection with the discussion of the cline of instantiation in the previous sub-section, we also need to look upwards towards context and sideways towards semiotic systems other than language, including bio-semiotic systems. This follows from the nature of semantics as an **interlevel**[36]; as Halliday (1973b: 64) points out, it is an ***interface to what lies outside language***:

> We shall define language as 'meaning potential': that is, as sets of options, or alternatives, in meaning, that are available to the speaker-hearer.

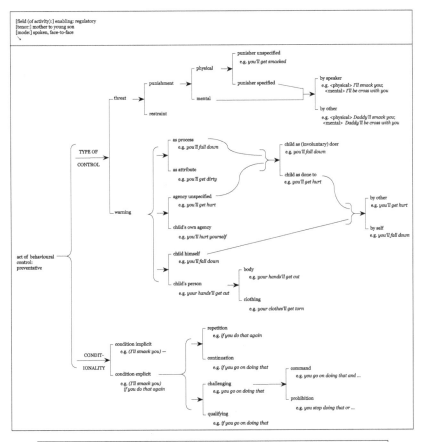
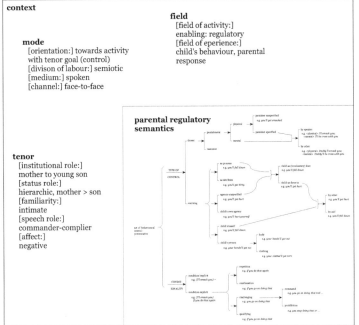

*Figure 3.37* Halliday's (1973b) description of maternal regulatory semantics, associated with a situation type characterized in terms of field, tenor and mode values

At each of the levels that make up the linguistic coding system, we can identify sets of options representing what the speaker 'can do' at that level. When we refer to grammar, or to phonology, each of these can be thought of as a range of strategies, with accompanying tactics of structure formation.

There are also sets of options at the two interfaces, the coding levels which relate language to non-language. We use 'semantics' to refer to one of these interfaces, that which represents the coding of the 'input' to the linguistic system. The range of options at the semantic level is the potentiality for encoding in language that which is not language.

The term 'meaning' has traditionally been restricted to the input end of the language system: the 'content plane', in Hjelmslev's terms, and more specifically to the relations of the semantic interface, Hjelmslev's 'content substance'. We will therefore use 'meaning potential' just to refer to the semantic options (although we would regard it as an adequate designation for language as a whole).

Semantics, then, is 'what the speaker can mean'. It is the strategy that is available for entering the language system.

One general implication for the account of semantics as an interface is that it needs to be modelled as **strategies** for transforming (construing, enacting) what lies outside language into linguistic meaning:

- the systemic description of semantics has to be such that it makes contact with its higher-order semiotic environment, i.e. with context; semantic terms must be contextually interpretable.
- the systemic description of semantics has to be such that it makes contact with denotative semiotic systems operating alongside language, and also by another step with bio-semiotic systems – sensorimotor systems (construing sensory information as meaning and enacting meaning as motor programmes).

*3.3.2.6.2 The Relationship between Semantics and Context*
Regarding the relationship to context, we have already seen an example of this, viz. Halliday's (1973b) description of a register-specific semantic system located midrange along the cline of instantiation – the system of maternal regulatory semantics (Figure 3.37). Since the semantic system is adapted to a particular situation type – a fairly restricted one, it is quite clear how it interfaces with the settings of the contextual parameters of field, tenor and mode. For example, it is adapted to a particular field of activity, viz. enabling: regulating; the strategic semantic options for regulating or controlling are 'threat' and 'warning' (cf. Figure 3.37). At the same time, it is also adapted to a particular tenor setting, including one of unequal power, with downward dominance (mother to young son), and a high degree of familiarity. The strategies of threatening and warning described in Figure 3.37 are adapted to the context of maternal control. It is possible to imagine other such register-specific regulatory semantic systems describing the resources adapted for control by heads of academic departments of the academic or non-academic staff, by tour guides leading tour groups around special places of interest, and so on. (Compare scenarios or prompts used in speech act realizations projects.)

But the relationship between context and semantics is more general, and adaptations can be stated in terms of descriptions of the general semantic system (the meaning potential) as long as they have been developed. There is a general **resonance** between the context and semantics based on correlations between their respective functional diversifications. Halliday (1978a: 143) characterizes the relationship as follows:

> Each of the components of the situation tends to determine the selection of options in a corresponding component of the semantics. In the typical instance, the field determines the selection of experiential meanings, the tenor determines the selection of interpersonal meanings, and the mode determines the selection of textual meanings.

| semiotic structures of situation | associated with | functional components of semantics |
|---|---|---|
| field (type of social action) | ' | experiential |
| tenor (role relationship) | ' | interpersonal |
| mode (symbolic organization) | ' | textual |

This is a fairly early characterization of what has come to be called the **context metafunction hook-up hypothesis** (e.g. Hasan 1995: 222), and since then there have been a number of related formulations of the relationship. It is a realizational type of relationship, but while realization is central to all semiotic systems since they are stratified systems (cf. Butt 2008), it is a challenging phenomenon to interpret theoretically and to model explicitly. And the realizational relationship between context and semantics is similar to but also different from that between semantics and lexicogrammar. It has been characterized as 'determination' and 'association' (by Halliday, as in the passage quoted above) and as 'activation' and 'construal' by Hasan (e.g. 2019: 222):

> Realization works somewhat differently in the two directions. In the encoding view, it is an **activation** of some possible choice at the next lower level: thus *in the production of an utterance, context activates meaning, meaning activates wording.* By contrast, in the reception of the utterance, realization is **construal** of the relevant choice at the higher level: thus *in decoding an utterance, the choice in wording construes meaning, the choice in meaning construes context.*

The term 'activation' might suggest instantiation rather than realization; but the two are distinct (see e.g. Halliday's 1992a, point that the two are – incorrectly, as it later turned out – combined in the older Firthian notion of exponence) and Hasan is exploring the relation of realization, not instantiation. The crucial point is that the relation between context and semantics is 'dialectic'; although it can of course be observed in the course of the instantiation of the system as text unfolding in context (and in the evolution of the system over longer periods of time), it is still a realizational relation, and the categories posited in the description of any particular language will need to make contact with the description of the context of culture.

The relationship between context and semantics is highlighted by Halliday's (1975b/2003: 79–80) discussion of speech act theory:

When the social context has been idealized out of the picture, a theory of speech acts provides a means of putting it back again. It celebrates the linguists' rediscovery that not only do people talk – they talk to each other.

The study of speech acts, which as Searle remarks is important in the philosophy of language, starts from the speaker as an isolate, performing a set of acts. These include, among others, illocutionary acts – questioning, asserting, predicting, promising and the like; and illocutionary acts can be expressed in rules. In Searle's (1965[37]) words,

> The hypothesis... is that the semantics of a language can be regarded as a series of systems of constitutive rules [i.e. rules that constitute (and also regulate) an activity the existence of which is logically dependent on the rules] and that illocutionary acts are performed in accordance with these sets of constitutive rules.

The meaning of a linguistic act thus comes within the scope of philosophical enquiry. But a language is not a system of linguistic acts; it is a system of meanings that defines (among other things) the potential for linguistic acts. The choice of a linguistic act – the speaker's adoption, assignment, and acceptance (or rejection) of speech roles – is constrained by the context, and the meaning of the choice is determined by the context. Consider a typical middle-class mother and child exchange: *Are you going to put those away when you've finished with them? – Yes. – Promise? – Yes.* The second of these yesses is at one level of interpretation a promise, a concept which (in Searle's now classic demonstration) can be explained by reference to conditions of three types: preparatory conditions, the sincerity condition and the essential condition. But its significance as an event depends on the social context: on modes of interaction in the family, socially accepted patterns of parental control, and so forth – and hence on the social system, Malinowski's 'context of culture'. To describe the potential from which this utterance derives its meaning, we should need to specify such things as (sub-culture) professional middle class, (socializing agency) family, (role relationship) mother–child, (situation type) regulatory, (orientation) object-oriented; and to interpret it as, at one level, a move in a child's strategy for coping with a parent's strategy of control. (How this may be done can be seen from the work of Bernstein and Turner, from one viewpoint, and of Sacks and Schegloff from another.) We shall not want to say that the child's utterance is 'insincere'; but nor shall we want to interpret it as 'one speech act conveying another', which introduces an artificial distinction between a speech act and its use, as if to say 'As an idealized structure, this is a promise; when it is instantiated, by being located in a social context, it functions as something else'.

This adds another crucial insight into the relationship between context and semantics: the meaning of systems in semantic system networks and of their terms can only be fully understood in relation to context the 'same' semantic system will have different higher-order contextual meanings in different types of context; as Halliday puts it, 'its significance as an event depends on the social context'. In terms of the tenor parameter within context and interpersonal semantic systems, this typically involves a multiplication of contextual meanings in the sense of significance according to the particular settings of values within the systems that make up the tenor parameter. Thus we can refer to tenor as a **meaning multiplier**.

This was demonstrated outside SFL and before its development as SFL began by Brown and Gilman (1960) in their well-known account of the 'pronouns of power of solidarity'. They showed that the 'same' pronominal contrast in languages with two addressee pronouns like (singular) French *tu* vs. *vous* or German *du* vs. *Sie* has different meanings depending on (in our systemic functional terms) the settings in tenor of power and familiarity (solidarity). For example, the choice of *tu* (or *du*) can enact a relationship where the speaker 'talks down' to the addressee if s/he holds a higher status in the system of roles of the community, but it can enact a relationship of solidarity if they are of equal status and are familiar (part of the same in-group).

Another example would be Ervin-Tripp's (1969) description of an American address system, presented and systemicized in Section 6.2 below. Her account brings out similar insights; for example, when a speaker uses the addressee's first name, this will have different significance depending on the tenor of the relationship. Thus to the 'pronouns of power and solidarity', we can add other interpersonal systems: the speech functions of power and solidarity, the modulations of power and solidarity, the judgements of power and solidarity, and so on. This is a crucial aspect of the relationship between semantics and context – one that is also brought out by Hasan's (1989, 2009) investigation of what she called 'semantic variation' (codal variation) in her study of the semantic selections made by mothers and their children from different social classes.

### 3.3.2.6.3 *The relationship between semantics and meaning in other semiotic systems*

Regarding the relationship between semantics and denotative semiotic systems operating alongside language within the same context, the semantic system must, in principle, be able to translate such systems into semantic categories and also be able to translate semantic categories into other denotative semiotic systems; the semantic system must provide the resources for construing meaning in such semiotic systems as linguistic meaning and of enacting linguistic meaning in other semiotic systems. Halliday (2013: 34–35) explores the limits of such inter-semiotic translation:

> Other, non-language, semiotic systems, as these are instantiated in the form of tables, charts, figures, plans, graphs, maps and formulae, tend to be designed so as to display meaning as choice, though not always in digital form; and they can often be 'read off' as verbalised text – though not uniquely, because their stratal location is in semantics, not in lexicogrammar.
>
> Other semiotic 'texts', whether visual, such as images and film, or in a different modality such as music, bear a more distant, indirect, relation to language. This does not mean that they cannot be illuminated by a linguistic theory; on the contrary, as O'Toole has shown in his highly original and imaginative excursus into the language of the 'displayed arts' of painting, architecture and sculpture, a great deal of additional insight is gained by using the concepts and methods of systemic linguistics to describe and analyse these artefacts (O'Toole 2010). Since the clientele for whom they are displayed also have language, this may turn out in the end to be the most effective way of explaining them. But that must be left open until there have been more attempts at theorising these other semiotics in their own terms – probably still using language in order to do so.

One of the many interesting issues to be explored is to what extent descriptions of meaning in semiotic systems other than language are separate from linguistic semantics or can be spliced into the linguistic semantic system. This is likely to vary considerably in terms of both semiotic systems and registers. (For example, analysing WHO's Weekly

Epidemiological Reports in English and French with tables, maps and charts, I found that there was a clear complementarity in the representation of certain meanings by language and the other semiotic systems and that all meanings in this domain could be construed in terms of the linguistic semantic system; see Matthiessen 2006b. For discussion, see also Section 6.3.4.)

Beyond denotative semiotic system that may operate multisemiotically (or 'multimodally') together with language or on their own but which may be translatable into language to some degree (and vice versa), we also need to consider **bio-semiotic systems** (Halliday and Matthiessen 2006) – sensorimotor systems: the description of the semantic system has to be such that it is possible to show how the information from sensory systems can be construed as ideational meaning, and related to other nodes in the semantic network, and also to show how the meanings can be enacted in motor programmes. This interface can be called **neurosemiotics** and researchers are now in a position to undertake investigations. For example, referring to SFL and the exploration in Halliday and Matthiessen (2006/1999), García and Ibáñez (2016) report on and discuss 'experimental studies on the neurocognitive basis of processes and verbs of doing', and they note that 'the evidence shows that (at least some of) the conceptual distinctions within semantics are naturally grounded in more basic (motor and perceptual) neurocognitive distinctions'.

The investigation of the relationship between semantic distinctions and 'more basic ... neurocognitive distinctions' is a crucial new avenue of research for systemic functional semantics (see also, approaches from systemic functional linguistics: e.g. Thibault 2004; Asp 2013). It involves an **embodied** interpretation of meaning (e.g. Pulvermüller 2013), which is entirely consistent with the systemic functional model of the ordered typology of systems.

Another way of exploring the relationship between semantics and sensorimotor systems is to model simulated embodiment in robotics research along the lines pursued and reported by Bateman et al. (2010). Focussing on the semantics of space ('spatial ontology'), they cover a number of theoretical and descriptive aspects of semantics as an interface to other systems that I have only been able to hint at here; as part of their conclusion (pp. 1066–1067) they note[38]:

> Our starting point in this paper was the extremely flexible relationship observed between spatial language and contextualized interpretations of that language. There is an urgent need for versatile and comprehensive accounts that support the contextualization process by pinpointing the information that needs to be anchored by context without prematurely over-committing to particular spatial interpretations. We have addressed this by considering the *linguistic* construction of space far more closely than has hitherto been the case. This has led to a 'linguistically responsible' characterization of the semantic distinctions that are carried by grammar (at least in English and German), couched as an extension of the Generalized Upper Model linguistic ontology and employing current ontological engineering principles.
>
> We have shown that this treatment covers a large proportion of naturally occurring linguistic expressions involving space. Simple inventories of linguistic terms (and their direct semantic interpretation in terms of physical spatial models) have been replaced by a richly structured characterization of linguistically-motivated spatial semantics that provides

strong support for active mediation between linguistic form and detailed spatial models. This characterization generalizes across contexts of use and applications, just as the corresponding linguistic expressions do. The Generalized Upper Model spatial extension is now accordingly employed as a level of linguistic semantics for both automatic generation and analysis within spatially-aware computational systems. [...]

We claim that an adequate account of linguistic spatial expressions will require at least the kinds of distinctions that our characterization has set out, independently of how these distinctions are then anchored in axiomatizations of space of particular kinds, in action routines for embodied behavior, or in perceptual models.

In general, the nature of the semantic system as an interlevel – as an interface between language and what lies outside language as far as the content plane is concerned – helps explain the need for 'hyphenated' studies of regions of semantics, including sociological semantics (or sociosemantics) and neurosemantics, or neurosemiotics.

## 3.4 Expression Plane System Networks

Expression plane system networks are located within the two expression strata of language, phonology and phonetics (in spoken language). In the illustration presented in Figure 3.1, the phonological network is the system of TONE but its manifestation at the stratum of phonetics is not included in the figure. I will review work on phonological system networks first, and then discuss the nature of phonetic system networks.

### 3.4.1 Phonological System Networks

Like lexicogrammar, phonology is an inner, or core, stratum – the form stratum of the expression plane, just as lexicogrammar is the form stratum of the content plane. As in the case of lexicogrammar, systemic representation and description started early in the development of SFL; Halliday developed a systemic description of the syllable in the Peking dialect of Mandarin starting in the 1950s with a Firthian prosodic analysis (Halliday 1959, 1970b) and later presenting a system network for syllable finals (Halliday 1992b); and around 1960 he turned to intonation in English, presenting a system network representing the system of TONE in Halliday (1963b), a version of which is included in Figure 3.1.

To understand systemic phonology, we need to recognize that the phonological system is conceptualized and theorized like other stratal systems – as a resource, in this case a resource for realizing content as sound. Thus the phonology of language is a **sounding potential**; and that is why it needs to be modelled by means of phonological system networks (rather than only as phonotactic patterns, such patterns being specified by phonological realization statements associated with terms in phonological systems). The description of the sounding potential of any one particular language should cover what speakers of that language 'can sound', just as the meaning potential of any one particular language should represent what its speakers 'can mean' (Halliday 1973b). Consequently, the systemic description of a particular language should include what is phonologically possible – both prosodically and articulatorily – not only those phonological patterns that have been deployed lexicogrammatically at a particular point in the history of the language[39]. For example, the systemic description of the sounding potential of English should predict not only *blip*, an existing lexical item, but also *blep*, *blap*, *blup* and *blop* even though they are not currently deployed in the realization of lexicogrammatical wordings.[40]

Phonological system networks have been presented for all phonological ranks in the SFL literature; in English, the phonological rank scale is: tone group > foot > syllable > phoneme, and in Mandarin, it is tone group > foot > syllable. There is clearly variation across languages in how they distribute their phonological systems compositionally in terms of a hierarchy of phonological units (just as there is variation in grammatical labour across the grammatical ranks scales of languages around the world). For example, Halliday (1992b) shows that Mandarin can be described most revealingly by stopping at the rank of syllable and accounting for patterns that have been interpreted phonemically by other linguistics prosodically in terms of the systems of the syllable as a movement between two postures.

Since the spectrum of metafunction is a principle of organization largely confined to the content plane of language, we cannot construct an overview of the phonological system of a given language by means of a function-rank matrix; but we can intersect the rank scale of the language with different phonological patterns, broadly prosodic and articulatory patterns, as illustrated for English in Table 3.23.

*Table 3.23* The division of phonological labour in terms of the phonological rank scale in English (from Matthiessen 2021)

| rank | prosodic | | ~ | articulatory |
|---|---|---|---|---|
| | pitch | rhythm | salience | articulation |
| **tone group** | TONE, TONICITY, TONALITY | | | |
| **foot** | | FOOT COMPOSITION, ICTUS STATE | | |
| **syllable** | | | SALIENCE | articulatory postures ('phonotactics') |
| **phoneme** | | | | PLACE, MANNER &c |

The differentiation between prosodic and articulatory modes of sounding is significant; and the distribution of these two modes across the phonological system of languages reflects the fact that that phonological systems are **natural** in relation to their adjacent substance stratum, just as lexicogrammatical ones are. In other words:

- form stands in a natural relation to substance :
- lexicogrammar stands in a natural relation to semantics :
- phonology stands in a natural relation to phonetics[41]

At the same time, phonological systems are **functional** in relation to their adjacent form stratum – lexicogrammar; as already noted, they provide the resources for 'transducing' patterns of wording as patterns of sounding. In addition, phonology can also be natural in relation to lexicogrammar in a more limited sense: the modes of expression of prosodic phonology may stand in a natural relationship to the modes of expression of the different metafunctions (Halliday 1979). This is the tendency at the highest rank, the rank of tone group: textual patterns are realized through the system of TONICITY, which assigns peaks of phonological prominence through the location of the major pitch movement, and interpersonal patterns are realized through the system of TONE, which assigns tone contours to extended stretches of wording, viz. a ranking clause in the default case[42].

Thus, in phonological systems, their terms are trinocularly related, as shown for one of the terms in the system of PRIMARY TONE in Figure 3.38. The term 'tone 3' is related upward to terms in lexicogrammatical systems; it signifies these terms, e.g. 'tentative' in the system of MARKED DECLARATIVE KEY. It is related downwards to phonetics; it is realized by a certain pitch contour – level or low rising. At the same time, it is related at its own level to terms in its own system, and by further degrees of separation to other terms in the same system network; it has a *valeur* in the phonological system. (For the contrast between this approach to the interpretation of intonation and approaches that foreground the view from below, 'bottom up', see Smith and Greaves 2015: 302–306.)

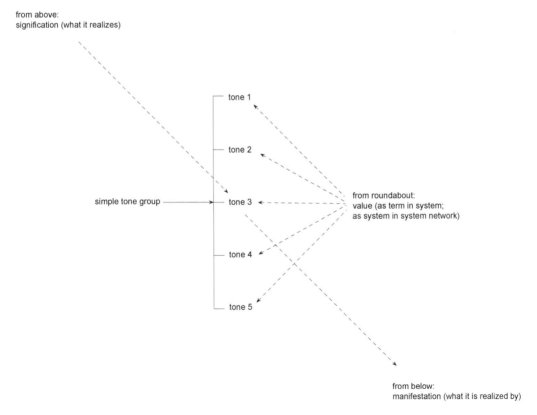

*Figure 3.38* Phonological systemic term viewed trinocularly

122 • *System in Systemic Functional Linguistics*

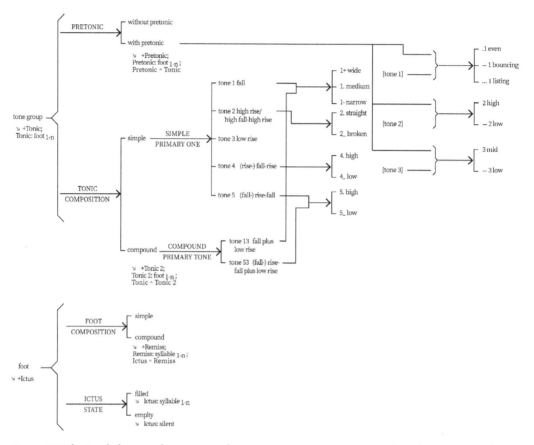

*Figure 3.39* The English prosody systems of INTONATION at tone group rank and RHYTHM at foot rank

So far, I have focussed on the systemic description of prosodic phonology, as illustrated for English in Figure 3.39. What about the systemic description of the articulatory domain of phonology? To explore the answer, let me return to the view of text unfolding for a moment – the view of text as ongoing choices that can be visualized as a text score (Figure 4.6) with parallel selections in simultaneous systems forming **systemic chords** – and also anticipate my summary of Catford's (1977) account of phonetic parameters in the next section. He helps us see speaking as process – as an activity creating patterns through simultaneous and successive choices (cf. Halliday 1961, on units as carriers of patterned activity).

The patterned activity of speaking can be modelled as ongoing simultaneous choices within different domains (represented by means of units along the phonological rank scale), and Catford's (1977: 227) visualization of these simultaneous choices in the articulation of the word *stand* is a helpful reminder of what we must capture in our account of the phonological system of a particular language and of language in general: see Figure 3.40. He characterizes this process as follows (Catford 1977: 226–228):

> ... we have presented the speech process as a complex event consisting of more or less constantly varying states, or 'values', of a number of parameters or ranges of conditions

of co-occurring components of the speech event. [...] there are moments of rapid change, which define for us, or tend to define for us, the limits of successive segments. [...] These 'moments of rapid change' are changes occurring in any one, or more, of the co-occurrent component parameters [...] The production of such a word as *stand* [st$^h$æǣndd$^h$] may be diagrammatically illustrated as in figure 60 [reproduced here as Figure 3.40, CMIMM]. Here, changing values are indicated for a number of parameters.

If we follow the line representing values along the parameter of *oral articulatory stricture type* we have the value 'fricative' for a time, then there is a sudden shift to *stop*, followed by a sudden switch to *resonant*, and later back to *stop* (since the oral stricture of [n] is, of course, of the stop type). As a result of the changes mentioned here, the parameter of stricture-type throughout this utterance is divided into four (numbered) parts, or four *spans*, as we shall call them, of relatively steady state, separated by three fairly rapid *transitions* from one state to the next.

For the parameter of *articulatory location* only two states are designated, namely *alveolar* (short for apicolamino-alveolar) and *palatal* (short for dorso-palatal). Each of these, of course, is a short-hand description of a tongue posture. It will be observed that in this case there are only three spans, the first stretching across to spans of stricture-type.

The parameter of state of the velic or nasal port has two values, *closed* and *open* and it can be seen that there is one short span of *open*, the start of which does not correspond to the start of any other span.

The phonation parameter again breaks down into three spans, a *voiceless* one, a *voiced* one starting almost immediately after the release of the [t], which, being preceded by [s], has minimal aspiration, and ending with a renewed short span of *voicelessness*. These spans are not quite co-extensive with any other spans.

Finally, there is a single pulse of the pulmonic initiator, a single rising-falling curve of initiator power, constituting a single span of initiator activity.

Each change in the state of one parameter is, of course, a change in the whole sound-productive event. Consequently, each such change defines the limits not only of one componential or parametric span, but also of the whole segment. On this basis, then, in *stand* we recognize eight segments, [s, t, h, æ, ǣ, n, d, ḍ], or nine, if we count the releasing [$^h$] at the end of the utterance. It is perfectly possible to perceive all the segments, auditorily or kinaesthetically, if one tries. Without giving special attention to what is going on, however, one may observe only five segments, [s, t, æ, n, d], these segments corresponding to so many minimal linear phonological units, or phonemes, of English.

Represented phonemically as /stænd/, the lexical item *stand*, might be thought of simply as a string of phonemes. But interpreted in terms of systemic functional phonology, it is patterned activity at two ranks, the rank of syllable and the rank of phoneme. As we develop the description of the articulatory phonology of English, we will have to decide how to distribute the account across these two ranks. For example, while phonation, 'voiced'/'voiceless', will surely be a phoneme rank system, will it also be a syllable rank one? If we posit it at syllable rank, we can say that the syllable /stænd/ has a 'voiceless' Onset but a 'voiced' Rhyme; and it will be prosodic in relation to phonemes in the sense of prosodies in Firth's prosodic analysis. Such decisions will have to be made on the evidence from particular languages. It is clear, however, that phonotactic patterns are part of the domain of the syllable. For example, the Onset of English syllables can be realized by certain consonant clusters, like fricative ^ stop (^ liquid) *st-*, *sp-*, *sk-* and *str-*, *spr-*, *skr-* but they are constrained (in ways that can be related to considerations of sonority and of articulation[43]); *ts-*, *ps-*, *ks-*, i.e. stop ^ fricatives are not possible realizations of Onsets in English.

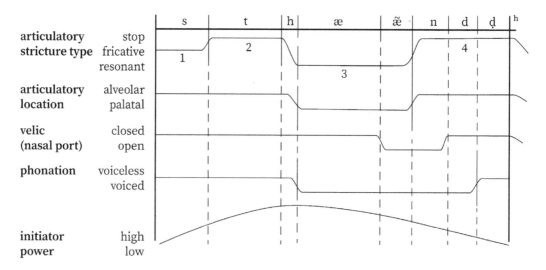

*Figure 3.40* Catford's (1977: 227) segmentation of articulation of the word 'stand' – interpretable as a visualization of speaking as the unfolding of simultaneous phonological choices in articulatory stricture type, articulatory location, resonance (velic closure), phonation and initiator power

In general – and here I will leave English as a source of illustration, syllables serve as the gateway between prosodic and articulatory phonology, as can be illustrated by a simplified version of my description of the syllable network of Akan: Figure 3.41. In Akan, the prosodic part is concerned with the prosodic system of TONE – of syllabic tone, i.e. with tone with the syllable as its domain, as is characteristic of 'tone languages' in general (as opposed to 'intonation languages' like English, where the tone group is the domain of tone[44]). The articulatory part is concerned with the syllable as an articulatory move, including phonotactic patterns. The maximal syllable structure is Onset ^ Peak ^ Coda; this is a phonological function structure: Onset, Peak and Coda are functions (elements) in the structure of the syllable, and they are realized by phonemes. If the Peak is 'nasal', then it is realized by a nasal phoneme (Peak: nasal), and no Coda is possible; but if it is 'vocalic', then there is the option of an Onset and also of a Coda, as shown in the system network. The Coda can only be realized by a nasal, but the Onset can be realized by a wider range of (single) consonant phonemes.

The syllabic specifications of the nature of the Onset, the Peak and the Coda are preselections of terms in the system network of phonemes, and these preselections are realizational relations, as visualized in Figure 3.42. As already noted, certain terms in the phoneme system network are realized at the rank of syllable, as indicated by the vertical downward pointing arrows. These capture syllabic (phonotactic) constraints on phoneme sequences. When terms in the phoneme system network are not preselected, this means that they are not constrained at syllable rank. For example, at phoneme rank, 'vowel' and 'consonant' are preselected, but in the vowel system of tongue root position, 'advanced' vs. 'neutral', the terms are not preselected.[45]

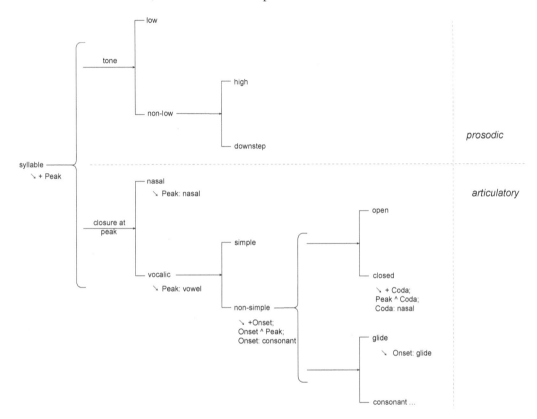

*Figure 3.41* The Akan syllable as a gateway between prosodic and articulatory phonology

The phoneme system network shown in Figure 3.42 is an abbreviated version of the full phoneme system network: Figure 3.43 (for the systemic terms, see Catford 1977). This system network includes certain systemic marking conventions: if 'central', then 'neutral'; if 'approximant', then 'tectal' (the whole roof of the mouth, contrasting with 'labial', the upper lip; cf. Figure 3.46 further below); and so on. Such marking conventions have been used in semantic, lexicogrammatical and phonological descriptions and are convenient ways of representing relations between systems on simultaneous 'tracks' within a system network, but they are problematic for traversal algorithms (see Matthiessen 1988a, and Section 6.4).

126 • *System in Systemic Functional Linguistics*

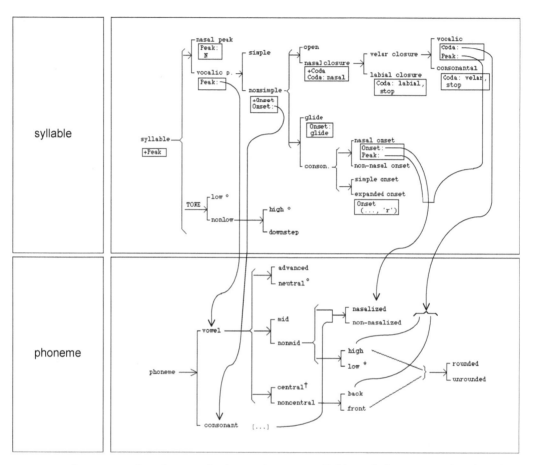

*Figure 3.42* The inter-rank realizational relations between syllable and phoneme in the phonology of Akan

In systemic descriptions of the phonological systems of different languages, the descriptive division of labour between syllable and phoneme is an interesting issue, especially in view of the point that many phonological theories posit the phoneme as a taken-for-granted part of their accounts (possibly further decomposed into bundles of distinctive features). Here Halliday's (1992b) systemic description of Peking syllable finals without positing the phoneme as a rank below that of phoneme is a crucial contribution to systemic phonology. Halliday's (1992b: 107–108) description of the Peking syllable gives a good sense of how an articulatory gesture – a movement from one articulatory posture to another – may operate in a particular language:

> The network [reproduced here as Figure 3.44, CMIMM] combines four principles of analysis. One is the Chinese phonological principle whereby all syllables are structured simply as initial plus final. The second is the Firthian prosodic principle whereby features such as posture (y/a/w) and resonance (nasal/oral) are treated non-segmentally. The third is the paradigmatic principle whereby features are interpreted as terms in systems, each system having a specified condition of entry. [Note that in Firthian system-structure theory the

entry condition is specified syntagmatically, whereas in a system network it is specified paradigmatically: entry to one system depends on selecting a certain term in (at least one) other.] The fourth is the dynamic principle whereby the syllable is envisaged as a wave, a periodic pattern of movement characterized by a kind of 'flow-and-return'. What this last means is that the syllable is construed as a movement from all initial state to a final state, each of these states is specified as a 'selection expression' (a cluster of features from different prosodic systems); and there is variation both temporally, in the extent to which a particular feature persists across the syllable, and spatially, in the route that is traversed from the initial to the final state.

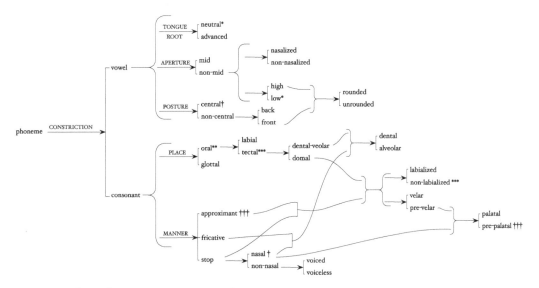

*Figure 3.43* Akan phoneme system network

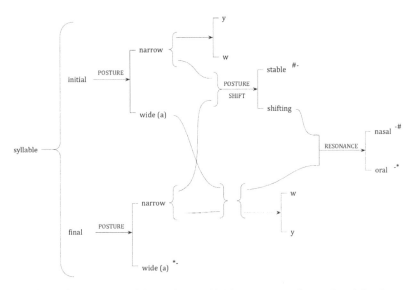

*Figure 3.44* Halliday's description of the Peking syllable in terms of initial and final posture, and the shift between them (Halliday 1992b: 107); the full version of his description is reproduced below as Figure 3.45

The full version of Halliday's (1992b) system of the Mandarin syllable is reproduced here as Figure 3.45. This system network covers articulatory systems, including ones that would be associated with phonemes in the description of a language such as English – systems of MANNER, ALIGNMENT, RESONANCE, APERTURE, and so on; but it does not include systems of syllabic tone, although Halliday discusses them. The issue of whether to stop at syllable rank or to posit a phoneme rank below it in the description of the phonological system of a given language is clarified by Halliday and Greave's (2008: 78, 79) comparison of English and Chinese; speaking of phonological units, they write:

> Such units in phonology are often not clearly delimited – in any given language there may be some that are more and some that are less determinate. [footnote:] For example, in Chinese the syllable is a clearly defined unit; but within the syllable the constituent structure is rather hazy: in Mandarin the entire system is framed as a move from an initial to a terminal posture, and there are no phonematic units at all. In English, on the other hand, the syllable is rather fuzzy (are words like *button, tower, police* one syllable or two?), but the phoneme-like segments are relatively clear – though not perhaps as clear as in Italian or Czech.

And this difference between English and Chinese can be related to how syllables are constituted as phonological gestures; Halliday (1992b: 110) contrasts them as follows:

> But the initial and final states are what constitute the essence of the syllable. Thus, whereas in English the peak of resonance in the syllable – the vowel nucleus – is also the most 'fixed' part, so that in a set like *seen, soon, sing, song*, the vowel posture is projected outwards on to the initial and final consonants, in the Mandarin syllable it is the other way round: the vowel 'nucleus' is simply a degree of aperture, and the initial and final postures of the syllable are 'projected' inwards to create a movement within this broad band of phonetic space.

Since the phoneme is the lowest-ranking unit (in languages that have this rank below that of the syllable), phonological features in phoneme systems such as PLACE and MANNER are realized inter-axially by phonemes. Phonemes, like other phonological units, are realized inter-stratally within the expression substance stratum of phonetics, by phonetic specifications. These specifications need to be mapped onto articulatory and auditory specifications (or in modelling speech, by the specifications needed by speech synthesizers and speech recognizers). This is an important task for the substance stratum of the expression plane, phonetics, as an interface between language and the bodily systems involved in sound production and perception. (I will discuss it the in the next subsection.)

Like semantics, phonetics is a substance stratum, serving as an interface to what lies outside language (see Figure 3.1 above); in the case of phonetics, the interface is to the bodily sound producing and perceiving potential in the first instance[46]. These somatic resources are studied in articulatory and auditory phonetics, and the next, physical phase of 'materialization' in acoustic phonetics and also aerodynamic considerations. There is thus a long tradition of investigation of the sound system of language in relation to extra-linguistic systems.

The System as a Fractal Principle • 129

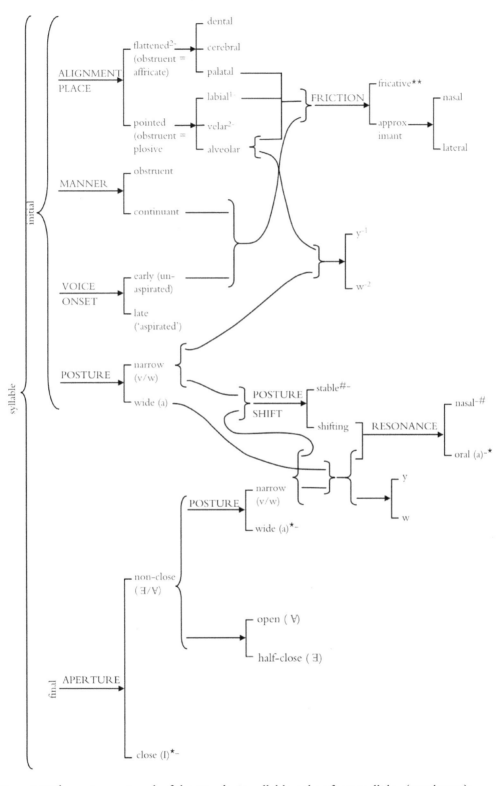

*Figure 3.45* The system network of the Mandarin syllable, taken from Halliday (1992b: 118): 'Figure 6.6 Network specifying Mandarin (Pekingese) syllables'

### 3.4.2 Phonetic system networks

In SFL, researchers have used the tools of acoustic phonetics in the investigation of prosodic patterns – intonation in particular, as in Watt (1992), Halliday and Greaves (2008), Bowcher and Smith (2014), Praat now being the go-to tool for acoustic analysis to support perceptual analysis. However, there is as yet no general framework of systemic functional phonetics. Therefore, we must imagine what such a framework would look like by examining contributions to the phonetics literature, and there are two excellent sources, viz. J.C. Catford and Peter Ladefoged. Both got their grounding at Edinburgh University, where David Abercrombie, who had studied with Daniel Jones and J.R. Firth, made foundational contributions to phonetics, including importantly in the present context his insights into English rhythm[47]. Both then went to the US, where they conducted research relevant to a systemic functional conception of phonetics – Ladefoged to UCLA and Catford to the University of Michigan.

Catford's (1977) *Fundamental Problems in Phonetics* would be a good starting point for the development of a systemic functional version of phonetics as an area of study. He offers the following preliminary remarks on phonetics (p. 1):

> Phonetics is generally, and correctly, considered to be a linguistic discipline – the study of all aspects of the phonic material of language. But, in order to cope efficiently with the vocal sounds that constitute the sound-systems of particular languages, phonetics must proceed from the most general possible consideration of the human sound-producing potential. Only thus can it be prepared to categorize and, in some sense, to explain not only the sounds used as the manifestation of all known languages, but also those of languages yet unstudied, as well as the 'pre-language' sounds of infants and the whole range of deviant sounds encountered in pathological speech.

The notion of 'the human sound-producing potential' is fundamental, and we can supplement it with the listener's complementary perspective – the human sound-perceiving potential. The emphasis on **potential** is an excellent starting point for a systemic approach to phonetics, and it is a continuation of the grounding in phonetics of pre-systemic Firthian phonology. (By positing prosodies, Firth was able to get closer to 'phonetic substance' than is possible in phonemic approaches.)

As an illustration, we can consider Catford's (1977: 162) chart of the oral articulation of English consonants. I have reproduced it in Figure 3.46 together with a system network representing the articulatory distinctions possible for the UPPER ARTICULATOR, the LOWER ARTICULATOR and the MANNER of articulation.

Figure 3.46 gives us a very clear sense of what aspects of the articulatory potential for consonants in general are deployed by English. However, the system networks 'overgenerates'; it embodies combinations that are not anatomically possible, like labio-velar articulation, thus specifying articulatory potential that will have to be restricted (try extending your lips backwards into the oral cavity to touch the soft palate!). This is brought out by Figure 3.47, which shows the English consonants in Figure 3.46 against the background of anatomically possible consonants (the shaded area).

This picture is very important because it gives an indication of how English has semioticized – more specifically, 'phonologized' – the articulatory human potential. While it's not possible to do the same at the other stratal interface, the content substance stratum of semantics (see Figure 3.1 above), it provides an interesting frame of comparison. One difference is clearly that while it is possible to map out the human articulatory resources, it is not possible to map out the extra-linguistic realm that semantics interfaces with in a similarly constrained way – perhaps to some extent for limited fields of concrete experience like colour vision. Crucially, semantics construes our experience as meaning, but phonetics does not construct our articulatory resources – or only in a very indirect sense in reference to adaptation of bodily resources to speech over long periods of evolution.

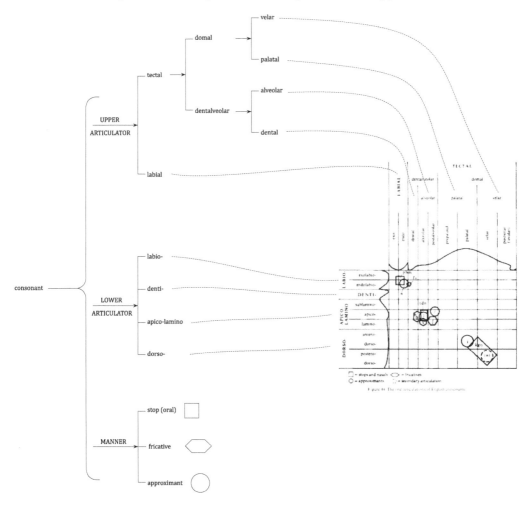

*Figure 3.46* Systemicized version of Catford's (1977: 162) chart of the oral articulation of English consonants

It would be possible to constrain the system network shown in Figure 3.46 in order to block systemic combinations that are anatomically impossible. We could block the combination of 'domal' and 'labio-' or 'denti-', of 'labial' and 'dorso-', and so on. This could provide an insight into the grouping of systems and systemic terms; for example, in one lower articulator environment, 'postalveolar' patterns with 'prepalatal' rather than with 'alveolar'. Such blocking can be achieved by revision of entry conditions and/or the use of conditions on systemic terms (cf. Section 6.4).

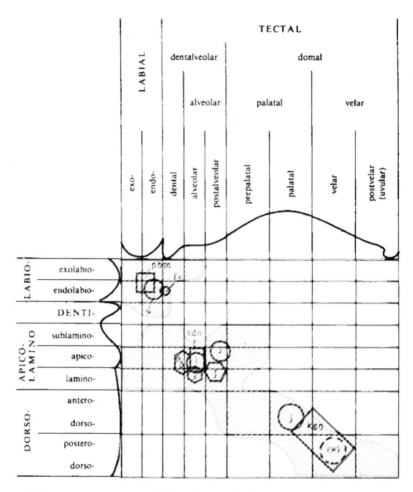

*Figure 3.47* English consonants against the background of anatomically possible consonants in terms of the oral cavity, based on a combination of Catford's (1977) Figures 43 and 44

In my own work developing a systemic description of the phonology of Akan, I found it helpful to 'ground' the phonological systems I postulated in Catford's articulatory phonetic account, using such articulatory parameters throughout rather than a mixture of features oriented towards articulatory and auditory considerations of the kind used in what might be called the Jakobsonian distinctive feature tradition (e.g. Jakobson, Fant and Halle 1952). Catford (1977: 13) is in fact explicit about the role of such parameters in the description of particular languages:

> General phonetics supplies a set of universally valid parameters which may be drawn upon (1) for the description of any specific piece of actual phonic substance, and (2) for the description of those particular types or ranges of phonic substance that may be utilised as distinctive features in the phonology of a given language. We refer here quite deliberately to 'universally valid parameters' rather than to 'universal features'. In the last decade or two a number of scholars have posited specific limited set of universal distinctive features (see Jakobson, Fant and Halle 1952, Chomsky and Halle 1968, and Ladefoged 1971). Of these, Ladefoged's multivalued 'features' are more akin to our 'parameters' than are the more restrictedly, more positively, defined features of Jakobson, Chomsky et al.

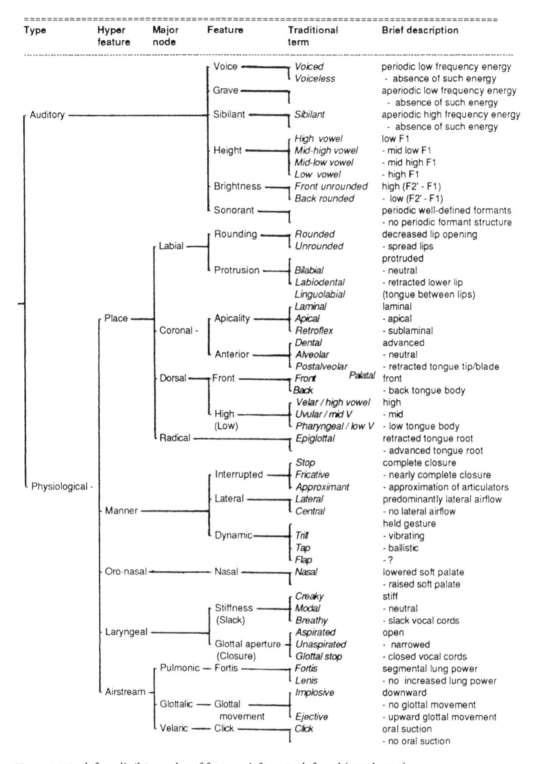

*Figure 3.48* Ladefoged's 'hierarchy of features', from Ladefoged (1988b: 128)

134 • *System in Systemic Functional Linguistics*

In his more introductory version of Catford (1977), Catford (2001: 9) suggests that this book could have been entitled 'componential-parametric' phonetics – which would be an apt title for a book on phonetics informed by SFL. The 'components' are initiation, articulation and (for certain sounds) phonation; and the 'parameters' are the 'ranges of variation' of the 'sub-components or features that characterize each of them'. Catford's 'parameters' can thus be interpreted as phonetic systems, as can Ladefoged's 'features'.

Ladefoged (e.g. 1988a: 16, 1988b: 128) has proposed a 'hierarchy of features', reproduced here as Figure 3.48. Here 'feature' covers both system and systemic term. The hierarchy can be interpreted as a step towards a phonetic system network; and it includes both the auditory and articulatory, or physiological, perspective on 'features'. Ladefoged (1988b: 127) comments:

> This tree structure represents a conjecture about the phonological resources, the features and their relations, that are available to the languages of the world at the level of segment. It should be emphasized that this figure gives only a tentative, incomplete view of the relations among features. Nevertheless, it forms part of a statement defining phonological possibilities that can occur. The arrangement of features into a tree structure has also been used by phonologists for other purposes, notably the grouping of properties that co-occur in spreading rules.

As I suggested above, we can think of the hierarchy in Figure 3.48 as a pre-systemic exploration of the general phonetic resources we could try to describe systemically (like the taxonomic part of hybrid lexicogrammatical system networks in Figure 3.23 discussed above). In undertaking such an attempt, we would also need to consider Ladefoged's (1988b: 129) further comments on the hierarchy as 'a first step towards defining the possible phonological segments in the world's languages':

> In order to serve this purpose a great deal has to be added to the tree structure in figure 2 [reproduced here as Figure 3.48, CMIMM]. In the first place we need to state the conventions governing the possible paths through the tree; but at the moment we do not know what these are. The general convention for reading the tree structure is that the maximum possible set of phonological segments is achieved by taking each path through every node except the terminal nodes (the features) where one of a set of choices has to be made. But this convention does not apply to the nodes in the third column. The Place node dominates a set of features such that for most sounds only one path has to be selected, but for some sounds more than one may be selected, and, arguably, for some, such as a glottal stop, none of the options is selected. Similar remarks apply to the choice of airstream mechanism ...
>
> There are several other cases, such as the properties determined by the Manner node, in which the inter-relations are too complex to be given in the form of a tree structure.

One possible solution to the problems Ladefoged identifies is to re-represent the auditory-articulatory space systemically. Conventions for traversing system networks have been worked out in great detail, especially in computational modelling (see Section 5.2.2). This would of course be a representation of our general human phonetic potential, and different languages will phonologize it in very diverse ways.

The brief exploration of Catford's and Ladefoged's description of phonetic parameters or 'features' in Ladefoged's sense has served to:

- illustrate the task of construing an anatomical map of articulatory resources systemically, taking a number of steps in delicacy and considering issues of distinguishing between what is anatomically possible and impossible;
- bring out the complementarity of articulatory (physiological) and auditory aspects of phonetics as an interlevel – as an interface between the system of phonology and bodily resources.

Just as with models of semantics and descriptions of the semantic systems of particular languages, accounts of phonetics must be relatable to extra-linguistic systems, in this case the articulatory and auditory systems in the first instance. We can, of course, also gain insights through simulations from models where phonological descriptions are linked to speech synthesizers, as in the exploratory systemic functional work by Teich, Watson and Pereira (2000).

Before leaving the exploration of a systemic functional approach to phonetics as an expression substance stratum, I would also like to note the possibilities opened up investigations of semiotic systems other than language. There is considerable potential for studies of 'paralanguage', like Wan's (2010) study of voice quality in call centre dialogue, and for studies of visible articulation such as lip rounding/spreading in relation to facial expressions.

## 3.5 Systemic Representation of Different Strata

In his discussion of system networks, Halliday (2013: 33–34) raises the issue of the extent to which the resources beyond the two inner, or 'core', strata of language, lexicogrammar and phonology, can be 'systemicized' or represented by system networks:

> I have largely restricted the discussion to the 'core' strata of language, lexicogrammar and phonology; and mainly to the lexicogrammar, Hjelmslev's 'form of the content', which is where the sense of 'meaning as choice' is most immediately perceived. Here the meaning potential is most fully systemicised. This is what grammar and phonology are about: ordering the processes of meaning, both 'content' and 'expression', into manageable networks of inter-connected choice.
> 
> [...]
> 
> Somewhere between the lexicogrammar and the context – the significant eco-social environment – we recognise an interface stratum, that of semantics, Hjelmslev's 'content substance'. Here the principle of organisation, following Martin and Matthiessen (1991), is not typological, as in the lexicogrammar, but topological; it is based on semantic domains, or realms of shared experience and interaction, whose formal reflexes may be scattered throughout the lexicogrammatical networks. A critical manifestation of this stratal boundary is provided by metaphor, both lexical and grammatical. Metaphor is a cross-coupling between the semantic and the lexicogrammatical, and therefore a rich resource for expanding the overall meaning potential.

I will discuss the complementarity of typological representations of stratal resources by means of system networks and topological representations below in Section 6.3 below. Halliday goes on to ask: 'Can one network the semantics?'. He answers it by pointing to the work by Ruqaiya Hasan on semantic networks (see above), key references being Hasan (1996), Hasan et al. (2007), Fung (2015); and we can of course add the semantic system networks presented by J.R. Martin (1992) and in subsequent publication drawing on these semantic networks, and by Martin and White (2005) as part of their description of appraisal. And, importantly, we can also add Halliday's (1973b) register-specific semantic system networks.

Halliday doesn't discuss the question 'Can one network the phonetics?', but I have already explored the possibility above. There is a generalization here: most system networks that have been published have been descriptions of either lexicogrammar or phonology – i.e. of the inner or 'core' strata of language. In Hjelmslevian terminology, they constitute form – content form (lexicogrammar) and expression form (phonology). When we ascend to content substance (semantics) and descend to expression substance (phonetics), any mode of representation of the resources must be held accountable not only to immediate linguistic stratal neighbours but also to external, extra-linguistic systems (see Table 3.24): that follows from the fact that the substance strata are interlevels – interfaces to what lies beyond language (for semantics as an interlevel, see Halliday 1973b).

*Table 3.24* The stratal neighbours of lexicogrammar, phonology, and semantics, phonetics

| plane | form | related to | substance | extra-linguistic systems | |
|---|---|---|---|---|---|
| content | lexico-grammar | ↖ | semantics | • context<br>• content of non-linguistic (denotative) semiotic systems | • somatic systems (sensorimotor systems) |
| expression | phonology | ↘ | phonetics | • expression of non-linguistic (denotative) semiotic systems (e.g. voice quality, facial expression) | • somatic systems (sensorimotor systems: articulatory, auditory) |

In order to understand the nature of system networks at different strata, we can again emphasize the parallel between the two stratal planes, the content plane and the expression plane. Within both planes, the relationship of the form stratum to the substance stratum is 'natural' (as opposed to 'conventional', or 'arbitrary'): lexicogrammar stands in a natural relationship to semantics, and phonology stands in a natural relationship to phonetics. As a result, from the point of view of linguists developing system networks there is some degree of indeterminacy between the strata within both planes; there is some degree of uncertainty as to whether a certain systemic description is lexicogrammatical or semantic and similarly whether a certain systemic description is phonological or phonetic. But this degree of indeterminacy is **inherent** in the phenomena themselves; it is not created by the theory – the role of the theory is to bring it out and to enable use to draw stratal boundaries in informed ways, weighing different criteria against one another.

Linguists have noted the uncertainty in relation to the content plane – sometimes criticizing Halliday's system network for being stratally ambivalent, but linguists (within SFL) have not tended to discuss such uncertainty in relation to the expression plane. Nevertheless, it is of fundamental importance to view these two 'planar' cases together; if we review the relation between lexicogrammatical and semantic networks in the light of the relation between phonological and phonetic system networks, we can shed light on the complementarity between form and substance, and we can also capture the principle of **double agnation** within both planes, manifested both in terms of semantics and lexicogrammar and in terms of phonology and phonetics. There will certainly be significant differences – the most important arguably being the existence of incongruent realizational relations between lexicogrammar and semantics (lexicogrammatical metaphor).

## 3.6 System Networks 'Outside' Language

Having sketched system networks within semantics, lexicogrammar, phonology and phonetics, let me now turn to regions outside language and ask to what extent they can be interpreted and described systemically by means of system networks.

### 3.6.1 Contextual System Networks

Moving upwards stratally, we can go on to ask 'Can one network the context?'. Halliday (2013: 34) comments on the systemic descriptions of context that have been put forward over the decades:

> With semantics, we are still locating ourselves squarely within language. What of other semiotic systems? The stratum of context, Firth's 'exterior relations of language', is treated by researchers in Systemic Functional Linguistics as falling within the domain of a linguistic theory; some context networks have been proposed (e.g. Hasan *et al.*, 2007: 724), but these appear rather as taxonomies of semiotic situation types than as options in the context of culture – and the former may well be their main theoretical value.

(Halliday's comment that context networks that have been proposed are 'taxonomies of situation types' rather than 'options in the context of culture' can be viewed against the background of his own sketch of the context of culture in the *Shall I tell you why the North Star stays still?* example at the end of Halliday 1984b.) So one interesting task is to complement the systemic descriptions of context he refers to by moving up the cline of instantiation from instance types (situation types) to the potential pole of the cline – to the **context of culture** or cultural system of a community. Is it possible, or desirable, to represent the cultural potential of a community by means of system networks? This is quite a daunting task, given the semiotic 'size' of a culture – cultures being construed and enacted through all the denotative semiotic systems that operate in their communities (their denotative meaning potentials), and also, by another step, by the social systems (their behaviour potentials).[48] In addition, there are questions similar to those that arise in the case of semantics having to do with the overall responsibility of the description in general and of the systemic one in particular.

To give an indication of contributions to the systemic description of the contextual parameters of field, tenor and mode, I have tabulated a few examples in Table 3.25. In the systemic functional literature, many characterizations of field, tenor mode are presented as discursive glosses on contexts of situation; they are instantial glosses that can stimulate thinking about what systemic descriptions would have to cover. For additional information, see also Wegener (2011: Appendix 1, 223–241).

The systemic descriptions offered by J.R. Martin (1992: Chapter 7) are accompanied by tables with lists of semantic and lexicogrammatical patterns, as indicated in Table 3.25. Those offered by Hasan, which have also fed into work by Butt and Wegener (cf. Butt and Wegener 2007; Wegener 2011), have not yet been enhanced with realization statements. What would such realization statements specify? It seems plausible that they would specify (fragments of) **contextual structure**, in the same way as linguistic system networks have systemic terms with associated realization networks that specify linguistic structure. Contextual structure has been characterized by means of a few different names, including 'generic structure' and 'schematic structure' and contextually more specific names like 'narrative structure' and 'argument structure'. They have tended to be specified by means of syntagmatic 'formulae' rather than by means of realization statements in the paradigmatic environment of systemic terms in contextual system networks. I'll come back to this approach. Meanwhile, let me suggest how systemic descriptions can be extended in delicacy to the point where it is possible to begin to associate realization statements with terms in the description. I will use one of the field parameters, viz. field of activity, as an example, focussing on one of the fields of activity that are oriented towards field itself, more specification field of experience. This is the field of activity of expounding 'knowledge' about field of experience in terms of general classes of phenomena: see Figure 3.49.

According to the description of field of activity in Figure 3.49,[49] the most general system specifies a contrast between activities that are essentially 'social' and ones that are essentially 'semiotic'. (i) The 'social' activities are those where the activity of a given situation type is constituted in social behaviour; it may be facilitated by language and/or other denotative semiotic systems, as when a team of removalists carrying a heavy and bulky piece of furniture give directions to one another by means of language or some form of gesture (possibly pointing with their noses or lips if their hands occupied with the task of carrying the furniture). This is the traditional notion of 'language in action'. (ii) The 'semiotic' activities are those where the activity of a given situation type is constituted in semiotic activity, i.e. in making meaning. Semiotic activity is always also constituted in social activity, but the situation type is constructed out of meaning in the first instance – even when the meaning-making may lead to social behaviour by 'recommending' or 'enabling' it.

There is a range of different semiotic activities, and it would be possible and desirable to differentiate them by means of a few steps in delicacy; but since this is only an illustration and I want to get to 'expounding' without too much expounding discourse on the way, I have represented the 'semiotic' activities in a single system. One of the seven terms is 'expounding': semiotic activities concerned with expounding 'knowledge' about general classes of phenomena by means of language and/or other semiotic systems such as taxonomic trees, schematic images annotated with arrows, mathematical representations (cf. Mohan 1986; Wignell, Martin and Eggins 1993).

Table 3.25 Contextual parameters – characterization and references to system networks

| | field | tenor | mode |
|---|---|---|---|
| Halliday (1978a: 142–143): characterization | **the social action**: that which is 'going on', and has recognizable meaning in the social system; typically a complex of acts in some ordered configuration, and in which the text is playing some part, and including 'subject-matter' as one special aspect; | **the role structure**: the cluster of socially meaningful participant relationships, both permanent attributes of the participants and role relationships that are specific to the situation, including the speech roles, those that come into being through the exchange of verbal meanings; | **the symbolic organization**: the particular status that is assigned to the text within the situation; its function in relation to the social action and the role structure, including the channel or medium, and the rhetorical mode. |
| J.R. Martin (1992), English Text | TRANSMISSION: oral (doing)/written (studying) oral: domestic/specialised [recreational/trades] written: administration/exploration<br><br>ACTIVITY SEQUENCE<br>• p. 539: 'Provisional classification of activity sequences for field of linguistics'<br>TAXONOMY<br>• p. 540: 'Composition taxonomy for members of an Australian linguistics department'<br>p. 541: 'Superordination taxonomy for theories of language'<br>• p. 544: 'A provisional classification of fields' | STATUS: equal/unequal<br>CONTACT: involved/distant<br>AFFECT: marked [positive/negative]/not marked<br><br>p. 526: 'Three dimensions of tenor'<br>STATUS<br>• p. 529: 'Aspects of the realisation of unequal status'<br>CONTACT<br>• p. 531: 'Tenor – CONTACT systems' & p. 532: 'Tenor – aspects of the realisation of contact'<br>AFFECT<br>• p. 536: 'Tenor – affect systems'; p. 534: 'Tenor – a provisional classification of affect' & p. 535: 'Tenor – aspects of the realisation of affect' | VISUAL: none/one-way/two-way & AURAL: none/one-way/two-way none & none: public/private & visually/aurally objectified field-structured<br>[ABSTRACTION: accompanying/constituting]/genre-structured<br>PROJECTION: projected/unprojected<br><br>• p. 515: 'Mode systems: speaking and writing focus';<br>p. 522: 'Mode – more delicate degrees of abstraction';<br>• p. 524: 'Mode – action, reflection and projection' & p. 525: 'Mode – aspects of the realisation of experiential distance' |
| Hasan (1999) – field and mode descriptions reviewed and discussed by Bowcher (2014) | MATERIAL ACTION: present/non-present [deferred/absent]<br>VERBAL ACTION: ancillary/constitutive [practical/conceptual]<br>SPHERE OF ACTION: specialised/quotidian [institutional/individuated]<br>ITERATION: stop/go [independent/aligned/integrated] | | |

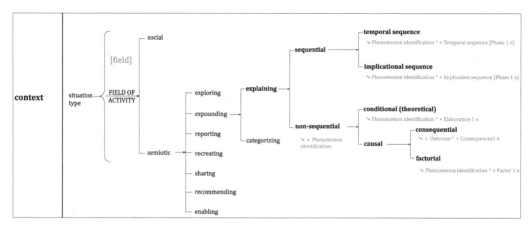

*Figure 3.49* Sketch of a system network for field of activity, extended in delicacy to the point where it makes contact with systemic functional description of explanations in education (Veel 1997)

At this point in delicacy, it is possible to make contact with descriptions in systemic functional educational linguistics – in particular, with descriptions of genres used in education (see Martin and Rose 2008). There are two broadly different modes of expounding 'knowledge', viz. 'explaining' and 'categorizing'. Drawing on Veel's (1997) account of explanation genres, we can identify a number of explanation strategies and represent them by systems as in Figure 3.49. The first system of choice is between 'sequential' and 'non-sequential' explanations, and each explanation strategy is further elaborated in delicacy. As we reach this region of delicacy, we can begin to specify contextual structures by means of realization statement associated with systemic term, as shown in the system network; for example, 'non-sequential' explanations are realized by the presence of a contextual element of 'Phenomenon Identification', and 'factorial' explanations include another element, 'Factor', which may be instantiated once or a number of times and is placed after 'Phenomenon Identification'.

Such elements are **contextual elements of structure**, and they will be realized either semiotically in the first instance if the field of activity is 'semiotic' or behaviourally in the first instance if the field of activity is 'social' (possibly or probably facilitated semiotically as already noted). The model of what such realizations look like was provided by Hasan (1984): she describes the semantic realization of the contextual element of Placement in a traditional nursery tale. This provides a promising framework for relating contextual patterns to semantic ones (for the contribution semantic logico-semantic complexing can make, see Matthiessen, forthcoming a).

The realization statements in Figure 3.49 serve to specify the contextual structures of different types of explanation. They would appear to be incompatible with the approach to the specification of contextual structures introduced by Hasan (1978) – GSP, or Generic Structure Potential (see also e.g. Halliday and Hasan 1985; Hasan 1984). GSP can be interpreted as a Firthian system-structure approach to the specification of the contextual structure characteristic of a particular situation type (cf. Mitchell 1957); it is comparable to the representation by such structures by means of RTNs (Recursive Transition Networks), developed around the same time in computational linguistics by Kathy McKeown (e.g. McKeown 1985). However, Hasan (personal communication) always thought of GSP as kind of placeholder to be replaced once contextual system networks had been developed to the point where it would be possible to specify contextual structure by means of realization statements associated with terms in contextual systems (as hinted at by the example in Figure 3.49).[50]

Before leaving the discussion of contextual system networks, I would like to note again Wegener (2011) and also her forthcoming book in the Equinox key concepts in SFL series. The further we move away from the 'form' strata of language – lexicogrammar and phonology – either upwards or downwards, the more likely we are to run into accounts from disciplines other than linguistics. This is certainly the case with context. In terms of disciplines, it has been approached and illuminated by anthropologists – in the case of SFL, Malinowski's contextual field observations and theory have been foundational, sociology and social psychology (e.g. Turner 1997; Argyle, Furnham and Graham 1981), philosophy (e.g. Barwise and Perry 1983) and AI, including modelling of context in the form of scripts and other schemata, situation-based and case-based reasoning, situational awareness and sensitivity (e.g. Schank and Abelson 1977; Gorniak and Roy 2007).

### 3.6.2 System Networks of Denotative Semiotic Systems Other than Language

Halliday (2013: 34–35) also considers the possibility of describing denotative semiotic systems other than language by means of system networks: see the passage quoted from his work above at the beginning of Section 3.2.2.6.3. If semiotic systems other than language are approached and interpreted systemically in the first instance rather than structurally, it is possible to bring out their organization as semiotic resources even though syntagmatically they may be very different from language and require distinct models of syntagmatic patterning, as in the case of rendering drawings and paintings. (And we can also explore the possibility of representing behaviour potentials within social systems by means of system networks, and even biological activity potentials and physical action potentials; but the nature of the contrasts being represented thus will of course change as we move down the ordered typology of systems – cf. 'phenomenal order' in Figure 1.2 above.)

On the use of system networks in descriptions of denotative semiotic systems other than language, see further Section 5.5 (with examples of semiotic systems having been described by means of system networks given in Table 5.1).

### 3.7 Summary of System as a Fractal Principle

In this chapter, I have shown that the notion of system applies to **all** strata of language in context and I have also referred to semiotic systems other than language. As far as paradigmatic patterns are concerned, the general principle is they can be modelled and described by means of system networks in all these different stratal environments. In other words, in this systemic approach all strata are handled according to the same **systemic template**. The key reason for this is that they are all conceived of as **resources**

– so as **potentials** at the potential pole of the cline of instantiation: the cultural potential of a community and the linguistic potential, i.e. the meaning potential, the wording potential and the sounding potential. This is one of the respects in which SFL is different from 'mainstream' linguistics, where different strata are usually handled in different ways. It is in this sense that the system is a **fractal principle**.[51]

The system network has been illustrated at work throughout the chapter – in the description of the linguistic strata and in the description of the context of language and other denotative semiotic systems; as noted immediately above, I will return to the use of system networks in the description of denotative semiotic systems other than language (for examples, see Table 5.1). These illustrations of the descriptive use of the system network will have given an indication of their potential as a cartographic tool in language description: having begun to flesh out the description of a language by means of system networks at different strata, one can arrive at a systemic map and use it to navigate the description of the language. This is the topic of the next chapter. After that chapter, I will be in a good position to exemplify the notion of the system in applications and to highlight the role of the system network in a few of the many areas of application of SFL.

# Chapter 4

# The System as a Navigational Tool in Language Description and Text Analysis

In the previous chapter, I have shown how language can be conceptualized as a resource and represented by means of systems forming system networks. These system networks are 'dispersed' throughout the stratal systems that make up language and also the extra-linguistic higher-order system of context. Systemic terms are related across strata by inter-stratal realization (illustrated in Figure 3.1) so that all of language in fact can be thought of as a gigantic system network (for more discussion, see Matthiessen, forthcoming b). This conception of language is one significant point of contact with Stratificational Linguistics and now Relational Network Theory (e.g. García, Sullivan and Tsiang 2017). In this chapter, I will discuss some of the consequences of modelling language systemically – of foregrounding the paradigmatic mode of axial order.

## 4.1 Systemic Terms as Nodes in Networks of Relations

In a system within a system network, any systemic term is multiply related along the semiotic dimensions that make up the 'architecture' of language (as shown for stratification in Figure 3.38 above):

- **systemically**, within a system that forms part of a system network: a given term contrasts with the other term or terms in its system, and it is related to the term or terms that serve as the entry condition to that system and it may be related to other terms by serving as (part of) the entry condition to one or more delicate systems (cf. Table 8.1). For example, in the system of MOOD (Figure 3.8 above), the systemic term 'declarative' contrasts with 'interrogative' in its own system, and is related to the term 'indicative' in the entry condition to that system, and through 'indicative' it is related to 'imperative' in in the system 'indicative'/'imperative'. In addition, the term 'declarative' is the entry condition leading to other, more delicate systems, viz. DECLARATIVE KEY ('neutral'/'marked') and MOOD TAGGING ('tagged'/'untagged').
- **axially**, within a system, one or more of its systemic terms are related inter-axially by means of realization statements to fragments of function structure (as in Table 3.2 above; cf. Table 8.2). For example, the term 'declarative' is related to the specification that Subject precedes Finite (Subject ^ Finite), as shown in Figure 3.8 above.
- **stratally**, across stratal subsystems of language, a given term may be related by inter-stratal realization upwards to the stratum next above and/or downwards

to the stratum next below. For example, the term 'declarative' is related by inter-stratal realization to 'statement' in the semantic system network of SPEECH FUNCTION and, indirectly after a couple of steps in further delicacy, to the terms in the phonological system of PRIMARY TONE, as with 'neutral' ↘ 'tone 1', 'protesting' ↘ 'tone 2', and so on (see Figure 3.1 and cf. Table 3.5).

- **instantially**, systemic terms in the system network representing some part of the system of language – the linguistic potential – are related by instantiation to instances of systemic terms selected in texts. Thus 'declarative' is related to innumerable instances of clauses that instantiate this systemic term, and these instances are 'distilled' in the system but the system is open and dynamic and thus subject to changes in patterns of instantiation (cf. Figure 4.12), changes that may be observed quantitatively as tendencies over time in relative frequencies and distilled as changes in systemic probabilities.

The first three relationships are illustrated in Figure 4.1. I'll return to the relationship of instantiation below – the relationship between systemic terms in the system network and their instantiation through actual choices in text.

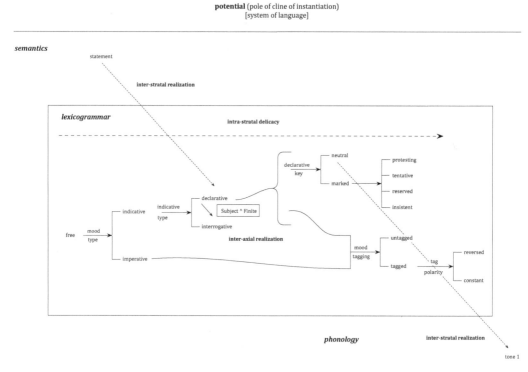

Figure 4.1 The systemic term 'declarative' as a node in a network of relations – multiply related in terms of (intra-stratal) delicacy in the system network of MOOD, in terms of inter-stratal realization to 'statement' in the semantic system of SPEECH FUNCTION, and in terms of inter-stratal realization to 'tone 1' in the phonological system of TONE

Thus, systemic terms are defined by the relationships they enter into; they are simply **nodes** in extensive networks, not 'things in themselves'. For example, 'declarative' is defined by being in contrast with 'interrogative' in the system of INDICATIVE TYPE, both being elaborations in delicacy of 'indicative', which contrasts with 'imperative' in the system of MOOD TYPE, by being the input to DECLARATIVE KEY and MOOD TAGGING, by being realized syntagmatically by the structural fragment Subject ^ Finite, by being realized phonologically by 'tone 1' in the system of PRIMARY TONE (in the case of 'neutral' declarative key), and by realizing 'statement' in the system of SPEECH FUNCTION.

## 4.2 Systemic Cartography: System Networks as Maps of Resources

Since systemic terms – and thus the systems that they are part of, including contrasting terms and entry condition and realization statements – are multiply related, one can move in at any point in one of the system networks that represents part of the overall organization of the linguistic system and follow the multiple 'threads' of relations, as illustrated for 'declarative' in Figure 4.1. Thus the systemic description of language supports 'Ariadne's thread':

> **Ariadne's thread**, named for the legend of Ariadne, is solving a problem by multiple means—such as a physical maze, a logic puzzle, or an ethical dilemma – through an exhaustive application of logic to all available routes. It is the particular method used that is able to follow completely through to trace steps or take point by point a series of found truths in a contingent, ordered search that reaches an end position. (Wikipedia entry[1])

I'm not suggesting that this is how a system network should be used – and a system network, while amazing, is not a maze! But it serves to underline the ***relational*** nature of systemic description. One can, as I said, start following a systemic thread at any point, but if one's task is to use the description as a reference account, it usually makes sense to start with the systems of primary delicacy that are identified in a function-rank matrix such as the one for the lexicogrammar of English presented as Table 3.6 above. Each cell of the matrix constitutes the 'semiotic address'[2] of one or more systems; for example, the cell located at the intersection of 'experiential' and 'clause' is the semiotic address of the system of TRANSITIVITY, and the cell immediately to the right of it is the home of interpersonal clause systems, the major one being one we are familiar with from the discussion above, the system of MOOD.

Thus the function-rank matrix of the lexicogrammatical system of a language can serve as a useful map of the resources of wording, identified by means of the names of the primary systems that collectively make up the total lexicogrammatical system. Since maps are the product of cartography, I have used the term **lexicogrammatical cartography** (Matthiessen 1995a) as a way of talking about views of the lexicogrammatical system. The function-rank map enables us to view the system from the vantage point of primary systemic delicacy (cf. the presentation of key clause systems in Section 3.2.1.2 above). An alternative view would be 'from below' based on an inventory of fragments of function structures specified by realization statements associated with systemic terms.

The cartographic potential of system networks turned out to be very important when we developed the computational Nigel grammar for the Penman text generation project[3] since it enabled us to get an overview of the grammar as we were developing it – helped by an enormous chart of the lexicogrammatical system network covering a whole wall in quite a large room. As I worked on the development of the description, based on Halliday's work, I started documenting it 'cartographically', surveying the lexicogrammatical system one system at a time. I adopted this form of documentation in my 1995 book *Lexicogrammatical cartography: English systems* (LexCart), which was intended to complement Halliday's IFG. The first and second editions of his IFG had very few system networks. As he invited me to join him in producing the third edition, we added system networks for all the major grammatical domains discussed in the book. However, IFG is still not organized principally around the systemic description, but LexCart is – so in a sense it reads like a taxonomic report.

In the documentation of English lexicogrammatical systems, I segmented systems differentiated according to metafunction and rank into **systemic regions**, as illustrated for the interpersonal clause systems of English in Figure 4.2. I presented the regions one by one, each with a magnified system networks: MOOD, KEY, DEPENDENCE (a bad name for the systems of 'bound' clauses – bad because bound clauses can be either dependent or down-ranked (embedded) and dependent is a structural-functional notion not one of systemic class), and MODALITY. Consequently, as the presentation progresses, readers can always move between the representation of the system network and the related documentation of it in the body of the text. The documentation includes a range of examples illustrating instances of each systemic term.

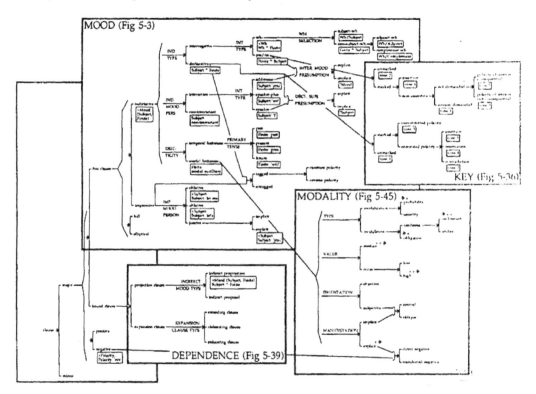

*Figure 4.2* The interpersonal clauses systems of English, segmented into regions in Matthiessen (1995a: 383)

In a way, I tried to replicate on the page what was possible to do on the computer; but of course the technology of the printed page was limiting: while cross references were possible, they only mimicked hyperlinks. I had a vision of an online system network where readers (viewers) could move around, shunting up and down in delicacy, and click on systemic terms (features) to see explanatory comments and/or examples, to access higher- or lower-stratal terms – or combinations of terms to view paradigms.

The vision was of a systemic functional linguist's work bench that would include various resources – prominently systemic functional descriptions – and tools. At some point, Wu Canzhong and I set out to create a first prototype using a database system. Part of this prototype is called SysAm, which is short for **Systemic Amanuensis** (I borrowed the notion of an 'amanuensis' from Martin Kay's idea of a translation amanuensis). SysAm supports both systemic functional reference resources (SysRef) – system networks, with examples and discursive documentation, and systemic functional analysis tools[4] (SysFan); see Wu (2000, 2009). SysRef is the cartographic part; it consists of linked databases for different parts of the overall account (we started the development before it was possible to do this with tables within a single database). Key aspects of the SysRef architecture are illustrated in Figure 4.3 and Figure 4.4.

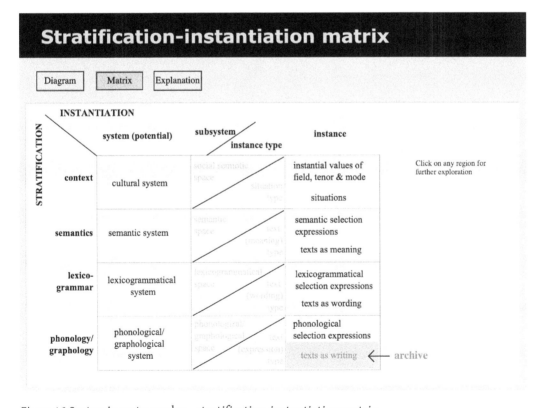

*Figure 4.3* Systemic cartography – stratification-instantiation matrix

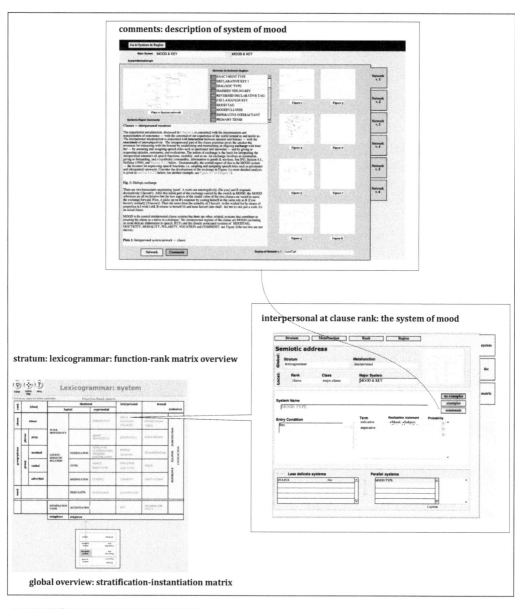
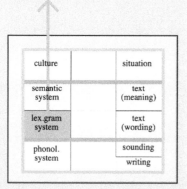

*Figure 4.4* Systemic cartography – function rank matrix, system of MOOD and discursive comments

In Figure 4.3, users will see a **stratification-instantiation matrix**; by clicking on any region within that matrix, they can access further detail. If they click on 'lexicogrammatical system' at the intersection of 'system (potential)' and 'lexicogrammar', they will reach the layout at the bottom of Figure 4.4. This layout is a lexicogrammatical function-rank matrix, just like the one in Figure 3.5 above, adapted from IFG4 (Halliday and Matthiessen 2014). But unlike the IFG function-rank matrix, this version is 'live': if users click on a system name such as MOOD, they will be taken to another layout, which provides a listing of individual mood systems within the overall mood system. These systems can be examined one by one, like the MOOD TYPE system in the example, and from the individual system layout, users can access examples and discursive comments documenting the system. The individual system layout also provides information about less delicate systems in the mood system network and more delicate ones.

Thus SysRef gives an indication of the cartographic potential of system networks in systemic descriptions of languages. It is, as noted, only a prototype; and a full-fledged implementation of a workbench along the lines of SysAm could certainly be a powerful environment for a whole range of linguistic activities. The navigation around system networks is, obviously, also supported by computational models of systemic functional grammars – notably in John Bateman's (e.g. 1997) KPML system, which incorporates the Nigel grammar (see Section 5.2).

## 4.3 Instantiation of Systemic Terms in Text

In the previous section, I showed that systems of system networks can be used as maps of the linguistic system, giving users the ability to navigate around the description, following different 'threads' according to their needs and interests, thus – in principle! – being freed from the technology of the printed page.

System networks can also be used to shed light on texts – on instances of the linguistic system. Texts unfold in their contexts of situation as processes of choice in the semantic system, and thus also (by dint of realization) in the lexicogrammatical system, and (by another link in the chair of realization) in the phonological or graphological system. Halliday (1977/2002: 48) characterizes **text as semantic choice**:

> By 'text', then, we understand a continuous process of semantic choice. Text is meaning and meaning is choice, an ongoing current of selections each in its paradigmatic environment of what **might have been** meant (but was not). It is the paradigmatic environment – the innumerable sub-systems that make up the semantic system – that must provide the basis of the description, if the text is to be related to higher orders of meaning, whether social, literary or of some other semiotic universe. The reason why descriptions based on structure are of limited value in text studies is that in such theories the paradigmatic environment is subordinated to a syntagmatic frame of reference; when paradigmatic concepts are introduced, such as transformation, they are embedded in what remains essentially a syntagmatic theory. [...] Here the description is based on system; and text is interpreted as the process of continuous movement through the system, a process which both expresses the higher orders of meaning that constitute the 'social semiotic', the meaning systems of the culture, and at the same time changes and modifies the system itself.

To get a sense of text 'as the process of continuous movement through the system', we can track successive selections of terms in systems, as illustrated for a passage from a telephonic service encounter in Figure 4.5. Here the most general interpersonal systems of the clause are represented as a system network to the left, and successive selections are shown to the right as a **score of choices** as the text unfolds from Clause [1] through Clause [17].[5] The analysis is presented in tabular format in Table 4.1.

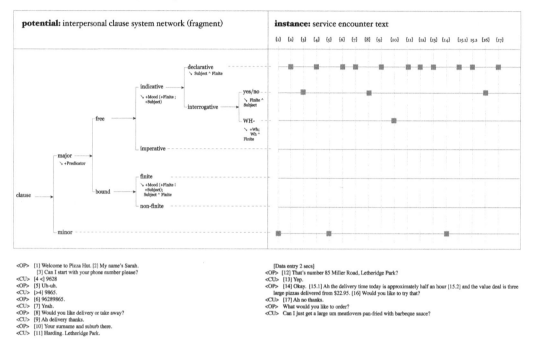

*Figure 4.5* Systemic text analysis – tracking choices in clauses as a service encounter unfolds in time

The analysis in Table 4.1 Systemic analysis of passage of a telephonic service encounter text (Clauses [1] through [17]) includes interpersonal selections from semantics (SPEECH FUNCTION), lexicogrammar (MOOD, and also the textual system of ELLIPSIS) and phonology (TONE). It is thus possible to follow the lexicogrammatical score set out in Figure 4.5 but also to refer to Figure 3.1 in Chapter 3 above, where the realizational relationships between semantics and lexicogrammar and between lexicogrammar and phonology are illustrated.

The selections shown in Figure 4.5 are within the interpersonal system of the clause, but of course the same picture of a score of selection emerges when we also consider experiential and textual systems in the same telephonic service encounter, as shown in Figure 4.6. Here selected terms are shown in darker shades. Patterns of selection stand out quite clearly; for example, we can see that experientially, 'relational' clauses are the most frequent choice, interpersonally, 'declarative' clauses are the most common, and textually, 'unmarked topical' (theme) occurs in all the clauses where it is an option, whereas the contrasting term, 'marked topical' (theme) is never selected in this passage. We can view selections for each system individually – for example noting a sequence of selections of 'material' in the system of process type around the middle of the passage shown in Figure 4.5; but we can also look for systemic patterns across systems, like the combinations of 'mental' and 'interrogative: yes/no', e.g. *would you like delivery or take-away?*. Such **co-selections** are like musical chords; they are **systemic chords**, and they can reveal significant moments or passages in texts.

Table 4.1 Systemic analysis of passage of a telephonic service encounter text (Clauses [1] through [17])

| context | | semantics | grammar | | phonology | text | |
|---|---|---|---|---|---|---|---|
| generic stages | | SPEECH FUNCTION | MOOD | ELLIPSIS | TONE | speaker | |
| Business Identification | | greeting | minor: salutation | | tone 3 | <OP> | [1] Welcome to **Pizza** Hut. |
| Server Identification | | initiate & demand & information | major: indicative: declarative | full | tone 2 | | [2] My name's **Sally**. |
| Phone Number Request | | initiate & demand & information | major: indicative: interrogative: yes/no | full | tone 1 | | [3] Can I start with your **phone** number please? |
| | | continuity | minor: continuity | | tone 1 | <CU> | [4 …] Yeah uh |
| | | respond & give & information | major: indicative: declarative | elliptical | tone 3 | | [… 4] 3419 |
| | | continuity | minor: continuity | | tone 2 | <OP> | [5] Uh-**uh**. |
| | | [cont'd] | [cont'd] | [cont'd] | tone 1 | <CU> | […4] 8856. |
| | | initiate & demand & information | major: indicative: declarative | elliptical | tone 3 tone 2 | <OP> | [6] 3419 // 8856. |
| | | respond & give & information | major: indicative: declarative | elliptical | tone 1 | <CU> | [7] **Yeah**. |
| Service Selection | | initiate & demand & information [question] | major: indicative: interrogative: y/n: alternative | full | tone 2 tone 1 | <OP> | [8] Would you like **delivery** or // **take** away? |
| | | respond & give & information [answer: statement] | major: indicative: declarative | elliptical | tone 1 | <CU> | [9] Ah **delivery** thanks. |
| Name and Address Request | | initiate & demand & information | major: indicative: interrogative: wh– | elliptical | tone 1 | <OP> | [10] Your surname and **suburb** there. |

| context | | semantics | grammar | | phonology | text | |
|---|---|---|---|---|---|---|---|
| generic stages | | SPEECH FUNCTION | MOOD | ELLIPSIS | TONE | speaker | |
| | | respond & give & information | major: indicative: declarative | elliptical | tone 3 tone 1 | <CU> | [11] **Comrie.** // Lethbridge **Park.** |
| | | | | | | <OP> | [Data entry 2 secs] |
| | | initiate & demand & information | major: indicative: declarative | full | tone 2 | <OP> | [12] That's number 73 Miller Road, Letheridge **Park?** |
| | | respond & give & information | major: indicative: declarative | elliptical | | <CU> | [13] **Yep.** |
| | | continuity | minor: continuity | | tone 3 | <OP> | [14] **Okay.** |
| Delivery Time | | initiate & give & information [statement] | major: indicative: declarative | full | tone 4 | | [15.1] Ah the delivery time today is approximately half an **hour** |
| Special Offer | | initiate & give & information [statement] | major: indicative: declarative | full | tone 5 | <OP> | [15.2] and the value deal is three large pizzas delivered from $22.95. |
| | | initiate & give & goods-&-services [offer] | major: indicative: interrogative; y/n | full | tone 2 | <OP> | [16] Would you like to **try** that? |
| | | respond [rejection] | major: indicative: declarative | elliptical | tone 1 | <CU> | [17] Ah **no** thanks. |

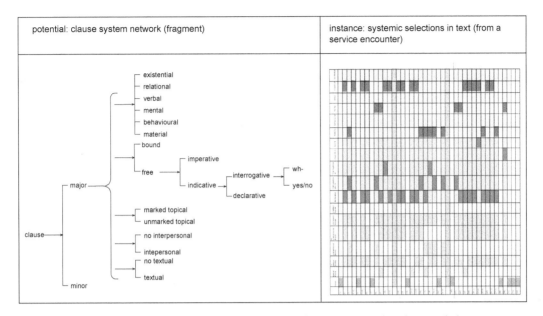

*Figure 4.6* Text score showing selections in experiential, interpersonal and textual clause systems for 'major' clauses and selections of 'minor' clauses in passage of a telephonic service encounter (Table 4.1 Systemic analysis of passage of a telephonic service encounter text (Clauses [1] through [17])). Darker shades indicate selections of systemic terms

The displays in Figure 4.5 and Figure 4.6 are designed to show the choice of systemic features clause by clause as the text unfolds so that it is possible to see how patterns of selections emerge logogenetically. I have referred to the patterns of selections in the systems shown in the figure as a **text score**, borrowing Weinreich's (e.g. 1978) term 'Textpartitur' (for additional examples, see e.g. Matthiessen 1995a, 1995c, 2002, 2014d, 2015d). Each systemic term, e.g. 'existential', 'imperative', 'marked topical', represents a 'note' that may be played as the text unfolds 'as the process of continuous movement through the system'. And simultaneously selected terms are, as noted, like a chord; they constitute a **systemic chord**.

The text score of systemic selections gives us a qualitative view of the unfolding text, but at the same time, it shows us how systemic terms emerge as more or less frequent selections. For example, after the first few clauses, it seems that 'declarative' is the most frequent selection in MOOD TYPE, overtaking 'interrogative' and 'imperative'. Obviously, selections may change as texts enter into new phases of development; but at the end of the process of unfolding, we can examine the finished text as a product, and count the number of selections of each systemic term. The frequencies of choices of experiential, interpersonal and textual systemic terms at the end of our service encounter are shown in Figure 4.7. The bars represent the counts for the systemic terms; for example, in the experiential system of PROCESS TYPE, the most frequently chosen term is 'relational', followed by 'material' and then by 'mental'.

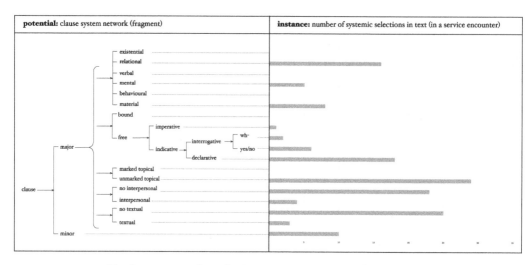

*Figure 4.7* Text profile showing number of selections in experiential, interpersonal and textual clause systems for 'major' clauses and selections of 'minor' clauses in passage of a telephonic service encounter (Table 4.1 Systemic analysis of passage of a telephonic service encounter text (Clauses [1] through [17])); the bars to the right of the system network represent the numbers of selections of each systemic term

The counts in Figure 4.7 are instantial; i.e. they are simply counts of the selections made by the server/operator and the customer/caller in the telephonic service encounter. And if we were to treat this service encounter text as an **artefact** – as a text of interest in its own right (which would be more likely if it were a passage from a highly-valued drama, like *Mystic Pizza: The Virtual Sequel*), we could stop at this point. However, if we treat this text as a **specimen** of something general – i.e. of a pattern further along the cline of instantiation, moving away from the instance pole towards the potential pole, then we treat the relative frequencies in this particular text as quantitative evidence for, say, the register of telephonic service encounters or service encounters in general, or (moving much further along the cline towards the potential pole) as quantitative evidence for probabilities in the linguistic system at the potential pole of the cline.

## 4.4 Systemic Probabilities and Frequencies of Selections of Systemic Terms

The frequencies of systemic terms we observe in the service encounter represented systemically in Figure 4.7 are instances of systemic probability. In one of his accounts of language as a probabilistic system, Halliday (1991a/2005: 45) explains this situation as follows:

> Frequency in text is the instantiation of probability in the system. A linguistic system is inherently probabilistic in nature. I tried to express this in my early work on Chinese grammar, using observed frequencies in the corpus and estimating probabilities for terms in grammatical systems (1956, 1959). Obviously, to interpret language in probabilistic terms, the grammar (that is, the theory of grammar, the *grammatics*) has to be paradigmatic: it has to be able to represent language as **choice**, since probability is the probability of "choosing" (not in any conscious sense, of course) one thing rather than another. Firth's

concept of "system", in the "system/structure" framework, already modelled language as choice. Once you say "choose for polarity: positive or negative?", or "choose for tense: past or present or future?", then each of these options could have a probability value attached.

By the same token, frequency in text accumulates to probability in the system, and small changes in frequency perturb systemic probability – significantly over time if the changes trend in the same direction, which is when these changes become noticeable as systemic changes (see further below)[6].

For example, in the service encounter text, the relative frequencies of selections of terms in the system of PROCESS TYPE are as follows: 'material' – 28%/'behavioural' – 0%/'mental' – 17%/'verbal' – 0%/'relational' – 55%/'existential' – 0%. But it is just one of myriads of texts out of which the systemic probabilities are 'distilled' – for service encounters, or for English in general. Since it is not yet possible to analyse very large samples of clauses in terms of PROCESS TYPE automatically, we still depend on manual analysis; but we can do manual analysis of clauses in registerially varied samples (cf. Matthiessen 2006a, 2014b). Figure 4.8 shows the relative frequencies of the process types in a sample of 10,382 clauses. Here the relative frequencies are, not surprisingly, quite different from those in the telephonic service encounter. The ordering in frequency is: material > relational > mental > verbal > behavioural > existential; this ordering is probably a fairly accurate reflection of probabilities in the general system of PROCESS TYPE.

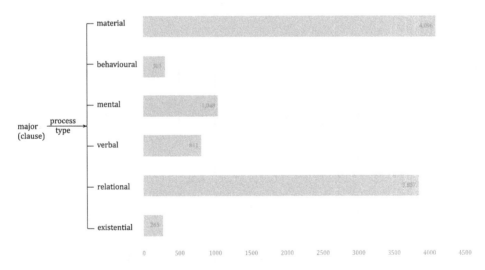

*Figure 4.8* Relative frequencies of terms in the system of PROCESS TYPE in a registerially varied sample of 10,382 clauses

Determining the frequency of the intersection of terms selected from simultaneous systems is also an important part of the study of the probabilistic nature of different systems. For example, we can intersect the system of PROCESS TYPE with the simultaneous system of AGENCY ('middle'/'effective'): the relative frequencies of the different combinations are shown in Figure 4.9. In 'material' clauses 'middle' and 'effective' agency are approximately balanced, but clauses of all other process types are predominantly 'middle', overwhelmingly so in the case of 'existential' and 'behavioural' clauses.

156 • *System in Systemic Functional Linguistics*

This quantitative systemic picture complements the qualitative one shown above in Figure 3.17 and Figure 3.19. As part of the discussion of those two figures, I suggested that there are no 'effective' clauses of the 'existential' and 'behavioural' process types; but we can now see that this is only almost the case in quantitative terms: it turns out that analytical 'effective' variants occur, with the sense of 'cause to behave' and 'cause to exist' although they are numerically almost negligible. (Such quantitative tendencies are also illuminating when we compare and contrast transitivity systems across languages. For example, in Chinese, there are no 'effective' clauses of the 'mental' process type, as pointed out by Halliday and McDonald 2004, and if we compare Chinese and English they may seem very different in this respect since English does have 'effective' 'mental' clauses; but once we add the quantitative information, the languages appear to be more similar, Chinese simply being the limiting case of a low probability of 'effective' 'mental' clauses. In general, low probability in one language may correspond to absence in another.)

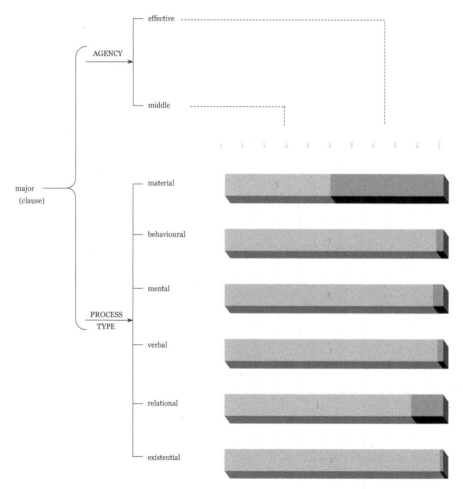

*Figure 4.9* Relative frequencies of the intersections of terms in the systems of process type and agency (N = 10,586 clauses)

There is obviously considerable variation in the selection of systemic terms such as those of the system of PROCESS TYPE at the instance pole of the cline of instantiation, but they are not purely instantial: they are 'distilled' as quantitative patterns characteristic of the registers that the texts instantiate. To get a very rough sense of what the **variation** across registers looks like, we can consider a small sample of texts belonging to five different registers (one spoken, casual conversation, and four written, scientific report, news report, narrative and topographic procedure): see Figure 4.10. Broadly, the quantitative preferences are predictable; for example, 'verbal' clauses have a higher relative frequency in news reports than in any other register, since 'attribution' to sources is important in journalism (it's an important aspect of the reporter's voice), and while 'material' clauses don't dip below 30%, they have the highest relative frequency in narratives, where they are central in construing the narrative backbone. If we were to explore the findings in Figure 4.10 further, we would discover that the variation in relative frequencies across registers can in fact consistently be interpreted also in qualitative terms by reference to the meanings at risk in a given register – the demands placed on it by its context of use.

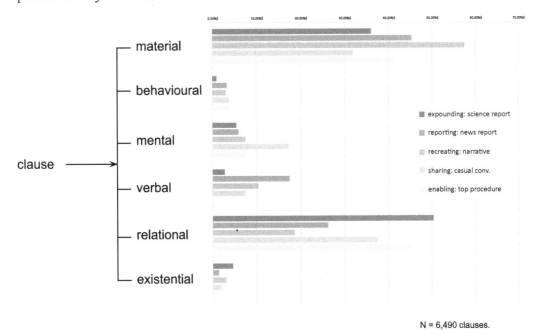

*Figure 4.10* Relative frequencies of terms in the system of PROCESS TYPE in a small sample of texts from different registers (N = 6,490 clauses)

The probabilistic interpretation of the linguistic system thus enables us to take account of variation in language. It also illuminates the linguistic system in terms of **population thinking**, as noted by Halliday (2013: 21–22):

> The concept of meaning as choice, or as choosing, whether or not it is being represented as a system network, may suggest a bias towards the individual meaner: the notion of an act of meaning, in particular, carries with it a suggestion of this kind. But choosing may be an activity of a whole population, as it is when they vote in an election or a referendum.

Meaning as choice can likewise be thought of in the context of a population – in the statistical sense: it may be concerned with very large quantities of acts of meaning, within which large-scale patterns and tendencies may be observed.

The network makes no prediction about what a particular person is going to mean on some particular occasion. It makes predictions about the behaviour of a population. It defines the range of options that is available to them as meaners, their meaning potential as producers and receivers in the social semiotic universe of language. And now that it is possible to observe patterns of relative frequency over a very large corpus of discourse, it can attach probabilities to each of the terms in a system – though only up to a certain degree of delicacy: there is a natural limitation here, in that for systems of greater delicacy the number of instances will be too small, and the conditioning factors too complex, to allow for any robust estimate of the probabilities involved.

(The probabilistic conception of the system of language is also fundamental to the study and interpretation of how children learn how to mean – and how to sound. Thanks to the advance in brain scanning technology and techniques, infants and young children can now be observed processing language, and the evidence is clear: even infants are statistical processors, tuning into the phonological and phonetic patterns they get extensive samples of in the language spoken around them. See e.g. the research conducted and reviewed by Patricia Kuhl, including Kuhl 2010a, b. This line of research is thus producing findings that are of course very compatible with the systemic understanding of ontogenesis developed by Halliday and other systemic functional researchers.)

## 4.5 Systemic Selection in Relation to the Cline of Instantiation

To recapitulate: systemic probabilities/frequencies are inherent in choice (or selection) – that is, in the instantiation in text of systemic terms in the system of language. At the instance pole of the cline of instantiation, we see quantitative patterns as relative frequencies in the selection of contrasting terms in systems such as PROCESS TYPE and MOOD TYPE, and we can observe trends emerging, and view them once the unfolding of a text has come to completion. At the potential pole, we can study quantitative patterns as probabilities inherent in systemic terms such as those in the systems of PROCESS TYPE and of MOOD TYPE. Intermediate between these two poles, we can investigate quantitative patterns either as **cumulative relative frequencies** emerging from texts as characteristic of registers or as **resettings of general systemic probabilities** in particular registers. These different views of quantitative patterns are visualized schematically in Figure 4.11. At the instance pole of the cline of instantiation, we can record selections of systemic terms as texts unfold in time; midway between the instance pole and the potential pole, we can distil these selections as systemic probabilities for different registers (thus treating registers as subpotentials of the overall potential of the language); and at the potential pole, we can in turn represent these aggregated registerial probabilities as overall systemic probabilities.

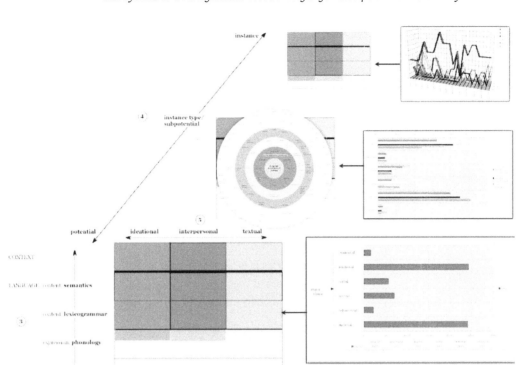

*Figure 4.11* Systemic selections in relation to the cline of instantiation – systemic probabilities, registerial probabilities/relative frequencies, and relative frequencies in texts unfolding through time

Figure 4.11 may give the impression, as may my paragraph immediately above, that while texts are 'dynamic' in the sense that they unfold in time – over fairly short periods of time, that systems are 'static' in the sense that they do not change through time – and consequently can be viewed synoptically. But this is the wrong impression. First of all, as Halliday has emphasized in many places over the years, text and system are one and the same phenomenon, not different phenomena; the difference lies in the **vantage point** we adopt as observers. Secondly, therefore, they both change through time; it is just that the timescales are different (e.g. Halliday and Matthiessen 2006, on the different timescales of processes of semogenesis). Texts unfold over short periods from less than a minute to several hours; but linguistic systems are constantly evolving, and changes that we can detect will take years or decades and more pervasive changes such as the great English vowel shift or the establishment of the modern use of 'do-support' may take hundreds of years. However, as just noted, languages are always evolving, and changes in systemic probabilities are an integral part of the phenomenon. Halliday (1991a/2005: 43) emphasizes that the system changes:

> From the point of view of European structuralism, a human system was a nexus of paradigmatic and syntagmatic relations that could be construed from the way they were manifested in patterns of behaviour. Saussure's langue/parole was one of the first formulations of this view. This clearly puts the system itself in a synoptic perspective. It is "held

together" by various metaphors: equilibrium, functional load, and the like. By contrast, the behaviour – the text, if we are talking about language – is viewed dynamically. This contrast is made explicit in Hjelmslev's "system/process" interpretation. Obviously the system changes; but it moves slowly along the time track, like a glacier, so the synoptic perspective, which enables us to examine it in fine detail, does not noticeably distort it. The text, on the other hand, is like the glacier stream, the water flowing out of the glacier; the natural perspective on text is a dynamic one, especially if our prototype of it is spoken rather than written text.

We can gain insight into change in constant progress from a pioneering study that is systemic in some fundamental respects although it appeared in Sweden in the early 1950s: Alvar Ellegård's (1953) PhD thesis. Using a historical corpus of English, he investigated 'the establishment and regulation of' *do* as an auxiliary over a period of three centuries, roughly from 1400 to 1700. The environment in which the auxiliary *do* is used as 'do-support' serving as Finite is characterized by the intersection of two interpersonal clause systems (Figure 3.8 above), viz. POLARITY ('positive'/'negative') and INDICATIVE TYPE ('declarative'/'interrogative'), as shown in Figure 4.12.

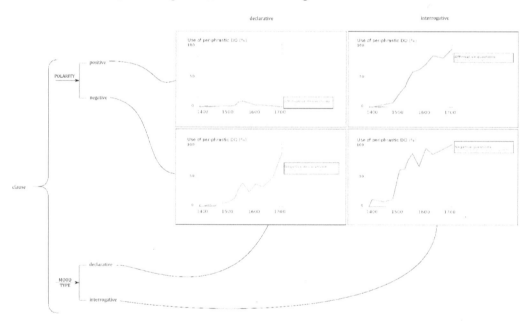

*Figure 4.12* The systemic environment of the auxiliary 'do' in 'do-support' defined by the intersection of the systems of POLARITY and INDICATIVE TYPE (MOOD TYPE)

In Figure 4.12, the systems of POLARITY and MOOD (indicative) TYPE are intersected in a table to show the systemic environments of *do*: the column headings are 'declarative' and 'interrogative', and the row headings are 'positive' and 'negative'; examples are given in Table 4.2. In the 'non-affirmative' combinations of 'negative' & 'declarative', 'interrogative' & 'positive'/'negative', the presence of *do* rose steadily from around 1400 to 1700. This was an increase in relative frequency; throughout the period, the likelihood that *do* would appear kept increasing, and by the end of the period, its presence had become (almost) categorical, as in present-day English. The 'affirmative' combination of 'positive' & 'declarative' engendered an interestingly different pattern. Throughout most of the period, *do* behaved like now – absent, except when 'positive' polarity is under marked focus; but there was an 'Elizabethan' period when *do* would appear with greater frequency in this systemic environment.

Of course there are other details to investigate, like the interplay with information focus and polarity and the form of 'imperative' clauses. However, the point of the reference to Ellegård's (1953) study is that the evolution of the system can be tracked over long periods of time by investigating gradual changes in relative frequency – interpreted in terms of the probabilistic nature of the system. (And of course we may become aware of such processes when they appear to accelerate and the equilibrium characteristic of gradual change is punctuated, just as we are now becoming aware of change in glaciers as they are melting as part of the syndrome of global climate change.) This also allows us to study the gradual development of new registers, as in Halliday's (1988) study of the emergence and changing nature of scientific English over a period of five centuries.

*Table 4.2* Absence and presence of 'periphrastic do' in the systemic environments of POLARITY and INDICATIVE TYPE; shaded options had largely disappeared by 1700

|  | INDICATIVE TYPE | | | |
|---|---|---|---|---|
| POLARITY | declarative | | interrogative | |
| positive | *you go* | *you **do** go* | ***do** you go?* | *go you?* |
| negative | *you go not* | *you **do** not go* | ***do** you not go?* | *go you not?* |
|  | *do* absent | *do* present | | |

## 4.6 Summary of the System as a Navigational Tool

Once Michael Halliday had designed the system network as representation of paradigmatic patterns as the primary patterns of axial order, it became a 'tool for thought' in C.H. Waddington's sense – or perhaps I should say a 'tool for meaning'. It expanded the metalinguistic meaning potential available to linguists (cf. Section 5.2.3), they (we) were empowered to view, observe, sample, describe, interpret and theorize language in new ways, leading to a number of discoveries such as the metafunctional organization of language. As a tool, system networks have now been put to uses Halliday had not – and could not have – anticipated when he first designed this 'tool for meaning', for example Phillips' (1986) use of system network to show subtle changes in ontogenesis (see also Halliday 2004a, for some discussion) or multilingual system networks (see Section 6.4.2 below).

One particular use of system networks has been the focus of this chapter – the system network as a navigational tool. In this respect, it might be thought of as a tool that is like the astrolabe – the topic of an early scientific text in English by Chaucer, illuminated linguistically by Halliday (1988) in his study of the evolution of scientific English. But the system network is not a material tool, it's a **semiotic tool** (a tool for thought, in Waddington's formulation); so it is ultimately part of the same family of designed semiotic systems as e.g. differential calculus, Boolean algebra, set theory, Venn diagrams, decision trees, flow charts, and frame-based inheritance networks – a couple of which will be discussed in relation to system networks in Chapter 6. As far as tools are concerned, the advancement of the scientific understanding(s) of the world has always depended on a combination of material tools (such as astrolabes, telescopes, microscopes, stethoscopes, particle accelerators and brain scanning devices) and semiotic ones (such as new branches of mathematics, projection systems in cartography, the system network, typed feature structures, LISP and network science).

As exemplified in this chapter and illustrated also in Section 3.2.1.2 in the previous chapter, the system network is an effective navigational tool because it enables us to draw comprehensive maps of the resources of any of the stratal systems of language (and in fact of any other semiotic systems). Such systemic maps can be indexed by means of function-rank matrices or comparable matrices identifying the key system of any stratum (e.g. Figure 3.5).

# Chapter 5

# The System in Different Domains of Application

The previous chapter has been concerned with the deployment of systems and system networks as navigational tools in the study of language in general terms, including different regions along the cline of instantiation. Here I will continue on this theme, but move to interfaces between linguistics and applications that are sometimes seen as on the borders between linguistics and other disciplines. Systemic Functional Linguistics has been developed as a resource capable of supporting a wide range of applications; Halliday (2002, 2008a) characterized this kind of linguistics as **appliable linguistics**, and I have detailed the attributes of appliable linguistics in the realm of discourse analysis – appliable discourse analysis, or ADA (Matthiessen 2014a). I need to emphasize that in this chapter I will be concerned with the notion of system in SFL in different domains of applications – centrally applications where system networks are used as representation of choice. As a kind of appliable linguistics, SFL has been deployed in a wide range of contexts, but I will only focus on examples of those where the system plays a central role. Thus in this chapter, I will only *illustrate* the appliability of 'system'; and I will not focus on other aspects of SFL that have turned out to be of crucial importance in various areas of application.

## 5.1 Pinpointing Choice

Since the 1960s, SFL has become engaged in an ever-increasing range of applications – translation and education being two early examples; many, or even most, of them can be characterized in terms of siting within institutions – e.g. family, education, healthcare, law, administration, politics, but there are also a number of applications of a fairly general nature that enhance the appliability to a range of institutional settings, perhaps in particular computational modelling and multimodal applications. There are now many overviews that contain information about applications, e.g. Hasan, Matthiessen and Webster (2005/7), Halliday and Webster (2009), Bartlett and O'Grady (2017), Thompson et al. (2019), Matthiessen and Teruya (2023).

Halliday (2012), in 'Pinpointing the choice: meaning and search for equivalents in a translated text', emphasizes the centrality of 'choice' to many applications; discussing his early engagement with questions about language in the 1950s in different contexts – as a language teacher, as a researcher in an early machine translation project, as a member of a group 'searching for a marxist, or at least marxism-compatible, linguistics' and as a lover of literature as art made of language, he takes a step back to identify a common motif (2012/2013: 145):

> If there was one motif that emerged as salient in all these different contexts, it was that of choice: language as meaning, and meaning as choice. In teaching a foreign language, one was always guiding the learners through networks of choices, opening up – or helping them to open up – an expanding range of meaning potential, increasing the delicacy of the choices they were making as they went along. [...] In translation, whether human or mechanical, the basic problem for the translator is the problem of choice – as is the decision of a writer whether to prefer this form of expression over that one. But these are just the occasions where the choice is, or can be brought, under focus of attention, as we can see in poets' notebooks, or in think-aloud protocol records of translators – they are choices that are made consciously.
> [...]
> If we look into some of the other domains where linguistics is being 'applied', the principle of choice is always likely to be in the foreground.

He then goes on to illustrate the centrality of choice in clinical and forensic contexts, and arrives at the following general principle of **pinpointing the choice** (2012/2013: 146):

> All use of language is a process of meaningful choice; and many of the applications of a linguistic theory depend on bringing out the specific choices that have been made, or that need to be made, in particular situational and textual contexts – in other words, on locating them in their function in the overall system of the language. This is what I meant by 'pinpointing the choice' in the title of this chapter.

In the remainder of his chapter, Halliday focusses on choice in translation – an area of application that I will discuss in Section 5.4. As noted by Halliday, systems of choice play a role in all applications, but the extent to which they draw on system networks is, naturally, varied. Here I will only give a few examples to indicate the power of system networks in applications – computational applications, educational applications, multilingual applications (with a focus on translation) and multimodal applications. I will start with computational applications since while they are less well-known than educational applications, they demand considerations that are, or could be, relevant to all applications – considerations of the theoretical modelling of system networks and interpretation of them as a representation of the theory of paradigmatic organization, the combination of which increases the potential for application.

## 5.2 Computational Applications

### 5.2.1 Computational Modelling of Language, Computational Tools for Linguistic Research

Computational applications are concerned with modelling some aspect of the linguistic system and linguistic processes, as in machine translation, text understanding, text generation, text summarization; so while they are ultimately related to the development of computational tools for doing linguistics, like concordancing tools in corpus linguistics and the application of machine learning techniques, they are fundamentally distinct from the development of tools precisely because they are concerned with modelling language as system-&-process.

Key examples of computational modelling of language informed by SFL and of computational tools for the development of accounts of language undertaken by SF linguists are set out in Table 5.1. (I have not included systemic functional research deploying computational tools developed outside SFL. A great deal of systemic functional research deploys standard tools such as WordSmith and ELAN, and techniques such as machine learning techniques.) Although, as just noted, the two are distinct, there are naturally areas of overlap, like the KPML system that can be used as a component in a text generation system but also as a workbench for developing systemic functional descriptions. Similarly, any breakthroughs in systemic functional parsing could lead to a major advance in computational tools for text analysis; it would lessen the distance between automated analysis and manual analysis, and give a huge boost to text-based research, including research into systemic probabilities.

*Table 5.1* Examples of computational modelling of language informed by SFL and computational tools developed by systemic functional linguists

| period | computational modelling | computational tools |
|---|---|---|
| 1950s | Halliday's (1956b) proposal for a mechanical thesaurus in machine translation | |
| 1960s | Henrici (1965) [systemic paradigms]; Winograd (1968) [tonal harmony] | |
| 1970s | Winograd (1972) [dialogue]; McCord (1975); Davey (1978) [text generation] | |
| 1980s | [text generation:] the Penman system, with the Nigel grammar at the Information Sciences Institute (Mann 1984; Matthiessen 1984; Mann and Matthiessen 1985; Matthiessen and Bateman 1991); [parsing:] representation in terms of a unification grammar formalism (Kasper 1988a,b) text generation as problem solving (Patten 1988) GENESYS at Cardiff University (Fawcett and Tucker 1990) [translation (and text generation):] Bateman et al. (1989) | |
| 1990s | [text generation:] the COMMUNAL project at Cardiff University (Fawcett, Tucker and Lin 1992); The KOMET system (Bateman, and Teich 1995; Teich, Bateman and Degand 1996); The KPML system (Bateman 1996, 1997) [parsing:] (O'Donnell 1994; Weerasinghe 1994) | Functional Grammar Processor (Webster 1993); KPML as a grammar development workbench (Bateman 1997) |
| 2000s | [parsing:] (O'Donnell 2005) [text generation and analysis:] Michio Sugeno's everyday computing project at RIKEN (e.g. Chang, Kobayashi and Sugeno 2001; Ito, Sugimoto and Sugeno 2004) [text categorization:] Jon Patrick's Scamseek Project at Sydney University (e.g. Whitelaw and Argamon 2004; Whitelaw, Herke-Couchman and Patrick 2005; Patrick 2008) | SysFan (Wu 2000); Systemics 1 (O'Halloran 2003); UAM CorpusTool (O'Donnell 2008, 2012) |
| 2010s | [parsing:] second-order systemic functional parsing (e.g. Costetchi 2013, 2020) [dialogue:] Couto-Vale (2017) | Multimodal Analysis (O'Halloran et al., 2012)[1] |

As Table 5.1 shows, in the history of the engagement between SFL and computing, the development of computational tools for doing linguistics has become more prominent while the computational modelling of language has arguably moved into the background as we proceed further into the twenty-first century (cf. Bateman et al. 2019). There are various reasons for this, but one has to do with a paradigm shift in computational linguistics/natural language processing: it is the move from symbolic design to statistical techniques, including approaches such as machine learning; the statistical approach has also been adopted in text generation (Bateman and Zock 2017). Thus while the probabilistic conception of language is central to SFL, and systems are taken to be distilled from text instances, and SFL is thus fully compatible with statistical NLP, the emphasis has tended to be on tools and techniques for constructing models out of large corpora of text (a manifestation of the theme of 'big data'). Another reason has to do with SFL itself. While researchers were successful in applying SFL to the task of modelling text generation by computer, in large part due to the systemic orientation of SFL, text analysis, including parsing, proved to be very hard (cf. Bateman 2008b, for an analysis in terms of the systemic functional 'architecture' of language, specifically in relation to axiality).

### 5.2.2 Beginnings of Computational Applications

Apart from Halliday's (1956b) proposal to use a 'mechanical thesaurus' in machine translation, the first computational engagement with system in SFL was Henrici's (1965) work on generating paradigms using system networks. This was already productive; for example, he identified and characterized the problem we encounter when we try to model recursive systems computationally. During the next decade and a half, there were a few interesting but fairly isolated attempts, including Winograd's (1972) use of system networks in his SHRDLU system, which became famous in AI as a milestone contribution, and Davey's (1978) pioneering use of system networks in a text generation system. Fawcett (1973) outlined a model on paper of a generative account based on system networks, and in the following decade his line of exploration led to a long-term research programme at Cardiff University of systemic functional modelling, one producing many publications, including PhD theses. The 1970s was also a period when scholars explored the formal or generative aspects of system networks (e.g. Hudson 1971; McCord 1975), but this line of investigation tended to be separate from computational modelling.

Computational modelling drawing on systems of system networks really took off in the 1980s with text generation projects – Fawcett's project noted above (e.g. Fawcett and Tucker 1990; Fawcett 1994) and our Penman project, directed by Bill Mann (e.g. Matthiessen and Bateman 1991). But let me pause for a moment to characterize the interesting issues that arise when system networks are used in computational models of language (for overviews, see O'Donnell and Bateman 2005; Teich 2009; Bateman and O'Donnell 2015; Bateman et al. 2019). The two central issues are arguably the following:

(i) To be used in computational models, system networks must be supplemented by theoretical accounts and explicit models of systemic processes.
(ii) To be used in computational models, system networks need to be made fully explicit, e.g. by being represented by means of some form of computational representation.

I will start with (i) since it actually reflects a gap in most linguistic theories; while linguistic theories may be strong at representing aspects of the linguistic system and annotations of texts, they tend to leave accounts of the relationship between the two less well articulated, including centrally the processes of moving between system and text (and text and system). But processes have been a central concern in computational linguistics since its beginnings in the 1960s – as is clear if one reviews parsing algorithms that have been proposed and implemented.

### 5.2.3 Processes

At the instance pole of the cline of instantiation, a text can be analysed segment by segment – e.g. clause by clause – showing the systemic terms selected for each segment, as illustrated in Figure 4.5 above for the major interpersonal system of the clause (MOOD) and in Figure 4.6 for the major textual, interpersonal and experiential systems of the clause. The analysis takes the form of a **systemic text score**, where each 'note' is a systemic term; the text score represents the systemic analysis of the text as a process unfolding through time – it represents the process of **logogenesis**. The segments are treated as phases in the unfolding of the text. At the completion of the final phase, the systemic analysis of the whole text can be represented as the systemic profile that has emerged by this point, as illustrated in Figure 4.7.

In computational modelling, we need to model the process of logogenesis – of the selection of terms in systems. In the discussion above of systemic text analysis, the systemic terms just appeared 'magically' in the text score; I did not spell out the process of deriving them by selection from the system network in focus in the analysis, like the system network of the clause. But in fact, the systemic terms recorded in the text score are the result of **passes** through the system network, or, to put this in terms used in computational SFL, **traversals** of the system network. These passes, or traversals, are processes of instantiation, either as part of text generation or as part of text analysis.

So let's examine how system network traversal works – adopting the direction of generation (rather than analysis). Consider Figure 5.1. This figure shows four successive states (or phases) in the system network of the clause (a greatly simplified version of this system network). The traversal starts with the systemic term 'clause', which is the systemic root of the system network of the clause (cf. Figure 3.4 and Figure 3.5 above). The selection of this term satisfies the entry condition of three simultaneous systems in Figure 5.1, viz. PROCESS TYPE: material/mental/verbal/relational, and MOOD TYPE: indicative/imperative, and THEME SELECTION: unmarked/marked. Since the entry condition of all three systems has been satisfied, they can be traversed in parallel: 'material', 'indicative' and 'unmarked' selected, leading to state 2 of the system network. The terms 'material' and 'indicative' satisfy the entry conditions of more delicate systems – material: dispositive/creative, indicative: declarative/interrogative & interactant/non–interactant. The selections are 'material', 'declarative' & 'non-interactant', as shown in state 3. The term 'dispositive' is the input to 'recipiency'/'non-recipiency', and 'declarative' to 'untagged'/'tagged'; the selections in these two more delicate systems are recorded as state 4 in Figure 5.1.

168 • *System in Systemic Functional Linguistics*

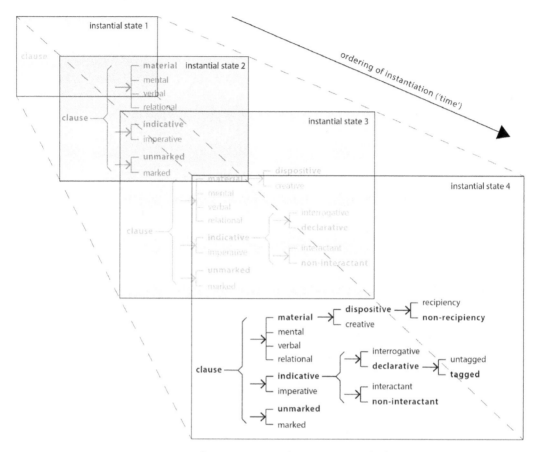

*Figure 5.1* Instantiating a system in the generation of text – traversal of a system network, system by system

Figure 5.1 shows successive states in the traversal of a simplified version of the clause system network. The system network is traversed from the least delicate systemic terms to the most delicate, in this example from 'clause' in state 1 to 'non-recipience', 'tagged', 'non-interactant' and 'unmarked' in state 4. As the system network is traversed, terms are selected in systems that become enterable; the terms selected are shown in bold. As an alternative to representing successive states of the traversal of a system network, we can simply show the **trace** of the traversal, marking systemic terms that are selected along the way. This is illustrated for the hypotactic conditional clause nexus (clause combination) *if there weren't trees on the earth, we would all be dead* in Figure 5.2.

The first term selected is 'clause'. This serves as input to three **simultaneous** systems, TAXIS, LOGICO-SEMANTIC TYPE and RECURSION; so they can be entered **in parallel**, and a choice made in each, in principle at the same time – in the case of the example, 'hypotaxis', 'expansion', and 'go on', the last of which opens up another pass through the system. The term 'hypotaxis' is terminal (in the system network represented in the figure), but 'expansion' leads to a choice in EXPANSION TYPE: 'elaborating'/'extending'/'enhancing'. In turn, 'enhancing' leads to a system representing different types of enhancing relations, and 'conditional' is selected. Finally, this is further specified by the choice of 'positive', which is realized by the binder *if* (contrasting with 'negative', *unless*, and 'concessive', *although*). The systemic terms that are selected as the system network is traversed are called a **selection expression**; in our example, the selection expression is {clause, hypotaxis, expansion, go on; enhancing, conditional, positive}.

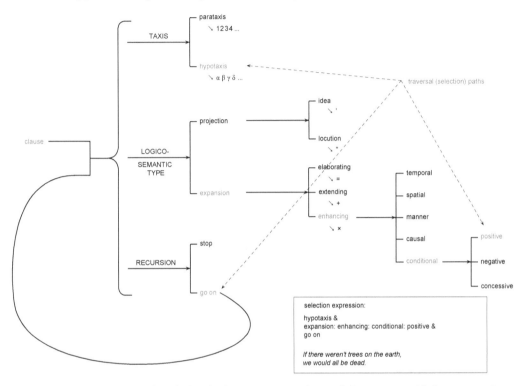

*Figure 5.2* Systemic traversal path for the hypotactic conditional clause nexus 'if there weren't trees on the earth, we would all be dead'

The two examples above are informal but give an indication of considerations that need to be taken account of in traversing system networks. In computational models, we must specify how system networks are traversed regardless of whether we are modelling generation or parsing (or more generally, text analysis). While some work has been done on systemic parsing, most work has dealt with text generation (e.g. O'Donnell and Bateman 2005; Bateman et al. 2019). In the Penman text generation system, we specified a procedure for traversing lexicogrammatical system networks – a **traversal algorithm**. One interesting finding was that simultaneous systems in system networks (as in Figure 5.2) can *in theory* be traversed in parallel; i.e. systems can be entered simultaneously and selections can be made simultaneously (see Tung, Matthiessen and Sondheimer 1988; Matthiessen and Bateman 1991). However, computer algorithms were typically restricted to sequential processing (unlike massively parallel processing in our brains), so we used a sequential traversal algorithm. It is presented as a flowchart-like represented in Figure 5.3.

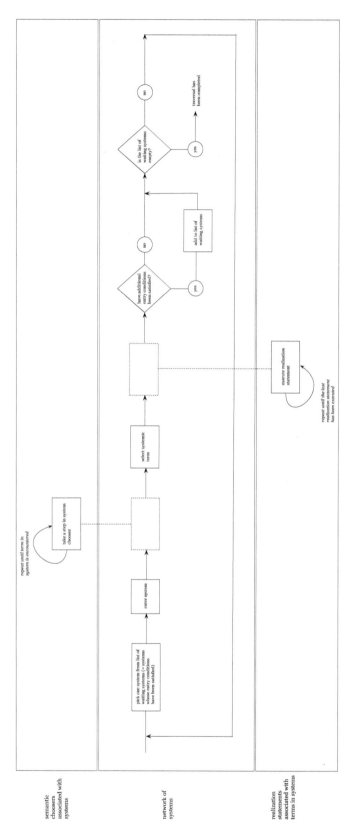

*Figure 5.3* A sequential algorithm for traversing system networks, adapted from Matthiessen and Bateman (1991: 106)

In this traversal algorithm, the traversal of systems in the system network is represented in the middle layer of the figure, and activities concerned with the basis for making the choice (see below) are shown above the network traversal itself and activities concerned with executing realization statements are shown below. As the system network is traversed,

- the traversal algorithm has to keep track of and update a list of systems whose entry conditions have been met – the list of waiting systems;
- the traversal will continue as long as there are systems on this waiting list, and will come to completion when no systems are left on the list;
- in each system, once entered, one of the two or more systemic terms must be chosen; in the algorithm in Figure 5.3, each system has a chooser – an expert on making the choice by consulting the semantics (see below);
- as a systemic term is selected, any realization statements associated with it will be executed.

As the traversal of the system network progresses, the systemic terms are, as noted, recorded as a selection expression, and the applications of the realization statements along the way are recorded as the gradually expanding function structure of the unit whose system network is being traversed.

The distinction between the system network and the algorithm for traversing the system network is one of fundamental importance. It reflects the view in computational linguistics since the 1970s that **declarative knowledge** and **procedural knowledge** need to be kept separate. The system network is 'declarative knowledge'; it is a resource without any procedural or processual commitments built in, so it can serve as a resource for different procedures or processes. Thus, while it can serve as a resource by generation algorithms such as the traversal algorithm sketched above, it can also be used as a resource by parsing algorithms (cf. Kasper 1988b; O'Donnell 1994; Fawcett 1994). And we can revise the traversal algorithm without changing the declarative representation of the system network. For example, to handle preselections of systemic terms, we can add a phase at the beginning of the traversal of backward chaining from preselected terms; e.g. if 'concessive' is preselected in the system network in Figure 5.2, the traversal algorithm would first determine that 'concessive' presupposes 'conditional', which presupposes 'enhancing', which presupposes 'expansion'. Such **path augmentation** is necessary to implement preselection 'from above' the unit whose system network is being traversed – above either in terms of stratum or in terms of rank (for further discussion, see e.g. Matthiessen and Bateman 1991).

## 5.2.4 Explicit Representations

The outline of the traversal algorithm in Figure 5.3 is actually quite informal. Still, it gives a hint of the need to spell out the steps in some degree of detail – as in a recipe written for children. I've already mentioned the challenge of recursive systems (as in Figure 3.33), noting that it was identified already by Henrici (1965). This is one of the issues that is brought out in the development of an account of the traversal algorithm; as an illustration, we can list a few such issues:

- **recursive systems:** the traversal algorithm needs to be able to differentiate between linear recursion (e.g. α β γ) and internal nesting (e.g. ααβ β), but this is not supported by the representation of recursive systems;
- **disjunctive entry conditions:** many systems have disjunctive entry conditions – does this mean that they could be entered more than once by the traversal algorithm?;
- **marking conventions:** as illustrated in the system networks in Figure 3.43 and Figure 3.45 above, systemic marking conventions are used to represent conditional relationships between systemic terms in different systems (see further Section 6.4.1 below), but how are they to be handled by the traversal algorithm? They presuppose a certain sequencing in the algorithm that is not made explicit by the entry conditions.

Such issues should be possible to address, and they have been discussed in the systemic functional literature concerned with computational modelling (e.g. Henrici 1965; Kasper 1988a,b; Matthiessen 1988a; Bateman 1989, 2008b; Teich 1999b)[2]. But they illustrate the general point that computational applications involving modelling of linguistic resources and processes place a demand on SFL in general and system networks in particular for a higher degree of explicitness as far as computational implementation is concerned. (There are, naturally, different kinds of need for explicitness that are inherent in different applications, like pedagogic explicitness in educational applications.)

Our response to this has been to propose a **model of the systemic functional metalanguage** used in theory, description and application that is stratified – just like language itself is stratified. The systemic functional metalanguage is a resource for engaging with language and other semiotic systems; like language, it operates in context and like language, it is stratified. When Halliday introduced system networks in the 1960s, he actually created a metalanguage that was stratified into the theory of axiality (i.e. of axial order), where the paradigmatic axis was given priority and the theoretical representation of system networks, and the representation of the theory axiality by means of system networks and realization statements: see Figure 5.4. This model had been worked out by the end of the 1990s, and has served as a resource in systemic functional metalinguistics since then.

Thanks to the work by Henrici (1965) in the 1960s and then to other researchers in the next decades, another stratum or level was added, viz. computational implementation. The addition of this level brought out issues with the theoretical representation of the kind mentioned above, but it also opened up the possibility of yet another level – a level of computational representation between the theoretical representation of system networks and the level of implementation in terms of some programming language (LISP being popular in computational linguistics and AI during this period). For example, system networks might be represented by production rules. (This happens not to be a good idea since production rules have an inherent procedural commitment which is undesirable in the representation of resources that should be usable by different processes of instantiation.)

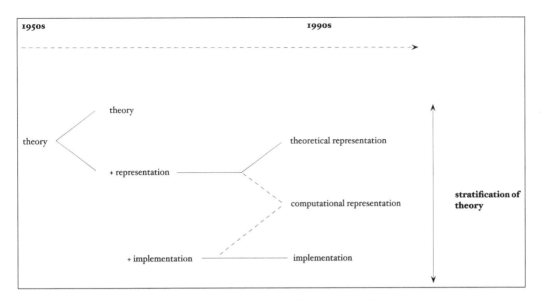

*Figure 5.4* The gradual increase in the stratification of the systemic functional metalanguage

Drawing inspiration from work on knowledge representation where comparable issues arise (e.g. Brachman 1979), I arrived at a model of the **systemic functional metalanguage stratified into four strata** or levels, represented diagrammatically in Figure 5.6. The theory of axial organization – more specifically of paradigmatic organization – is realized by the system network at the level of theoretical representation. There has been some exploration and experimentation (e.g. Hudson 1976; McCord 1975), but there is essentially only one type of theoretical representation in this domain of the metalanguage – the system network. One step in the direction of supporting realization by more explicit forms of representation is to specify system networks by means of algebraic notation, as shown informally in Table 8.1 and Table 8.2 of the Appendix. The algebraic representation of Halliday's original set of clause systems that became the basis of the Nigel grammar is provided by him in Halliday (2004b: 268–284), as illustrated in Figure 5.5. These representations were translated as lists in LISP files[3] in the Nigel grammar.

In contexts of computational modelling, the system network needs to be realized – re-represented – by some type of **computational representation** such as production rules, unification grammar, frame-based inheritance networks or typed feature structures (all of which have been discussed in the computational SFL literature). Significantly, at this level there is a choice among alternatives, each with different properties (I've already mentioned the problem with production rules: they embody an undesirable procedural commitment). And these alternatives have been used to represent other theoretical constructs besides system networks.

MOOD                    systems 200–299              201–209: mood type

200   # System:    MOOD
      Condition:   Node
      Input:       clause
      Outputs:     1 finite 0.9                      M. + Mood
                                                     Mood (+ Finite)
                                                     Mood ^ Residue

                   2 non-finite 0.1

201   # System:    MOOD TYPE
      Condition:   Node
      Input:       finite
      Outputs:     1 indicative 0.9                  M. Mood (+ Subject)
                   2 imperative 0.1

202   # System:    INDICATIVE TYPE
      Condition:   Node
      Input:       indicative
      Outputs:     1 declarative                     M. Subject ^ Finite
                   2 interrogative

203   # System:    INTERROGATIVE TYPE
      Condition:   Node
      Input:       interrogative
      Outputs:     1 yes/no                          M. Finite ^ Subject
                   2 wh-                             M. + WH
                                                     Wh ^ Finite

204   # System:    WH-FUNCTION
      Condition:   Node
      Input:       wh-
      Outputs:     1 wh- subject                     M. Wh / Subject
                   2 wh- other                       M. Wh / Residual
                                                     Finite ^ Subject

*Figure 5.5* Example of Halliday's (2004b) listing of systems represented algebraically (rather than graphically)

By another step in stratal descent, we arrive at the level of **implementation**. Again, we are faced with a choice – this time a choice among programming languages. As I mentioned above, LISP used to be the unmarked selection in computational linguistics and AI (Winograd's 1972, SHRDLU being one example) – it had, after all, been designed by John McCarthy as a list programming language. Then Prolog was added, and other alternatives were introduced such as C++; the choice of programming language would likely be influenced by the stage of software development, with a distinction between developmental research systems and software for everyday use (whether publicly available or more restricted). Today, linguists would very likely turn to Python; but there is a wide range of programming languages and to a certain extent, we can understand them in registerial terms, viz. as adaptations to contextual demands. For instance, in programming involving statistics, R is used across disciplines. In our area, there's been a general move towards object-oriented programming languages with some kind of type hierarchy. Thus earlier contributions where system networks were represented by means of production rules would not be repeated now since such rules embody an undesirable procedural commitment.

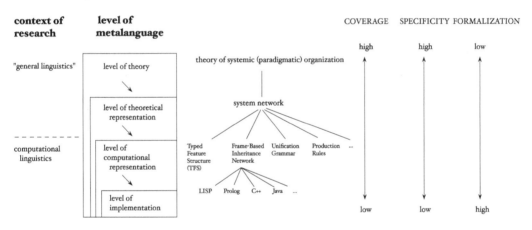

*Figure 5.6* The stratification of the systemic functional metalanguage, illustrated by reference to the paradigmatic part of the theory

As the diagram in Figure 5.6 shows, there are trade-offs across the levels of the metalanguage. I have suggested three scales, viz. coverage, specificity and formalization.

- **Coverage:** At the level of theory, coverage of linguistic and other semiotic phenomena is high since that is precisely what the theory has been designed to do for us, and in the case of SFL, it has been designed from the start to be a holistic theory of language supporting comprehensive descriptions of particular languages. At the level of implementation, coverage of semiotic phenomena is low simply because there are theoretical domains that we do not yet know how to specify in such a way that they can be implemented – which of course depends on advances at the intermediate levels of theoretical representation and computational representation.

- **Specificity:** At the level of theory, specificity is high since the theory has been designed as a theory of language and now also other semiotic systems; various theoretical constructs would certainly seem to be specific to language, like the spectrum of metafunction, the theory of lexicogrammatical metaphor, the theory of ontogenesis in three phases. At the level of implementation, the specificity is low since programming languages can be used to implement a great range of models in different domains.
- **Formalization:** At the level of implementation, formalization is high since the high degree of formalization is a pre-condition for implementation. All higher-level indeterminacies have been removed at this level, so that computer programmes can run without human intervention. At the level of theory it is low since the theory must be a resource with a holistic orientation, empowering us to observe and conceptualize language and other semiotic systems even where there is still a great deal of indeterminacy.

The trade-offs represented by these three scales are natural and inevitable. For example, in work on parsing, there is a need for 'robust' formalization of syntagmatic patterns (e.g. Bateman 2008b)[4], and researchers have experimented with computational representations that can support the view of the lexicogrammatical resources essential to parsing (cf. the early work by Kasper 1987, 1988a,b)[5] and with staged parsing, starting with a generally available non-systemic parser such as the Stanford dependency parser or with a parsed corpus (a 'tree-bank') (e.g. Honnibal 2004; Honnibal and Curran 2005; O'Donnell 2005; Costetchi 2013, 2020). Of course researchers always strive to increase coverage also at the lower levels, and this will place demands on the theory. In fact, the scales represent dialectic relationships. For example, insights from the application of computational representations in domains other than that of the system network as a theoretical representation of paradigmatic theory can lead to new insights. And as a theory, SFL is oriented towards general systems thinking – it is not designed to insulate language from other complex adaptive systems but rather to support the identification of general principles manifested in the different orders of system.

The stratified model of the systemic functional metalanguage is highly relevant not only to systemic computational modelling but also to theoretical and descriptive work dealing with subsystems of the overall system of language in context. Thus the demands placed on theory and description in the development of the interlevel aspects of semantics and also of accounts of semantic reasoning can be illuminated by accounts involving the representation of semantics by means of frame-based inheritance networks (e.g. Bateman 1990; Halliday and Matthiessen 2006). Similarly, it seems clear that accounts of context will need powers of representation that may not be met by system networks.

## 5.3 Educational Applications

There have been innumerable applications of SFL to educational contexts, and it is impossible to review them here, but they are well documented (Hasan, Matthiessen and Webster 2005/7; Halliday and Webster 2009; Rose and Martin 2012; Bartlett and O'Grady 2017; Thompson et al. 2019). The degree to which they have involved system networks has varied, but there is considerable scope for more educational applications based specifically on system networks, and I will focus on one 'classic' study where the system network plays the central role – a resource teachers can use in analysing their students' output to diagnose problems. This is Gibbons and Markwick-Smith's (1992) demonstration of the value of Halliday's systemic description of modality in English (first presented in Halliday 1970a, and then in revised form in the editions of Halliday's IFG, Chapters 4 and 10).

Their contribution can be seen against the background of Wilkins' (1976) proposal for a notional syllabus (cf. the much earlier contribution by Hornby 1954: Part 5 'Various concepts and how to express them'). Gibbons and Markwick-Smith's (1992: 39) emphasize the value of the systemic organization of the resources of modality[6]:

> To illustrate the nature and use of a Systemic semantic description, the area of modality in English will be used. This area traditionally causes considerable problems for second-language learners, particularly the meaning and use of modal verbs themselves. For comparison one must look at Wilkins (1976: 40–41). It can be seen that Wilkins' taxonomy is in essence a list, although the numbering indicates more organisation than Brumfit allows. Formal realisations are numerous and are examples only, and no semantic or stylistic differentiation is made among them. Some of the semantic contrasts are embedded in running text. All of this makes it difficult to base teaching on this taxonomy and renders the semantic analysis of error almost impossible.

They then present Halliday's (1985a) description of the system of MODALITY, and include his system network, which I have presented here in an adapted version together with a paradigm of examples: Figure 5.7. They comment on the advantage of the systemic description of modality, or any system of language, over a list of notions – even if it embodies some further organization; they write (p. 39):

> It can be seen that this is a system rather than a list, meeting one of Brumfit's strongest objections [to Wilkins's notional syllable, CMIMM]. It presents a clear picture of the major choices available in the English modality system. An important difference from Wilkins' model is that several semantic choices must be made simultaneously in order to arrive at a possible formal exponent [i.e. realization, CMIMM]. The left-to-right axis is one of increasing semantic delicacy. In as far as the language system itself can predict acquisition order (this must always be balanced against external demands and psychological factors such a processing constraints), it would predict the acquisition of the left-hand grosser distinctions before the right-hand more delicate semantic distinctions.

Based on these and other comments in their article, we can again see the value of the system network as a 'cartographic tool'; it gives us a very clear and explicit map of the resources in the language – resources that second/foreign language learners must gradually master. However, they then go on to demonstrate additional value of the system network: they show that it can be used as a **diagnostic tool** in the analysis of learner output – to 'analyse error and absence' as they put it. Using system networks like the system network of MODALITY, it is possible to analyse written (or indeed) spoken output by learners in order to profile their selections – making possible a comparison with the output by native speakers addressing the same tasks. In their article, the use an illustration drawing 'two compositions by a Hong Kong secondary school pupil with Cantonese as her mother tongue' (p. 41).

178 • *System in Systemic Functional Linguistics*

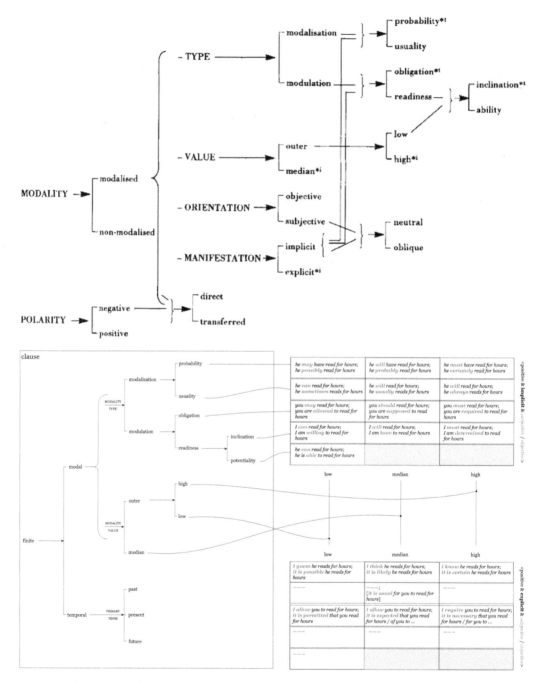

*Figure 5.7* The system of MODALITY in English (adapted from Halliday and Matthiessen 2014)

Gibbons and Markwick-Smith (1992: 43) report on the findings of their analysis of the two compositions:

> In the two compositions by the Hong Kong learner, there is a noticeable and sometimes inappropriate under-use of modality. Some areas of the modality system are reasonably represented however – she does not appear to have problems with adverbial exponents of

'usuality' – she uses *often, never, always* and *seldom*. Similarly, there are a number of correct uses of **explicit** markers of modality, both **objective** e.g. *it is possible that* and **subjective** e.g. *I think that, I find that*. It is in the **implicit** area – in practice this usually means modal verbs – that the problem is found. Notice, incidentally, the utility of the network display in detecting both developed and underdeveloped areas. Although the learner is of intermediate standard and has an extensive vocabulary, the only modal verb used correctly is *can* ...

Once problems in learner output have been diagnosed systemically, one can move on to a consideration of treatment, or 'remedies'; Gibbons and Markwick-Smith (1992: 44) comment: 'Using the system network, then, we are able to show that remedial treatment is required in the 'subjective implicit' expression of various types of modality.' They then go on to suggest four stages in an 'instructional cycle' (Gibbons 1989): Stage 1 – Focusing > Stage 2 – Recognition > Stage 3 – Guided practice > Stage 4 – Application. Throughout this staged process, the system network can serve as a point of reference – a map of the resources to be taught and learned.

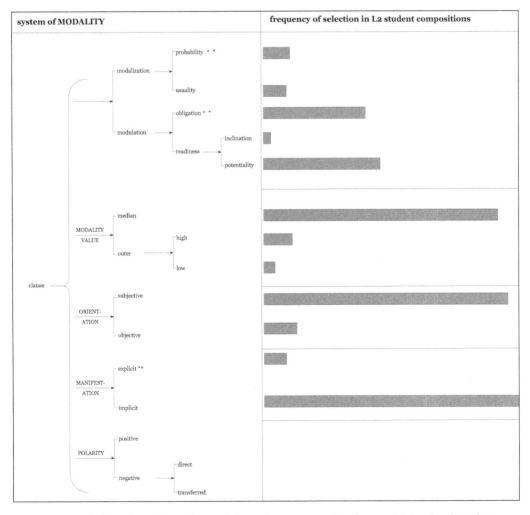

*Figure 5.8* Xuan's (2015) modal analysis of the written output by Chinese high school students learning English over a year of writing

180 • *System in Systemic Functional Linguistics*

Since I am concerned with the application of systems and system networks, let me leave Gibbons and Markwick-Smith's (1992) pedagogic advice at this point, and briefly refer to another educational linguistic study where the systemic description of modality has played an important role: Xuan (2015). Xuan's study is a pioneering longitudinal investigation of essays written by Chinese high school students writing in English over a period of one year. He analysed their output in terms of the system of MODALITY – among other systems, categorizing their written compositions throughout the year based on field of activity within context (using the account presented in Matthiessen 2015a; see also Figure 3.49 above). While he did not have access to a reference group of native English writers, his findings in the area of the system of modality also seemed to indicate both over-use and under-use: see the bar chart in Figure 5.8.

As we can see from Figure 5.8, the Chinese learners' choices were predominantly as follows: MODALITY TYPE: 'modulation', either 'obligation' or 'potentiality' & MODALITY VALUE: 'median' & ORIENTATION: 'subjective' & MANIFESTATION: 'implicit'. The most common realization was Finite: *can*, followed by Finite: *should*. Thus it would seem that over a period of a year's schooling, the learners did not vary their modal selections greatly. Why would this be the case? Xuan found that the writing tasks that the students were asked to undertake, either practice or test tasks, were registerially quite narrow, and there was no obvious principle of registerial progression over the year. He classified the ten writing tasks he investigated in his one-year longitudinal sample according to field of activity within context: see Figure 5.9. The two commonest tasks fell within contexts of sharing (3 tasks) and of recommending – more specifically advising (5 tasks). There was no obvious registerial progression in tasks that would have helped the students to gain access to and master more options within the system of MODALITY.

*Figure 5.9* Ten writing tasks given to Chinese high school students studying English over one year sorted according to fields of activity in Xuan's (2015) study

Xuan's (2015) study suggests that system networks representing the description of linguistic resources can be important diagnostic tools not only in tracking individual learners, but in tracking whole cohorts of learners longitudinally. The diagnostic outcomes may point not only to remedial tasks for individual learners or groups of learners but also to a reconceptualization of syllabi and curricula along registerial lines (cf. Byrnes, Maxim and Norris 2010). Based on Xuan's (2015) findings, one could imagine curricular revisions taking into account both the complementary learning opportunities presented by different registers and the progression from one register to another – a progression designed to enable learners to expand their mastery of the system based on their engagements with registers where different parts of the system are systematically deployed.

Thus in order to give students a gateway to the part of the system of MODALITY devoted to assignment of 'obligation', we might include texts in regulatory contexts – such as laws and legally bindings agreements. For example, consider the text score representing the analysis of an excerpt from the constitution of a parent-school association of a high school in Australia: Figure 5.10. As the text unfolds, it become increasingly clear that it will give students exposure to 'obligation' – and that it will give them examples of the most frequent use of the increasingly rare modal operator *shall* (cf. Leech 2003).

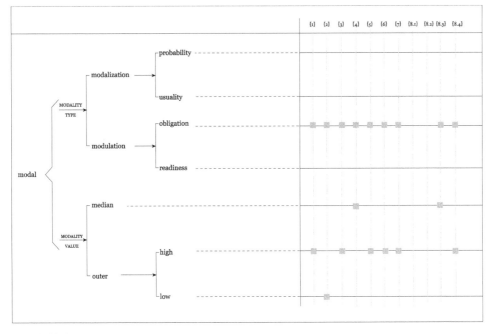

3. SCHOOL STAFF

[1] The Association **shall** not exercise any authority over the teaching staff or any matter relating to the control or management of the school. [2] School staff **may** become members of the Association. [3] The Principal of the school, or the Principal's nominee **shall** be a member, ex-officio, of the Association and all its committees.

4. MEMBERSHIP

[4] Membership **will** be open to all parents of pupils attending the school and to all citizens within the school community. [5] The Association **shall** maintain a register of members. [6] A person whose name appears in the register and who has paid the annual subscription **shall** be a member of the Association. [7] The register **shall** be updated after each general meeting by the Secretary or the Secretary's nominee. [8.1] If the name of a person has been omitted from the register [8.2] when that person is otherwise entitled to be a member [8.3] and their name **should** have been recorded in the register, [8.4] then that person **shall** be a member of the Association.

*Figure 5.10* Successive selections in the system of MODALITY in a text regulating a parent-school association

## 5.4 Translation and Comparative Studies

Translation has been an area of application in SFL since the 1960s, even going back to Halliday's (1956b) suggestion that a 'mechanical thesaurus' could be valuable in machine translation (for overviews, see Steiner 2005, 2015; Wang and Ma 2021[7]). If we take as a starting point the characterization of translation as the **recreation of meanings in context** (Matthiessen 2001), then this implicates systemic choice both in the interpretation of the source language text in its context of situation and in the generation of the target language text in its context of situation: Halliday (2012), Matthiessen (2014c). In other words, systems and system networks are central to conception of and research into translation (and interpreting) – including the systemic probabilities that are theoretically inherent in system networks, the value of which was emphasized by Toury (2004) in reference to Halliday's work on systemic probability.

Returning now to Halliday's notion of **pinpointing choice** in applications of SFL, let me quote him (Halliday 2012: 149–150) as he explains what this means in translation:

> When we talk of 'pinpointing the choice', in the theory and practice of translation, this means locating, within the systems of the two languages concerned, the moments of equivalence and shift that come to our attention. These may, of course, be almost any moments in any pair of texts that are related as source and target texts in translation, since equivalence on all dimensions is rather improbable. At the same time, the concept of translation, as process and as product, depends on the search for equivalence and the assumption that equivalence can be achieved in at least certain respects. There will always be a trade-off, such that we are able to say that, in the given context, the greatest value is carried by equivalence of this or that particular kind: usually in some combination of stratum and metafunction. (My first published translation was an English rendering of a Chinese song; since this was done for performance at a recital, it had to fit the rhythm and spirit of the music.) The translator will give these forms of equivalence priority, in making choices, and accept the resulting shift in other locations. All work of translating is the exercise of choice, conscious or unconscious. But then, so is every other performance of language.

In his study, Halliday gives a number of examples of pinpointing choice in translating from Chinese into English, but I will turn to an example involving the system of MODALITY in translation of *Alice in Wonderland* from English into German (presented in more detail in Matthiessen 2014c). If we assume heuristically that the German system of MODALITY is roughly the same systemically as the English system[8], then we can compare selections in the English source texts with selections recreating them in the German text, as illustrated in Figure 5.11. This figure shows the mapping of English selections onto German ones; it captures a tendency that I found for 'explicit' 'subjective' modalities of 'probability' to be translated as 'implicit' 'objective' ones: *I'm sure* is translated by the modal adverbs *sicherlich*, *bestimmt* or *wahrlich*. Having identified such apparently systematic differences, we should then go on to check the German system of MODALITY in this particular area and also investigate registerially comparable original texts in German. We should ideally include relative frequencies of selection, and the systemic probabilities we can induce from them.

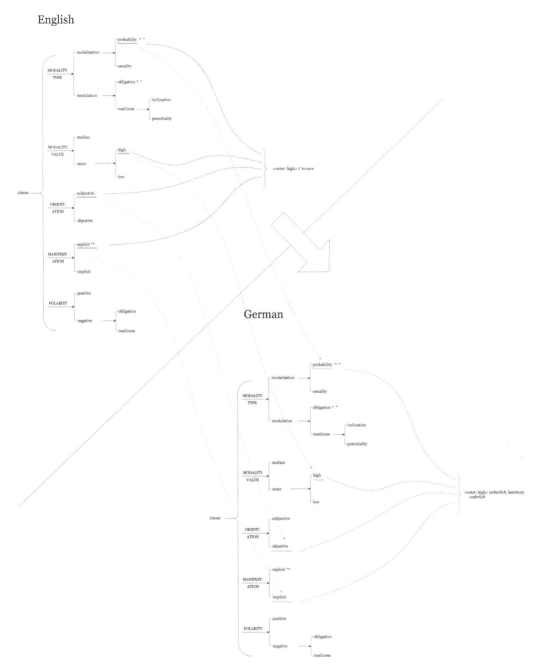

*Figure 5.11* Choices in translation – system of MODALITY in English, system of MODALITY in German

The choices recreated in translation shown in Figure 5.11 are lexicogrammatical although of course in a grammatical system that is semantically 'transparent'. But choices in translation are semantic choices in the first instance – semantic choices in context; and when we examine choices made by translators, we often need to ascend to semantics to examine choices in meaning and their environment one stratum up, in context. I will just give one brief example, drawing on an exploration of topographic procedures in English and German. In topographic procedures, readers are told to move around some region by walking or driving, and this procedure is interrupted at intervals by the introduction of places of interest along the way. How are such places of interest introduced into the text? There are a number of semantic strategies, shown in Figure 5.12: a place of interest can be introduced as the destination of movement or it can be represented as an entity encountered along the way, either subjectively by reference to what the reader will see or objectively by reference to the location of the place of interest. Both 'encountered' strategies are possible in both English and German, but English seems to prefer the 'objective location' option and German the 'subjective view':

English
In the Cathedral itself, **there is** the Chapel of Santa Llúcia, opposite the Archdeacon's Palace, which itself contains a Romanesque gallery with arches supported by 12$^{th}$- and 13$^{th}$-century columns.

German
In der Kathedrale selbst **kann** man die Kapelle Santa Llúcia (Heilige Luzie) **bewundern**, gegenüber dem Palast von l'Ardiaca (Erzdiakon). Heute noch **kann** man im Palast des Erzbischofs eine romanische Galerie mit Bogen **sehen**, die auf Säulen des XII. und XIII. Jh. ruhen.

English translation of the German version
In the Cathedral itself, you **can admire** the Chapel of Santa Llúcia, opposite the Archdeacon's Palace. Today you **can** still **see** a Romanesque gallery which rests on 12$^{th}$- and 13$^{th}$-century columns, in Archdeacon's Palace.

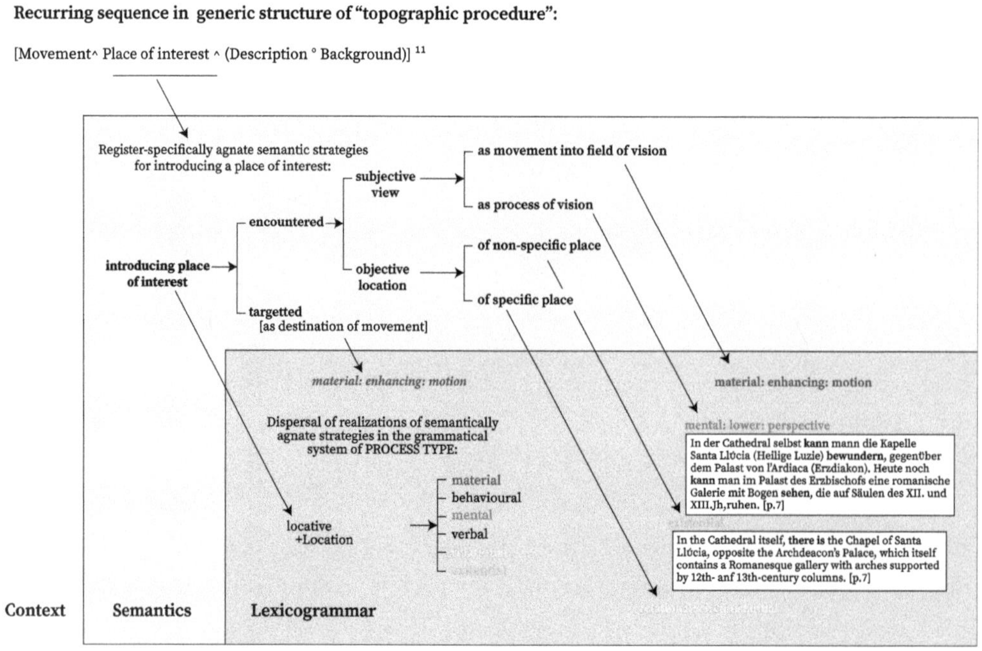

**Recurring sequence in generic structure of "topographic procedure":**

[Movement^ Place of interest ^ (Description ° Background)] [11]

*Figure 5.12* Semantic choices in the construal of Place of Interest in the contextual structure of topographic procedures

The contextual conditions under which the choices are made are obviously quite specific, but we can note that there is a 'convergence' in the grammar between 'existential' clauses and 'mental: perceptive' ones as configurations lending themselves to the presentation of the place of interest as New information towards the end of the clause: Theme/Place (cathedral) + New/Existent or Phenomenon (chapel).

The example given just now is most likely typical of choice in translation: when we translate, we choose among options in meaning in reference to the register that the source text instantiates and in reference to the **comparable register** in the target language that the text we are recreating instantiates. This principle was illuminated by three important systemic studies at the turn of the century, which have provided guidance since then: Teich (1999a), Lavid (2000) and Murcia-Bielsa (2000); see also Matthiessen, Teruya and Wu (2008).

For example, Lavid (2000: 74–75) reports on the 'realization patterns for requests' in 'administrative forms' in English, German and Italian. As far as the mood systems of these languages at the potential pole of instantiation are concerned, there is no immediately obvious reason why the languages should differ in their realization of the speech function of request (a delicate type of command), but they do. Lavid (2000: 74) characterizes the difference between English vs. German and Italian:

> The speech act of requesting action from users is the most frequent one in administrative forms. The English forms, which, as was explained above, have been written following specific guidelines which recommend the use of simple, direct and polite language, tend to minimise the social distance and to level out the social roles between the Administration and the users by using the *imperative* mood structure, often preceded by the politeness marker 'please', as in (1) below:

(1) Please tick all the boxes that apply to you. (DLAA2)

> By contrast, the Italian/German forms, produced in a socio-cultural setting where the administration is only now beginning to be sensitive to the users' needs, still opt for indirect patterns of realisation, which create a distant, impersonal tone. Examples (2) for Italian, and (3) for German illustrate this.

(2) La cartolina deve essere utilizzata anche per la segnalazione alta Sede INPS di inesattezze od emissioni nei periodi assicurative riportati sull'estratto.

'The card must also be used to inform the INPS office of any inaccuracy or omission in the insurance periods reports in the extract.' (INPS 2)

(3) Der Berichtigungsabschnitt muss bei der Landestelle NISF oder bei einem der Patronate der Provinz abgegeben werden.

'The claim for correction must be sent to the regional NISF office or to one of the Patronats of the province.' (COM 1)

The relative frequencies of the realization of request by either imperative or declarative (mood) in Italian, English, German instructional texts are set out in Figure 5.13, which is based on Lavid (2000: Figure 1, p. 74).

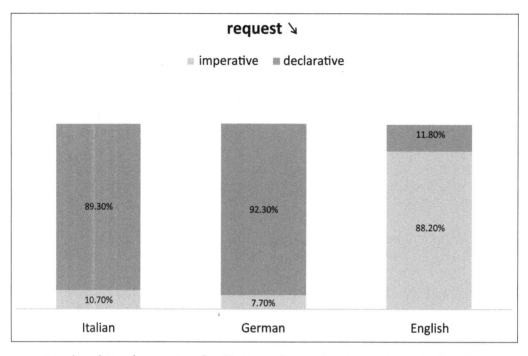

*Figure 5.13* The relative frequencies of realizations of request by imperative or declarative clauses in Italian, German and English, based on Lavid (2000: Figure 1, p. 74)

By taking the probabilistic nature of language into consideration and by conceptualizing registers also as probabilistic settings, it is thus possible to bring out potentially subtle differences among languages in registerial patterns. This is clearly information that is valuable to translators, and also to researchers developing and fine-tuning machine translation systems. (In the literature on machine translation, register has been discussed under the heading of 'sub-language', as in Kittredge 1987.)

## 5.5 Multisemiotic Studies

The applications considered so far have been concerned with language: the modelling of the system network and use of systemic descriptions in computational linguistics, systemic descriptions used to diagnose problems in language learner output and systemic descriptions in the characterization of the recreation of meaning in context through choice in translation. However, system networks have also turned out to be crucial in applications to **semiotic systems other than language** (cf. Section 3.5.2), as already illustrated by their use in the description of protolanguage and in the description of context (as a connotative semiotic system) in Chapter 2. In the description of protolanguage, we can abstract away from differences in syntagmatic realization – either vocalization or gesture (cf. Section 2.3 above); these syntagmatic patterns can vary and be of different kinds as long as they provide the resources for realizing systemic contrast (*valeur*). For example, in the case of the child studied by Halliday, at around 9 months, he had a protolinguistic system with two terms realized vocally (interactional 'let's be together'/ personal 'look, that's interesting') and three terms realized gesturally (instrumental, positive 'I want that'/instrumental, negative 'I don't want that'/regulatory 'do that') (Halliday 2004a: e.g. 91, 145). In this way, the expression plane was multimodal. This is the same aspect of system networks that made it possible for Halliday to integrate intonation into his account of both phonology and lexicogrammar (e.g. Halliday 1967; Halliday and Greaves 2008). Just as the paradigmatic organization of protolanguage can be abstracted away from the syntagmatic mode of realization as either vocal or gestural, so the paradigmatic organization of language can be abstracted away from the syntagmatic mode of realization, say the realization of terms in mood systems by intonation, by structural elements (e.g. modal particles) or by sequence (e.g. the relative sequence of Subject and Finite).

Thus system networks enable us to detach paradigmatic patterns from syntagmatic ones, and we can handle **different modes of syntagmatic patterns** as realizations of terms in systems as long as the terms are differentiated by the syntagmatic patterns. For example, the systemic contrast between 'declarative' and 'interrogative: yes/no' may be realized by a contrast in tone, falling/rising, a contrast in modal particle, e.g. no particle/interrogative particle, or a contrast in sequence, e.g. *it is/is it*. (For the importance of this in language typology, see Matthiessen 2004; Teruya and Matthiessen 2015.) This property has turned out to be crucial to their 'appliability' to semiotic systems other than language. System networks can be used to make the *valeur* of systemic contrasts explicit even if syntagmatic patterns are still beyond the reach of some kind of formalization. They thus help make the distinction between 'emic' and 'etic' contrasts clearer, which is a potential challenge in descriptions of semiotic systems other than language, as in the pioneering work by Birdwhistell (1952, 1970). For example, Birdwhistell (1952: 18–120) discusses whether facial expressions ('kines') are 'morphologically significant' or 'insignificant', which would be brought out in systemic representations (cf. discussion of comparable issues in Halliday's 1967, description of tones in English).

Table 5.2 Examples of systemic descriptions of semiotic systems other than language

| semiotic system | domain | reference |
|---|---|---|
| music | tonal harmony | Winograd (1968) |
| | semantics of intervals | Steiner (1988) |
| pictorial | images of various kinds | Kress and van Leeuwen (2006) |
| | narrative structures | p. 74 |
| | analytical structures | p. 104 |
| | interactive meanings | p. 149 |
| | composition | p. 210 |
| | images in children's picture books | Painter, Martin and Unsworth (2014) |
| | graphics | Lim (2004: 236) |
| graphology | typography | Lim (2004: 235) |
| | hyperlinks | Djonov (2008) |
| gesture | gestures accompanying speech | Martinec (2001, 2004) |
| gaze | video | Baldry and Thibault (2010: 171, 196) |

188 • *System in Systemic Functional Linguistics*

Among the various multisemiotic studies, I will only discuss a few of those where system networks have been a central part of the description (see Table 5.1).

## 5.5.1 Winograd's Systemic Description of Tonal Harmony

The first systemic description of a semiotic system other than language is almost certainly Winograd's (1968) systemic description of tonal harmony[9]; his system network for a chord is shown in Figure 5.14. While his pioneering account has not been picked up in multisemiotic, or multimodal, studies in SFL, it has been recognized in music theory.

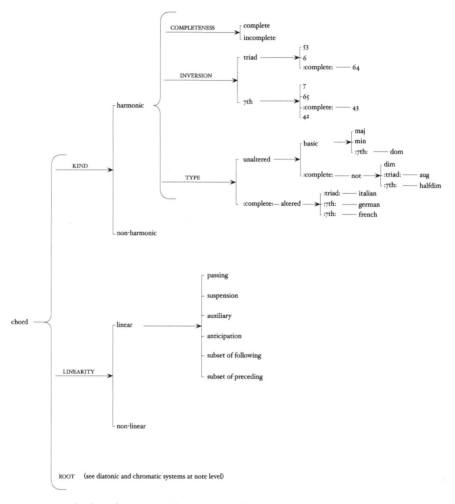

*Figure 5.14* Winograd's (1968) systemic description of a chord in music

As researchers began to investigate semiotic systems other than language based on SFL in the second half of the 1980s, some of them used system networks – notably, Kress and van Leeuwen (1996, 2006) presented their description of images as (what we might call) a pictorial system by means of system networks, and in our computational work (cf. Section 5.2) we also employed system networks in Multex, our multilingual text generation system capable of also presenting information using maps (e.g. Matthiessen et al. 1998).

## 5.5.2 Kress and van Leeuwen's Systemic Description of Images

As just noted, Kress and van Leeuwen use system networks to describe the pictorial meaning potential of images; as an illustration of their contribution, I have reproduced their systemic description of options in the depictive construal of narratives as Figure 5.15. A number of the labels they use are familiar from Halliday's description of the system of TRANSITIVITY in English, like 'process', 'circumstance', 'agentive', 'mental', 'verbal'. There is clearly an interesting issue as to how to interpret the system network. It would make sense to interpret it as a representation of the pictorial resources for construing our experience of a quantum of change narratively by means of an image; but 'processes' and 'circumstances' are in fact not mutually exclusive options: processes may be augmented by circumstances; Kress and van Leeuwen (2006: 72) write 'narrative images may contain secondary participants, participants related to the main participants, not by means of vectors, but in other ways'. Since this is the case, it would make sense to revise the system network to include two primary systems, one concerned with process types and the other with the option of representing a circumstantial augmentation. (And again, the different types of circumstance, 'setting', 'means' and 'accompaniment', are not mutually alternative options.) Arguably, the system network in Figure 5.15 is used like a taxonomy rather than like a full-fledged system network (cf. Section 6.2.1).

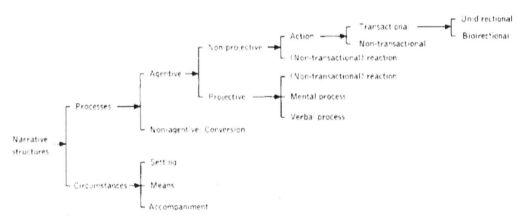

*Figure 5.15* Example of the use of a system network to describe an aspect of the depictive system, showing systemic options in the depictive construal of narratives – Kress and van Leeuwen's (2006: 74) 'narrative structures in visual communication'

Kress and van Leeuwen (1996, 2006) also provide realization statements associated with the terms in the system networks they present. But these realization statements are informal discursive ones, as can be seen from the realization statements related to the system network in Figure 5.15: see Table 5.3. They include realization statements that refer not to systemic terms but to 'participants' mentioned in realization statements associated with systemic terms. To make this important distinction easier to detect, I have adapted their table and separated into two columns, statements concerning systemic terms in their system network and ones concerning participants mentioned in other realization statements. I have also bolded mentions of participants and circumstances in the realization statements to make it easier to identify them (there is no realization statement given for 'Relay'). In the case of circumstances, they appear as systemic terms in the system network, and also mentioned in the realization statements associated with these terms.

In a way, the informal nature of their realization statements underlines the value in being able to free the specification of paradigmatic patterns from syntagmatic ones: even though it may not yet be possible to formulate realization statements comparable in explicitness to those used in descriptions of languages, researcher can develop systemic descriptions of semiotic systems other than language – as long as they include realization statements of some kind.

*Table 5.3* Realization statements (discursive specifications) associated with systemic terms in the system network reproduced in Figure 5.15 – adapted from Kress and van Leeuwen's (2006: 74–75)

| systemic term or participant | | realization statement |
| --- | --- | --- |
| unidirectional transactional action | | A vector, formed by a (usually diagonal) depicted element, or an arrow, connects two participants, an **Actor** and a **Goal** |
| bidirectional transactional action | | A vector, formed by a (usually diagonal) depicted element, or a double-headed arrow, connects two **Interactors**. |
| non-transactional action | | A vector, formed by a (usually diagonal) depicted element, or an arrow, emanates from a participant, the **Actor**, but does not point at any other participant. |
| | Actor | The active participant in an action process is the participant from which the vector emanates or which is fused with the vector. |
| | Goal | The passive participant in an action process is the participant at which the vector is directed. |
| | Interactors | The participants in a transactional action process where the vector could be said to emanate from, *and* be directed at, both participants. |
| transactional reaction | | An eyeline vector connects two participants, a **Reacter** and a **Phenomenon**. |
| non-transactional reaction | | An eyeline vector emanates from a participant, the **Reacter**, but does not point at another participant. |
| | Reacter | The active participant in a reaction process is the participant whose look creates the eyeline. |
| | Phenomenon | The passive participant in a (transactional) reaction is the participant at which the eyeline is directed; in other words, the participant which forms the object of the Reacter's look. The same term is used for the participant (verbal or non-verbal) enclosed in a 'thought bubble'. |
| conversion | | A process in which a participant, the **Relay**, is the **Goal** of one action and the **Actor** of another. This involves a change of state in the participant. |

| systemic term or participant | | realization statement |
|---|---|---|
| mental process | | A vector formed by a 'thought bubble' or a similar conventional device connects two participants, the **Senser** and the **Phenomenon**. |
| | Senser | The participant from whom the 'thought bubble' vector emanates. |
| verbal process | | A vector formed by the arrow-like protrusion of a 'dialogue balloon' or similar device connects two participants, a **Sayer** and an **Utterance**. |
| | Sayer | The participant in a verbal process from whom the 'dialogue balloon' emanates. |
| | Utterance | The (verbal) participant enclosed in the 'dialogue balloon'. |
| setting | | The **Setting** of a process is recognizable because the participants in the foreground overlap and hence partially obscure it; because it is often drawn or painted in less detail, or, in the case of photography, has a softer focus; and because of contrasts in colour saturation and overall darkness or lightness between foreground and background. |
| means | | The **Means** of a process is formed by the tool with which the action is executed. It usually also forms the vector. |
| accompaniment | | An Accompaniment is a participant in a narrative structure which has no vectorial relation with other participants and cannot be interpreted as a Symbolic Attribute (see Chapter 3). |

As I have noted, the realization statements are informal discursive ones. Unlike the realization statements used in the description of lexicogrammatical systems, they are not represented by means of operators such as 'insert', 'order', 'expand' and one or more operands, either functions such as 'Subject', 'Finite', and 'Mood' or systemic terms (features) such as 'bound', 'modal', 'nominal group'. Instead they refer to elements of an image such as objects like 'vector', 'arrow', 'dialogue balloon' that might be part of the menu of a drawing programme, representational phenomena such as 'participant', 'process', relationships between in particular 'participant' and 'vector' like 'emanate', 'be directed at', 'be fused with', viewer perspective including 'eyeline', 'background', 'foreground' and aspects of colour and brightness, e.g. 'saturation' and 'darkness/lightness'.

Some of these elements seem to belong to the expression plane, e.g. 'arrow', 'vector', 'emanate' while others seem to belong to the content plane, e.g. 'participant', 'process'. The differentiation would be clearer if it was made explicit for example by networking not only the content plane as but also the expression plane, as in Lim's (2004) system network description of 'graphics' and as in Martinec's (2004) system network description of gestures that accompany speech, referred to below in Section 5.5.4.

### 5.5.3 Multimodal Text Generation

In our computational multimodal work in the 1990s, we took a somewhat different approach from that outlined by Kress and van Leeuwen (1996). To enable us to develop an explicit model of how to generate texts (in English and Chinese) accompanied by maps, we chose to focus on particular registers, such as weather forecasts and the weekly epidemiological records, WERs, published by WHO. We produced system networks registerially tailored to such tasks, and defined graphic realization operator for graphic realization, or 'rendering', statements. In the registers we explored, it turned out that it was possible to describe the meaning potential of the multisemiotic combinations we worked with.

For example, in ideational semantic domain model of weather forecasts, we could describe the domain by specifying the domain in terms of sequences, figures and elements, using the same kind of representation of system networks that we had designed earlier for multilingual systems. In other words, we used the multilingual version of system networks (Bateman et al. 1991; Bateman, Matthiessen and Zeng 1999; Matthiessen 2018a) to represent the multimodal meaning potential of weather forecasts[10]. As an illustration, I have represented the multi-semiotic system network for figures in the domain of weather forecasts as Figure 5.16. Here the options included in the system network can be realized linguistically, and the options in the shaded partitions can also be represented cartographically. The same turned out to be the case when I modelled the domain of monitoring outbreaks of communicable diseases published by WHO (Matthiessen 2006b), summarized in Section 6.4.4.1.7 below in terms of complementarities across semiotic systems; but there are clearly registers where the overall domain model within the ideation based is determined by a semiotic system other than language, with language playing a subsidiary role.

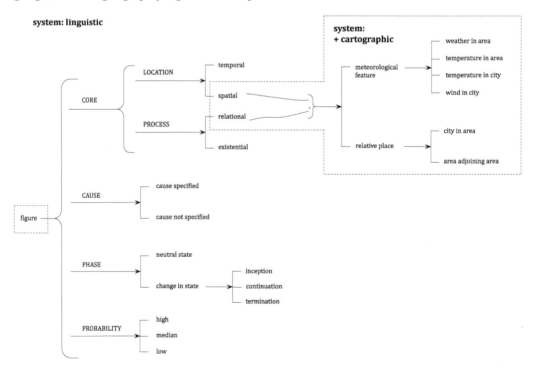

*Figure 5.16* Example of multisemiotic meaning potential, with partitions for the sub-potential that can be construed by weather maps (as well as by language), adapted from Matthiessen, Kobayashi and Zeng (1995)

As shown in n Figure 5.16, the semantic description of the domain of weather forecasting sketched by means of a system network is purely paradigmatic; it does not include realization statements. Thanks to the separation of the paradigmatic axis and the syntagmatic one in SFL, it is possible to represent the shared linguistic and cartographic potential by means of the system network itself, while we factor out the syntagmatic differences and represent them by means of distinct sets of realization statements. Such statements are of course necessary to relate the specification of the domain system to the syntagmatic realizations of terms in the system in texts and maps (in the register of weather forecasts); without them, it would not be possible to generate multimodal weather forecasts or any other kinds of multimodal document.

Realization statements consist of a **operator** and one or more **operands**, as shown for linguistic realization statements in Table 8.2 in the Appendix. Cartographic realization statements are concerned with the rendering of maps, for example [operator:] drawing [operand:] objects on the map and [operator:] plotting [operand:] objects [operand:] at locations. They are set out in Table 5.3 together with the established operators used in linguistic realization statements (as in Matthiessen and Bateman 1991). The two sets are arranged to indicate certain points of comparison, but exploring similarities and differences between the cartographic and linguistic modes of expression would obviously require a significantly more detailed presentation, and the point here is merely to illustrate the possibilities that are opened up when system networks with explicit realization statements are applied to the description of semiotic systems other than language, in conjunction with language.

*Table 5.4* Realization statements used in description of a cartographic and linguistic system for generating weather forecasts (adapted from Matthiessen, Kobayashi and Zeng 1995)

| cartographic realization statements | | | | linguistic realization statements | | |
|---|---|---|---|---|---|---|
| operator | operand 1 | operand 2 | operand 3 | operator | operand 1 | operand 2 |
| draw | object | | | insert | function | |
| paint | object | pattern | | preselect | function | term (in system network) |
| erase | object | | | | | |
| invert | object | | | order | # | function |
| | | | | | function | # |
| boundary | object | | | | | |
| combine | object | object | location | order | function | function |
| plot | object | location | | | | |
| overlap | object | object | location | conflate | function | function |

The domain of weather forecasts is characteristic of fairly restricted registers, and thus good as an illustration. We also used it in Halliday and Matthiessen (2006), where we offered a somewhat fuller account of the ideational semantics of the domain. Such restricted registers range over only part of the overall linguistic meaning potential, and they may deploy denotative semiotic systems other than language that have been adapted to the particular context of use in which they operate – as in the case of weather maps. When we need to increase the explicitness and formalization of the description of non-linguistic semiotic systems, focussing on particular registers can serve as a very practical way forward. But it is also a motivated one in that many semiotic systems are in fact fairly register specific, as noted in Matthiessen (2009b). Other simple examples include the semiotic system of time lines used in historical recounts, the semiotic system of flowcharts used in procedures, and of course system networks used in linguistic descriptions (cf. also Doran 2016). (For educational implications, cf. Mohan 1986.) The focus on register – or 'genre' – is central to the GeM model developed by John Bateman and his collaborators in a context of multimodal text generation but adapted to the task of explicit systematic analysis of multimodal discourse (e.g. Delin and Bateman 2002; Bateman 2008a; Bateman, Wildfeuer and Hiippala 2017).

### 5.5.4 Systemic Description of Gesture

While descriptions of semiotic systems other than language have tended to focus on images (Kress and van Leeuwen 1996) or 'displayed art' (O'Toole 1994), some important systemic studies have focussed on the exchange of meanings in face-to-face interaction, including a few pioneering studies: Martinec (2004) on gesture and Martin and Zappavigna (2019) on paralanguage. Martinec (2004) includes a helpful review of non-systemic functional work on gesture, positioning his own contribution relative to those by Adam Kendon, David McNeill and other leaders in the field. He raises interesting points that are foundational to the interpretation of gesture, centrally the issue of how systemic/instantial gestures are (location along the cline of instantiation, in our terms).

Drawing on a corpus of sports commentary (but tested against other registerial samples), Martinec (2004) offers part of the foundation for the description of gestures accompanying spoken language, especially indexical gestures (as opposed to emblematic ones) used in construing experience; cf. also Muntigl (2004). Importantly, he offers systemic descriptions of both the content plane and the expression plane, thus taking a step beyond descriptions other than language only providing systemic descriptions of one plane or the other (usually the content plane); and he specifies realization statements relating systemic terms in the content system network and the expression system network.

In terms of the content plane system, which he characterizes as 'semantics', he deals with aspects analogous to the lexicogrammatical system of transitivity and the semantic system of figuration in language. Specifically, he describes a system of process type and a system of location, called 'circumstance'. The process system provides a primary distinction between 'action' and 'state', with further elaboration in delicacy of 'action'.

The circumstance system is simply the choice between specifying the location of the process or not.

In terms of the expression plane, which he characterizes as 'form', Martinec postulates three simultaneous systems, one representing the expressive potential of the forearm, one of the hand and one of the fingers. He characterizes these as three ranks, but they are not ranks in the technical sense of SFL: they are not ranked units on a compositional hierarchy. Instead, they are comparable to three simultaneous phonological systems, oriented towards articulatory phonetics rather than auditory phonetics. For example, terms in systems in grammar are realized phonologically by TONE, and these tone systems cover the direction of the pitch movement, the width of the movement, and also options within the pretonic, if present (see Figure 3.39 above). The analogy with the system of TONE is motivated. Tone is an expressive resource in interpersonal service. In contrast, the aspects of gesture described by Martinec is an expressive resource in experiential service (he notes other metafunctional uses of gesture), and both have protolinguistic origins as expressive resources (Halliday 1992a). (If we take the expression plane of indexical gesture interpreted in terms of three simultaneous systems, it would seem that the forearm systems are primarily realizations of the nature of the process, and the hand and finger systems with the circumstantial specification of location, i.e. location or no location.)

Naturally, one question that arises is whether gesture can be integrated as an expressive resource in the description of language on the model of Halliday's integration of intonation – or whether it is better treated as a parallel semiotic system. However it is treated, it is clear from research outside SFL that the task of construing our experience of the flow of events may be parcelled out in different ways in different lexicogrammar-gesture combinations, as indicated by the comparison of English and Spanish reported by Lantolf (2010) (cf. also brief reference in Section 2.5). For example, in English it is perfectly possible and common to construe directed motion through space in a clause where the Process represents manner of motion (e.g. *he wobbled into the kitchen*). It isn't in Spanish, but Spanish speakers may represent the manner of motion gesturally. (For a systemic functional discussion, see Matthiessen 2015e, with references to the extensive non-SFL literature, developing original observations by Talmy 1985. For a study of translation of 'material' clauses of motion from English into Spanish, see Matthiessen, Arús-Hita and Teruya 2021.)

As noted above, Martinec provides systemic descriptions of both the content and expression resources of gesture. I have put these two system networks together in Figure 5.17, and represented the realizational relationship between one set of content terms and one set of expression terms. The full set of realizations are set out in Table 5.5, which I have compiled from the list of realization statements associated with terms in the content system provided by Martinec (2004: 211). (Representing all the inter-stratal realizational relationships diagrammatically would be quite visually informative – the kind of networking that would reveal patterns of double articulations, but it would make the figure hard to read unless the inter-stratal lines could be separated by colours or some other graphic resource.) From Table 5.5, we can see that Martinec's description brings out natural realizational relations between content and expression by means of the forearm, notably:

action ↘ movement
        active ↘ force
        passive ↘ no force
state ↘   hold

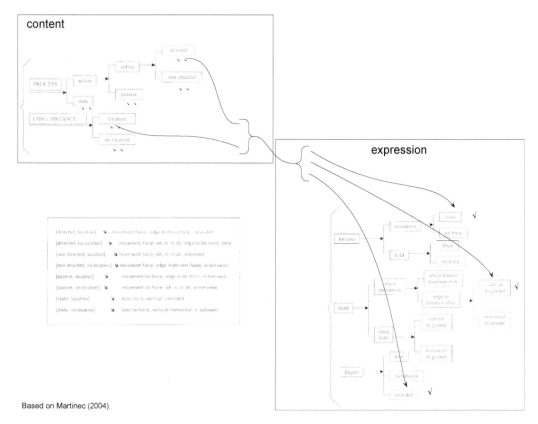

Based on Martinec (2004).

*Figure 5.17* System networks for gestures – content plane: indexical experiential gestures at the content plane; expression plane: forearm, hand and finger systems. Composition of system networks from Martinec (2004)

Thanks to Martinec's (2004) description, it is possible to begin to explore to what extent indexical gesture is integrated with spoken language in face-to-face interaction as an expressive resource just as intonation is (Halliday and Greaves 2008). And if we focus on gesture on its own, we can also ask whether it is possible to interpret it as a primary semiotic (like protolanguage), a higher-order semiotic (like post-infancy adult language), or an intermediate semiotic or possibly a different kind of semiotic. To address this, we would need to expand Martinec's description, but it is possible to make a couple of observations. (1) As described by him so far, indexical gesture can be interpreted as a bi-stratal system, content and expression (or in his terms, semantics and form), rather than a quadristratal one like language. In this respect, it would appear to be a primary semiotic like protolanguage. (2) However, unlike protolanguage, the expression plane is systemicized in his description. (In protolanguage, there may be a general distinction between vocalization and gesture, and as it develops, vocalizations may be deconstructed into articulation and prosody, but that would happen at a fairly late stage.) (3) At least certain realizational relations between content and expression appear to be natural (rather than conventional, or 'arbitrary'), as in the case of tone realizing interpersonal contrasts.

*Table 5.5* Relationship between content and expression in Martinec's (2004) description of gesture

| expression: | | | | content: | | | state |
|---|---|---|---|---|---|---|---|
| | | | | action | | | |
| | | | | active | | passive | |
| | | | | directed | non-directed | | |
| forearm | movement | force | | & location/& *no location* | & location/& *no location* | | |
| | | no force | | | | & location/& *no location* | |
| | hold | force | | | | | & location |
| | | no force | | | | | & *no location* |
| hand | when movement | whole hand in direction of movement | | & *no location* | & location | & *no location* | |
| | | edge in direction of movement | vertical to ground | & location | & *no location* | | & location & *no location* |
| | | | horizontal to ground | | | & location | |
| | when hold | vertical to ground | | | | | |
| | | horizontal to ground | | | | | |
| fingers | bent | | | & *no location* | | | |
| | in-between | | | | & *no location* | & location/& *no location* | & *no location* |
| | extended | | | & location | & location | | & location |

## 5.5.5 Function-Rank Matrices for Semiotic Systems Other than Language

Having examined the application of 'system' in the study of different semiotic systems other than language – or operating together with language, I would now like to take a step back to ask to what extent semiotic systems other than language can be described comprehensively by refence to systemic maps – specifically to function-rank matrices, since such matrices have played such a central role in the development of comprehensive descriptions of a reasonably wide range of languages.

During the second half of the 1980s and the 1990s, we find a number of pioneering systemic functional contributions to the systemic functional description of semiotic systems other than language appearing for the first time (the semiotic foundation having been provided by Halliday 1978a,b). Two complementary lines of research began to be developed. One was the framework by Kress and van Leeuwen (1990, 1996, 2006) – already touched on above; the other was the framework for analysing 'displayed art' developed by O'Toole (1994).

These two frameworks complement one another in important respects in the description of images – paintings in particular. While Kress and van Leeuwen introduce system networks that can be used in the analysis of images (as illustrated in Figure 5.15), O'Toole does not; but he establishes a rank scale in the description of the system of paintings, with four ranks: work > episode > figure > member, and he intersects this rank scale with a spectrum of metafunctions to construct a function-rank matrix, reproduced here as Table 5.6. Each cell is the 'semiotic address' of one or more systems. This depictive function-rank matrix can be compared with the linguistic one presented above as Table 3.6. The names of the functions are different from the names of the linguistic metafunctions, but the functions are comparable: ideational – representational, interpersonal – modal, and textual – compositional.

*Table 5.6* O'Toole's (1994) function-rank matrix for the systemic description of painting

| unit/function | representational | modal | compositional |
|---|---|---|---|
| work | narrative themes<br>scenes<br>portrayals<br>interplay of episodes | rhythm          modality<br>gaze<br>frame<br>light<br>perspective | gestalt:       proposition<br>framing        geometry<br>horizontals   line<br>verticals        rhythm<br>diagonals      colour |
| episode | actions, events<br>agents – patients – goals<br>focal/side sequence<br>interplay of actions | relative prominence<br>scale<br>centrality<br>interplay of modalities | relative position in work<br>alignment<br>interplay       of forms<br>coherence |
| figure | character      object<br>act/stance/gesture<br>clothing components | gaze       contrast: scale<br>stance                 line<br>characterization    light<br>colour | relative position in episode<br>parallelism/opposition<br>subframing |
| member | part of body/object<br>natural form | stylization | cohesion:       reference<br>(parallel/contrast/rhythm) |

O'Toole's (1994) cartographic approach to the characterization of the systems that make up different semiotic systems has proved to be helpful in systemic functional research into different semiotic systems and multisemiotic (or 'multimodal') texts, as can be seen e.g. in contributions to O'Halloran and Smith (2011), O'Halloran et al. (2016).

## 5.6 Summary of the System in Different Domains of Application

In the previous chapters, I examined the systemic approach in terms of theory – e.g. the fractal principle – and at work in description – e.g. the description of the key systems of English clause grammar: I have presented the system network as a mode of representing paradigmatic patterns as the primary form of axial order, and I have illustrated how they have been used in the description of the resources of language in context. Building on these accounts, in this chapter, I have turned to the systemic approach in applications and the system network as a tool that expands the potential for applications in different domains. Out of a wide range of applications, I have selected only four examples: computational modelling, educational applications (more specifically, the use of the system network as a diagnostic tool), choice in translation and the systemic description of semiotic systems other than language. These examples are applied in somewhat different ways, but they all illustrate the potential for the expansion of uses of the system network beyond language description and text analysis.

Many applications have a clear site or set of sites within an institution, as in the case of educational applications – and also applications in translation as a professional activity, in healthcare, administration, marketing, courtroom discourse and other areas studied in forensic linguistics. Other applications extend the uses of the system approach and system networks in such a way that they can be taken up in new applications across a wide range of institutional sites.

Computational applications have been of this kind, opening up the possibility of using system networks in text generation, text understanding and machine translation. So far such applications have generally remained within 'laboratories', but in future work they may find their way into applied AI. (In computational linguistics and natural language processing, there has been a shift away in the last couple of decades from the traditional approach of manual symbolic modelling to statistical NLP and machine learning techniques. In principle, this is compatible with SFL – in particular the systemic functional conception of language as a probabilistic system. One challenge is to articulate and then profit from the complementarity of such approaches and theory-empowered manual modelling.)

Multisemiotic, or 'multimodal', applications have similarly increased the potential not only for MDA, 'Multimodal Discourse Analysis', but also for work in institutional settings where such analysis can lead to insights that can inform future applications, e.g. Zhang's (2018) comparative study of public health posters in Hong Kong and New York.

Against the background of systemic theory, description and application, I will turn to challenges to and possibilities for the systemic approach in the next chapter.

# Chapter 6

# The System: Challenges and Possibilities

In the previous chapters, I have presented the systemic functional conception of language, and also of other semiotic systems, and illustrated how system networks have been used to represent ontogenesis and learning how to mean (Chapter 2), to describe all of the strata of language in context (Chapter 3), to map out the resources of language (Chapter 4) and to engage in different fields of application (Chapter 5). Along the way, I have identified various challenges such as the interpretation of recursive system networks used in the representation of logical resources and of marking conventions while I have highlighted possibilities opened up by the systemic angle of approach and the representation of axial order in language by means of system networks. In this chapter, I will focus on both challenges and possibilities, starting with a review of the benefits of what we might call the 'systemic turn' in linguistics contributed by systemic functional linguistics as a way of understanding language and other semiotic systems as resources.

## 6.1 Orientation of Axial Patterns

The notion of system in Systemic Functional Linguistics goes back to pre-SFL days – to Firth's system-structure theory. Halliday's 'transformation' of this theory into one where system is given priority over structure – where the paradigmatic axis is treated as primary in the modelling of axial order and syntagmatic patterns are derived by means of realization statements – was introduced almost six decades ago. Firth's system-structure theory was a variant of the European structuralist approach to axiality – the differentiation of the paradigmatic and syntagmatic axes as modes of linguistic order. In this approach, there is an emphasis on the paradigmatic axis, but the two axes are balanced, given equal weight.

In contrast, in US American structuralism, the syntagmatic axis is treated as primary, as in American structuralist accounts of phonology and morphology. As attention shifted to syntax and Chomsky (1957) introduced what was to become generative linguistics, generative linguists concentrated on rule systems for specifying syntagmatic patterns. In these rule systems, paradigmatic relations were in a sense parasitic on syntactic structures. For example, many transformational rules can be interpreted as paradigmatic relations stated in syntagmatic terms, relying on the metaphor of transformation (which had of course also been used in traditional grammar). The fact that many transformations in fact represent paradigmatic relations in syntagmatic terms is reflected in the re-interpretation of transformations as meta-rules in Generalized Phrase Structure Grammar (GPSG; Gazdar et al. 1985) in order to create a non-transformational representation of grammar. In other words, one way of viewing paradigmatic patterns in relation to syntagmatic ones is that they are of a more abstract order; they are 'meta' to syntagmatic structures.

In contrast with both European and American structuralists, Halliday's unique contribution was to make the paradigmatic axis primary. Focussing on this axial shift, Halliday (1966a/2002) makes this move in terms that could make sense to linguists basing their theory of grammar on the syntagmatic axis. He makes a distinction between two kinds of syntagmatic specifications, viz. syntagms and structures. Syntagms are 'arrangements of classes in sequence' and structures are 'configurations of functions'. He then begins to explore paradigmatic patterns; he writes (1966a/2002: 108–112), referring to syntagmatic specifications:

> While many other formulations are possible, the recognition in some form of other of two distinct types of representation, linked by some form of 'realization' relation, is relevant to the understanding of syntagmatic patterns, and the distinction can be made and discussed solely in terms of relations on the syntagmatic axis. Clearly, however, it is relevant also to relations on the paradigmatic axis. It may be helpful to relate this point to the distinctions made by Hjelmslev and by Firth. [...] Firth likewise makes a terminological distinction, referring (1957: 17) to syntagmatic relations as relations of structure and to paradigmatic relations as relations of system.
> [...]
> The paradigmatic contrasts associated with a given, defined environment may be thought of as being accounted for either in a single representation of 'deep' grammar, in which are incorporated both syntagmatic and paradigmatic function, or in a separate form of statement, distinct from, but related via the specification of the environment to, the statement of syntagmatic relations. Firth's concept of the system embodies the second approach. The **system** may be glossed informally as a 'deep paradigm', a paradigm dependent on functional environment; in a sense, and *mutatis mutandis*, the relation of system to paradigm is analogous to that of structure to syntagm as these terms were used above. [...] A system is thus a representation of relations on the paradigmatic axis, a set of features contrastive in a given environment. Function in the system is defined by the total configuration: for example 'past' by reference to 'present' and 'future' in a three-term tense system, as structural function is defined by reference to the total structural configuration for example 'modifier' by reference to 'head'.
> If paradigmatic relations are represented separately in this way, this implies that the full grammatical description of a linguistic item should contain both a structural and a systemic component. It may be useful therefore to consider the notion of a **systemic description** as one form of representation of a linguistic item, the assumption being that it complements but does not replace its structural description.
> [...]
> For any set of systems associated with a given environment it is possible to construct a **system network** in which each system, other than those simultaneous at the point of origin, is hierarchically ordered with respect to at least one other system.
> [...]
> Systemic description may be thought of as complementary to structural description, the one concerned with paradigmatic and the other with syntagmatic relations. On the other hand it might be useful to consider some possible consequences of regarding systemic description as the underlying form of representation, if it turned out that the structural description could be shown to be derivable from it. In that case structure would be fully predictable, and the form of a structural representation could be considered in the light of this.

This long passage by Halliday shows his attempt at the time to make the foundation of systemic grammar accessible to linguists focussed on structure, starting with syntagmatic axis. This is quite different from the way in the systemic functional conception of grammar, and of language more generally, that has now become familiar. The starting point is the conception of language as a resource for making meaning – a meaning potential; and this interpretation of language 'invites' an approach where the paradigmatic axis is given priority. This was indeed the way in I chose in Chapter 2, showing how the paradigmatic interpretation of language as a resource lends itself to an account of language development as learning how to mean. Was Halliday's syntagmatic gateway to the theory of the paradigmatic axis as primary, characterized as 'deep grammar' successful at the time? The evidence suggests that it was not. When we discussed this formative period of early SFL, Michael Halliday emphasized to me that the article was designed to be accessible to generative linguists – hence the notion of paradigmatic relations 'deep grammar', and he went on to note that Paul Postal had entirely misunderstood system networks as some kind of strange version of phrase structure rules. (This was of course the decade during which generative linguists seemed to be on a mission to discredit other linguistic theories, one strategy being to interpret them according to their own conception of a linguistic theory.)

To recap, I have summarized the conception and treatment of axiality, of the paradigmatic axis and the syntagmatic axis, in Table 6.1. (For further detailed discussion along these lines, see Matthiessen, forthcoming b; Matthiessen et al., forthcoming; Matthiessen et al. 2018.) The column headings represent the possible foregrounding of axiality – the paradigmatic axis is treated as primary, the syntagmatic axis is treated as primary, or the two are treated as balanced. The rows specify (1) linguistic theories and schools representative of the three different positions, and (2) the specification of paradigmatic and syntagmatic patterns in terms of the three different positions.

Table 6.1 Linguistic theories and schools in relation to their focus on axiality, the differentiation of and specification of paradigmatic and syntagmatic patterns

|  |  | axial primacy: | | |
|---|---|---|---|---|
|  |  | paradigmatic axis primary | balanced | syntagmatic axis primary |
| linguistic theories and schools | | *Systemic Functional Linguistics* (SFL) | European structuralists, including Firthian system-structure theory and also, in this respect, Sydney Lamb's Stratificational Linguistics | US American structuralists, and then generativists |
| specification of axes | paradigmatic axis specified by | systems of options, represented by system networks | Firth: syntagmatically local systems located in places in syntagmatic specifications[1] | alternation in syntagmatic rule systems (e.g. transformations, metarules) |
| | syntagmatic axis specified by | realization statements attached to terms in systems | structures | syntagmatic rule systems |

If the topic of this book had been the different conceptions of and approaches to patterns in language in terms of axiality – in terms of the differentiation of paradigmatic patterns and syntagmatic ones, I would trace the history of ideas and add many threads to the discussion. For example, in the domain of word grammar (morphology), Robin's (1959) addition of word-&-paradigm to supplement Hockett's (1954) syntagmatically-oriented distinction between item-&-arrangement and item-&-process is very helpful. But the topic could and should be illuminated by a wider view – for example, exploring Roget's essentially paradigmatic interpretation of lexis, Hjelmslev's renaming of Saussure's 'associative relations' (evocative of psychoanalysis) as 'paradigmatic relations', the Apoha in the Buddhist theory of meaning (Prakasam 1985: Chapter 11), Jakobson's (1949) fundamental misstep in reinterpreting paradigmatic values in phonology and feature components of phonemes ('distinctive features', imported into generative phonology), Heller and Macris' (1967) insights embodied in their 'parametric linguistics', the syntagmatic orientation in the conception of 'probabilistic linguistics' offered by Bod, Hay and Jannedy (2003). This further exploration of patterns in language in terms of axiality in the history is very tempting to pursue (especially in view of the role it played in my own early attempts to come to terms with apparently irreconcilable insights into language; cf. Matthiessen 2015b; Matthiessen et al., forthcoming); but I'll resist this temptation and now turn to the benefits of the systemic turn, presented by Halliday (1966a) to linguists viewing language through the 'lens' of syntagmatic patterns.

## 6.2 The Benefits of the Systemic Turn

The conception of language as system in the sense of prioritising the paradigmatic axis and of representing paradigmatic organization by means of system networks has led to new possibilities and insights, in terms both of the general theory of language in context and of descriptions of particular languages. There is now an extensive body of both theoretical and descriptive experience with, and results from, this approach to the conceptualization and representation of the organization of language in context and now also of that of semiotic systems other than language. I have discussed the new possibilities and insights in various places throughout the book, but let me list a number of central ones here:

- Halliday's systemic description of the lexicogrammar of English – the first ever of any language in the history of linguistics led to his discovery of clusters of systems (Section 3.2.1.1), which prompted him to develop his theory of **metafunction**.
- Halliday's systemic theory enabled him to conceptualize and represent language as an inherently **probabilistic system** (Section 4.4) – one that could be studied quantitatively once it became possible to compile corpora of a reasonable size (e.g. Halliday and James 1993).
- Halliday's invention of the system network as a representation of paradigmatic organization enabled him to integrate **intonation** (and prosodic phonology more generally) into the overall account of language even though it had been difficult for linguists to accommodate in syntagmatically based theories (e.g. Halliday 1967; Halliday and Greaves 2008; Smith and Greaves 2015).

- Halliday's systemic orientation enabled him to conceive of **lexicogrammar as a continuum** along the cline of delicacy (see Section 3.2.1.5) rather than treating grammar (syntax and morphology) and lexis as separate components or modules (which is how they tend to be conceived of in the commonsense folk model of everyday language users – backed up by Bloomfield's, 1933, conception of the lexicon as a repository of idiosyncratic information).
- Halliday's focus on system (rather than on structure) gave him unique insight into the **ontogenesis** of language – into how young children learn how to mean, starting with an initial phase of a protolanguage that they construct in interaction with their care givers, their immediate meaning group (Chapter 2), rather than starting with 'first words' (which don't appear until children make the transition from protolanguage to post-infancy adult language).
- Halliday's design of system networks has made it possible for him and other systemic functional linguists to develop comprehensive descriptions of particular languages – comprehensive up to a certain point in delicacy, and to apply **systems thinking** to such description, leading to the discovery of **fractal systems** such as the system of logico-semantic type and the thematic principle (Section 3.2.1.3).
- Halliday's system network representation has made it possible for us to model multilingualism by means of **multilingual system networks**, where both potential shared across languages and language-specific resources are represented (Bateman, Matthiessen and Zeng 1999; Matthiessen 2018a; see further Section 6.4.2 below), and also **multimodal system networks** (see Section 5.5.3 above).
- Halliday's invention of the system network as a representation of paradigmatic organization has enabled other scholars to develop descriptions of **semiotic systems other than language** with very different modes of expression such as gesture, painting and music (Section 5.5).

These possibilities and insights are shown diagrammatically in Figure 6.1. I have designed it to bring out the way that the choice of the 'paradigmatic base' opens up new possibilities of representing axial order leading to new insights. (See also Matthiessen 2015b, for a discussion of a version of this diagram and Matthiessen et al. 2018, on Halliday's 'axial re-think'.)

## 6.3 System Networks, Taxonomies and Flow Charts

We can learn a good deal about paradigmatic organization and system networks as a form of representation of this mode of organization by engaging in 'metalinguistic translation' – by translating other forms of representation by means of system networks and by translating system networks by means of other forms of representation – typically computational ones (but cf. also Lamb 2013). There have been a number of solutions to the task of representing system networks in computational models – by production rules, typed feature structures, and other computational forms of representation: see Section 5.2.3 on explicit representations (Figure 5.6).

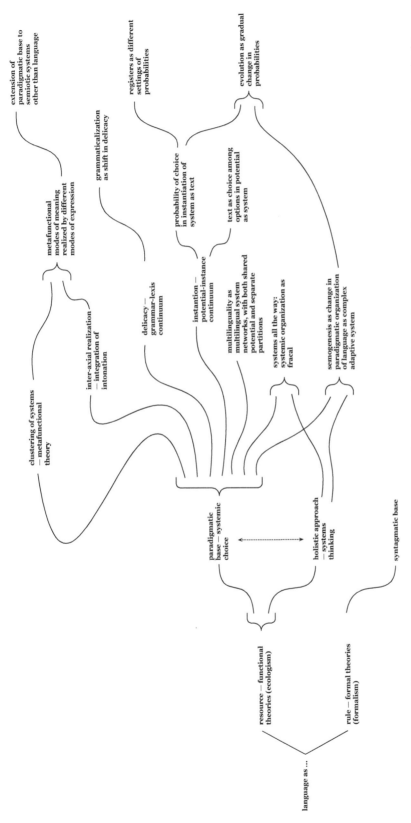

*Figure 6.1* Conception of language as resource – possibilities opened up by modelling it based on paradigmatic organization and systems thinking

### 6.3.1 System Networks, Taxonomies and Mind Maps

System networks are not taxonomies, nor are they decision trees. They embody simultaneous systems and complex entry conditions that may involve disjunctions and/or conjunctions of systemic terms, as illustrated in e.g. Figure 3.8 (e.g. disjunction of 'imperative' and 'declarative' in the entry condition of the system of MOOD TAGGING), Figure 3.13 (conjunction of 'non-predicator theme' and 'focussed' in the entry condition of the system of THEME REPRISE). Here it is important to remember that system networks were developed to represent language as a meaning potential. Halliday (2013: 21) emphasizes this aspect of system networks:

> A system network is the theoretical representation of a potential, the potential that is inherent in some particular set of circumstances; since a language is a resource for making meaning, I referred to it as a **meaning potential** (Halliday 1973). The network may be read either procedurally, with meaning as choosing (in circumstance a, choose either x or y or z), or declaratively, with meaning as choice (in circumstance a, either x or y or z is on the cards); 'system' is really short for 'system-&-process'. The network is not a schema of classification – it cannot be reduced to a strict taxonomy; rather, it offers a model, or map, of what human populations are doing when they mean.

Thus system networks cannot be translated straightforwardly into taxonomies – including 'mind maps'. Since mind maps are available through various applications, they can provide a quick and easy way of displaying system networks as if they were taxonomies, possibly enhanced with descriptions and examples. This is illustrated by the mind map display in Figure 6.2 (a). It represents the clause systems of THEME, of MOOD and other interpersonal systems and of TRANSITIVITY. The interpersonal clause systems can be compared with the interpersonal system network of the clause set out in Figure 3.8 above. In addition to the possibility of using the mind map representation to navigate around the systemic description and view any attached information – metadata, e.g. descriptions and examples, one can also choose another mode of visualization of the same data, e.g. a radial display, as in Figure 6.2 (b). This turns out to be very helpful in the development of systemic descriptions since alternative visual representations make it possible to view different aspects of the description. For example, the radial display makes it possible to identify varying degrees of delicacy across the description since the layout is uniform throughout, whereas the mind map display makes it possible at least to 'simulate' systemic interdependencies. (A possible analogy would be D'Arcy Thompson's, 1917, geometric transformations of drawings of animals, like his well-known fish transformations in Chapter XVII.) Importantly, if the mind mapping application is powerful enough, it will allow user to export the data in different formats including spreadsheet representation, which can then be imported into a database, and slide presentations.[2]

# The System: Challenges and Possibilities • 207

(a) Mind map diagram

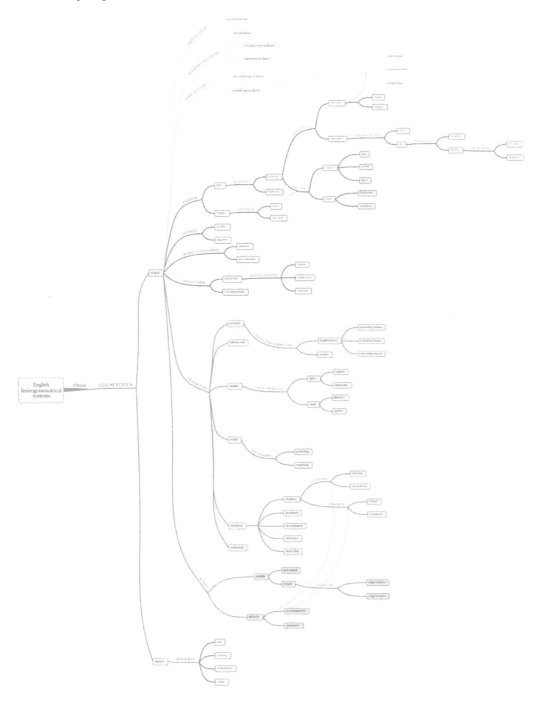

(b) Radial display

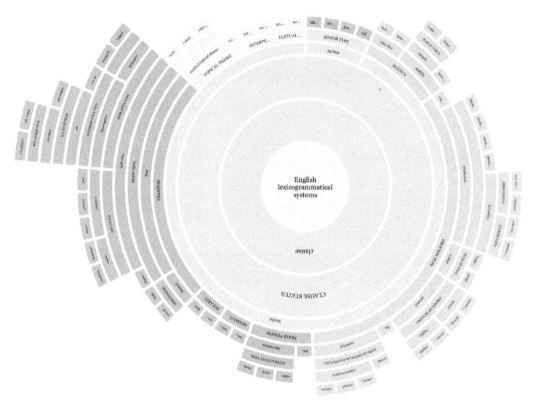

Figure 6.2 A 'mind map' version of English clause systems, (a) visualized as a mind map, and (b) as a radial display

The mind map in Figure 6.2 captures the simultaneity of textual, interpersonal and experiential systems, but it does not and cannot distinguish between simultaneous systems and contrasting terms within a given system – except that I have used branch labels to represent system names like TEXTUAL THEME, FREEDOM, and PROCESS TYPE. The mind map can show steps in delicacy, but it cannot show complex entry conditions. I have simulated complex entry conditions with arrows directed at branching points, e.g. the systemic contrast in DEICTICITY between 'temporal' and 'modal' emanates from 'declarative', but also has an arrow directed at it emanating from 'imperative' since MOOD TAGGING is available in either 'declarative' or 'imperative' clauses.

As the example in Figure 6.2 illustrates, there is thus a *loss* of information when we 'translate' system networks into strictly taxonomic representations. However, obviously, strict taxonomies can be translated into system networks even though the opposite is not the case; but such translation may involve some re-arrangement, as when the same taxonomic distinctions are repeated in more than one taxonomic location precisely because taxonomies do not allow simultaneous systems or disjunctive entry conditions to capture systemic sharing of contrasts.

People often think in terms of taxonomies rather than system networks, and this even applies to people who are linguists. Thus in their review of critical evaluations of

Doug Biber's 'MD methodology', McEnery and Hardie (2012: 114) comment on the choice of features to include in the automatic analysis of corpora:

> So we might argue that the MD methodology could be more solidly founded if based on a selection of features which is both *principled* and *exhaustive* – a standard which Biber's feature-lists approach but do not reach. How might such a fully motivated list of lexico-grammatical features be derived? At this point we move into the realm of hypothesis. However, one possible approach is to consider the functions of a language as a feature tree. This could start at the very high level of nominal components versus verbal components (since the noun–verb distinction is one of the most universal features of language structure), and then diversify from there, with attention to contrasting linguistic options and category alternatives at each branch in the tree. Figure 5.2 illustrates part of what such a feature tree, rooted at the most absolutely general linguistic function (expression of 'meaning' in the very broadest sense), and containing several of the features Biber in fact includes in his MD model for English, might look like.

Their Figure 5.2 is a 'fragment of a feature tree for English'; formally, it is a strict taxonomy, with a first taxonomic split between 'actions (verbs)' and 'entities (nouns)' as an illustration. They go on to comment (still p. 114):

> It would be conceptually straightforward, if practically extremely challenging, to develop an ordered tree that could encompass all of the features used by Biber, that would be consistent between languages at the upper levels, and would make it obvious where features have been overlooked.

Their suggestion to organize features in terms of feature trees appeared around 45 years after Halliday (e.g. 1963b, 1964, 1966a, 1967/8) had introduced system networks in linguistics and used them in systemic descriptions precisely of the kind that could guide corpus investigations along the lines McEnery and Hardie suggest – except that system networks are representationally more powerful than feature trees. Since the 1960s, system networks have been used extensively in the description of English and quite a range of other languages: the extreme practical challenge they note has already been met innumerable times, also in computational applications. Thus when they write (p. 115): 'surely, a comprehensive feature set should be the ideal starting point for the MD method', we might consider the alternative: surely, comprehensive system networks (of 'features', i.e. systemic terms) 'should be the ideal starting point for the MD method'. Such starting points are available for a growing number of languages from different genetic families and with different typological characteristics (see e.g. Teruya and Matthiessen 2015; Mwinlaaru and Xuan 2016; Kashyap 2019).

## 6.3.2 System Networks and Flow Charts

Like taxonomies, flow charts may be able to be translated into system networks, but this raises the interesting issue of what they represent in the first place. If flow charts are used to represent some aspect of the meaning potential of language, then re-representing them by means of system networks can be a helpful and illuminating exercise. As an illustration, I have chosen Ervin-Tripp's (1969) discussion of address systems in general and specifically her detailed flow chart representation of 'an American address system', more specifically her 'rules', which 'seem to apply fairly narrowly within the academic circle I know' (p. 97). This example also serves as an illuminating illustration of the description of an interpersonal linguistic system and at the same time the tenor considerations within context that it evokes since the interpersonal choices enact distinctions in tenor. Ervin-Tripp's (1969: 95) flow chart representation is reproduced here as Figure 6.3.

Ervin-Tripp refers to Brown and Ford's (1964) 'pioneering and ingenious research on forms of address in American English, using as corpora American plays, observed usage in a Boston business firm, and reported usage of business executives' and then, building on their description, presents her own account (1969: 94):

> Expanding their analysis from my own rules of address, I have found the structure expressed in the diagram in Fig. 1 [reproduced here as Figure 6.3, CMIMM]. The advantage of formal diagraming is that it offers precision greater than that of discursive description (Hymes 1967). The type of diagram presented here, following Geoghegan (in press), is to be read like a computer flow chart. The entrance point is on the left, and from left to right there is a series of selectors, usually binary. Each path through the diagram leads to a possible outcome, that is, one of the possible alternative forms of address.
> [...]
> The person whose knowledge of address is represented in Fig. 1 is assumed to be a competent adult member of a western American academic community. The address forms which are the 'outcomes' to be accounted for might fit in frames like 'Look, - - - -, it's time to leave.' The outcomes themselves are formal sets, with alternative realizations. For example, first names may alternate with nicknames, as will be indicated in a later section. One possible outcome is no-naming, indicated in Fig. 1 by the linguistic symbol for zero [Ø].
>
> The diamonds indicate selectors. They are points where the social categories allow different paths. At first glance, some selectors look like simple external features, but the social determinants vary according to the system. and the specific nature of the categories must be discovered by ethnographic means. For example, 'older' implies knowledge of the range of age defined as contemporary. In some southeast Asian systems, even one day makes a person socially older.

In translating Ervin-Tripp's (1969) flow chart of her American address system, we can simply re-represent selector diamonds as systems and interpret the representations to the right as realization statements. For example, Married ± is translated as female: married/unmarried, and if 'married', then the realization is + Mrs ^ Last name, and if 'unmarried', then it is + Miss ^ Last name.[3] My system network translation of the flow chart is presented as Figure 6.4.

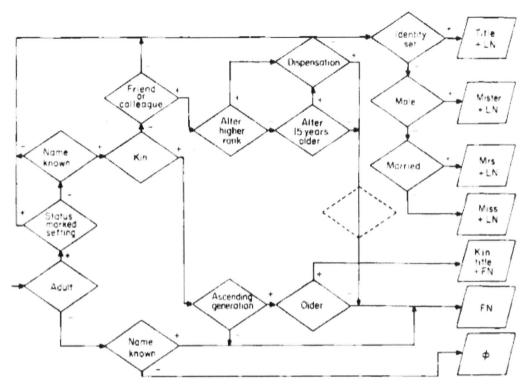

*Figure 6.3* Ervin-Tripp's (1969: 95) flow chart representation of an American address system

The two representations of Ervin-Tripp's American system of address in Figure 6.3 and Figure 6.4 could of course be seen simply as different visualizations of the same system. If so, it would be a matter of choosing which one provides the clearest picture of the resources; and it would be helpful to have graphing software that would allow us to switch among different visual displays, and many mapping tools in fact do (but sadly without an option for system networks). However, it turns out that while there is a repetition of the choice between 'name known' and 'name unknown' in both the original flow chart version and my system network translation of it, this is actually a case of the source language 'shining through' in the translation: as I have illustrated at various points throughout the book, system networks can have simultaneous systems – i.e. systems with the same entry condition (as in the system of speech function in Figure 3.26 above). Since simultaneous systems are formally possible in system networks, we can ask if the repetition of the systemic contrast between 'name known' and 'name unknown' could be avoided by changing the entry condition of the system so that it become simultaneous with 'adult'/'non-adult'. This revised version is shown in Figure 6.5.

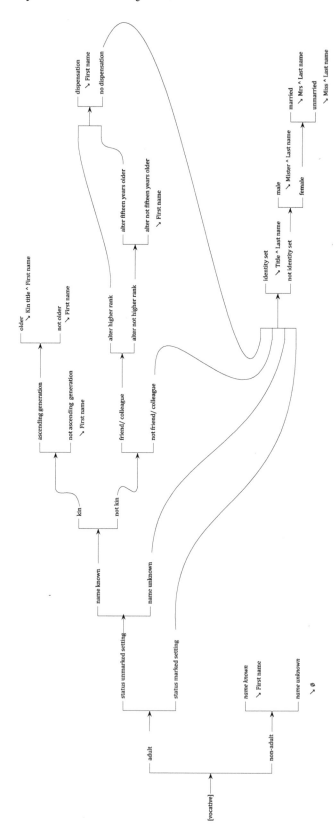

Figure 6.4 System network 'translation' of Ervin-Tripp's (1969: 95) flow chart representation of an American address system (Figure 6.3)

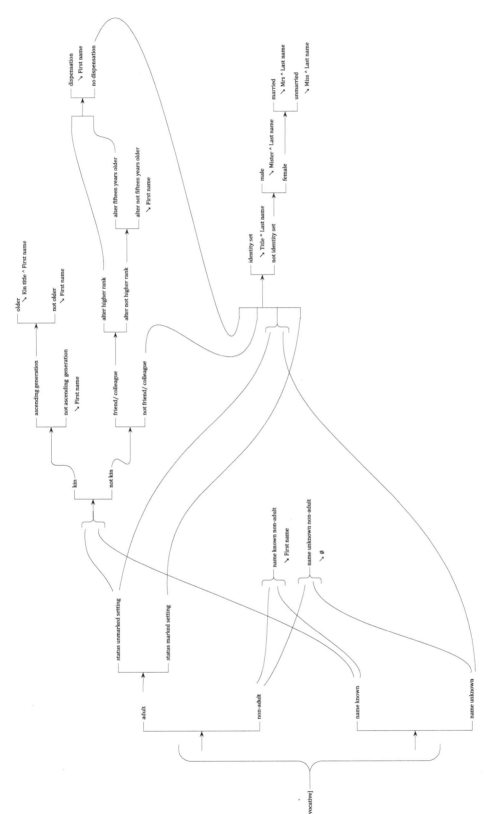

*Figure 6.5* Redrawing of the system network in Figure 6.4, now with 'adult'/'non-adult' and 'name known'/'name unknown' as simultaneous systems

The revised version arguably makes good contextual sense: in choosing how to address a person, one would simultaneously have to consider their age and one's familiarity with their name. And yet, the version in Figure 6.5 indicates that if the setting is 'status marked setting', the contrast between 'name known' and 'name unknown' makes no difference. However, it turns out that it actually makes a difference with respect to more delicate distinctions within the identity set system ('identity set'/'non-identity set'). Even though this difference is left implicit in Ervin-Tripp's flow chart, her comments on the identity set makes it clear that the nature of the realizations depends on whether the name is known or not (Ervin-Tripp 1969: 96–97):

> The **identity** set refers to a list of occupational titles or courtesy titles accorded people in certain statuses. Examples are Judge, Doctor, and Professor. A priest, physician, dentist, or judge may be addressed by title alone, but a plain citizen or an academic person may not. In the latter cases, if the name is unknown, there is no address form (or zero, Ø) available and we simply no-name the addressee. The parentheses below refer to optional elements, the bracketed elements to social selectional categories.
>
> | | |
> |---:|:---|
> | [Cardinal]: | Your excellency |
> | [U.S. President]: | Mr. President |
> | [Priest]: | Father (+ LN) |
> | [Nun]: | Sister (+ religious name) |
> | [Physician]: | Doctor (+ LN) |
> | [Ph.D., Ed.D.], etc.: | (Doctor + LN) |
> | [Professor]: | (Professor + LN) |
> | [Adult], etc.: | (Mister + LN) |
> | | (Mrs. + LN) |
> | | (Miss + LN) |
>
> Wherever the parenthetical items cannot be fully realized, as when last name (LN) is unknown, and there is no lone title, the addressee is no-named by a set of rules of the form as follows: Father + Ø → Father, Professor + Ø → Ø, Mister + Ø → Ø, etc. An older male addressee may be called 'sir' if deference is intended, as an optional extra marking.
>
> These are my rules, and seem to apply fairly narrowly within the academic circle I know. Non-academic university personnel can be heard saying 'Professor' or 'Doctor' without LN, as can school teachers. These delicate differences in sociolinguistic rules are sensitive indicators of the communication net.
>
> The zero forms imply that often no address form is available to follow routines like 'yes,' 'no,' 'pardon me,' and 'thank you.' Speakers of languages or dialects where all such routines must contain an address form are likely in English either to use full name or to adopt forms like "sir" and 'ma'am,' which are either not used or used only to elderly addressees in this system.

It would be possible – even desirable – to further elaborate the system network to take account of these more delicate distinctions depending on whether the name is 'known' or 'unknown'. If we took this step, we could also 'collect' instances of the same realization statement and represent them within gates with disjunctive entry conditions, e.g. ↘ +First name would be located in a gate with the following disjunctive entry condition:

'name known non-adult'/'not ascending generation'/'not older'/'dispensation'/'alter not fifteen years older'. This would not just be systemic spring cleaning or bookkeeping, but it would actually reflect the systemic conditions under which a speaker can address the listener using his or her first name alone – a combination of status and in-group.

It would be possible to investigate further revisions of the system network; for example, we could try to capture the proportionality between kin and friend/colleague considerations:

kin : not kin :: friend-colleague : not friend-colleague
ascending generation : not ascending generation :: alter higher rank : alter not higher rank
older : not older :: alter fifteen years older : alter not fifteen years older

This proportionality suggests that we could abstract out two systems, one concerned with relationship and the other with generalized rank:

related (as kin, friend or colleague)/not related
related: higher (generation, rank, age)/not higher

Such a version would generalize and highlight the tenor-based distinctions having to do with power ('vertical relations') and familiarity ('horizontal relations').

This exercise in meta-translation – re-representing Ervin-Tripp's description of an American address system couched in terms of a flowchart by means of successive system network versions – has demonstrated that issues of descriptive interest arise in the course of such an exercise. It has also indicated that the system network is a better form of paradigmatic representation of a resource than the flowchart. Flowcharts have, of course, been used to represent different kinds of 'knowledge'; but they are most suited to the represented of procedural knowledge rather than to the representation of declarative resources (cf. Mohan 1986). In fact, they have been used in SFL to represent procedural knowledge, as in Ventola (1987); Fawcett, van der Mije and van Wissen (1988); Fawcett (1989).

## 6.4 The Complementarity of Typology and Topology

In the previous section, we considered system networks in comparison with other forms of representation involving discrete distinctions. Let's now take one step further to consider non-discrete distinctions or continua along the paradigmatic axis.

### 6.4.1 Agnation Again

Patterns along the paradigmatic axis are concerned with relatedness or agnation. Agnation is represented by systems in system networks. For example, in Figure 3.1 above, within its own lexicogrammatical clause system network, the term 'declarative' is:

- immediately agnate with the contrasting term 'interrogative' in the system of INDICATIVE TYPE;
- by another step in delicacy, it is agnate with 'neutral' and 'marked' in the system DECLARATIVE KEY,
- and by one further step in delicacy to the terms in the system that differentiates types of marked declarative key, i.e. to 'protesting', 'tentative', 'reserved' and 'insistent';
- and by one step 'backwards' in delicacy to the term 'indicative' in the system MOOD TYPE.

At the same time, 'declarative' is also agnate with systemic terms in other system networks through the realizational relation of preselection:

- 'declarative' is agnate 'upwards' to 'statement' in the semantic system of SPEECH FUNCTION;
- and 'declarative' is agnate 'downwards' to systemic terms in the system SIMPLE PRIMARY TONE – indirectly through the more delicate terms in the system of MOOD that 'declarative' is agnate with.

I touched on the multiple relationships that systemic terms enter into in Section 4.1, emphasizing that systemic terms are not 'things in themselves' but are rather defined by reference to the relationships they are nodes in, as illustrated again for the term 'declarative' in Figure 4.1. In other words, whether we are concerned with the *valeur* or the signification of a systemic term (cf. Hasan 1985b), it's all captured by the relationships it enters into.

### 6.4.2 Patterns of Agnation Not Captured by Systems in System Networks

Does this systemic account of relations of agnation capture all insights into paradigmatic patterns? Not quite. The system network as a resource of theoretical representation forces us to draw paradigmatic boundaries where we would theoretically conceive of a continuum, and it makes it difficult to capture what we might think of as **convergent evolution**.[4] I have actually already smuggled in some examples of these issues:

- When we try to represent the articulatory space of the oral cavity systemically by means of a system network, we are forced to draw boundaries, as illustrated above in Figure 3.46. One can address this need for boundaries by increasing the delicacy of the systemic description, but this still means drawing boundaries somewhere within a continuum.
- When we develop the description of the system of PROCESS TYPE, we need to make a primary cut – distinguishing four or six primary process types, as in the six term system in Halliday's IFG description of English (Halliday and Matthiessen 2014: Chapter 5): 'material'/'behavioural'/'mental'/'verbal'/'relational'/'existential'; but as we extend the primary description in delicacy, we may find that some more delicate process types converge, possibly within certain registers, even though

they were separated at birth in primary delicacy (cf. Martin and Matthiessen, 1991, on the complementarity of typology and topology; Matthiessen, 1995a, in relation to process types; and see further below). This situation is illustrated in Figure 5.12: in the register of topographic procedures, mental clauses of perception and existential clauses converge in the sense that they both provide a transitivity configuration of process + participant, where the participant can be given the status of Focus (of new information – Process + Phenomenon or Existent/Focus of New.

Examples of the kind just given have led systemic functional linguists to explore representational resources that will allow us to capture the paradigmatic theory of agnation in terms of continua. This is a representational investigation that is of interest even if we take double agnation within the content plane into consideration – an important property of the stratification of this plane into semantics and lexicogrammar: see Section 3.2.2 above.

### 6.4.3 Topologies and Fuzzy Sets

At least two ultimately related possibilities have been suggested and investigated in a preliminary way – the use as representational resources of **topologies** and of **fuzzy sets**.

(1) The possibilities of topological representation of agnation by means of continuous spaces was inspired by Lemke's (1987) manuscript on genre typology: Martin and Matthiessen (1991) put forward **topology** as a complement to typology in the representation of paradigmatic patterns. (Thus topology and typology constitute different views of, representations of, the same range of phenomena, each foregrounding somewhat different aspects of the phenomena.) Since then, topological representations have been used *informally* as a mode of capturing continua in agnation, as in Martin's (2003) topology of history genres (see also Martin and Rose 2008) and our topological representation of fields of activity (e.g. Matthiessen and Teruya 2016).

The notion of topology comes from mathematics, and the use of abstract space as a way of construing meaning is of course widespread in linguistics (cf. Matthiessen, 1992, on 'topos' in interpretation of the textual metafunction). The general characterization of topology in the Wikipedia entry is relevant:

> In mathematics, **topology** (from the Greek words τόπος, 'place, location', and λόγος, 'study') is concerned with the properties of a geometric object that are preserved under continuous deformations, such as stretching, twisting, crumpling and bending, but not tearing or gluing.
>
> A topological space is a set endowed with a structure, called a *topology*, which allows defining continuous deformation of subspaces, and, more generally, all kinds of continuity.

This continuity complements the typological discontinuity imposed by system networks. However, up to now, the use of topological representations in SFL have remained 'figurative' – a source of insight into the visualization of semantic regions of language in context, and semiotic regions more generally. I've referred to the use of topologies in the representation of genre families, but let me begin with an example from the description of the system of PROCESS TYPE in the clause grammar of English. Before introducing this example, I would just like to note that continuity is the norm in language in context, as in evolved systems in general: indeterminacy is pervasive, and our theory of language must treat this condition as a central property of language. I could equally well have chosen examples of continuities inherent in interpersonal and textual systems.

The experiential system of PROCESS TYPE is one of the three primary systems in the description of TRANSITIVITY in English, the other systems being AGENCY and CIRCUMSTANTIATION (see Section 3.2.1.2.3 above). There are six primary process types – 'material'/'behavioural'/'mental'/'verbal'/'relational'/'existential'; and the major ones of these in terms of frequency in text and distinctive characteristics are 'material'/'mental'/'relational'. When we represent them typologically by means of a system with six terms, they are all of course quite distinct; but the system actually construes a continuous space of our experience of quanta of change in the flow of events. The process types shade into one another; minor types are intermediate between the major types: 'behavioural' is intermediate between 'material' and 'mental', 'verbal' is intermediate between 'mental' and 'relational' and 'existential' is intermediate between 'relational' and 'material'. This continuity is brought out when we visualize the system of process type as a topology; the typological and topological views on the system are shown together in Figure 6.6. The cover of the 2nd edition of Halliday's IFG features a similar version of the continuous space of process types.

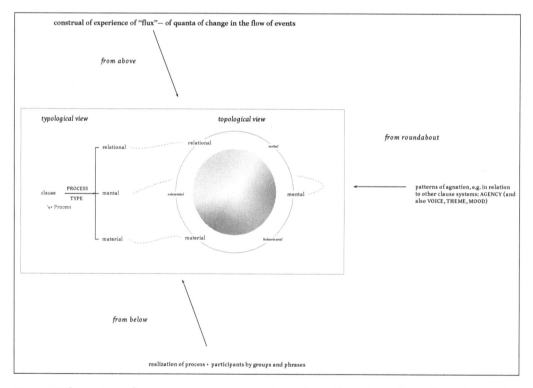

*Figure 6.6* The system of PROCESS TYPE represented typologically and topologically and viewed trinocularly

The topological representation is, of course, based on lexicogrammatical criteria – some overt, some covert involving reactances. They are summarized in Halliday and Matthiessen (2014: 354), and to these can be added other considerations such as the likelihood of different types of circumstance occurring with different process types (see Matthiessen 1999) and considerations 'from above' concerning contributions to the creation of meaning of text (such as the very specific role played by 'existential' clauses in the realization of the Placement text segment in traditional narratives). Martin (1996a) explains why distinctions among process types are made based on a number of different considerations and highlights the significance of this systemic approach to description.

Another area where the topological approach has been a helpful complement to a typological representation is the contextual parameter of FIELD OF ACTIVITY – see e.g. Figure 5.9 above. Like process types in the system of transitivity, fields of activity shade into one another within context; a well-known example is the way reporting and promoting shade into one another in so-called infomercials. In Matthiessen and Teruya (2016) we interpret this indeterminacy in terms of the **typology of indeterminacy** proposed in Halliday and Matthiessen (2006), which I will return to below – see Table 6.2 Types of indeterminacy (adapted from Halliday and Matthiessen 2006: 549 ff).

To bring out the fact that fields of activity shade into one another, we can represent them topologically by means of a diagram I have called the discursive pie of fortune: see Figure 6.7. In this diagram, there are eight primary distinctions and within each of them two or three secondary distinctions. They shade into one another; adjacent sectors shade into one another, e.g. partly fictional biographies in between 'reporting' and 'recreating', and opposing sectors also shade into one another, one interesting example being the blurring between sharing private opinions and exploring public values due to the new technologies of channels of communication.

Figure 6.7 Fields of activity as regions within semiotic space shading into one another

220 • *System in Systemic Functional Linguistics*

When we try to translate the 'topology' in Figure 6.7 into a system network, we find that there are various systemic choices we can make among alternative versions of the system network. We could simply postulate a single system to capture the eight fields of activity at primary delicacy: 'expounding'/'reporting'/'recreating'/'sharing'/'doing'/'enabling'/'recommending'/'exploring'. Since terms in systems are not ordered, adjacency in the system is arbitrary. Thus we would lose the information about adjacent segments in the topological display, which has been designed precisely with adjacency in mind – e.g. 'expounding' shading into 'reporting' and 'reporting' shading into 'recreating'.

At the same time, other possibilities present themselves. For example, we can set up as a primary distinction the difference between fields of activity that are primarily social in nature being manifested through social behaviour – 'doing' – and fields of activity that primary semiotic in nature being manifested through the exchange of meaning – 'expounding'/'reporting'/'sharing'/'enabling'/'recommending'/'exploring'. This systemic representation is shown in Figure 6.8.

But there are other possibilities as well. Within 'semiotic activity', we could make another systemic cut, differentiation 'enabling' and 'recommending' from the rest since they commonly lead to 'doing' contexts – doing being either recommended or enabled. Alternatively, we could make a primary distinction between 'recreating' and the rest, since 'recreating' is an activity that imaginatively creates other contexts, as in a courtroom drama. As always, descriptive decisions reflect considerations from different vantage points (cf. Martin's, 1996a, discussion of approaches to the description of process types), and will be made to optimize these considerations.

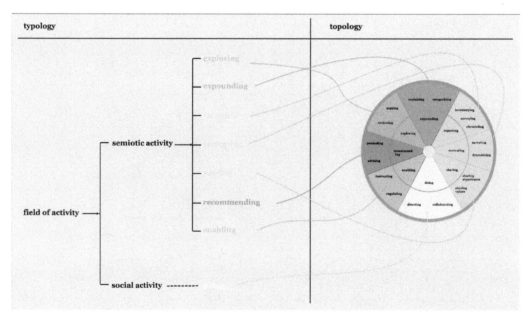

*Figure 6.8* Field of activity represented typologically and topologically – one possible systemicization of the discursive pie of fortune

The general principle here is to view the phenomena under investigation in terms of **trinocular vision** along different semiotic dimensions (on trinocular vision, cf. also Section 3.3.1.5 above, Section 3.4.1 – Figure 3.38, and Section 7.1 – Figure 7.1). Typically, we try to develop accounts that are balanced in terms of considerations 'from above', 'from below' and 'from roundabout'; but there may be reasons to foreground one of these views, and in functional theories, the view 'from above' tends to be given special attention because it reflects the nature of language as a resource for making meaning.

(2) The experiments with **fuzzy sets** took place in, and in interaction with the members of, Michio Sugeno's laboratory at Tokyo Institute of Technology in the 1990s and later his laboratory at the Brain Science Division of the RIKEN Institute in Tokyo (2000–2005). Fuzzy set theory was first proposed by Lotfi Zadeh (1965) as an advance over traditional crisp set theory, or standard set theory, introduced into mathematics by Georg Cantor in the 1870s. In crisp set theory, an element is either a member of a set or not; in fuzzy set theory, an element can be a member of a set to a certain degree, ranging from not being a member to being a full member. Zadeh was at UC Berkeley, and his work resonated with work at the time on prototypes, in particular Eleanor Rosch's prototype theory. Introductory examples given as illustrations often involve natural kinds; for example, a sparrow is a member of the set of birds to a higher degree than penguins and emus because it can fly; and penguins, dolphins, sharks, sturgeons and seals may be members of a fuzzy set of swimming creatures to various degrees.

Fuzzy set theory was applied to a variety of engineering tasks quite successfully, like fuzzy control systems, and the theory was expanded to include fuzzy logic (e.g. Yager and Zadeh 1992). As far as systems in system networks are concerned, one possibility is to treat systemic terms as (names of) fuzzy sets. Exactly how this is done will depend on the nature of the system to be represented fuzzily. For example, if the system of PROCESS TYPE is to be represented fuzzily (cf. Figure 6.6 above), the major types might be represented by fuzzy sets, and the minor ones might be represented by degrees of membership in these sets – in particular, 'behavioural' might be interpreted as being a member of the 'material' and 'mental' sets to varying degrees. This would be one way of interpreting and representing overlaps as one of the types of indeterminacy, to be discussed in the next subsection.

Rounding off this section, I would like to point out that the notion of continuity was part of the theory from the beginning, even going back to the pre-systemic days of scale-&-category theory; Halliday (1961: 42) characterizes clines as the type of scale that construes continua (footnotes omitted):

> In discussing these I have used the terms 'hierarchy', 'taxonomy' and 'cline' as general scale-types. A hierarchy is taken to mean a system of terms related along a single dimension which must be one involving some form of logical precedence (such as inclusion). A taxonomy is taken to mean a special type of hierarchy, one with two additional characteristics: (i) there is a constant relation of each term to the term immediately following it, and a constant reciprocal relation of each to that immediately preceding it; and (ii) degree is significant, so that the place in order of each of the terms, statable as the distance in number of steps from either end, is a defining characteristic of that term. A cline resembles a hierarchy in that it involves relation along a single dimension; but instead of being made up of a number of discrete terms a cline is a continuum carrying potentially infinite gradation.

Thus in this section, I have been concerned with representing 'a continuum carrying potentially infinite gradation'.

### 6.4.4 Indeterminacy

The explorations with topological visualizations of systemic agnation and fuzzy set representations of terms in systems reflect the need to come to grips with **indeterminacy** in languages – not as a bug but as a positive feature. Ideationally, indeterminacy enables us to construe our experience of the world as 'fuzzy' rather than as 'crisp'; semiotic indeterminacy is needed to construe our experience of the world as pervasively indeterminate. Interpersonally, indeterminacy enables us to enact our roles and relations in a fluid way, one that is open to ongoing negotiation and calibration. Textually, indeterminacy enables us to engender ideational and interpersonal meanings as degrees of prominence, manifested syntagmatically as waves of information with peaks of prominence gradually yielding to troughs of non-prominence (cf. Halliday 1985b).

*6.4.4.1 Types of Indeterminacy*

It will be helpful to identify different types of indeterminacy that play a role in theorizing language systemically and in developing descriptions represented by system networks. I have summarized the discussion in Halliday and Matthiessen (2006: 547–562) in tabular form: Table 6.2.

As an initial illustration of indeterminacy, let me return to the contextual parameter of field of activity, approached above in terms of the complementary representations of agnation of typology and topology (Figure 6.7 and Figure 6.8). In Matthiessen and Teruya (2016), we discuss four kinds of indeterminacy – ambiguity, neutralization, overlap, and blend: see Figure 6.9.

The activity may be **ambiguous**, a prominent example being the possible ambiguity that may arise between chronicling within the reporting sector and narrating within the recreating sector – reporting facts or narrating fiction. Here there is a sense that they can be told apart (as happened when people argued about the status of Defoe's *Journal of the Plague Year* as fact or fiction), but the two activities may even blend as happens in imaginative recounts of events – highlighting the point that 'facts' are semiotic constructs and subject to acceptance by consensus.

The distinction between two different activities may be **neutralized**, as happens under certain conditions pertaining to the contextual parameter of mode when sharing personal opinions and exploring public values are no longer distinct – the private and public realms shade into one another. The mode conditions have to do with the technology of the channel within mode – the world wide web supported by the internet and mobile devices operating various social platforms.

The activity may be a **blend** of two different activities, as when soft-sell advertisements also masquerade as news reports – infomercials. Here promotion is blended with objective reporting (or at least the appearance of objective reporting!): 'commercial' + 'information'.

Table 6.2 Types of indeterminacy (adapted from Halliday and Matthiessen 2006: 549 ff)

| # | type | gloss | characterization | example | |
|---|---|---|---|---|---|
| (1) | ambiguities | 'either a or p' | one form of wording construes two distinct meanings, each of which is exclusive of the other. | modal operator *must* as either 'high' 'obligation' or 'probability', e.g. *you must be very thoughtful* (ambiguous, but obligation likely) vs. *you must be very thoughtless* (ambiguous, but probability likely) | MODALITY |
| (2) | blends | 'both b and q' | one form of wording construes two different meanings, both of which are blended into a single whole. | modal operator *might* combining 'potentiality' & 'probability', e.g. *he might finish the painting next week* | MODALITY |
| (3) | overlaps [borderline cases] | 'partly c, partly r' | two categories overlap so that certain members display some features of each. | 'behavioural' clauses: partly like 'material', partly like 'mental' (construing sensing as activity) | PROCESS TYPE |
| (4) | neutralizations | 'd = x in environment s' | in certain contexts the difference between two categories disappears. | in 'non-finite' clauses, the distinction 'condition'/'cause'/'time' may be neutralized: *I get tired running* ['finite': *if I run/because I run/ when I run*] | TYPE OF ENHANCEMENT |
| (5) | complementarities | 'e ≠ y but they both apply' | certain semantic features or domains are construed in two contradictory ways. | transitive/ergative models of transitivity | TRANSITIVITY |
| | | | | tense/aspect models of process time | TEMPORALITY |
| | | | | modalization: probability (belief in information)/evidentiality (source of information) | MODAL ASSESSMENT |

The activity may represent an **overlap** between two different activities, as when reviewing within the exploring section also involves some degree of promoting within the recommending sector. For example, a reviewer may praise and book and at the same time recommend it to his or her readers.

What about complementarities in the domain of fields of activity? They can arguably also be found, as in physics education: the teacher instructing students in how to undertake a lab experiment within the enabling sector, before they pour into the lab; the teacher directing them while they are undertaking the experiment in the lab (doing sector); and the students chronicling their experiment in procedural recounts (reporting). These activities are all complementary to the activity of expounding physical theory. And there is also the complementarity of spoken and written physics discourses, involving different modes of construing knowledge in physics.

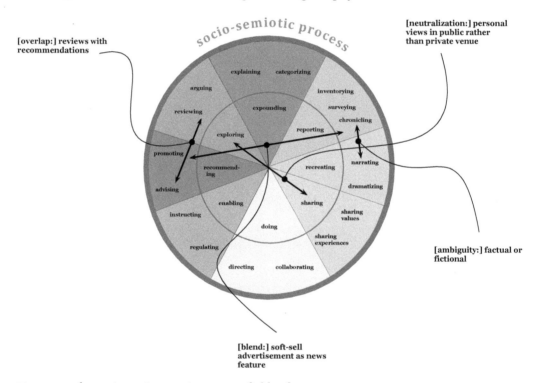

*Figure 6.9* Indeterminacy in agnation among fields of activity

Indeterminacy is a general property of the system of language, of its context and of other denotative semiotic systems,[5] and the different types characterized in Table 6.2 may be manifested at various points throughout these systems, from phonetics to semantics and also including context (cf. again Matthiessen and Teruya 2016). I will discuss them briefly one by one, focussing on how they show up within the content plane of language.

### 6.4.4.2 Ambiguities

**Ambiguities** typically show up when we view some pattern 'from below' and find that it can be assigned more than one analysis in reference to the relevant system at the higher level (axis, rank or stratum). The pattern may be a single item such as *will* or *can*, as grammatical or lexical items, a (part of a) syntagm in the sense of a sequence of classes (Halliday 1966a), a (part of a) function structure or a (part of a) selection expression.

The simplest case is that of a polysemous item such as *will, can, must; escape, stand for*. The case of *will* is depicted in Figure 6.10. The orthographic word *will* realizes either a lexicogrammatical verb or a noun; and the verb is either a grammatical one, the operator *will*, or a lexical one. The noun *will* typically functions as Thing in the structure of a nominal group (although it might serve as Classifier), in either of two senses, viz. 'mental faculty' (e.g. *how much of it is the will of the gods*) or 'legal document' (e.g. *in the second it was the absence of a signed 'living will' or advance directive document that wreaked havoc with my cousin*); the nominal group can serve in a clause of any process type and of any mood type. The lexical verb *will* has two distinct senses, either 'bequeath', in which case it serves in a 'benefactive' 'material' clause, or 'desire', in which case it serves in a 'desiderative' 'mental' clause (e.g. *it would follow, that if God had willed, or should will the direct opposite of what he does, it would impose obligation upon us*).

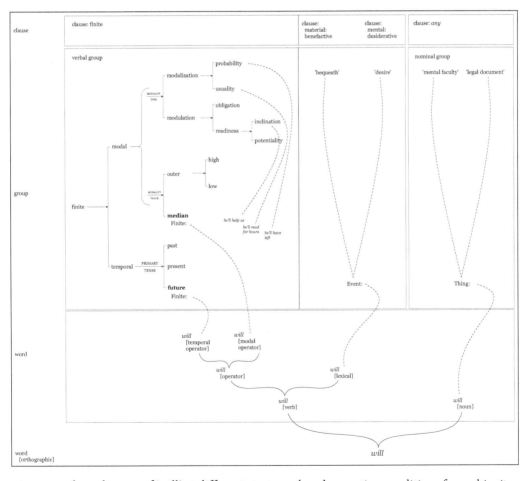

*Figure 6.10* The polysemy of 'will' at different strata and ranks creating conditions for ambiguity

The grammatical verb *will* is either a temporal or modal operator (auxiliary); the different senses are captured in the system network of verbal groups serving in 'finite' clauses to the left in Figure 6.10:

- temporal: future: *The boat **will** be salvaged*; *I think that politically the world is mad; always has been, probably always **will** be.*
- modal: modalization: probability: *The ozone hole may get worse, and there **will** be more hemispheric, and possibly global, ramifications.*
- modal: modalization: probability [usuality]: *It is a metaphor for what we have all observed, that a very weak father **will** generally produce a very strong son. And a very strong father **will** generally produce a weak son.*
- modal: modulation: readiness: *Well, a hungry man **will** even eat lasagne*; *But I **will** save you because you are good.*

According to the general principle of agnation, the analysis of any given instance can involve a probe checking close agnates; for example, temporal: future: *the boat will be salvaged* ~ temporal: (primary) present, secondary future *the boat is going to be salvaged*; modal: modulation: readiness: inclination *I will save you* ~ temporal: present, (non-finite) inclination *I'm determined to save you*. Such probing by search for agnates may, of course, suggest alternative analyses, revealing indeterminacy in the example being probed.

Ambiguity also goes beyond single grammatical or lexical items, as already noted. For example, the syntagm 'nominal group + verbal group [Event: make] + nominal group + nominal group' can realize different function structures, e.g. (using an old textbook type example) material: creative & effective: benefactive: cliency: Actor: *he* + Process: *will make* + Client: *her* + Goal: *a new computer desk* 'he will build a new computer desk for her' or relational: intensive & attributive & benefactive: Carrier: *he* + Process: *will make* + Beneficiary: *her* + Attribute: *a good husband* 'he will be a good husband to her'. In naturally occurring texts unfolding in their contexts, many potential ambiguities are, of course, resolved because of the meanings available in the co-text and the context. As a specimen in a museum of theoretical linguistics, an example may be ambiguous, but in its environment, the potential ambiguities may not arise. For example, if we meet:

made her a shining star

this could be in a passage about making Christmas decorations, so the example would be material: creative & effective: benefactive: cliency; but the co-text immediately makes us favour the 'relational' reading of 'cause her to be' (relational: intensive & attributive: attributed):

The media has put her up on a pedestal and made her a shining star – well past her 15 minutes of fame.

This example set out alongside the textbook example above with the three different systemic analyses, represented by selection expressions in Figure 6.11. The three analyses are not equally likely for both examples; as already noted, the co-text of the corpus example favours analysis (2). This is supported by likely agnates like *the media turned her into a shining star*; in contrast, *the media made her* would be 'material' (cf. Graham Greene's novel *England made me*). Language in context is a **fault tolerant system** – it's an **ambiguity tolerant system**.

|     | selection expression | [the media] | made | her | a shining star |
|-----|---------------------|-------------|------|-----|----------------|
| (1) | material: creative & effective: benefactive: cliency | Actor | Process | Client | Goal |
| (2) | relational: intensive & attributive: attributed | Attributor | Process | Carrier | Attribute |
| (3) | relational: intensive & attributive & benefactive | Carrier | Process | Beneficiary | Attribute |
|     |                     | he          | made | her | a good husband |

*Figure 6.11* Syntagmatic ambiguity – different systemic analyses represented by selection expressions realized by function structures

### 6.4.4.3 Blends

**Blends** will often appear to be systemically impossible because they involve systemic terms on disjunctive paths through a system network. Thus 'either b or q' is resystemicized as 'both b and q' under certain conditions. We can draw an example from the system of MODALITY again. The systems of MODALITY TYPE and MODALITY VALUE are simultaneous in the system network of MODALITY. Certain combinations do not occur; in particular, if the type is 'modulation: readiness: potentiality', the value is 'low'; there are no 'median' and 'high' instances of potentiality. This is a general property of the system.

There is another general property involving the two systems having to do with indeterminacy. When the value is 'high', we find clear instances of ambiguities involving 'probability', 'obligation' and 'readiness'. For example, *you must be happy* could mean either 'probability', agnate with *I'm sure you're happy*, or 'obligation', agnate with *you're obliged to be happy*. Of course, the systemic environment plays a role in creating the potential for the perception of such ambiguities and for helping listeners resolve them. Here the setting of the interpersonal system of SUBJECT PERSON to 'interactant: addressee' helps create the potential for the perception of the ambiguity. If the selection is 'non-interactant', the example is most likely heard as 'probability': *he must be happy*, agnate with *I'm sure he's happy*, with a co-text including positive assessment, e.g. *He has won the lottery. He must be happy.* (But contrast: *When he arrives, make sure that he's well taken care of. He must be happy.*) Compare also the contrast between the examples given in Table 6.2 between *you must be very thoughtful* (where high obligation is the likely interpretation) and *you must be very thoughtless* (where high probability is the likely interpretation). Here the positive vs. negative interpersonal connotations of *thoughtful* (positive) vs. *thoughtless* (negative) play a role. Similarly, choices of expansions of the clause can resolve the ambiguity: *you must be happy* [expansion: enhancing: reason] *since your granddad gives you presents* vs. *you must be very happy* [expansion: enhancing: conditional] *if your granddad gives you presents*. Three possible systemic analyses of *she must complain* are set out in Table 6.2.

228 • System in Systemic Functional Linguistics

Table 6.3 Ambiguities of high value modal operator 'must'

| preceding co-text | example | systemic term | gloss |
|---|---|---|---|
| I wonder why they take all that trouble just for her? | She must complain. | probability | 'the reason is certainly that she complains' |
| I don't think they'll let her return it! | She must complain. | obligation | 'it is essential that she should complain' |
| Whatever happens she's never satisfied. | She must complain. | readiness: inclination | 'she insists on complaining' |

In contrast, when the value is 'low', we find clear examples of blends involving 'probability', 'obligation' and/or 'readiness'. For example, *she might complain* can be analysed as a blend of 'probability' ('it is possible that she'll complain') and 'obligation' ('she's allowed to complain'). Here is another example, developed in more detail, from Halliday and Matthiessen (2006: 558–559):

> But at the opposite corner, so to speak, if we combine low value with oblique (remote), the result is typically blending rather than ambiguity: e.g. *it couldn't hurt you to apologize* is a blend of 'it would not be able to hurt you' (readiness: ability), 'it is unlikely that it would hurt you' (probability) and even perhaps [it would not be allowed to hurt you' (obligation). In other words, looking at it from the point of view of blending, in the region of 'what I think'/'what is wanted', it is easiest to blend the low values 'what I can conceive of' with 'what is permitted', especially in 'remote' conditions (hypothetical, projected or tentative) [realized as *could, might*] and hardest to blend the high values 'what I am convinced of' with 'what is required', especially when 'immediate' [realized as *must*]. This is diagrammed in Figure 13.3 [reproduced here as Figure 6.12, CMIMM]. This shows that, in modality, a very complex region where the metafunctions themselves overlap ('what I think is' and 'what ought to be' blending in 'what I think ought to be'), the indeterminacy even extends to indeterminacy between the different types of indeterminacy!

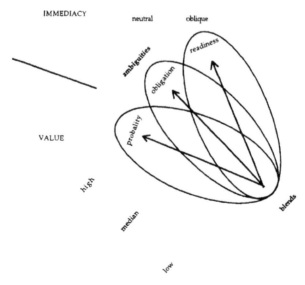

*Figure 6.12* The intersection of MODALITY TYPE and MODALITY VALUE and different types of indeterminacy

How do we represent blends systemically? As noted above, the systemic terms that are blended are on disjunctive paths through the system network, in the case of our example, disjunctive paths through the system of MODALITY. That's why I said that 'either b or q' is resystemicized as 'both b and q' under certain conditions. The nature of the blend of 'probability' and 'potentiality' in 'low' value modality is illustrated in Figure 6.13. The illustration shows that the blend is systemically impossible in the sense that 'probability' and 'potentiality' are on different paths, separated at primary delicacy by the contrast between 'modalization' and 'modulation'. If we visualize the situation topologically, we could represent a continuum: usuality – probability – potentiality – inclination – obligation, where probability and potentiality blend if the value is 'low'. Typologically, in a system network, we would either have to redraw the system network to capture the blend or treat it as a case of double analysis, i.e. *he might finish the painting by tomorrow* would be analysed twice, both as 'probability' and as 'potentiality'.

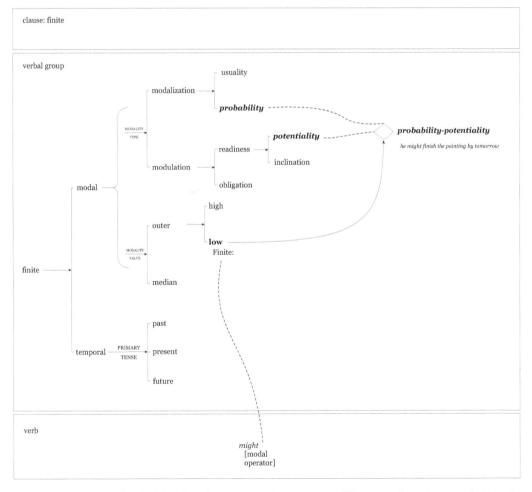

*Figure 6.13* An example of a blend in the system of MODALITY: if 'low' in value, then 'probability' and 'potentiality' might blend

### 6.4.4.4 Overlaps

**Overlaps** can in principle be handled systemically by the introduction of finer systemic differentiation, either by an increase in the number of terms in a given system or by increased delicacy of differentiation 'downstream'. A well-known example from the systemic description of English comes from the system of PROCESS TYPE – viz. the systemic interpretation of 'behavioural' clauses. Topologically, 'behavioural' clauses can be visualized as a region between 'material' and 'mental' clauses, as in Figure 6.6 above. Since they constitute an overlap category, they are 'partly material, and partly mental', as shown in Table 6.4. The table brings out the intermediate status of 'behavioural' clauses; in some respect they behave like 'material' one but in other they behave like 'mental' ones. We can capture a key aspect of their nature by characterizing them as construing sensing as activity – rather than as inert, as 'mental' clauses do. The table is, clearly, not exhaustive; it would be possible to add other properties. For example, in the construal of perception, 'mental' clauses have an interesting unique characteristic[6]: temporal clauses in the simple present and modal clauses of the subtype modulation: readiness: potentiality are very close agnates, e.g. *I hear the birds singing* vs. *I can hear the birds singing*. In this respect, they are quite distinct from 'behavioural' and 'material' clauses; thus *I'm waiting* is quite distinct from *I can wait*, as is *I'm listening* from *I can listen*.

*Table 6.4* 'Behavioural' clauses as an overlap category, with some properties of 'material' clauses and some of 'mental' ones (adapted from Halliday and Matthiessen 2006: 551)

| | PROCESS TYPE | | |
|---|---|---|---|
| **property** | **material** | **behavioural** | **mental** |
| category meaning | doing-&-happening | behaving | sensing |
| unmarked present tense | present-in-present | | simple present |
| | | (or simple present) | |
| | I'm waiting | I'm listening | I hear |
| potential for projection | cannot project | | can project |
| | *I'm waiting that they're away | *I'm listening that they're way | I hear that they are away |
| potential for macro-phenomenal Range | cannot be configured with macro-phenomenal Range | can be configured with macro-phenomenal Range | |
| | *I'm waiting the birds singing | I'm listening to the birds singing | I hear the birds singing |
| Medium construed as endowed with consciousness | not construed as endowed with consciousness | construed as endowed with consciousness | |
| | it (= the bus) waited | it (= the cat) listened | it (= the cat) heard |
| clause probed by *do* | is probed by *do* | ? | is not probed by *do* |
| | the best thing to do is wait | | *the best thing to do is hear |

In systemic descriptions of the system of PROCESS TYPE, 'behavioural' clauses were not recognized as a distinct type in the early work – not surprisingly, since a number of the properties involve reactances and are shared between the more easily identifiable 'material' and 'mental' process types. Once recognized as a distinct type, they have been treated in two different ways, either as a subtype of 'material' clauses (contrasting with 'eventive' clauses) or as one of the primary process types. In the 'Nigel grammar' (the computational grammar of the Penman text generation project), they were described as a more delicate subtype of 'material' clauses, and when I expanded and documented this description in Matthiessen (1995a), I retained this description. But since the early work on the Nigel grammar, Halliday had 'promoted' 'behavioural' to the status of a primary process type, which is how it is handled in all four editions of Halliday's IFG. Naturally, consumer considerations are always part of the picture (Halliday 1964), but on balance, describing the 'behavioural' process type as one of the primary ones in English best brings out its status in the system as a whole as an 'overlap' category. In fact, this allows also to recognize an overlap between 'material' and 'verbal' clauses, as well as 'mental' ones; for example, 'behavioural' clauses can, arguably, be used to construe saying as activity just as they can be used to construe sensing as activity, and they can be pressed into service as projecting clauses in a restricted way, viz. projecting quoted locutions with the sense of 'say' + accompanying behavioural activity representing a facial expression or voice quality, as in *'It will not be necessary,' the attendant smiled.*

Reviewing the systemic functional literature on TRANSITIVITY (cf. Matthiessen 2018b), we find that descriptions have chosen different points in delicacy for the system of primary process type, as indicated in Figure 6.14. These low-delicacy process types represent combinations of properties, as discussed by Martin (1996a); they are brought out in overviews such as Table 6.4 and Table 5.45, 'Criteria for distinguishing process types', in Halliday and Matthiessen (2014: 354). Similar descriptive variation can be expected in different descriptions of languages other than English (cf. discussion by Halliday and McDonald 2004: 378–380, regarding decisions about the description of process type in Chinese). Such decisions will be influenced by various considerations, involving an optimization of properties revealed by trinocular vision (Figure 6.6) – i.e. seeing the system of process type 'from above' in terms of category meanings (doing-&-happening, sensing-&-saying, and being-&-having), 'from below' in terms of realizations (e.g. the number and nature of participants, as with 'existential' + (one participant, interpretable as) Existent, contrasting with 'attributive' (two participants, interpretable as) +Carrier, +Attribute and 'identifying' (two participants, interpretable as) +Token, +Value), and 'from roundabout' in terms of systemic interaction (e.g. the opening up of the option of 'project' for 'desiderative' and 'cognitive' mental clauses as being concerned with 'higher' sensing than 'perceptive' and 'emotive' ones).[7]

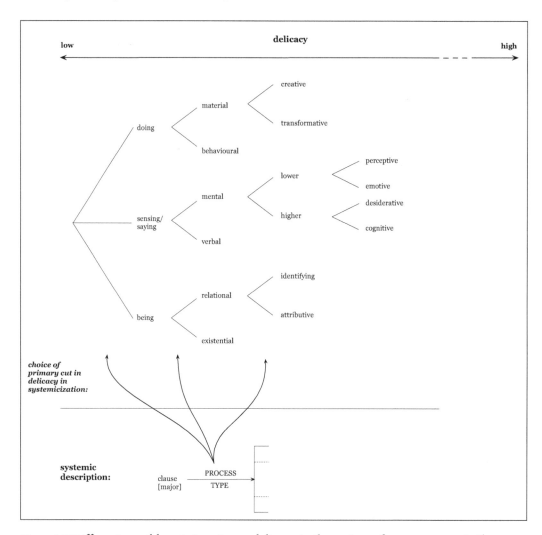

*Figure 6.14* Different possible cuts in primary delicacy in the system of PROCESS TYPE in the systemic description of English

### 6.4.4.5 Neutralizations

**Neutralizations** can typically be interpreted as reduction in the specification of delicacy in some systemic environment. The example in Table 6.2 Types of indeterminacy (adapted from Halliday and Matthiessen 2006: 549 ff) involves the system of FINITENESS in 'bound' clauses, and it is an instance of a more general contrast between 'finite' and 'non-finite' clauses. While 'finite' clauses select in the system of DEICTICITY between 'modal' and 'temporal' (as shown in the interpersonal grammar of the clause in Figure 3.8 above), 'non-finite' clauses don't: the distinction between 'modal' and 'temporal' is thus neutralized. In addition, in both 'modal' clauses and 'non-finite' ones, the distinction between primary 'past'/'present'/'future' and secondary 'past'/'present'/'future' is neutralized. For example, *they finished* and *they have finished* both correspond to (modal) *they may have finished* and to (non-finite) *having finished* (*they trooped off to dinner*). This situation was noted already by Halliday (1970a/2005: 178):

If expressed verbally, by *must* etc., then the modality replaces the primary tense and the tense system with which it combines is the non-finite one, in which the absence of primary tense leads to some neutralization. One non-finite tense corresponds to up to three finite ones, e.g. *must have built* corresponds to (i) *surely ... built*, (ii) *surely ... has built*, and (iii) *surely ... had built*, as the following makes clear:

(12.1) surely he left yesterday  he must have left yesterday
(12.2) surely he has left already  he must have left already
(12.3) surely he had left before you came  he must have left before you came

(Systemic neutralization is distinct from another type of non-specification, viz. **elective systems**. Such systems involve specifications of different values within some domain, but making the distinction is not obligatory and not making it has no value in the system. Halliday and McDonald (2004) discuss such systems as part of their description of Chinese, one example being the system of ASPECT and another being the system of DETERMINATION. Thus while in English, the absence of the Deictic element in the nominal group has a systemic value in the system of DETERMINATION, in Chinese it just means that the nominal group is not determined.)

## 6.4.4.6 Complementarities

**Complementarities** are treated in detail in Halliday's (2008b) book on that topic based on a series of lectures dealing with very general complementarities: the complementarity between system and text, between grammar and lexis, between spoken and written language. To these, we can add other very general complementarities, like the complementarity between the logical and experiential modes of construing experience. These complementarities are, in principle, relevant to the engagement with any language, and the complementarity between grammar and lexis is very much a systemic complementarity in that it can be interpreted by reference to the system network (cf. Section 3.2.1.5 above). Halliday (2008b: 3–4) writes:

> It seemed to me that the lexis and the grammar were complementary, at least in their reality-construing, **ideational** function. In principle, any phenomenon of human experience could be construed either way: either lexically, as specific and open-ended, or grammatically, as generalized and closed; and hence, if some phenomenon showed a high degree of complexity, it might be construed in both ways at once. One example I had given was that of pain. Pain is an extraordinarily complex and difficult feature of human experience; it is a phenomenon that is very hard to comprehend, yet we have to construe it in language – to make it meaning-full – if we want to come to terms with it. The result is an elaborate mix of grammatical and lexical strategies, as I found when I studied the lexicogrammar of pain in modern English, using both data from the corpus and paradigm construction (Halliday 1998b/2005); and Motoko Hori found a comparably rich – but different – mixture in Japanese (Hori 2006). There is a complementarity here: the lexicogrammar of our ordinary, everyday discourse is telling us that we can construe pain in this way, or we can construe it that way; and that even if the construals can't all be right (because at least some of them contradict each other), it is only by construing it in many ways at once that we can get a satisfactorily rounded picture of it.

Here, in the case of pain, we can see how the lexis and the grammar complement each other. There is a lexical inventory of different kinds of pain: quite a small one, at least in everyday use, based on the items *hurt, pain, ache, sore* and *tender*; these may then be elaborated by other terms transferred from elsewhere and used in simile or as metaphor: *burning, throbbing, stabbing* and a few others. Also lexicalized, of course, are the parts of the body where pain is found to be located. But the relation between the pain and the sufferer is grammaticalized, through the systemic resources of transitivity and voice; and there is quite a large paradigm of pain expressions, formed by combining simple oppositions such as *it hurts/it's hurting; it hurts/I hurt; it hurt me/I hurt myself; my leg hurts/I hurt my leg*, and so on. Any one such expression is a combination of the lexical and the grammatical resources that intersect to construe the experience of pain.

The lexicogrammar of pain is an example of the general complementarity of grammar and lexis (see also Lascaratou 2007, on the construal of pain in Greek). But there are also complementarities that appear when we work on systemic descriptions of particular languages, like the complementarity of the transitive and the ergative models of the system of TRANSITIVITY, the complementarity of THEME and INFORMATION as principles for organizing a quantum of information, or the complementarity of singular vs. non-singular and plural vs. non-plural as models of number. Such complementarities vary across languages with respect to how the complementary models are 'mixed', so systemic descriptions will have to take the nature of the mixture into account separately for each language being explored. In the description of the system of TRANSITIVITY in English, the transitive and ergative models can be treated as complementary perspectives covering the whole system, described systemically in terms of AGENCY (ergative perspective) and PROCESS TYPE (transitive perspective), as in the successive editions of Halliday's IFG and Matthiessen (1995a).[8] Alternatively, they can be networked in such a way that they apply to different domains or partially different domains of the overall system, as in Davidse (1999).

When we compare languages, we are also likely to find complementarities, like the complementarity of logical serialization and experiential classification for construing the flow of events (cf. Halliday and Matthiessen 2006: Chapter 7), TENSE and ASPECT systems as strategies for construing process time and of MODALITY and EVIDENTIALITY systems as strategies for assessing the validity of propositions. For example, both English and Chinese have grammaticalized systems for construing processes unfolding through time; but the English system is concerned with the temporal location of the process – it is a tense system, and the Chinese system is concerned with the temporal bounding of the process – it is an aspect system (see Halliday and McDonald 2004; and cf. Matthiessen 2015c): see Figure 6.15. (The English tense system is organized logically as serial tense rather than experientially as taxonomic tense, whereas the Chinese aspect system is organized experientially; but there are also 'tense languages' with experiential tense systems, e.g. classifying 'past' tense into subtypes according to their degree of remoteness from the now of speaking: see Matthiessen 2004, for discussion and references.)

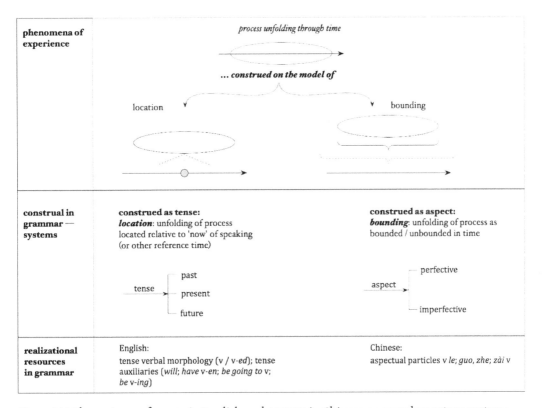

*Figure 6.15* The systems of TENSE in English and ASPECT in Chinese as complementary systems for construing processes unfolding through time

The English system of TENSE and the Chinese system of ASPECT would appear to be incompatible in the sense that they do not share any systems when we represent them systemically in a multilingual system network (see Section 6.4.2 below), and this indeed turns out to be the case, as shown in Figure 6.16. The temporal systems of English and Chinese are both largely 'pure' systems, with little mixture of the two temporal models of tense and aspect, and in this respect, they represent tendencies towards the western and eastern poles of Eurasia. For example, while English is somewhat extreme in its logical modelling of tense, we also find tense systems in e.g. French (Caffarel 1992) and Spanish. In contrast, in East and South-East Asia, we find a number of languages from different families operating with the aspect model, including Tagalog, Vietnamese and Thai. This suggests that these complementary temporal models are 'areal features', and this impression is reinforced when we meet mixed systems in between the outer poles of Eurasia (and North Africa): there are examples of mixed tense-aspect systems in Slavic languages, Indo-Aryan languages and (at least, in my view) in Modern Standard Arabic.

The complementarity illustrated in Figure 6.16 is located within the lexicogrammatical stratum. It represents two complementary models for construing the unfolding of processes in time. It will need to be resolved at the stratum of semantics: language learners going in either direction, bilingual speakers and translator & interpreters must clearly have mastered a multilingual semantic meaning potential that enables them to operate with both grammatical systems and to move between them when necessary.

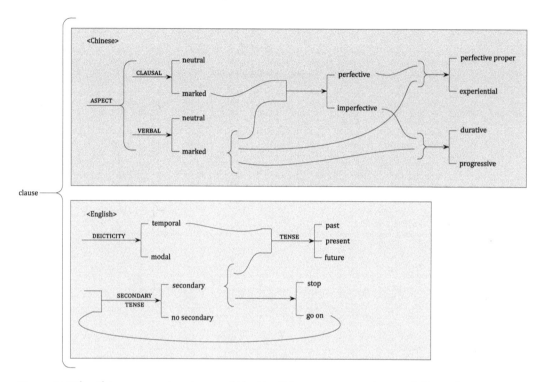

*Figure 6.16* The Chinese aspect system and the English tense system in a multilingual system network – each in its own separate systemic partition

### 6.4.4.7 Complementarities Across Semiotic Systems

A similar task needs to be addressed by multi-semiotic systems: different semiotic systems complement one another in the making of meaning, and at least if they are clearly coordinated in the making of meaning, as e.g. language and gesture are, then there must be a kind of semantic system that enables users of such semiotic systems to coordinate and integrate the meanings they make while at the same time dividing the semiotic labour of making meaning among them, as suggested for linguistic and pictorial systems in Figure 6.17. The complementarity of such systems has typically been discussed in terms of the relationship between them – often at the instantial pole of the cline of instantiation, i.e. relationships that obtain between written text and 'images' of different kinds (e.g. Royce 1998, 1999; Martinec and Salway 2005; Bateman 2008a). But we also need accounts of the complementarity of the modes of meaning made by two or more semiotic systems operating together – showing how the work of making meaning is divided among them and how different kinds of meaning are apportioned to one semiotic system or another.

One strategy for developing accounts of multi-semiotic complementarity is to focus on one register at a time (see Section 3.2.2.5 on register-specific semantic systems). Within the ideational metafunction at the stratum of semantics, such accounts have been referred to as **domain models** in computational linguistics and AI (see Halliday and Matthiessen 2006, where the domains of weather forecasts and recipes are sketched). As an example, I will draw briefly on a domain model based on the analysis of a sample of WHO's Weekly Epidemiological Records (WER; see Matthiessen 2006b; and Cross et al., 1998, on the HINTS system that this domain model was part of). These reports are published in English and French and also include language, tables, statistical charts and maps. The ideational domain of that register can be modelled in a unified way, and the meanings that may be construed non-linguistically can be located within the overall domain model. A schematic representation of the domain model is set out in Figure 6.18. There are three regions that are realized by the non-linguistic semiotic systems, viz. numbers of cases and of deaths, the percentage or ratio of case fatalities and morbidities, and people as cases in relation to places.

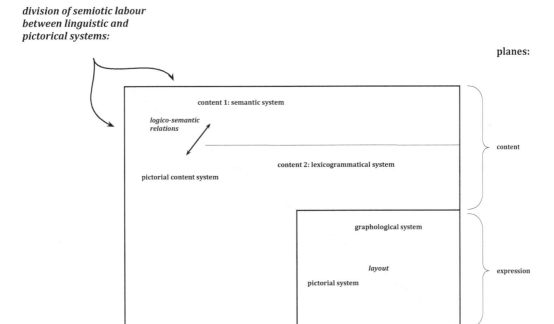

*Figure 6.17* The complementarity of semiotic systems in the making of meaning, illustrated by the complementarity of language and a pictorial system

Here a key multisemiotic role played by language is to 'gloss' non-linguistic displays, indicating how they are to be interpreted (by means of identifying clauses where the Token represents the non-linguistic semiotic construct and the Value provides the 'gloss'). References to maps, figures (charts) and tables are often just given in brackets in the verbal text, but they may be construed by identifying relational clauses with the name of the semiotic artefact as Token and the interpretation of it as Value, as in *Map 1 and Fig. 1 present the global distribution of the estimated total number of adult AIDS cases from the late 1970s until the end of 1996.*, shown in Figure 6.19. In terms of the complementarity between language and the other semiotic systems in the multisemiotic WERs, language is used to make the links to maps, charts, and tables; and it provides the resources, when necessary, to provide a general interpretation of their meaning. In the example diagrammed in Figure 6.19, the map and the chart elaborate on the number of AIDS cases with details regarding numbers and geographic location; the chart restates some of the information shown by the map. The verbal text also provides an elaboration of details, indicating the conditions of the estimated numbers.

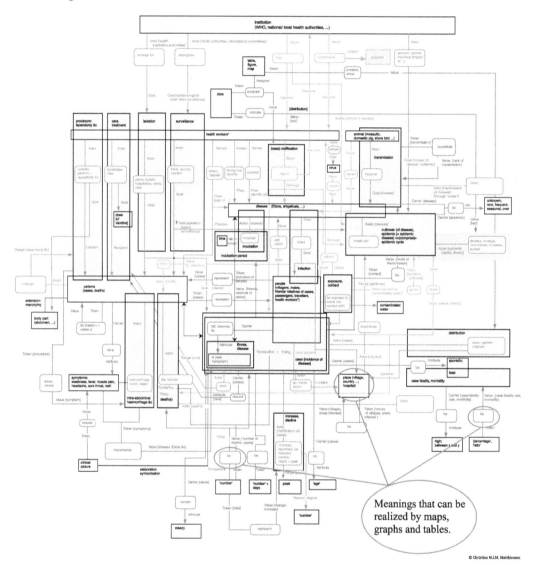

*Figure 6.18* Semantic domain model based on sample of WER by WHO, with regions also realized by non-linguistic semiotic systems indicated

*The System: Challenges and Possibilities* • 239

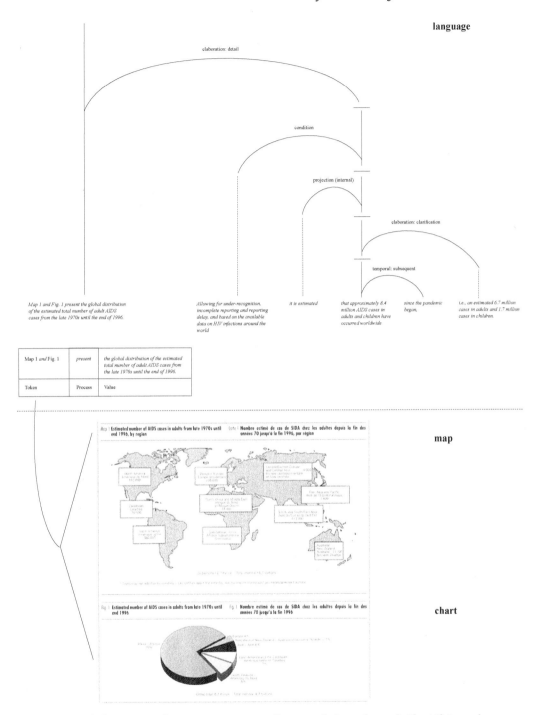

*Figure 6.19* Verbal text providing interpretation of map and chart through identifying relationship, and further textual elaboration (WHO's Weekly Epidemiological Record, No. 48, 29 November 1996)

## 6.5 Enhancement of Representational Power of System Networks

Throughout this book, I have introduced and used 'standard' system networks. They have remained quite stable since Halliday designed them in the 1960s; the conventions have remained the same, and are set out in Table 8.1 in the Appendix, with the realization statements associated with systemic terms specified in Table 8.2. Naturally, there have been particular research contexts where special pressure has been applied to system networks – computational applications in particular, as sketched in Section 5.2 above. The computational work has included investigations of the formalization of system networks and the re-representations of them by computational representations such as typed feature structures and frame-based inheritance networks. However, these investigations have tended not to be picked up outside computational SFL even though they are relevant to various tasks such as the investigation of the discursive construction of knowledge in educational linguistics. Along the way, we have met some particular variants of system networks:

- **displayed system networks**, where simultaneous systems or systems with disjunctive entry conditions are displayed as more delicate systems within the systems they are simultaneous with or can be reached from through disjunctive entry conditions (Figure 6.21), thereby being displayed more than once in the system network (Fawcett 1988a).
- **hybrid system networks**, where system networks are extended in delicacy by strict taxonomies, serving as stepping stones used in the development of systemic descriptions of lexis (Figure 3.18 and Figure 3.19).

And in this chapter, I have discussed the translation between flow charts, taxonomies and mind maps on the one hand and system networks on the other. As we have seen, different modes of visualization of paradigmatic patterns can be quite helpful.

### 6.5.1 Conditional Marking Conventions

There is one system network convention that has appeared a few times in systemic descriptions that I have presented – **conditional marking conventions**, as in Halliday's (1992b) description of Peking syllable finals (Figure 3.45). I have only mentioned them, referring forward to this section. They usually accord with the following template: if systemic term $a$, then systemic term $p$, where $a$ and $p$ are terms on simultaneous paths through the system network. For example:

- in the Akan phoneme system network in Figure 3.43, there are four conditional markings, e.g. if 'central', then 'neutral', which captures the constraint that only non-central vowels allow for a distinction between neutral tongue root position and advanced tongue root position – only 'non-central' ones ('back' and 'front') allow for a contrast in tongue root position.
- in the English interpersonal clause system network in Figure 3.8, if the clause has a 'subjective' modality assessment, then the clause is 'modal' in deicticity; and if its 'readiness' is of the 'potentiality' type, then it is 'low' in modality value.

In Figure 3.8, I have used a graphic convention that I have introduced since it makes it easier to visualize and thus keep track of conditional marking relationships: a dotted arrow leads from the conditioning term to the conditioned one. I have set out a simple example in Figure 6.20 showing a conditioning relationship between MOOD TYPE and POLARITY: if a clause is 'exclamative' in mood type, it is 'positive' in polarity (rather than 'negative'). The impossibility of negative exclamatives is illustrated in the paradigm of examples set out in Table 6.4.[9] A convenient way of blocking such impossible systemic combinations is to use a conditional marking convention, as illustrated in Figure 6.20.

Such conventions have been used fairly often in systemic descriptions over the years since the 1960s. In a way, they capture gaps in paradigms 'elegantly'. However, there is an issue that will need to be taken care of: they impose a 'hidden' constraint on traversal algorithms (Figure 5.3 above). In principle, simultaneous systems can be traversed in any sequence. Thus if the system of POLARITY is entered first, and 'negative' is selected, and the system 'non-exclamative/ 'exclamative' is entered later and 'exclamative' is selected, there is a **systemic selection clash**: the selection would be 'exclamative' and 'negative', which is blocked. For this reason, working on the development of the systemic text generation system referred to above in Section 5.2, I revised the system network used in the Nigel grammar to remove all instance of conditional marking conventions. The revised versions are less elegant, but they will work straightforwardly with the traversal algorithm we designed.

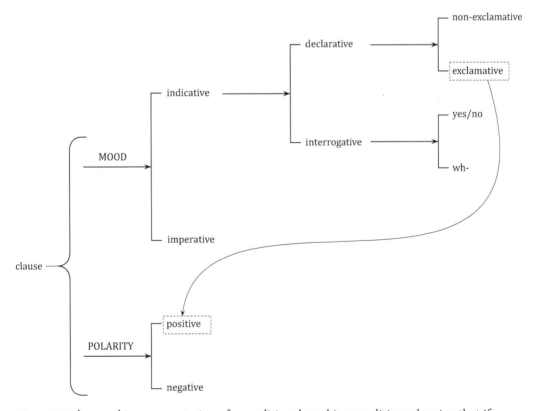

*Figure 6.20* The graphic representation of a conditional marking conditions showing that if a clause is 'exclamative', then it is 'positive' (rather than 'negative') in polarity

Table 6.5 Paradigm showing the intersection of polarity and mood type, with one impossible combination

| MOOD TYPE | | | POLARITY | |
|---|---|---|---|---|
| | | | positive | negative |
| indicative | declarative | non-exclamative | *he's very generous* | *he isn't very generous* |
| | | exclamative | *who generous he is!* | *\*how generous he isn't!* |
| | interrogative | yes/no | *is he very generous?* | *isn't he very generous?* |
| | | wh- | *who is very generous?* | *who isn't very generous?* |
| imperative | | | *be generous!* | *don't be generous!* |

### 6.5.2 Multilingual System Network

Conditional marking conventions add to the representational power of system networks, but they can be replaced by alternative 'wiring'. However, there is one representational enhancement of system networks that cannot be replaced – one that genuinely and unproblematically enhances their representational power: **multilingual system networks**. This enhancement of the representational power of system networks started in computational SFL around 30 years ago. We faced the task of developing multilingual text generation systems, both in Germany and in Australia; and we reported the development in Bateman et al. (1991) and then expanded on it in Bateman, Matthiessen and Zeng (1999). However, even though this enhancement of system networks originated in computational applications, multilingual system networks are important for a variety of tasks, including language description, language comparison and contrast, translation studies and other areas of activity where two or more languages are brought into contact with one another[10]: see Teruya et al. (2007); Matthiessen (2014c, 2015c, 2018a). Thus multilingual system networks are needed to account for various semiotic activities multilingual speakers may engage in, like code-switching, code-mixing, translation and interpreting – cf. the notion of 'translanguaging' (e.g. Mazzaferro 2018), and of course also the activity of a meaner learner to mean in a new (second or foreign) language (Matthiessen 2015c).

The basic idea is very simple: the system network of each language being described is represented in such a way that its own language-specific integrity is maintained, and when the system networks of different languages are 'unified', the parts that are shared or congruent with one another are represented as common potential and the parts where the languages differ and allocated to distinct **partitions** that conditioned in terms of the language of languages that they apply to. Such partitions may include just realization statements or systems with any associated realization statements. (If terms in systems in different languages seem to be the same, but actually have different systemic values, different *valeurs*, the systems will of course be represented in language-specific partitions. See Matthiessen 2004: 597, for an illustration of this point in relation to 'cognitive' in the 'mental' clause grammars of English, Tagalog and Japanese: the *valeurs* of 'cognitive' is different in the systemic description of each language.) This approach clearly depends on the priority of paradigmatic organization quite centrally; and, as a representation of a multilingual meaning potential, it is a significant advance over approaches based on syntagmatically oriented theories of grammar, as in the pioneering work on the 'syntax of code-switching' by David Sankoff and collaborators (e.g. Sankoff and Poplack 1981; Sankoff and Mainville 1986).

As an illustration of multilingual system networks, let me start with the description of personal pronouns – an area of the lexicogrammar that has been used for illustrative purposes in discussions of system networks in SFL by Fawcett (1988b) and Martin (2013).[11] (This choice of illustration will also relate to the refence to Brown and Gilman, 1960, in Section 3.2.2.6.2 above and the discussion of the relationship between interpersonal systems and the contextual parameter of tenor.) Let me give a fairly simple example of a multilingual system network involving differences in simultaneity as well as in delicacy in the description of the system of personal pronouns in English and Indonesian[12]: see Figure 6.21. This system network represents the integration of the systems of personal pronouns in English and Indonesian. Drawing on descriptions of personal pronouns in Indonesian in various standard reference sources, I have tried to 'systemicize' them. It is perfectly possible that I got it wrong, but the description is only an illustration of theoretical points concerning the concept of the multilingual meaning potential and the focus is not on descriptive details.

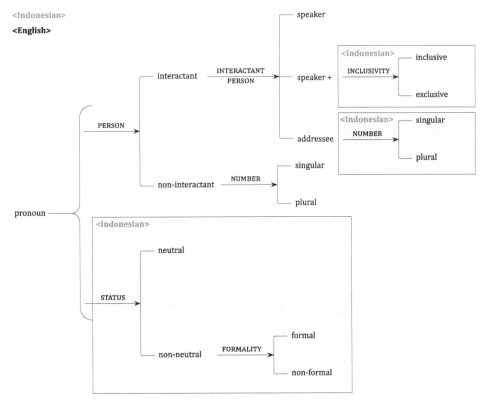

*Figure 6.21* A fragment of a multilingual system network – the system of personal pronouns in English and Indonesian unified in a multilingual system network. The system network includes three partitions that are specific to Indonesian (represented by <Indonesian>), viz. the systems of INCLUSIVITY, NUMBER, STATUS (and the dependent system of FORMALITY); the other systems of the system network are shared by English and Indonesian (in a common partition, represented by <Indonesian>, <English>)

The multilingual system network in Figure 6.21 represents the integration of English and Indonesian. The two languages share three systems, viz. PERSON, INTERACTANT PERSON and NUMBER. These three systems are represented in the partition of the system network that is common to both languages: <Indonesian> and <English>. Here <Indonesian> and <English> are the conditions associated with the partition. But there are a number of systems that are specific to Indonesian. There are two systems specific to Indonesian that have systemic terms in shared systems as their entry conditions: INCLUSIVITY, with 'speaker+' (i.e. speaker plus others) as the entry condition, and NUMBER with 'addressee' as the entry condition. And there is another system that is simultaneous with the system of PERSON; this is the system of STATUS, one of whose terms ('non-neutral') leads to another more delicate system, FORMALITY.

The realizations of combinations of systemic terms in Figure 6.21 are set out for English and Indonesian in Table 6.6.[13] This table shows clearly that the Indonesian pronouns are defined by the intersection of terms from two simultaneous systems, PERSON and STATUS. These realizations could be represented in the system network in Figure 6.21 as systemic gates. A gate is like an ordinary system except that is always as a complex entry condition, not a single feature, and only one term; one or more realization statements are associated with this term. I will illustrate the use of gates in multilingual system networks below (Figure 6.22).

Table 6.6 Personal pronouns in English and Indonesian – grammatical items realizing the systemic terms in Figure 6.21

| PERSON | | | English | Indonesian | | |
|---|---|---|---|---|---|---|
| | | | | non-formal | neutral | formal |
| interactant | speaker | | | aku | | saya |
| | speaker+ | inclusive | I | | kita | |
| | | exclusive | | | kami | |
| | addressee | singular | you | kamu; engkau | anda | saudara |
| | | plural | | kalian | | |
| non-interactant | singular | | he, she, it | | dia, ia | beliau |
| | plural | | they | | meréka | |

The situation illustrated in Figure 6.21 above is quite common in the representation of multilingual meaning potentials. In a multilingual meaning potential, the languages making up the potential often differ in terms of the number of parameters they use in organizing some domain, e.g. a single parameter represented by one system with delicacy-dependent systems or two parameters represented by two simultaneous systems with delicacy-dependent systems. Thus English organizes personal reference in terms of only the system of PERSON but Indonesian organizes it in terms of the simultaneous systems of PERSON and STATUS. We find status distinctions in the pronominal systems of many languages – predictably, given their importance in terms of tenor in societies bloated in terms of hierarchy, but there is variation across languages in terms of how independent PERSON and STATUS are of each other (cf. Brown and Gilman 1960). For example, in a number of languages spoken in Europe, the status distinction applies only to the 'addressee' person – the well-known *tu/vous* distinction found in e.g. French, Spanish and German; so in multilingual system networks that cover the system of personal pronouns in English and in one or more of these languages, the STATUS distinction would be represented as a more delicate system with 'addressee' as its entry condition rather than as a system simultaneous with PERSON.

Let me give one more example of a multilingual system network where two languages, English, and Korean, differ in terms of the number of simultaneous systems that are involved in organizing a domain, adding one more language, Chinese, to illustrate difference in delicacy: see Figure 6.22. This example relates to another interpersonal domain – the grammar of SPEECH FUNCTION (i.e. MOOD), and the variation between Korean and English & Chinese is very similar to the variation in status illustrated in Figure 6.21.

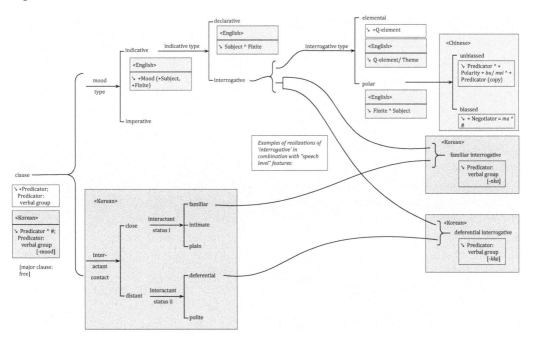

*Figure 6.22* Multilingual system network of MOOD – English, Chinese, and Korean, with speech level in Korean (the system of interactant contact) and the gates with the terms 'familiar interrogative' and 'deferential interrogative' as examples of the systemic interaction with the system of mood type

English, Chinese and Korean share the basic MOOD system (for Korean, see e.g. Sohn 1999; S.E. Martin 1992), but Chinese elaborates polar interrogatives in terms of the speaker's expectation as to the answer, viz. 'unbiased' or 'biased' (see Halliday and McDonald 2004).[14] However, the three languages differ in how the various mood types are realized. In English, the realization statements, which appear in English-specific partitions, involve the Mood element; but in Korean, they involve the verbal group serving as the

Predicator of the clause and in Chinese a final Negotiator function may be involved in the realization. The Predicator in Korean comes at the end of the clause, as specified by the Korean-specific realization statement associated with 'clause' at the far left of the system network in Figure 6.22; and it is an important site for interpersonal realizations in the clause, giving the clause an interpersonal 'finale' at the point at which the current speaker in a dialogue may hand over to the addressee to become the next speaker. Mood types are realized by verbal suffixes, but these suffixes may also realize terms in an interpersonal system simultaneous with the system of MOOD, viz. INTERACTANT CONTACT.

The system of INTERACTANT CONTACT is concerned with tenor relations between speaker and addressee having to do with contact ('horizontal relations', essentially in-group vs. out-group) and status ('vertical relations', social hierarchy); these distinctions are often described under the heading of 'speech level' in accounts of Korean. Thus every time a speaker of Korean makes a selection in the system of MOOD, s/he also has to make a selection in the system of INTERACTANT CONTACT, locating herself or himself in social space relative to the addressee. Mood markers – the verbal mood suffixes – may differ according to the 'speech level' (see e.g. S.E. Martin's 1992: 306, 'mood shift table'): I have illustrated this for two combinations, the contrast between 'polar' interrogative clauses that are 'familiar' and those that are 'deferential'. I have represented these combinations by means of systemic gates (see above), with associate realization statements – 'familiar interrogative' and 'deferential interrogative'.

The examples in Figure 6.21 and Figure 6.22 illustrate how multilingual system networks can be used to show what interpersonal concerns multilingual speakers must have incorporated in their multilingual meaning potentials. In the interpersonal metafunction, languages vary with respect to what aspects of tenor they grammaticalize. The description of English, Chinese and Korean in Figure 6.22 does not, of course, mean that speakers of English and Chinese cannot and do not make selections concerned with contact and status within tenor; they do make such selections, but the relevant systems are not built into the core of the interpersonal clause grammar but instead depend on the meaning potential that is opened up through interpersonal metaphors of mood (e.g. Halliday 1984a; Halliday and Matthiessen 2014: Chapter 10).

As we develop descriptions of two or more languages using multilingual system networks, we may of course find that there is no shared potential at all. Such a case has already been illustrated. The systems of TENSE in English and of ASPECT in Mandarin are completely complementary systems: see Figure 6.15 and the multilingual system network in Figure 6.16. Since these two systems are grammatical ones, the task of relating them to one another will have to reside in the multilingual semantics, where it may be recognized e.g. that under certain conditions the perfective aspect in Chinese can be related to the secondary past in English. The challenge of relating systems that appear to be very different is discussed in Halliday and Matthiessen (2006: Chapter 7), with references to Pawley's account of Kalam – in contrast with English (e.g. Pawley 1987, 2008; cf. also Lane 2007; Grace 1981).

Multilingual system networks have usually been used to represent a small handful of languages although the implementation provided by John Bateman's (e.g. 1997) KLPM system has no limit on the number of languages that can be represented by multilingual system networks. The descriptive explorations undertaken with small numbers of languages represented by means of multilingual system networks suggests two **tendencies**:

- In terms of axial order, languages tend to be more congruent with one another systemically than structurally; that is, languages can achieve comparable systemic contrasts such as 'hypotactic' vs. 'paratactic', 'declarative' vs. 'interrogative', 'positive' vs. 'negative', 'material' vs. 'relational' by different syntagmatic means. Consequently, realization statements are more likely to be located within language-specific partitions, as in the case of realization statements for English in the multilingual system network in Figure 6.22.
- In terms of paradigmatic order, languages tend to be more congruent with one another towards the lower-delicacy pole of the cline of delicacy and less congruent with one another as the delicacy increases, and as it extends towards the lexical zone. Consequently, high-delicacy systems are more likely to be located within language-specific partitions, as in the case of the Chinese partition for polar interrogative types in Figure 6.22.

There are clearly other considerations as well, such as the difference between foundational interpersonal systems of exchange – lexicogrammatical mood systems – and variably extended systems enacted by/in tenor parameters of 'power and solidarity' (cf. the Korean-specific partition in the multilingual mood system network in Figure 6.22). But here I'll focus briefly on the two tendencies set out above.

In terms of axial order, there are abundant examples of language construing/enacting/encapsulating comparable systemic contrasts realized by means of different syntagmatic patterns.[15] To test this generalization, we need access to a good typological database – WALS being an obvious candidate,[16] but we also need to identify accounts in such databases that can be interpreted both systemically (paradigmatically) and structurally (syntagmatically). In WALS, one of the candidates of such accounts is the realization of 'polar' interrogatives (as opposed to 'elemental' ones). In one language after another, there is clear evidence of the systemic contrast between 'polar' and 'elemental' interrogatives, as with English 'yes/no' vs. 'wh-' interrogatives; but there's considerable variation in the syntagmatic realization of 'polar' interrogatives.

Let me just illustrate this variation for a partial sample of languages spoken in West Africa, based on information from WALS: see Figure 6.23. There are three syntagmatic patterns: a Negotiator function realized by an interrogative particle (as in Ewe), which is by far the most common and widely spread pattern; the Predicator realized by a verb including an interrogative affix (as in Beria); or a phonological prosody, more specifically rising tone (as in Yoruba).[17] One syntagmatic pattern that does not occur is the ordering of Finite before Subject – not surprisingly, since this is quite an 'exotic' tactic pattern largely restricted to Germanic languages such as English (and possibly languages that have been in areal contact over long period of time). Other linguistic areas ('Sprachbund') are also very interesting to examine; I have chosen part of West Africa as an example partly because we have surveyed mood systems in that region in Mwinlaaru, Matthiessen and Akerejola (2018). Again the key point shown by samples like the one presented in Figure 6.23 is that the systemic valeur inherent in two or more terms in the same system may be achieved syntagmatically in a variety of ways – but what matters is that it is manifested syntagmatically. (Of course, the realizational differences we find within the system of MOOD TYPE are not restricted to that system; they tend to cut across systems belonging to different regions of the grammar.)

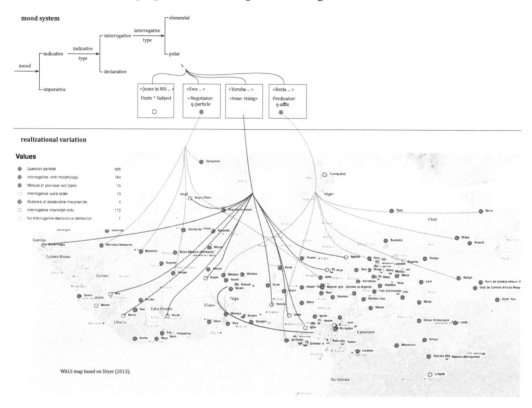

*Figure 6.23* The system of MOOD: geographic spread of types of realization of polar interrogative in western West Africa (based on WALS)

This brief reference to the variation in the realization of mood systems around the languages of the world can serve as a transition to a brief note on 'system' and typological generalizations. When we examine the mood systems of languages spoken around the world (e.g. Sadock and Zwicky 1985; König and Siemund 2007) in relation to multilingual system networks, we can begin to discern certain broad generalizations, including:

- the interpersonal grammars of languages around the world tend to be more congruent in terms of low-delicacy systems of mood type that capture the basic interpersonal logic of reciprocity but less congruent in terms of more delicate distinctions;
- while the general systemic distinctions tend to be fairly congruent, the syntagmatic ('tactic') realizations of these distinction indicate a considerably larger envelope of variation – though within the general mode of prosodic expression;
- while the grammar of all languages are likely to grammaticalize speech function, languages vary considerably with respect to which they grammaticalize with distinctions in tenor relations.

As we examine the mood systems of different languages, we can identify a range of possible expansions of the primary mood types, as illustrated in Figure 6.24. These possible expansions are represented pre-systemically, merely as possible more delicate elaborations of the primary mood types, e.g. having to do with the validity (evidentiality), force and interactive stance of a declarative realizing a statement or the expected compliance with an imperative realizing a command. In addition, there may, as we have seen for Korean, be another interpersonal vector – one concerned with the tenor of the relation between speaker and addressee (distinctions in 'speech level'). The hybrid system network in in Figure 6.24 clearly needs to be refined based on more extensive typological studies of a larger varied samples of mood systems than are currently available. But for systemic functional linguists embarking on the description of the interpersonal clause grammar of a 'new' language, it can serve as a guide to distinctions to look for in naturally occurring dialogues in different contexts or to probe for in the elicitation of examples in the description of mood paradigms.

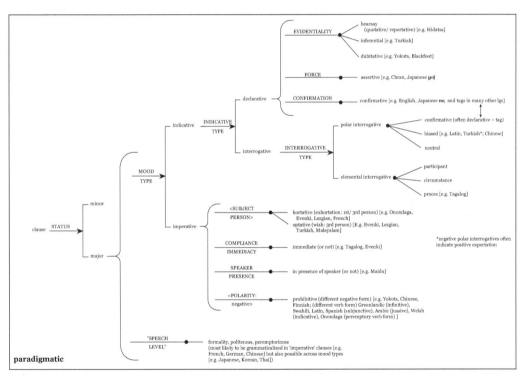

*Figure 6.24* Systemic options for the interpersonal clause grammars of languages around the world

Many generalizations in the typological literature can, however, be interpreted as statements about the order of elaboration of grammatical and phonological systems. For example, Comrie and Keenan's (e.g. 1979) noun phrase accessibility hierarchy in relative clause formation can be interpreted for relatives as an ordering of systemic elaborations, as in Figure 6.25. This says that languages will have a relative that serve as Subject in the relative clause. If this is further elaborated, it will be a choice between Subject and Complement; and if this is further elaborated, the non-subject relative will be Complement or an 'oblique' element. I use their account here merely to illustrate

250 • *System in Systemic Functional Linguistics*

how such accounts can be interpreted systemically. Or to put it more forcefully, such accounts are actually systemic typologies – i.e. generalizations about the systemic potential of some area of grammar (or phonology).

Thus many of the patterns found in the WALS database can be restated systemically, with information about the number of languages in the samples in the database. For example, most languages do not make tenor-related distinctions for 'addressee' in their pronominal systems, but some do, and then the systemic distinction can be characterized as 'respectful'/'intimate'. An even smaller number of languages elaborate 'respectful' in terms of the degree of respect, 'elevated status'/'higher status'. This ordering of systems is set out in Figure 6.26 together with a chart showing the number of languages in the sample for each type.

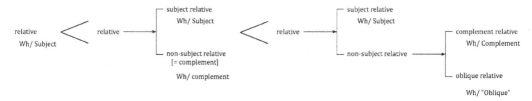

*Figure 6.25* Systemic interpretation of the accessibility hierarchy for relatives

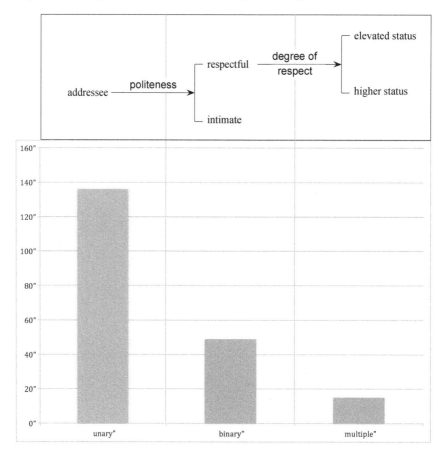

*Figure 6.26* Systemic elaboration of addressee pronouns, based on the WALS database

There is clearly much more to say about systemic functional typology, but this brief excursion is only intended to illustrate those aspects that can be related to multilingual system networks.

## 6.6 Summary of Challenges and Opportunities

In this chapter, I have taken a step back from the fundamental theoretical notion of the system, its representation by system networks and applications in a number of domains. I have tried to discern and bring attention to both challenges and opportunities. One could in fact do a SWAT analysis along the lines I sketched for SFL in general in Matthiessen (2010); but I swatted the temptation to walk the path of management think here, and instead focussed on challenges and opportunities.

As it turns out, on balance, challenges are located primarily at the level of theoretical representation within the systemic functional metalanguage, as set out in Figure 5.6 above, whereas opportunities are on the whole due to systemic theory, one metalinguistic stratum higher. In other words, many challenges have to do with the task of doing full representational justice to the theory of system, e.g. capturing theoretical insights into systemic clines, systemic indeterminacy, conditioning probabilities, auto-generative systems, as was illustrated in Section 6.3 above. This is of course one reason why the metatheoretical model of metalanguage as a stratified system is crucial; as we try to increase the power of the system network as a system of theoretical representation, we can gain new insights from the next level down, i.e. the level of computational representation.

At the same time, we also need to recognize, of course, that the relation between the levels of theory and theoretical representation in the shape of system networks is a dialogic or dialectic one – much like the relationship between semantics and lexicogrammar. Like other graphic representations and forms of visualization, system networks are an excellent tool for thinking with, working out paradigmatic patterns and relationships. One can get a sense of this empowering nature of system networks as one tries to develop a systemic description of some region of a particular language, or of course of some other semiotic system. This empowering effect also becomes very evident when one undertakes the task of translating other systems of representation that can be used to visualize paradigmatic patterns, as in the case of taxonomies, mind maps and flow charts illustrated in Section 6.2 above.

System networks are not, of course, a closed chapter in SFL; they are very much 'live' and open to further development (as well as the possibility of wholesale replacement if a good candidate presents itself – or is designed). This was touched on in Section 6.4 – with particular reference to our development of multilingual system networks. As I noted a long time ago (Matthiessen 1993), this representational enhancement can also be used to represent variation within a given language of the registerial kind – or indeed any other kind of variation (dialectal, codal), and even possibly the complementarity of different semiotic systems within a unified semantic network, as briefly illustrated above with reference to Figure 6.18 (and cf. also Section 5.5.3, Figure 5.16).

# Chapter 7

# Conclusion

Each chapter of this book has its own summary, and, to a certain extent, the chapters can be read independently of one another (hence the many cross references). Instead of summarizing the book here, touching on the presentation in the previous chapters on the distinct but related senses of 'system' set out in Figure 1.2, I will take a step back and try to contextualize, or even recontextualize, 'system' in the light of the previous chapters but with additional perspectives that are possible to adopt only at this point. I will begin by viewing axiality, i.e. axial order (paradigmatic vs. syntagmatic) trinocularly. I will then suggest an analogy between the distinction between paradigmatic and syntagmatic order and David Bohm's distinction between implicate and explicate order. Finally, I will return to the view of 'system' in an ordered typology of systems, again noting the connection between SFL and different manifestations of systems thinking – as one possible preamble to future research.

## 7.1 Angles of Axial Order: Trinocular Vision

The major theme of this book has been 'system', which derives from **axiality** – the distinction between the paradigmatic axis and the syntagmatic one. If we take one step back, then we can see that this is about **order** – order in language as a resource for making meaning. Like everything else in language, this order can be viewed **trinocularly**, from different vantage points – from above, from below and from roundabout, as shown in Figure 7.1. The vantage point we adopt will determine our *perspective on this order*, which perspective that we foreground based on our point of vision (cf. also Table 6.1 above):

- If we see the order **from below**, we will see it in the first instance as syntagmatic patterns; this is the view that is foregrounded in American structuralist theories. Seen from this vantage point, paradigmatic patterns will appear as parasitic on syntagmatic patterns (e.g. like alternatives in structural rules).
- If we view the order **from above**, we will see it in the first instance as paradigmatic patterns; this is the view foregrounded in systemic theories. Seen from this vantage point, syntagmatic patterns will appear as manifestations of paradigmatic patterns.
- If we view the order **from roundabout**, we will see it in the first instance as a balance between paradigmatic patterns and syntagmatic ones; this is the view foregrounded in system-structure theories. Seen from this vantage point, paradigmatic patterns will appear as located or placed within syntagmatic ones (as

in Firth's system-structure theory, Hasan's GSP – and possibly the meta-rules of GPSG).

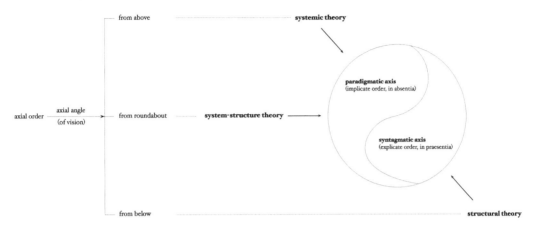

*Figure 7.1* Trinocular view of axial order – seen 'from above': systemic theory, seen 'from below': structural theory, seen 'from roundabout': system-structure theory

The different vantage points will foreground different manifestations of order; for example, adopting the view from above, we will see patterns of agnation (and to bring out such patterns, scholars devised the **commutation test** in phonology), but adopting the view from below, patterns of distribution will come to the fore, as in the development of distributionalism in US structuralist linguistics, associated with Bloomfield (1933), Harris (e.g. 1954) and other structuralist linguists (see e.g. Matthews 1993: in particular Chapter 3, on 'distributional syntax', spanning post-Bloomfieldians and Chomskyans up through the 1970s). For example, in his preface to a collection of his papers, Harris (1970: v) characterizes the **distributional method** as follows:

> The papers reprinted in this volume carry out what has been called the distributional method, i.e. the analysis of occurrence-restrictions, beyond phonemics. The establishment of the phoneme marked the beginning of structural linguistics both in content and in method. [...] Phonemics showed that new entities, the phonemes, could be defined as classifications of these sounds based on their occurrence-relations. The occurrence-restrictions (i.e., the restrictions on combination) of the originally observed sounds are thereupon replaced, equivalently, by the occurrence-restriction which determines membership of sounds in phonemes, plus the occurrence-restrictions on the phonemes.
>
> This methodological approach, of defining more freely combining new elements on the basis of occurrence-restrictions of old elements, has proved applicable in many further situations in structural linguistics.

Thus viewed from below, order manifests itself partly in terms of syntagmatic co-occurrences, and this invites the development of distributionalism as an approach, but also later developments in US generative linguistics concerned with rules manipulating segments of syntagms, for example moving them or deleting them in syntactic syntagms or changing distinctive features within phonemes (conceived of as feature bundles) in phonological syntagms.

The different angles of vision shown in Figure 7.1 have served as points of departure for a range of linguistic theories, a number of which are listed as examples in Table 7.1 (cf. also Table 6.1 above). The examples include both whole theories and theoretical methods such as distributionalism. A particular school or tradition may embody more than one angle of vision; for example, the Prague School covered systemic patterns in Trubetzkoy's (1939) phonology, but focussed on syntagmatic patterns in its Functional Sentence Perspective. And Jakobson (1949), a founding member of the Prague Linguistic Circle, reinterpreted Trubetzkoy's paradigmatic phonological values as components of phonemes, his 'distinctive features' – a move that illustrates the point being made here that order may be **interpreted *from different vantage points*.** Jakobson (1949/1962: 420) introduces his interpretation of phonemes as consisting of distinctive features as follows:

> Long ago the neurologists distinguished two kinds of complexes (*Simultankomplexe* und *Sukzessivkomplexe* in K. Kleist's terminology) which underlie our speech-ability, which are differently located in the brain and which may be respectively compared with the chords and sequences in music. Meanwhile the science of language continued to treat the phoneme as the most minute (further indivisible) linguistic unit.

> However, as the phonemes of a given language form a system of sequences, so the system of phonemes, in turn, is formed by their constituents, i.e. by distinctive features. And the breaking up of the phonemes into distinctive features follows precisely the same tested devices as the division of morphemes into phonemes.

He then goes on to suggest that commutations show that phonemes can be 'decomposed' into 'commutable elements'. A bit further on his account, he continues (1949/1962: 422):

> In dissociating the phoneme into distinctive features we isolate the ultimate linguistic constituents charged with semiotic value.

In adopting the view from below (Figure 7.1), Jakobson thus reinterpreted terms in systems representing patterns along the paradigmatic axis (i.e. paradigmatic *valeurs*) as syntagmatic components or constituents of phonemes, and he addressed the possible objection that while phonemes occur in sequence and distinctive features don't by invoking the notion of simultaneous complexes (*Simultankomplexe*) in addition to sequential complexes.[1]

But while we can adopt the different views just outlined above, does this mean that one view can be derived from another by simply adjusting our observer perspective? The answer is 'no' because the different views are not equally informative, i.e. they do not equally capture all aspects of axial order (cf. Matthiessen 1995a). The view from above embodies more information because it includes relations that are not visible from below or even from roundabout. For example, if distinctive features are treated as component parts of phonemes, the systemic relations among terms in systems are not visible, so they are not represented. Phonologists have represented distinctive features in taxonomies; for example, Fant (2004: 181), who had worked with Jakobson and Halle in the 1950s (Jakobson, Fant and Halle 1952), presents a 'distinctive feature coding tree of Swedish vowels' but precisely because it is a tree, distinctive feature oppositions are repeated, occurring in more than one place in the tree, so generalizations are not captured as they would be in a system network (cf. Section 6.3.1 above).

*Table 7.1* Examples of different theories of axial order

| axial angle of vision | theory | examples |
|---|---|---|
| from above | systemic theory | systemic functional theory [system networks, with realization statements] |
| from roundabout | system-structure theory | [linguistics:] Firth's system-structure theory, Hasan's GSP; [computational linguistics:] RTNs (Recursive Transition Networks); frame-based inheritance networks |
| from below | structural theory | Distributionalism; Immediate Constituency analysis; Transformational grammar (including phrase structure rules) [embodying 'alternation rules']; GPSG (with metarules for paradigmatic statements); LFG; RRG; FG; Construction Grammar; Autosegmental phonology; Jakobsonian phonology; componential analysis (in [lexical] semantics) |

Ideally, then, the view from above – in our case, the systemic view – should be the **canonical view**, capturing all aspects of axial order, and other views should be possible to *compile out* from it as the need arises (cf. Matthiessen 1995a; Matthiessen and Nesbitt 1996). Thus while the systemic view attracted researchers in computational linguistics as they began to model text generation and build text generation systems (for computational applications, see Section 5.2), researchers developing computational models capable of parsing and text understanding need a robust representation of the view from below to support parsers in their tasks like the segmentation of units (see e.g. Bateman et al. 2019; Kasper 1988b; O'Donnell and Bateman 2005; O'Donnell 2017).

As we compare the three views defined by trinocular vision in Figure 7.1, we can try to determine how similar they are – how congruent they are with one another. This appears to vary across strata, ranks and metafunctions. For example, in articulatory phonology it would appear that they are fairly close to one another in the sense that phonemic systems can be located in structural places; in other words, their entry conditions can be characterized syntagmatically. This was after all a key domain of description in Firth's system-structure theory. And it is possible to imagine how phonotactic patterns could be represented by means of recursive transition networks (although patterns of a more prosodic nature might be backgrounded; cf. Figure 3.38 above). In contrast, in clause grammar, the views from above and from below are in general fairly distant from one another since systemic terms can be realized by a variety of syntagmatic patterns belonging to different 'modes of expression' (Halliday 1979), patterns that are also often dispersed along the rank scale. Here locating systems within structural places is impossible in the general case (which is reflected indirectly in the complex syntagmatic rule systems developed within generative linguistics).

## 7.2 Axial Order: Implicate and Explicate Order

Approaches to axial order can arguably – even productively – be compared to the physicist David Bohm's distinction between **implicate order** and **explicate order**. He develops the distinction in the context of physical systems, but indicates that it is of general relevance (cf. Pribram's 2013 review of Bohm's influence on his conception of the brain). Importantly, he gives priority to implicate order, suggesting that most attention has been given to explicate order. Here is his preview of his account – Bohm (1979: xviii):

> In chapter 6 we go further to begin a more concrete development of a new notion of order, that may be appropriate to a universe of unbroken wholeness. This is the *implicate* or *enfolded* order. In the enfolded order, space and time are no longer the dominant factors determining the relationships of dependence or independence of different elements. Rather, an entirely different sort of basic connection of elements is possible, from which our ordinary notions of space and time, along with those of separately existent material particles, are abstracted as forms derived from the deeper order. These ordinary notions in fact appear in what is called the *explicate* or *unfolded* order, which is a special and distinguished form contained within the general totality of all the implicate orders.

And in Chapter 6, he writes (Bohm 1979: 190):

> Now, we are proposing that in the formulation of the laws of physics, primary relevance is to be given to the implicate order, while the explicate order is to have a secondary kind of significance (e.g., as happened with Aristotle's notion of movement, after the development of classical physics).

One way of interpreting Bohm's distinction between implicate and explicate order within semiotic systems is to take it as analogous to the axial distinction between paradigmatic and syntagmatic patterns: **implicate order = paradigmatic order**, and **explicate order = syntagmatic order**. Bohm's (1979: 189) observation about what physicists have tended to focus on – 'Generally speaking, the laws of physics have thus far referred mainly to the explicate order.' – can by analogy be extended to linguistics: linguists have tended to view language 'from below' in terms of the trinocular vision set out in Figure 7.1, i.e. the more exposed and easily observable aspects of language, where space and time are 'dominant factors determining the relationships of dependence or independence of different elements' – a fair characterization also of syntagmatic patterns.

Since paradigmatic order is modelled in SFL by means of system networks (at the metalinguistic level of theoretical representation; cf. Figure 5.6 above) and they include realization statements associated with systemic terms, this analogy makes particularly good sense: as system networks are traversed, syntagmatic or explicate order is unfolded. I have added the analogy to the linguistic characterizations of the two axial order in Table 1.3 above, restating it as Table 7.2. I have also added characterizations by Michael Halliday couched in terms of chain vs. choice and strategic vs. tactic, and in addition I have added the differentiation within the fractal type of expansion into the subtypes of 'elaborating', 'extending', 'enhancing'.

Paradigmatic relations can be interpreted as predominantly 'elaborating', although extending relations are manifested in conjunction and disjunction; in contrast, syntagmatic relations can be interpreted as predominantly 'extending' (constituency) and 'enhancing' (sequence). This needs more discussion but instead let me turn to insights that come from B.L. Whorf, an important and ingenious contributor to the US American tradition of anthropological linguistics (see e.g. Martin 1988).

*Table 7.2* Axiality – different sets of terms for the two axes of organization

|  |  | axis: | |
|---|---|---|---|
|  |  | **paradigmatic** | **syntagmatic** |
| characteristics | gloss | choice | chain |
|  | manifestation | covert; cryptotypic categories | overt (revealing phenotypic categories) |
|  | evidence | reactances | markings, 'signals' |
|  | fractal type | elaborating | extending & enhancing |
| scholars: linguists | Saussure | associative (in absentia) | syntagmatic (in praesentia) |
|  | Hjelmslev | paradigmatic | syntagmatic |
|  | Firth | system | structure |
|  | Halliday | system – system networks, given priority as axial order | syntagms and function structures, derived by means of realization statements associated with systemic terms |
|  | | strategic | tactic |
| scholar: physicist | Bohm | implicate (enfolded) order – primary relevance | explicate (unfolded) order – secondary significance |

The interpretation of paradigmatic organization in Bohm's (1979) terms as implicate order – enfolded order – also fits well with insights from Whorf (1956), taken over by systemic functional linguists and elaborated within SFL, in particular his insights into **overt** vs. **covert** categories, **cryptotypes** within covert categories (contrasting with **phenotypes**), and **reactances** vs. **explicit marking**. The following passage from one of Whorf's papers collected in Whorf (1956: 70–71) can serve as a representative example (the editor's footnotes omitted):

> A covert linguistic class may not deal with any grand dichotomy of objects, it may have a very subtle meaning, and it may have no overt mark other than certain distinctive 'reactances' with certain overtly marked forms. It is then what I call a CRYPTOTYPE. It is a submerged, subtle, and elusive meaning, corresponding to no actual word, yet shown by linguistic analysis to be functionally important in the grammar. For example, the English particle UP meaning 'completely, to a finish', as in 'break it up, cover it up, eat it up, twist it up, open it up' can be applied to any verb of one or two syllables initially accented, EXCEPTING verb belonging to four special cryptotypes. One is the cryptotype of dispersion without boundary; hence one does not say 'spread it up, waste it up, spend it up, scatter it

up, drain it up, or filter it up'. [Footnote: 'Burst' belongs to this cryptotype; the colloquial 'bust' does not.] Another is the cryptotype of oscillation without agitation of parts; we don't say 'rock up a cradle, wave up a flag, wiggle up a finger, nod up one's head', etc. The third is the cryptotype of nondurative impact which also includes psychological reaction: kill, fight, etc., hence we don't say 'whack it up, tap it up, stab it up, slam it up, wrestle him up, hate him up.' The fourth is the verb of directed motion, move, lift, pull, push, put, etc., with which UP has the directional sense 'upward', or derived senses, even though this sense may be contradicted by the verb and hence produce an effect of absurdity, as in 'drip it up'. Outside this set of cryptotypes, UP may be freely used with transitives in the completive-intensive sense.

This example comes from the system of TRANSITIVITY, and cryptotypes discussed by Whorf seem to be largely from the experiential lexicogrammar (but he also cites other examples like 'demonstrative particles'). Cryptotypes are implicate in nature; in contrast, Whorf's (1956: 72) **phenotypes** are revealed in explicate order:

> In contrast to the cryptotype I give the name PHENOTYPE to the linguistic category with a clearly apparent class meaning and a formal mark or morpheme which accompanies it; i.e., the phenotype is the 'classical' morphological category. The meaning of 'up' and 'un-' are phenotypes, and so are the various tenses, aspects, voices, modes, and other marked forms which all grammars study. Grammatical research up to the present time has been concerned chiefly with study of phenotypes.

Elsewhere Whorf (1956: 132) notes that 'determination of cryptotypes usually requires deep study of a language'. That is certainly consistent with the notion of implicate order – and the experience of the development of systemic descriptions of the lexicogrammars of various languages. Systemic functional linguists have, as noted, taken up and developed Whorf's work on covert categories – cryptotypes, reactances; for examples, see Halliday (1967/8), Martin (1996b), Matthiessen (1995a), Davidse (1999), Rose (2001), Teruya (2007).

## 7.3 Search for Order: Systems All the Way Down?

The short detour above into Bohm's (1979) search for a deeper order behind the patterns that are most readily observable – his 'explicate order' – can serve as an example of the potential benefits of viewing language in context ***holistically***, not only within their own realm of meaning, but also at one further remove where we can consider principles of organization in all realms of phenomena. Engaging in **systems thinking**, we can try to identify principles of organization that are common to systems of all orders as they increase in complexity (see 'phenomenal order' in Figure 1.2 above), from one order to another, e.g.

- the cline of instantiation, extending from physical/biological/social/semiotic potentials to instances within these different realms of phenomena;
- compositional organization, ranging from the macro scale via the meso scale to the micro scale;

and principles of organization that emerge somewhere in the ascendance of systems, e.g.

- the dispersal of resources within collectives of individuals in complementary roles organized into role networks emerging with 'life' and characteristic of biological, social and semiotic systems.

Thus in the course of searching for principles of organization of complex adaptive systems in general, we can try to identify principles that are specific to language or to all semiotic systems – like the stratification into content and expression as a property needed by semiotic systems to be able to 'carry' meaning. Importantly, we look for principles of organization that emerge with the move towards greater complexity – and also more 'power'. In his empirical study of the ontogenesis of language, of learning how to mean (see above, Chapter 2), Halliday (1975a, 2004a) shows how instantiation, stratification, axial differentiation and metafunctional organization gradually emerge as distinct dimensions of organization in the phases of ontogenesis.

The search for general principles of organization that apply to all complex adaptive systems depends on the fundamental notion of **system** itself, in the sense of 'phenomenal' order identified in Figure 1.2 – the organization of phenomenal realm into systems of increasing complexity: physical < biological [physical + life] < social [biological + order] < semiotic [social + meaning]. These are all **emergent differentiations** of the general notion of system with the sense of phenomenal order; the sequence reflects their emergence in the history of our universe – the sequence of cosmogenesis (cf. Layzer 1990). That is, each new order of system represents the emergence of a new fundamental property made possible by a new form of organization. Significantly, each new order of system 'inherits' the features of lower order systems, adding a characteristic property and a characteristic form of organization creating the conditions for this property. Thus semiotic systems are also social systems, and by another move down the ordered typology, also biological systems, and finally also physical systems. Language is socially enacted, biologically embodied and physically manifested. For a pioneering systemic functional exploration with a focus on phonology, see Cléirigh (1998).

The features of the four orders of system are set out in Table 7.3. The table specifies the time of emergence of each new systemic order; in the case of physical and biological systems, current scientific research seems to indicate **monogenesis** within a period of time that can be estimated roughly. In the case of social systems and primary semiotic systems, **polygenesis** seems much more likely – multiple cases of emergence from the system of the immediately lower order, probably over an extended period of time. In the case of higher-order semiotic systems – language in particular – alternative hypotheses have been put forward over the decades, but there now seems to be a consensus around some version of monogenesis in Africa on the order of 200 to 250 K years ago – the 'East Side Story', as Corballis (2002) calls it.

*Table 7.3* Properties of systems of increasing complexity operating in different phenomenal realms

| systemic property | material | | immaterial | | |
|---|---|---|---|---|---|
| | physical systems | biological systems | social systems | semiotic systems | |
| | | | | primary | higher-order |
| emergence | big bang, c. 13.8 billion years ago | beginning, c. 3.5 billion years ago | multiple times of emergence | multiple times of emergence | c. 200–250 K years ago, in Homo sapiens sapiens (AMHs) |
| mode of cosmogenesis | | evolution | | | |
| domain of operation | cosmos | planet earth | certain biological populations | certain social groups | groups of Anatomically Modern Humans (AMHs) |
| characteristic property | | + life | + value (social order) | + meaning | |
| | | | | microfunctional mode of meaning | metafunctional mode of meaning |
| characteristic form of organization | | | relational role networks | stratification: content and expression | + 'form' between outer substance strata: lexicogrammar & phonology |
| nature of potential | event potential | action potential | behaviour potential | meaning potential | |
| nature of individual | – | biological organism | person (as aggregate of personae [social roles]) | meaner (as aggregate of meaning roles in meaning groups) | |

To recapitulate: the notion of system in the sense of phenomenal order in Figure 1.2 above is a general one, common to all phenomenal realms in the ordered typology in Table 7.3. And it seems clear that systems of all orders display certain common principles of organization including those of the cline of instantiation (all systems are extended from the potential pole to the instance pole, with intermediate patterns such as registers and weather patterns) and of compositional hierarchies (like the rank-based ones of language and biology [organism > organ > tissue > cell]). But what about system in the sense of paradigmatic axial order – 'the organizing concept for modelling paradigmatic relations in language', in Halliday's (2009: 232) formulation?

According to this formulation, system in this sense would appear to be unique to the organization of language, or rather (as we have seen), to the organization of semiotic systems in general. However, if we explore the interpretation of system in terms of implicate (enfolded) order, it would appear to be a general property of systemic order. To the extent that different **phenomenal potentials** – physical event potentials, biological action potentials, social behaviour potentials and semiotic meaning potentials – can be modelled 'implicately' by systems, and by systems forming system networks, this makes sense. Clearly, choice among two or more systemic terms cannot imply intention in the case of physical systems, but this is similarly true of systems of all orders: many choices are automated choices below the level of consciousness (in organisms with consciousness) and do not involve intentional choice – i.e. decisions – as generally understood. (I have put it like this since research has indicated that what we ourselves may experience as conscious choices may have been made by our brains before we become aware of them; e.g. Bode et al. 2014; Soon et al. 2008.)

It is certainly clear that systems thinking in the specific sense of construing phenomenal realms of all orders is a theme for the twenty-first century, one that has come increasingly clearly into focus. Barabási (2016) provides an informative wide-ranging introduction to **network science**; as part of the introduction, he observes (p. 5):

> We are surrounded by systems that are hopelessly complicated. Consider for example the society that requires cooperation between billions of individuals, or communications infrastructures that integrate billions of cell phones with computers and satellites. Our ability to reason and comprehend our world requires the coherent activity of billions of neurons in our brain. Our biological existence is rooted in seamless interactions between thousands of genes and metabolites within our cells.
>
> These systems are collectively called *complex systems*, capturing the fact that it is difficult to derive their collective behavior from a knowledge of the system's components. Given the important role complex systems play in our daily life, in science and in economy, their understanding, mathematical description, prediction, and eventually control is one of the major intellectual and scientific challenges of the 21st century.
>
> The emergence of network science at the dawn of the 21st century is a vivid demonstration that science can live up to this challenge. Indeed, behind each complex system there is an intricate network that encodes the interactions between the system's components: ...

As initial examples, he lists cellular networks, neural networks, social networks, communication networks, power grids and trade networks. While communication networks imply semiotic networks and they are implicated also at least in social networks (the phenomenal order immediately below semiotic systems) and in neural networks (one order further below), I would of course want to add semiotic networks to his list of introductory illustrations. As far as language is concerned, this means a pervasively relational conception of language as a network of networks – a network of the stratal and rank-based subsystems and their interrelationships, but also of the relations between language and other systems, both other semiotic systems and other systems of a lower phenomenal order. Such a conception would enable us to investigate what Barabási (2016: 8) calls the 'universality of network characteristics' (italics in original):

> A key discovery of network science is that *the architecture of networks emerging in various domains of science, nature, and technology are similar to each other, a consequence of being*

*governed by the same organizing principles. Consequently we can use a common set of mathematical tools to explore these systems.*

Thus even if it may not be system networks – or turtles – all the way down, it seems very likely that it is networks all the way down. That is: two decades into the twenty-first century, metatheoretically speaking.

# Chapter 8

# Appendix: Systemic Conventions

This appendix provides an overview of systemic conventions – system networks and their associated realization statements. Helpful discussions of different aspects of system networks include Martin (1987, 2013), Fawcett (1988a), Matthiessen and Bateman (1991), Halliday (2013).

## 8.1 System Networks and Realization Statements

**System networks** can be represented algebraically or graphically; both conventions are set out with brief glosses in Table 8.1. See also Figure 2.1 above.

*Table 8.1* Systems in system networks

| algebraic representation | graphic representation | gloss |
|---|---|---|
| a: x/y | term *a* →NAME→ term *x* / term *y* | entry condition *a*, terms *x* or *y* |
| a/b: x/y | term *a* / term *b* →NAME→ term *x* / term *y* | **system with disjunctive entry condition** entry condition *a* or *b*, terms *x* or *y* |

264 • System in Systemic Functional Linguistics

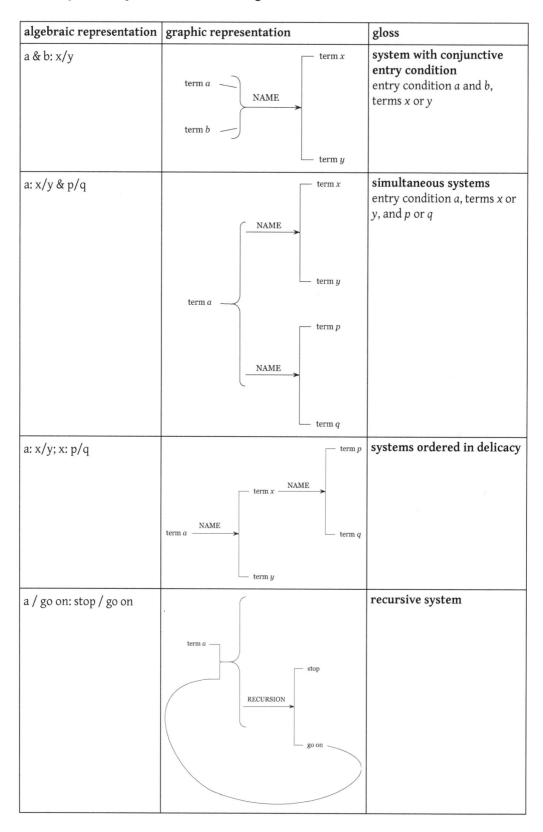

| algebraic representation | graphic representation | gloss |
|---|---|---|
| a & b: x/y | | **system with conjunctive entry condition** entry condition *a* and *b*, terms *x* or *y* |
| a: x/y & p/q | | **simultaneous systems** entry condition *a*, terms *x* or *y*, and *p* or *q* |
| a: x/y; x: p/q | | **systems ordered in delicacy** |
| a / go on: stop / go on | | **recursive system** |

Appendix: Systemic Conventions • 265

For additions to these basic system network conventions, see:

- For **marking conventions** used in system networks, see Section 6.4.1. Note the proposal introduced here for graphic representation of marking conventions, illustrated in Figure 6.20.
- For **multilingual system networks** (involving systemic partitions), see Section 6.4.2.

**Systemic probabilities** can be shown in brackets after systemic terms, as in Figure 3.8. Graphic representations of relative frequencies in text can also be incorporated in system networks as illustrated in e.g. Figure 4.8, Figure 4.9, Figure 4.10, Figure 5.8 and in Figure 8.1.

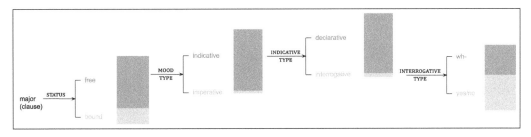

*Figure 8.1* The system of mood with charts representing relative frequencies in text included

Examples of systems presented in this book are tabulated in Table 1.4. Large system networks can be represented with systems 'collapsed' as schematic overviews: see Figure 3.4, which presents a **systemic index** of clausal systems described in Halliday and Matthiessen (2014). Systems across metafunctions and ranks can be presented in a **function-rank matrix**, as in Table 3.6. The two are related in Figure 3.5: The function-rank matrix as a directory to systems in the overall system network of the clause.

In representations of system networks, we can also recognize variants and annotated versions used in overviews:

- **displayed system networks**: Fawcett (1988a), as in Figure 6.21;
- system networks annotated in terms of **systemic regions** as an aid in discursive presentations, as in Figure 4.2;
- **hybrid system networks** and taxonomies (as a descriptive developmental stage), e.g. Figure 3.18, Figure 3.19.

Terms in systems may have associated **realization statements**. They consist of a realization operator and one or two realization operands. The realization statements used in a wide range of accounts are set out in Table 8.2.

While the realization operators have been given names that suggest actions, e.g. the action of inserting a function, they can in fact all be interpreted declaratively as involving existence and relations of expansion, as shown in the typology in Figure 8.2. For example, 'Insert' specifies the existence of a function in a function structure; it is a constraint on that structure having to do with the presence of the function, and 'Order' specifies a sequential relationship between two functions. The types of expansion in the typology are the ones familiar from the characterization of expansion as a fractal type, i.e. elaborating, extending and enhancing relations.

Table 8.2 Realization statements

| Operator |        | Operand(s)                         | Examples                                    | Gloss                                                                                                        |
|----------|--------|------------------------------------|---------------------------------------------|--------------------------------------------------------------------------------------------------------------|
| name     | symbol |                                    |                                             |                                                                                                              |
| Insert   | +      | Function                           | +Mood                                       | The presence of a structural function is specified.                                                          |
| Order    | ^      | Function, Function                 | Subject ^ Finite                            | The order of two structural functions is specified.                                                          |
| Expand   | ( )    | Function, Function                 | Mood (Subject, Finite)                      | The expansion of a structural function by two or more structural functions is specified.                     |
| Preselect| :      | Function, systemic term ('feature')| Finite: negative; Process: verbal group     | The preselection of a structural function to be realized by a unit with a particular systemic term is specified. |

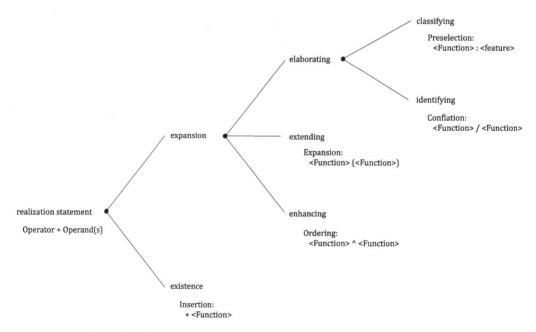

Figure 8.2 Typology of realization statements

## 8.2 'Good' System Networks

In the SFL literature, there have naturally been many examples of system networks; and there have been some publications dealing specifically with the question of what constitutes a 'good' system network, reflected in the title of the valuable contribution by Fawcett (1988a). Good system networks should minimally include:

- root terms specified – i.e. the domain of any system network must be specified, preferably as the root or initial entry condition;
- realization statements specified, either associated with systemic terms in system network or in separate table.

If any system network presented in the literature does not meet these two conditions, it should be treated with caution. If the information is lacking, perhaps it is possible to retrieve it from the account that accompanies it. But if the information is not available, this suggests that there is still work to be done – work that may suggest revisions of the system network.

If the domain of operation of the system network cannot be determined, it is unclear how the system network relates to other aspects of the overall description of language or of other semiotic systems and the system network fails to provide a more general account of patterns of agnation. If realization statements are lacking, this means that the systemic description fails to include fundamental empirical evidence for the account given. Realization statements include all types – intra-stratal and inter-stratal ones, and within intra-stratal ones both inter-axial ones and inter-rank ones. Perhaps the greatest danger (temptation) is producing contextual and semantic system networks without realization statements, but just as for lexicogrammatical and phonological ones without realization statements, this actually means that important evidence for drawing systemic distinctions has been left out, so the status of such description will need to be problematized.

Incomplete system networks may be a natural and even necessary part of the development of systemic descriptions, but it is advisable – and more transparent – to present them as hybrid system networks or even as taxonomies of some kind.

A good way of testing a system network is to produce a paradigm based on it. This may reveal problems. Problems may be somewhat hidden, as when the terms of a system turn out not be mutually exclusive. If this is the case, the system should perhaps be represented as a taxonomy until the actual systemic contrasts have been worked out.

## 8.3 Displays of Paradigms and Systemic Analyses

System networks define paradigms, and they can be displayed in various ways so as to enable viewers to visualize paradigmatic patterns and of course to test the predictions about paradigmatic patterns that any given system network makes:

- **Tabular paradigms**: paradigms can be displayed by means of tables, with systemic terms as column and row headings, e.g. Table 1.2, Table 6.5; tables can be shown together with system networks, as in Figure 3.33, Figure 5.7 (cf. also Figure 3.46).

- **Circular paradigms:** paradigms can be displayed by means of concentric circles, e.g. Figure 3.10, Figure 3.14.

There are other ways of displaying paradigms that can be quite helpful. For example, Halliday (1998b: 28) uses a fan-like diagram to represent the options within the lexicogrammar of pain.

Systemic analysis of texts can be displayed in a variety of ways, e.g.

- as **enhanced box diagrams** with selection expressions and function structures, e.g. Figure 3.6: Systemic and structural analyses of two clauses (from the dialogue in Table 3.7 below);
- as **tables** with selection expressions represented in columns, as in Table 4.1: Systemic analysis of passage of a telephonic service encounter text (Clauses [1] through [17]);
- as system networks with highlighted **traversal paths**, as in Figure 3.28, Figure 5.2 (cf. also the successive traversal states shown in Figure 5.1);
- as system networks accompanied by **systemic scores**, as in Figure 4.5, Figure 4.6, Figure 5.10.

# Notes

## Preface

1  See: https://www.equinoxpub.com/home/key-concepts-in-systemic-functional-linguistics/

## Chapter 1

1  Apologies to any readers who would have preferred an introduction dealing with the **study** of system as a phenomenon rather than this introduction, where I attempt at least to give a flavour of the phenomenon itself. My choice is clearly intentional (though 'choice' does not – unlike 'decision' – embody intentionality); I've made it to avoid reifying our conception of system and to ensure connection with the phenomena themselves.
2  *Trump sinks in polls, protesters call to defund the police: A closer look.* URL: https://youtu.be/YV5srZTCX9k
3  This is also reflected in the terminology used by phonologists. While many terms can be related to articulatory manifestations, other terms reflect auditory considerations, like 'sibilant', 'sonorant'. Cf. Section 3.4.
4  Speaking of choice: Michael Halliday belonged to a generation of speakers of English for whom *he* could be used as a personal pronoun 'unmarked' in terms of gender, as in *a child ... he*; nowadays writers, including linguists, will often add a disapproving '[sic]', arguably somewhat anachronistically, to quotes from writers who belonged to generations with a different pronominal system and who had not been brought up with the focus on such choices. In my own case, as a nascent writer of academic English, I remember Sandy Thompson drawing our attention to this in the 1980s – and she also pointed me to the work by Betty Friedan. Michael and I discussed such issues; his only concern was that people's attention might be diverted from deeper systemic manifestations like the cryptogrammatical patterns in the system of TRANSITIVITY construing biases such as gender/sex biases in terms of participant roles assignment (cf. Halliday 1990).
5  Koerner (1971: 157) comments: 'Saussure's example shows the affinity of his concept of associative relations with Kruszewski's formulation of the law of contiguity operating in language, but also (sows the seed) for a further abstraction of his findings by Hjelmslev who introduced the term "paradigmatic" to replace the less formal but surely more adequate (in terms of the nature of language) Saussurean expression "associative".' And Van der Walle, Williams and Willems (2006) write: 'In modern linguistics, the distinction is better known as the syntagmatic/paradigmatic dichotomy, the term "paradigmatic" going back to Hjelmslev who proposed this substitution of "associative" in order to avoid the undesirable psychological connotations of that word (Hjelmslev 1938a:161n3 [Hjelmslev 1938]).' What Hjelmslev (p. 152, fn. 3 in my edition) wrote is: 'C'est pour éviter le psychologisme adopté dans *le Cours* de F. de Saussure que je substitue le terme « rapport paradigmatique » à celui de « rapport associatif ».' That is, he distances himself of Saussure's psychologism in general: 'It is to avoid the psychologism adopted in the *Cours* by F. de Saussure that I substitute the term "paradigmatic relation" for "associative relation".' Cf. association theory in psychology that was around in Saussure's time, discussed by Wundt (1902).
6  For discussion of terminological issues, see also Fontaine, Bartlett and O'Grady (2013).
7  Terms in system such as 'indicative'/'declarative' have also been called (systemic) features or options.

## Chapter 2

1. Halliday (1975a) gives a number of examples of how semiotic acts emerge from material acts, the material acts often providing expressive resources for the realization of the content of the semiotic acts. This process of emergence is an important aspect of understanding that semiotic acts are inherently stratified. For example, when young infants gaze at objects, grab them, and pull them towards themselves, these are material acts; but when they gaze at another person as an intended addressee, and 'pretend' to grab the object they want but don't make contact with it and thus can't pull it towards them, this is now emerging as the expression of content, 'I want that'. This is what Halliday has called 'borrowing from the material domain': see below.
2. In discussion 'ontogenetic origins', Tomasello (2003: 19) claims 'The human adaptation for symbolic communication emerges in human ontogeny quite predictably across cultures at around 1 year of age (Tomasello 1995, 1999).' This is around 4 months after the starting period based on the evidence provided by Halliday and other systemic functional linguists who have undertaken longitudinal case studies of young children learn how to mean.
3. This obviously applies to the development of spoken language. In the case of sign languages of deaf communities, the expression plane is constituted visually, involving gesture and face: see Johnston (1992) for a metafunctional interpretation.

## Chapter 3

1. That is, a 'free' clause as opposed to a 'bound' one. This is the contrast in the system of FREEDOM: while 'free' clauses make direct contributions to the development of dialogue since they realize dialogic moves with their speech-functional selections (e.g. *The moon is a balloon, isn't it? – It can't be.*), 'bound' clauses do not: they are grammatically constrained, either by serving as dependent clauses in hypotactic clause combinations (clause nexuses, e.g. *David said → that the moon was a balloon*) or by being embedded (down-ranked) to serve as if they were groups or words in clauses or groups (e.g. *David's claim [[that the moon is a balloon]] fascinated people*).
2. The system of SPEECH FUNCTION and the system of MOOD TYPE are thus located within the two strata of the content plane, semantics and lexicogrammar respectively. In a brief characterization of Halliday's account, referring to Halliday (1994), Collins (2005: 3) writes: 'Halliday's four-term mood system is based on two intersecting parameters, one involving the two basic types of speech act ('demanding' and 'giving'), and the other involving the two types of 'commodities' which may be exchanged by speakers ('information' and 'goods-and-services'). Unfortunately the correlation with the grammatical system of clause type described above is partial: offers of goods-and-services are realised by the same clause type as information demands and there is, moreover, no place in the system for exclamatives (which involve a giving of information, but one which is secondary to the expression of the speaker's emotional state or attitude).' There is potential terminological confusion here since what Collins refers to as 'mood system' is the system of speech function and what he refers to as 'clause type' is the system of mood type. But the real problem with this characterization is that what he presents as a problem, i.e. there is 'unfortunately' a partial correlation between the two, with offers being realized 'by the same clause type as information demands' is in fact a demonstration of the power of double agnation. Offers have no mood category of their own in English, and this turns out to be a very general pattern around the languages of the world. And Collins' claim that there is 'no place in the system for exclamatives' is simply false.
3. Double agnation can be related to the interpretation of stratification in terms of **metaredundancy**. This line of interpretation was originally suggested by Jay Lemke, and then further explored by Halliday (1992a). Lemke explains context in terms of redundancy, probability distributions and metaredundancy on YouTube: https://www.youtube.com/watch?v=DhC85hvNjxM For discussion, see also Matthiessen (forthcoming b).
4. As in the case of other illustrations here, this one is taken from English; but the valeur in content of the expressive contrast between falling and rising tone is quite common among languages, and Bolinger (e.g. 1986, 1989) suggests a correlation with bodily relaxation vs. tension.

5   The identity of the Subject is revealed by the 'question tag' (technically the Moodtag): *let me do your homework, shall I?* (This is thus quite distinct from *let me* in the sense of 'allow, permit me', as in *let me borrow your skateboard, will you?*). See Halliday and Matthiessen (2014: 164–165).
6   The system of DEICTICITY is the systemic contrast between 'temporal' and 'modal'. It is available to 'indicative' clauses and 'finite bound' clauses – but not to 'imperative' clauses (although they are also finite). It is concerned with the dimension according to which the validity of the proposition of a clause is argued in relation to the nub of the argument, the Subject. The validity of the proposition is argued either in terms of time in relation to the 'now' of speaking (e.g. *the moon is a balloon/the moon was a balloon/the moon will be a balloon*) or the actuality of speaking (e.g. *the moon may be a balloon/the moon should be a balloon/the moon must be a balloon*). The choice is realized by the Finite element of the clause (which forms the Mood element together with the Subject). See Halliday and Matthiessen (2014: Section 4.2).
7   In English, the delicate options in mood represented by the systems of KEY distributed systemically across the mood types are realized by terms in the system of tone operating within the tone group (intonation unit) in phonology. But in languages such as Cantonese and Vietnamese where pitch movement is largely used up within the syllable as the phonological unit, comparable contrasts in key are realized by interpersonal particles (see e.g. Matthiessen 2004) – interpersonal contrasts that are interactive in nature, relating to the ongoing exchanges of meaning in dialogue.
8   Compound tone 13 with the sense of 'request' – marked polarity, with tonic on Finite (*do/don't*).
9   Here message, move and figure refer to the semantic units realized by the clause (cf. Halliday and Matthiessen 2006, 2014). In Halliday's (1985a) *Introduction to Functional grammar*, these metafunctional perspectives on the clause are characterized as clause as messages (textual), clause as exchange (interpersonal) and clause as representation (experiential). The term 'message' has also been used in another sense in SFL, in Hasan's (e.g. 1996) 'message semantics'; here 'message' is a unit on her semantic rank scale.
10  Systems are presented here as 'system name': 'term 1/term 2/... term n', for example FREEDOM: free/bound; MOOD TYPE: indicative/imperative. The entry condition is specified in the system network in Figure 3.8.
11  As elsewhere in the presentation here of lexicogrammatical systems, I have drawn on the description of English. The system of THEME is one area where English has 'diverged' from its Germanic siblings. More generally, there is considerable variation across languages (see e.g. Matthiessen 2004), as for any other area of the grammar, and the account of a specific language must be grounded in empirical evidence from text in that language.
12  It is important to interpret the system of THEME (and other textual systems) along these lines as strategies available to speakers (and writers) to guide their listeners (and readers) in the interpretation of the clause as a message, indicating how such **guiding textual statuses** can be modelled, as in Matthiessen (1992) and various subsequent publications drawing on insights from computational modelling. This is a way of transcending discussions that focus on interpreting the descriptive labels and glosses used, like 'what the clause is about' or 'the point of departure of the clause' (cf. Halliday, 1984b, on the ineffability of grammatical categories). They tend to be metaphorical in nature and need to be grounded in models of textual statuses as processing guides. Thus to understand the category of theme, we need to study how it is used in the processing of text, rather than build our account on attempts to understand glosses – an ever-present temptation in linguistics. In other words, the primary task is to study a linguistic phenomenon, not the label or gloss it has been given (unless we are doing metalinguistics). Once we have arrived as a rich account of theme as a strategy for guiding the processing of text, we are in a position to model the notion of 'the point of departure of the clause' as part of an explicit model of text generation and text understanding. And as always in systemic account, we need to focus on the systemic valeurs in addition to their higher-stratal signification, as argued by Hasan (1985b).
13  The system in Figure 3.13 is perhaps a better model when linguists start describing the system of THEME in languages other than English. They tend to ask which elements are marked vs. unmarked topical Themes, but this is not a good question to start with: descriptive decisions about thematic markedness should emerge from discourse evidence and interaction with other systems.
14  This potential for an information unit boundary after the topical Theme, whether it is marked or unmarked, has been noted by Halliday since the 1960s; but although it is very significant, it tends to be overlooked by systemic linguists who argue that when the topical Theme is marked, the Theme extends

up to and includes the Subject. Although this line of analysis reflects the nature of Theme as the peak of a textual wave (Halliday, 1979; Matthiessen, 1992), it disregards the fact that in text analysis, the identification of Subjects complements the identification of Themes, as shown very powerfully by Halliday (1992c).

15  As noted above, the systemic descriptions of English included here are merely illustrative. Thus interesting details, many of which are covered in Halliday and Matthiessen (2014), are left out. Similarly, references to other languages are not included. If the focus of this book had included systemic comparison of different languages and generalizations across different languages, it would have been interesting to note that there are languages that separate the relative marker and the anaphoric pronoun in relative clause, Arabic being one prominent example. But since such observations fall outside the focus of the book, I will try to resist the temptation of making them.

16  This is thematically agnate with *the dog it was that died*, from Oliver Goldsmith's 'An Elegy on the Death of a Mad Dog': *The man recovered of the bite, The dog it was that died*. In terms of Goldsmith's satirical elegy, the theme selection makes excellent sense and serves to counter the expectation that the man would have died after being bitten by a rabid dog. (Tom Stoppard used this thematic variant as the title of one of his plays.)

17  Note that both the ergative model and the transitive one are models of transitivity, so it is misleading to contrast the terms 'ergativity' and 'transitivity'.

18  Languages vary in how they generalize across different process types (see Matthiessen 2004). The envelope of variation is illuminated by Martin's (1996b) description of the system of TRANSITIVITY in Tagalog. The variation also needs to be seen in the light of the complementarity of the experiential and logical modes of construing experience, as brought out in Halliday and Matthiessen (2006/1999: Chapter 7).

19  Here there is an experiential motif the cuts across process types – the motif of joint activity, viz. social or semiotic interaction. In fact, it can be related to a fractal type in the content system of English – the logico-semantic notion of extension, which is manifested within different semantic and lexicogrammatical domains. Such joint activity may be modelled materially as action, behaviourally as behaviour or verbally as saying. For example, in a 'material' clause one of the entities involved in the joint activity may be construed as a Goal, as in *Romeo hugged Juliet* (cf. with the *do to/with* probe for Goals: *what Romeo did with Juliet was hug her*) as an agnate variant of *Romeo and Juliet hugged*; and in a 'verbal' clause, there is often an additional agnate variant where the co-participant is construed participantally as a Receiver, as in *Rome spoke to Juliet*; and in addition, the language of the semiotic interaction may be specified circumstantially or even in some cases participantally as Verbiage, as in *Romeo and Juliet spoke (chatted, gossiped, argued) in Italian* and *Romeo and Juliet spoke Italian*. At the same time, certain patterns of wording are manifested within more than one process type, e.g. the manifestation of 'extension' either experientially as a circumstance of Accompaniment or logically as an extending nominal group complex service as a participant (Medium); for example, *Romeo and Juliet fought : Romeo fought with Juliet :: Romeo and Juliet chatted : Romeo chatted with Juliet* (but only *Romeo and Juliet hugged*, not normally **Romeo hugged with Juliet*). In this way, the grammar construes a continuum from 'material' clauses via 'behavioural' ones to 'verbal' clauses. They share certain patterns that are manifestations of the motif of 'extension', e.g. either as co-participation or as accompaniment; but each process type model has one or more distinctive properties, like the possibility of (material:) a Goal, (verbal:) a Receiver or a Verbiage. There are a number of other such experiential motifs that cut across process types, being construed on the models provided by the different process types, like the motifs of perception, emotion and pain (for the grammar of pain, see Halliday, 1998b). In each case, there is likely to be indeterminacy (see Halliday and Matthiessen 2006: Section 13.3). Whenever there is indeterminacy in the language, linguists will face decisions about where to draw paradigmatic lines between terms in systems. Each term will capture a combination of properties, as illustrated by Martin (1996a). As always, systemic functional descriptivist will operate with trinocular vision, view the properties 'from above', 'from below' and 'from roundabout'. Different descriptive decisions taken in the account of the system of PROCESS TYPE since the 1960s are surveyed in Matthiessen (2018b), and Banks (2016) details different descriptions of 'behavioural' clauses in English in terms of their location in the system of PROCESS TYPE. (He favours one of the descriptive positions, but does not actually review complex evidence from the phenomena themselves.)

20 Note that the experiential clause system is called the system of TRANSITIVITY – regardless of the mixture of the transitive model and the ergative one. Thus it is confusing to call these two models 'transitivity' and 'ergativity', since the label 'transitivity' is already in use for the system in general, whether it is modelled by a particular language transitively or ergatively. The term 'ergativity' is also used in descriptive linguistics (including language typology) to refer to ergative-absolutive case marking (or 'alignment').

21 Halliday (1981, 1985a) identifies fractal patterns manifested within text and clause, and within different grammatical domains, but he does not yet use the term fractal. In our work together, for example in preparing Halliday and Matthiessen (2006/1999), we decided that the notion of fractal was a helpful theoretical interpretation of such similar patterns manifested across different domains with some degree of variation. We drew on Benoit Mandelbrot's (e.g. 1982) work on fractals though of course without his mathematical modelling and sophistication. It is certainly possible to interpret earlier insights into recurrent patterns along similar lines, e.g. Otto Jespersen's notion of rank and X-bar theory in generative linguistics.

22 This cell can be filled by metaphorical wordings, e.g. *John's claim was* [[*that he had run away*]] as an incongruent version of *John claimed that he had run away*.

23 They are clearly not ideationally synonymous. In addition, the ideational fractal patterns are manifested in distinct interpersonal and textual environments. For example, when they are manifested in the clause, they are enacted interpersonally as a proposition or proposal, and are thus open to negotiation – but they are not when they are manifested within the domain of the nominal group.

24 Neale (2002: 236–237) writes: 'Matthiessen's (1995[a]) Lexicogrammatical Cartography, which includes tables for the categorization of verbs – though, interestingly, he does not transfer them to system networks', adding in a footnote: 'I say 'interestingly', because he is working in the systemic tradition, and so we would expect him to present his classification in a system network.' The reason I did not 'transfer' the categorization of verbs 'to system networks' is straightforward: just as in the case of Figure 3.23, I had not systemicized the categorization – and it is a classification of verbs serving as (the Event of) the verbal group functioning as Process, not yet an account of delicate PROCESS TYPE as a clause-rank system involving not only the Process but configurations of Process and another transitivity role – in particular, Process + Medium, but also Process + Range and Process + certain 'inner' circumstances. The taxonomies in Matthiessen (1995a) and in Figure 3.23 are **pre-systemic**, and cannot simply be 'transferred' to systemic networks. Such taxonomies simply constitute a step towards systemic descriptions.

25 Tucker's (2007) approach is formulated in terms of the 'Cardiff Grammar', where there is one level of system networks within the content plane of language – interpreted as semantic system networks. In contrast, the 'Hallidayan' version of SFL presented in this book operates with both semantic system networks and lexicogrammatical ones; there are two strata of agnation within the content plane, making statements of double agnation possible (see Section 3.1.2), with statements of paradigmatic *valeur* both within semantics and within lexicogrammar. This bi-systemic approach has been essential in the interpretation of grammatical metaphor (Section 3.2.1.4), and it is of course also relevant to the interpretation and description of lexical metaphor. In fact, 'phraseology' often involves both lexical and grammatical metaphor.

26 She calls this description 'message semantics', but I don't use that name here since 'message' here refers to the semantic textual correlate of a clause (following Halliday, e.g. his IFG), and 'move' refers to its interpersonal correlate (see Figure 3.26).

27 This film is a highly valued verbal artefact, admired for its witty dialogue. It is a good source to study from the point of view of interpersonal choices enacting complex tenor relations; it is a satire, brimming with sarcasm and irony – features characteristic of the interpersonal multiplication of meanings in different settings of tenor values. Thus the dialogue has to be read – listened to and viewed – as interpersonally layered, and any analysis of the screenplay as an artefact would have to bring this out. The screenplay is available from different web sources; see: https://scripts-onscreen.com/tag/all-about-eve-script/

28 Martin's (1992: 49) is based on Berry's (1981) systemic description of exchange, which she adapted from the Birmingham School account dialogue – the pioneering study by Sinclair and Coulthard (1975) on classroom discourse, couched in terms of Halliday's (pre-systemic) scale and category theory, and other contributions including Burton (1980) and Tsui (1986). Berry also uses a distinction between A-events

and B-events, taken from the work by Labov (1972) and Labov and Fanshel (1977), and represents exchange structure in terms of functional 'slots' realized by moves labelled Dx1, X1, X2, X1f etc. Since the point of my adapted system network is simply to illustrate the approach, I have replaced the labels with more transparent terms.

29 Of course, it would be possible to retain exchange as a unit, but to model it in terms of dependency structure rather than in terms of constituency structure.

30 The contrast between the synoptic and dynamic perspectives on language (or 'languaging') is of course not restricted to the interpersonal resources of semantics. It is simply one area where the contrast has been illuminated and discussed, and it would be possible and interesting to examine other areas, within other metafunctions and within other strata. The dynamic perspective has arguably been foregrounded in accounts in linguistic traditions embracing emergentist approaches to language (e.g. MacWhinney and O'Grady 2015). In SFL, the dynamic perspective has been developed in reference to the cline of instantiation, including the different semogenic time frames (phylogenesis, ontogenesis, logogenesis; Halliday and Matthiessen 2006): see Chapter 2 and see also Section 4.3. In a foundational contribution, Halliday (1977) characterized and modelled text as choice, showing how texts can be analysed as successive selections in systems, which can be related to his (1961) view of language as patterned activity. In addition, Michael Gregory's phasal analysis brings out logogenetic patterns that emerge as texts unfold (e.g. Gregory 2002; Cloran, Stuart-Smith and Young 2007; Malcolm 2010; Bartlett 2016; O'Donnell 2019: 224–225). Naturally, in computational modelling of language in SFL, dynamic considerations have been of central concern, prominently in the modelling of generation and parsing: see Section 5.2.

31 In early descriptions of English (and some other languages), the sentence was posited as a rank above that of the clause; but in subsequent research, Halliday and other scholars working with his description found that patterns 'above' the clause within grammar can be handled by a rich account of clause complexing, as in Chapter 7 of all the editions of Halliday's IFG. This contrasts with some tagmemic work and also some systemic contributions where 'sentence' is treated as a level or rank above that of the clause (cf. Longacre, 1970). In the IFG tradition, the term 'sentence' is reserved as the name of a unit of graphology, the orthographic sentence (Halliday and Matthiessen 2014: Chapter 1). It is also important to remember that while rank-based composition in terms of a rank scale is part of the general theory of language, the particular ranks of the rank scales used in the description of particular languages is **not** part of the general theory of grammar; rank scales are posited based on empirical evidence in the description of particular languages. This is important since one of the ways in which languages vary is precisely the division of grammatical labour across ranks, e.g. between group rank and word rank (see e.g. Matthiessen 2004).

32 I will use this well-established line of investigation in SFL as a point of reference for comparison with the interpretation of composition in text in terms of logico-semantic complexing. There have been many other relevant discussions of semantic composition, including contributions from SFL, Tagmemics (e.g. Pike, 1967), related work by Longacre (e.g. 1970, 1976, 1979, 1996), and other approaches concerned with the organization of text (e.g. Hinds, 1977), also in computational linguistics (an early influential contribution being Grosz and Sidner, 1986, distinguishing between attentional and intentional patterns in the organization of discourse). One issue has been the stratal allocation of compositional hierarchies, as noted early on by Halliday and Hasan (1976). There has also been work on phonological composition above the tone group. Halliday (1961: 78) indicated that it would be helpful to recognize paraphones; and a number of scholars dealing with prosodic phonology have explored phonological patterns beyond the tone group with possible semantic significance, including Ken Pike, Elizabeth Couper-Kuhlen, David Brazil, Radan Martinec, Gerard O'Grady. For a recent overview of rhythmic patterns in relation to semantic ones, see Martinec (2018).

33 Noting, however, that a text is defined as 'language functioning in context', so it's defined by reference to context – and thus variable according to the nature of a given type of context. This is related to my point about the registerial variation in composition at the semantic stratum.

34 Hasan's 'message semantics'.

35 Compare Bohm's (1979: 191) discussion of descriptions of order in physical systems (but with implications for other kinds of system as well): 'each theory will abstract a certain aspect that is *relevant* only in some limited context, which is indicated by some appropriate measure. [...] We can thus say in a particular context that may be under consideration, the general modes of description that belong

to a given theory serve to *relevate* a certain content, i.e., to lift it into attention so that it stands out 'in relief'.' By 'relevate', he means 'lift up', related to 'make relevant'. Analogously, we might characterize the description of contextually adapted semantic systems as register relevation.

36  In an early statement of the 'levels of language', Halliday (1961: 39) referred to semantics as 'context' and to context as 'situation' ('extra-textual features'). He later regarded these terminological choices as bad, and by the time of Halliday (1973b), he used 'semantics' and 'context' in their now established senses, with semantics as an interlevel between context and the rest of language. (In Halliday, McIntosh and Strevens, 1964: 18, 'semantics' is used alongside 'context', which is characterized as 'relation of form to situation'; and 'situation' is still used in the sense of 'non-linguistic phenomena'.)

37  Published in Black (1964), and listed in references here as Searle (1964).

38  For the 'upper model' mentioned in the quoted passage, see e.g. Bateman (1990). It grew out of the work Michael Halliday and I began in 1986 in the context of the Penman text generation project (e.g. Matthiessen, 1987), the first version being the 'Bloomington Lattice': see Halliday and Matthiessen (2006/1999).

39  This is obviously very different from a conception of the phonological 'module' of a language operating with underlying phonological representations that occur in lexicon entries.

40  A nice example is the liquid soap named *Bliw*, introduced in Sweden in 1968: http://vitterhetsakad.se/ckeditor_assets/attachments/505/smutshygien.pdf The name given to the soap didn't exist in Swedish, but it's a possible syllable – and it sounds kind of nice, suitably including a liquid as part of the syllabic Onset.

41  This is clearly how these two expression strata have evolved, and how they emerge in ontogenesis. Pointing out that phonology is natural (rather than conventional) in relation to phonetics does not undermine the crucial insight that phonology is a system of linguistic form, to put it in Hjelmslevian terms. The 'features' or 'options' in phonological systems are characterized by their *valeur*; this is the view of phonology from its own level, 'from roundabout' (cf. Figure 3.38). This was a crucial insight brought out by Saussure in his ground-breaking and justly famous 1878 *Mémoire sur le système primitif des voyelles dans les langues indo-européennes* ('Dissertation on the Original System of Vowels in the Indo-European Languages'). I remember a seminar at Lund University in the second half of the 1970s where a scholar discussed Saussure's contribution in the *Mémoire*, and commented that it was a pity that he had not specified the phonetic manifestations. The leading Swedish expert on European structuralism and linguist who introduced it into Swedish linguistics, Bertil Malmberg, was in the audience, and commented, energetically and frustratedly, that that was the fundamental point of Saussure's account – the relational nature of phonological systems based on differentiation in *valeur*.

42  To be more accurate: over an information unit, which in the unmarked case corresponds to a ranking clause (see e.g. Halliday, 1967; Halliday and Greaves 2008; Halliday and Matthiessen 2014).

43  Like the phoneme and other phonological units, the syllable needs to be interpreted in terms of trinocular vision in reference to the relevant semiotic dimensions; but is also needs to be viewed in reference to both speech production and speech perception, again like other phonological units. Indeed, like any other linguistic category, the syllable is not a 'thing in itself' but rather a node in a network of relationships, so if it is approached from only one vantage point, it is likely to appear illusory.

44  And of course there are languages where there are two phonological domains, the tone group and the syllable, as in Mandarin Chinese (e.g. Halliday and McDonald 2004).

45  These particular terms, 'advanced' vs. 'neutral', are subject to vowel harmony: complexes of syllables that realize a given grammatical word have the same tongue root selection, either 'advanced' or 'neutral', which can be interpreted as a phonological marker of grammatical word-hood.

46  Both perspectives are clearly relevant and crucial; but the examples given here will involve the articulatory perspective on the bodily sound potential. This perspective is foregrounded in introductions to phonetics, and it is easier to explore through 'phonetic yoga'. However, auditory practice is equally crucial in phonetic training.

47  Ladefoged (1996: 239) characterizes Abercrombie's standing in the field as follows: 'David Abercrombie was *the* British phonetician following Daniel Jones in the second half of the twentieth century. He redefined the subject, creating general phonetics as a university discipline that had not previously existed.'

48  As always, we must be aware of the metacontext – following Halliday's (1964) discussion of 'syntax and the consumer', we need to consider 'context and the consumer'. For example, while they certainly face

49  Which, following Halliday (2013: 34), we can locate midway along the cline of instantiation as a representation of situation types focussed on field of activity, which is why it possible to specify structures characteristic of different situation types – like Hasan's GSP. Thus it does not cover the more general considerations we need to take into account in describing the cultural potential of a community – cf. again Halliday (1984b) on the North Star text.

50  As far as contextual structures are concerned, Mitchell (1957) is a forerunner in the Firthian tradition. He developed a description of service encounters in a market in Cyrenaica. While Hasan's GSP model seems to draw on this work, it was actually only after she had developed her model that Hasan (p.c.) realized the similarities to Mitchell's description.

51  There are, obviously, syntagmatic patterns that can also be interpreted as fractal even if the term has not been used. Thus linguists have explored syntagmatic generalizations across different syntagmatic environments, e.g. Otto Jespersen's notion of rank, X-bar theory; implicational universals of the kind introduced by Joseph Greenberg, Johanna Nichols' head marking vs. dependent marking patterns.

a number of shared demands on the account of context, contributions to the description of context in educational linguistics and the description of context in computational linguistics (in the sense of the explicit computational modelling of language in context) diverge considerably.

# Chapter 4

1  URL: https://en.wikipedia.org/wiki/Ariadne%27s_thread_(logic)
2  This term is due to David Butt.
3  See: https://www.isi.edu/natural-language/penman/penman.html
4  In this section, I'm concerned with reference tools. The standard analysis tools used in SFL include prominently O'Donnell's (2012) UAM Corpus Tool: http://www.corpustool.com
5  The selections of systemic terms shown to the right in the figure are actually simply passes through the system. I will return to the conceptualization and representation of selections in Section 5.2, where I review computational modelling of system networks and processes of instantiation ('traversal algorithms').
6  Halliday (1959) used his corpus of Chinese to count relative frequencies of terms in a number of systems and infer probabilities. In the 1950s, there was interest in linguistics in the implications of Shannon's **information theory** (e.g. Shannon and Weaver 1949). The theory was explored by both Halliday (see 1991a/2005: 45–46, 1991b/2005: 67–68, 69, 1993b/2005: 138–139, 142) and Roman Jakobson, who of course had only recently arrived in the US when information theory and related developments came into focus there (cf. Van de Walle 2008), but linguistics developed in a different way starting in the 1960s because Chomsky and other generative linguists were not interested in, or even hostile towards, language as a probabilistic system – a stance that arguably set back the development in linguistics in general about four decades. In a paper given at a special colloquium on the history of phonology, John Goldsmith suggested that phonologists should go back to Jakobson's ideas in the 1950s. Halliday was also one of the presenters (Halliday 1998c), and I remember that in the question period after Goldsmith's presentation, Janet Pierrehumbert, who was in the audience, suggested that Halliday's systemic theory would be best suited to accommodate probabilities. A few years later, the book *Probabilistic Linguistics* was published (Bod, Hay and Jannedy 2003). By then the negative attitude towards language as a probabilistic system due to generative linguistics in the 1960s had largely disappeared, and corpus data and analysis techniques had made it possible to investigate the probabilistic nature of language (cf. also the development of statistical NLP: Manning and Schütze 1999). Meanwhile, Halliday and other systemic functional linguists had developed the notion of language as a probabilistic system and undertaken empirical studies (see e.g. Plum and Cowling 1987; Nesbitt and Plum 1988; Halliday 1991a,b, 1993b; Halliday and James 1993; Fine 1992; Weerasinghe 1994; Matthiessen 1999, 2006a; Jesus and Pagano 2006; for an overview, see Matthiessen 2015f).

## Chapter 5

1. Developed at the Multimodal Analysis Lab under the direction of Kay O'Halloran (2008–2013).
2. Issues of the kind exemplified here had been identified by the end of the 1990s, and while they had not generally been solved, there were indications of possible solutions and they were reasonably well understood. They can be seen as important findings resulting from the interaction between SFL and computation up through the 1990s. Such issues are still relevant (cf. Bateman 2008b), but the attention in the interaction between SFL and computation has shifted to other concerns. For example, the issues are not a focus in the recent overview by Bateman et al. (2019).
3. At the time LISP was the default programming language used in computational linguistics and AI. See further below.
4. As a tiny example, consider the challenge of disambiguating *will* represented in Figure 6.10 below. If syntagmatic patterns are only approached from below, the number of alternative analyses will certainly become daunting. However, from a systemic functional point of view, parsing should in principle be bi-axial, multi-functional and multi-stratal (cf. O'Donoghue 1994).
5. Interestingly but not surprisingly, approaches to parsing have tended to be more influenced by formal considerations in linguistics and approaches to generation than by functional considerations: see Fawcett (1994: 370–371).
6. Before the quoted passage, Gibbons and Markwick-Smith have referred to Brumfit's (1979) critique of Wilkins' (1976) notional syllabus and his rejection of the proposal to replace the 'syntactic syllabus' with a notional one.
7. In keeping with the theme of this book, I focus here on applications of different aspects of 'system' in translation and comparative studies informed by SFL (which is part of multilingual studies; see Matthiessen, Teruya and Wu 2008); translation studies informed by SFL have also drawn on other aspects of SFL, but I have not included them here since I'm concerned with 'system'. In this area of research, contributions are concerned with different sets of languages, and they are, quite naturally, published in a range of different languages. This reflects the fact that there are different SFL research communities around the world, typically dealing with translation from and into English (but not only English) and the regional major language; so there are publications not only in English, but also in Portuguese, Spanish, Indonesian, Vietnamese, Chinese and other languages. For a recent overview of systemic functional translation studies involving different language pairs, see Matthiessen et al. (2022 Chapter 10, Table 10.1).
8. There are clearly interesting differences between the two systems of MODALITY, English having moved away from the Germanic mode in evolving modal operators without non-finite forms and German having retained the subjunctive as an option in the verbal system. One additional noticeable detail is that German 'splices' evidentiality into its system of modality (in uses of *sollen*, complementing the subjunctive mode) but English doesn't.
9. For an interesting and relevant pre-SFL Firthian study of songs in Yurok, see Robins and McLeod (1956).
10. This was an obvious extension of the representational power of system networks designed to represent more than one language. I had already suggested that partitions could be used to represent register-specific areas of a system network (Matthiessen 1993).

## Chapter 6

1. Here we can also include Hasan's (e.g. 1978, 1984) GSP, offered by her as a stepping stone towards systemicized characterizations of context.
2. This is an example of the application of a very important general principle in the management of systemic descriptions, systemic analyses and in fact any descriptive data: the data should always be represented in such a way that that format can be changed – so that the information is not 'trapped' in one application, possibly dependent on a proprietary format, but can be exported in various formats, and then imported into other applications. One way of ensuring this is to use shareware developed by teams and with large user communities.

3  Ervin-Tripp's description was produced before *Ms.* gained general currency; the use of this title seems to have been spread after the launch of the *Ms.* magazine in 1972. See: https://en.wikipedia.org/wiki/Ms.

4  The Wikipedia characterizes 'convergent evolution' thus: '**Convergent evolution** is the independent evolution of similar features in species of different periods or epochs in time. Convergent evolution creates **analogous structures** that have similar form or function but were not present in the last common ancestor of those groups.' See: https://en.wikipedia.org/wiki/Convergent_evolution An example is the evolution of the wings of birds and the wings of bats.

5  Unless they have been designed to get rid of all modes of indeterminacy, as happened in the move from the evolved grammatical logic of clause complexing to the designed logic of propositional calculus.

6  This is restricted to 'perceptive' 'mental' clauses. Thus in the English translation of Herman Hesse's Siddharta, *I can think. I can wait. I can fast.* is not a close agnate of *I think. I can wait. I can fast* since the clause *I can think* is 'cognitive' rather than 'perceptive'. The exchange is as follows: Kamala: *What might you be able to do?* - Siddharta: *I can think. I can wait. I can fast.* And in the original German: Kamala: *Was kannst du denn?* - Siddharta: *Ich kann denken. Ich kann warten. Ich kann fasten.*

7  The view 'from below' has tended to be foregrounded in parsers. More specifically, they have tended to rely on specifications of syntagms in the first instance, which is one reason why some systemic functional explorations of parsing have involved two stages: first a non-SFL parser doing a syntagm-based parse, like the Stanford Dependency Parser, and then a systemic functional analysis of the output of this parse: cf. Section 5.2.4.

8  In the description of English, it turns out that the ergative model can be generalized across process types (Process + Medium ± Agent) while the transitive model in a sense takes 'material' clauses as the prototype (Actor + Process ± Goal), a prototype that leads to differentiation among process types. But this is a pattern specific to English, and the situation may be different for various other languages (cf. Halliday and McDonald 2004: 354, on the transitive and ergative models in Mandarin; and Martin's, 1996b, description of the system of TRANSITIVITY of Tagalog, suggesting yet other models).

9  Or, rather than 'impossibility', perhaps improbability – low probability of 'exclamative' clauses; see e.g. Quirk et al. (1985: 88). The issue of the intersection of MOOD TYPE and POLARITY is brought out by a systemic description where the two systems are described as simultaneous (since POLARITY is simultaneous with the system of FREEDOM and the term 'free' is the entry condition to MOOD TYPE, as shown in Figure 3.7). Thus the description immediately invites us to ask whether 'positive' and 'negative' can combine with all mood types, which I have probed in Table 6.5. Descriptions of English generally note the special semantics of negative yes/no interrogatives, but not the possibility of the combination of 'negative' and 'exclamative'. For example, it is not discussed in the context of the account of exclamative clauses by Huddleston and Pullum (2002) in their reference grammar of English, and Collin's (2005) article on exclamative clauses in English does not raise the issue, nor does Siemund's (2015) helpful corpus-based study of 'exclamative' clauses. The best way of probing the existence of positive vs. negative exclamative clauses empirically is of course to analyses a large corpus. The difficulty that presents itself is to find *how* or *what* in exclamative clauses that are either 'positive' or 'negative' since both *how* and *what* have other uses as well, in particular interrogative and relative ones. However, the sequence *what a* is much more likely to occur in an exclamative clause, so in an exploratory study I examined 1,000 instances of *what a* in COCA (out of the 61,356 occurrences in the corpus). While there are non-exclamative clauses, most clauses with *what a* are exclamative. All of them are 'positive'; none of them are 'negative'. Naturally, we need to study a much larger sample, including *how* and all instances of *what*, not only *what a*. However, it seems safe to assume that the frequency of the combination of 'exclamative' and 'negative' will be very low – very likely considerable less that 1%, so highly marked in terms of probability. (In terms of probability, 0.1 constitutes marked, as in positive 0.9/negative 0.1.) Now, this is a nice illustration of descriptive decisions one has to make in developing system networks: assuming that the frequency of 'negative' exclamatives is less than 1% or even less than 0.1%, is it reasonable not to allow for the combination of 'negative' and 'exclamative' in the systemic description, as indicated in Figure 6.20? This does not mean that the system is static; as shown in Section 4.5 (see Figure 4.12), being probabilistic systems, languages change gradually in terms of changing probabilities, which can be detected as changes in relative frequencies in historical corpora.

10 An important application would be as part of contrastive linguistics for the twenty-first century as a resource in second/foreign language teaching: see Matthiessen (2015c).
11 This region of the lexicogrammar of different languages can be a good source of comparison represented in terms of multilingual system networks, but it is important to note that while it is highly grammaticalized in many languages, including English and Indonesian, as represented here, it is in fact a region of typological variation: languages vary in their pronominal resources from highly grammaticalized systems of a small number of options to systems that are located further towards the lexical zone of lexicogrammar, with many more options, as in the case of Thai (e.g. Iwasaki and Ingkaphirom 2005). And even languages with highly grammaticalized pronominal systems may have a strategy for referring to the addressee(s) using non-interactant strategies as a way of increasing the resources for negotiating the tenor of the relationships, by providing systemic access to various titles. For example, in Swedish – at least traditionally, one would not address one's doctor using either of the two addressee pronouns, *du* [cf. French 'tu', German 'du'] or *ni* [cf. French 'vous', German 'Sie'], but rather a non-interactant strategy: *vad skulle Dr. Arent rekommendera?* 'what would you [Dr. Arent] recommend?'; using *ni* would have suggested some kind of master and servant relation in terms of tenor. And this non-interactant strategy can then serve as the source of polite pronouns like *usted, ustedes* in Spanish. In view of the very high premium on tenor relations, it seems natural that languages evolve rich resources for negotiating such relations – especially certainly in the highly hierarchical societies that began to evolve with city-based civilizations around 5,000 years ago, societies where the notion of strangerhood began to emerge.
12 I have drawn on a passage from the manuscript of my Matthiessen (2018a) chapter on multilingual system networks – a passage that had to be deleted from the published version to keep within the word limit.
13 There are certain conditional relationship between systemic terms that can be inferred from Table 6.5 and which could be represented in the system network in Figure 6.21. For example, if the person is 'speaker', then the status is 'non-neutral'; if the person is 'speaker+' or 'non-interactant', then the status is 'neutral'.
14 Cf. a similar effect in the intersection of MOOD TYPE: interrogative: yes/no and POLARITY: negative in English, as in A: *I think isn't vitamin D the vitamin you get from the sun?* - B: *That's right, yes.*; see e.g. Matthiessen (1995a: 488–489) and Halliday and Matthiessen (2014: 174). But note that Chinese is significantly different in that the distinction is embodied as an elaboration in delicacy of 'polar' interrogatives: whenever speakers select 'polar', they must make a further choice (rather than just go with the unmarked, or default, polarity of 'positive', as in the case of speakers of English). Cf. the point below about the significance of the simultaneity of the grammaticalization of speech function and tenor relations in Korean.
15 Even though syntagmatic patterns appear to vary considerably across languages, there is arguably more similarity than might at first appear to be the case. To pursue this, we need two syntagmatic notions, **modes of expression** (e.g. Halliday 1979; Martin 1996c) and also **media of expression**. For relevant discussion of modes of expression and means of expression, see Matthiessen (2004).
16 See: https://wals.info
17 For tone as a medium of expression of systemic contrasts in grammar, cf. Section 3.2.1 above. The prosodic mode of expression characteristic of the interpersonal metafunction (Halliday 1979) may be carried by different media of expression – segments, intonation, sequence (Matthiessen 2004). As noted above, while operating with the prosodic mode of expression, languages vary with respect to the medium of expression, and the medium of expression may change over time in a given language. In the case of French, polar interrogatives may be realized segmentally by a modal 'particle', sequentially by Finite before Subject and/or intonationally by rising tone: see Caffarel (2006). Irrespective of how the systemic contrast between 'declarative' and 'polar interrogative' is realized, the two terms will lead to more delicate systemic distinctions, e.g. in the areas of modal assessments (ranges of options and the orientation, either giving or demanding assessments) and elicitations of responses, 'declarative' clauses having some kind of option since unlike 'interrogative' ones they do not embody the sense 'demand'.

## Chapter 7

1   Fischer-Jørgensen (1975: 146) draws attention to the point that this echoes Bloomfield's (1933) statement that 'the distinctive features occur in lumps and bundles each one of which we call a phoneme'. This contrasts with Trubetzkoy's (1939: 35) paradigmatic characterization of the phoneme: 'Und da jedes Phonem ein Glied einer phonologischen Opposition sein muß, so folgt daraus, daß sich das Phonem nicht mit einem konkreten Lautgebilde, sondern nur mit seinen phonologisch relevanten Eigenschaften deckt. Man darf sagen, daß *das Phonem die Gesamtheit der phonologisch relevanten Eigenschaften eines Lautgebildes ist.*' In Baltaxe's (1969: 36) translation: 'And since every phoneme must be a member of a distinctive opposition, it follows that the phoneme is not identical with an actual sound but only with its phonologically relevant properties. One can say that the phoneme is *the sum of the phonologically relevant properties of a sound (Lautgebilde).*'

# References

Akerejola, Ernest. 2005. *A systemic functional grammar of Òkó*. PhD thesis. Macquarie University.

Allerton, David J. 2002. *Stretched verb constructions in English*. London: Routledge. https://doi.org/10.4324/9780203167649

Argyle, Michael, Adrian Furnham and Jean Ann Graham. 1981. *Social situations*. Cambridge: Cambridge University Press. https://doi.org/10.1017/CBO9780511558283

Asp, Elissa. 2013. The twin paradoxes of unconscious choice and unintentional agents: What neurosciences say about choice and agency in action. In Lise M. Fontaine, Tom A.M. Bartlett and Gerard N. O'Grady (eds), *Systemic functional linguistics: Exploring choice*, Chapter 8. Cambridge: Cambridge University Press.

Baldry, Anthony and Paul J. Thibault. 2010. *Multimodal transcription and text analysis: A multimedia toolkit and coursebook*. London & Oakville: Equinox Publishing Ltd.

Banks, David. 2016. On the (non)necessity of the hybrid category behavioural process. In Donna Miller and Paul Bayley (eds), *Permeable contexts and hybrid discourses*, 21–40. London: Equinox Publishing Ltd.

Barabási, Albert László. 2016. *Network science*. Cambridge: Cambridge University Press.

Bardi, Mohamed Ali. 2008. *A systemic functional description of the grammar of Arabic*. PhD thesis. Macquarie University.

Bartlett, Tom. 2016. Phasal dynamism and the unfolding of meaning as text. *English Text Construction* 9(1): 143–164. https://doi.org/10.1075/etc.9.1.08bar

Bartlett, Tom and Gerard O'Grady (eds). 2017. *The Routledge handbook of systemic functional linguistics*. Milton Park: Routledge. https://doi.org/10.4324/9781315413891

Barwise, Jon and John Perry. 1983. *Situations and attitudes*. Cambridge, MA: MIT Press.

Bateman, John A. 1985. *Utterances in context: Towards a systemic theory of the intersubjective achievement of discourse*. PhD thesis. Department of Artificial Intelligence/School of Epistemics, University of Edinburgh.

Bateman, John A. 1989. Dynamic systemic-functional grammar: A new frontier. *Word* 40(1–2): 263–287. https://doi.org/10.1080/00437956.1989.11435808

Bateman, John A. 1990. *Upper modelling: Current states of theory and practice*. University of Southern California/Information Sciences Institute.

Bateman, John A. 1996. KPML: The KOMET-Penman (Multilingual) Development Environment: Support for multilingual linguistic resource development and sentence generation. GMD/Institut für Integrierte Publikations- und Informationssysteme (IPSI), Darmstadt. (Release 1.0). {Studie der GMD}, {302}. 1996. 276p. (ISBN 3-88457-304-7; ISSN 0170-8120).

Bateman, John A. 1997. Enabling technology for multilingual natural language generation: The KPML development environment. *Natural Language Engineering* 1(1): 1–42. https://doi.org/10.1017/S1351324997001514

Bateman, John A. 2008a. *Multimodality and genre: A foundation for the systematic analysis of multimodal documents*. London & New York: Palgrave Macmillan.

Bateman, John A. 2008b. Systemic functional linguistics and the notion of linguistic structure: Unanswered questions, new possibilities. In Jonathan J. Webster (ed.), *Meaning in context: Implementing intelligent applications of language studies*, 24–58. London & New York: Continuum.

Bateman, John A., Joana Hois, Robert Ross and Thora Tenbrink. 2010. A linguistic ontology of space for natural language processing. *Artificial Intelligence* 174: 1027–1071. https://doi.org/10.1016/j.artint.2010.05.008

Bateman, John, Robert Kasper, J. Schütz and Erich Steiner. 1989. A new view on the process of translation. *The 4th Annual Meeting of the European Chapter of the Association for Computational Linguistics*. UMIST: Manchester, UK. https://doi.org/10.3115/976815.976853

Bateman, John, Daniel McDonald, Tuomo Hiippala, Daniel Couto-Vale and Eugeniu Costetchi. 2019. Systemic functional linguistics and computation: New directions, new challenges. In Geoff Thompson, Wendy L. Bowcher, Lise Fontaine and David Schöntal (eds), *The Cambridge handbook of systemic functional linguistics*, 561–586. Cambridge: Cambridge University Press. https://doi.org/10.1017/9781316337936.024

Bateman, John A. and Christian M.I.M. Matthiessen. 1993. The text base in generation. In Keqi Hao, Keqi Hao, Hermann Bluhme and Renzhi Li (ed.), *Proceedings of the international conference on texts and language research*, Xi'an, 29–31 March 1989, 3–45. Xi'an: Xi'an Jiaotong University Press.

Bateman, John, Christian Matthiessen, Keizo Nanri and Licheng Zeng. 1991. The rapid prototyping of natural language generation components: An application of functional typology. *Proceedings of the 12th international conference on artificial intelligence*, Sydney, 24–30 August 1991, 966–971. San Mateo, CA: Morgan Kaufman.

Bateman, John A., Christian M.I.M. Matthiessen and Zeng Licheng. 1999. Multilingual language generation for multilingual software: A functional linguistic approach. *Applied Artificial Intelligence: An International Journal* 13(6): 607–639. https://doi.org/10.1080/088395199117289

Bateman, John A. and Michael O'Donnell. 2015. Computational linguistics: The Halliday connection. In Jonathan J. Webster (ed.), *The Bloomsbury companion to M.A.K. Halliday*, 453–466. London: Bloomsbury.

Bateman, John A. and Elke Teich. 1995. Selective information presentation in an integrated publication system: An application of genre-driven text generation. *Information Processing and Management* 31(5): 753–768. https://doi.org/10.1016/0306-4573(95)00053-J

Bateman, John A., Janina Wildfeuer and Tuomo Hiippala. 2017. *Multimodality: Foundations, research and analysis - A problem-oriented introduction*. Berlin: Mouton de Gruyter.

Bateman, John A. and Michael Zock. 2017. Natural language generation. In Ruslan Mitkov (ed.), *Oxford handbook of computational linguistics*. 2nd ed., 284–304. Oxford: Oxford University Press. https://doi.org/10.1093/oxfordhb/9780199573691.013.010

Bateson, M. Catherine. 1979. The epigenesis of conversational interaction: A personal account of research development. In Margaret Bullowa (ed.), *Before speech: The beginning of human communication*, 63–77. London: Cambridge University Press.

Berry, Margaret. 1981. Systemic linguistics and discourse analysis: A multi-layered approach to exchange structure. In Malcolm Coulthard and Michael Montgomery (eds), *Studies in discourse analysis*, 120–145. London: Routledge & Kegan Paul.

Bickerton, Derek. 1995. *Language and human behaviour*. London: UCL Press.

Birdwhistell, Ray L. 1952. *Introduction to kinesics: An annotated system for analysis of body motion and gesture*. Washington, DC: Dept. of State, Foreign Service Institute.

Birdwhistell, Ray L. 1970. *Kinesics and context: Essays on body-motion communication*. London: Allen Lane the Penguin Press. https://doi.org/10.9783/9780812201284

Black, Max. 1964. *Philosophy in America*. London: George Allen & Unwin.

Bloomfield, Leonard. 1933. *Language*. London: Allen & Unwin.

Bod, Rens, Jennifer Hay and Stefanie Jannedy (eds). 2003. *Probabilistic linguistics*. Cambridge, MA: MIT Press. https://doi.org/10.7551/mitpress/5582.001.0001

Bode, Stefan, Carsten Murawski, Chun Siong Soon, Philipp Bode, Jutta Stahl and Philip L. Smith. 2014. Demystifying 'free will': The role of contextual information and evidence accumulation for predictive brain activity. *Neuroscience and Biobehavioural Reviews* 47: 636–645. https://doi.org/10.1016/j.neubiorev.2014.10.017

Bohm, David. 1979. *Wholeness and the implicate order*. London: Routledge & Kegan Paul.

Bolinger, Dwight. 1986. *Intonation and its parts: Melody in spoken English*. Stanford, CA: Stanford University Press. https://doi.org/10.1515/9781503622906

Bolinger, Dwight. 1989. *Intonation and its uses: Melody in grammar and discourse*. Stanford: Stanford University Press. https://doi.org/10.1515/9781503623125

Bowcher, Wendy L. 2014. Issues in developing unified systems for contextual field and mode. *Functions of Language* 21(2): 176–209. https://doi.org/10.1075/fol.21.2.02bow

Bowcher, Wendy L. and Meena Debashish. 2019. Intonation. In Geoff Thompson, Wendy L. Bowcher, Lise Fontaine and David Schöntal (eds), *The Cambridge handbook of systemic functional linguistics*, 171–203. Cambridge: Cambridge University Press. https://doi.org/10.1017/9781316337936.009

Bowcher, Wendy L. and Bradley Smith (eds). 2014. *Systemic phonology: Recent studies in English*. Sheffield: Equinox Publishing Ltd.

Brachman, Ronald J. 1979. On the epistemological status of semantic networks. In Nicholas V. Findler (ed.), *Associative networks: Representation and use of knowledge by computers*, 3–50. New York: Academic Press.

Brown, Roger and Marguerite Ford. 1964. Address in American English. In Dell Hymes (1964), *Language in culture and society*, 234–244. New York: Harper and Row.

Brown, Roger and Albert Gilman. 1960. The pronouns of power and solidarity. In Thomas A. Sebeok (ed.), *Style in language*, 253–276. Cambridge, MA: MIT Press.

Brumfit, Christopher J. 1979. Notional syllabuses – a reassessment. *System* 7(2): 111–116. https://doi.org/10.1016/0346-251X(79)90033-2

Burton, Deidre. 1980. *Dialogue and discourse*. London: Routledge & Kegan Paul.

Butt, David G. 2008. The robustness of realizational systems. In Jonathan J. Webster (ed.), *Meaning in context: Implementing intelligent applications in language studies*, 59–83. London & New York: Continuum.

Butt, David G. and Rebekah Kate Ardley Wegener. 2007. The work of concepts: Context and metafunction in the systemic functional model. In Ruqaiya Hasan, Christian M.I.M. Matthiessen and Jonathan Webster (eds), *Continuing discourse on language: A functional perspective*, Volume 2, 589–618. London: Equinox Publishing Ltd.

Byrnes, Heidi, Hiram H. Maxim and John Norris. 2010. Realizing advanced foreign language writing development in collegiate education: Curricular design, pedagogy, assessment. *The Modern Language Journal* 94, Supplement. https://doi.org/10.1111/j.1540-4781.2010.01137.x

Caffarel, Alice. 1992. Interacting between a generalized tense semantics and register-specific semantic tense systems: A bi-stratal exploration of the semantics of French tense. *Language Sciences* 14(4): 385–418. https://doi.org/10.1016/0388-0001(92)90023-8

Caffarel, Alice. 2006. *A systemic functional grammar of French: From grammar to discourse*. London & New York: Continuum.

Caffarel, Alice, J.R. Martin and Christian M.I.M. Matthiessen (eds). 2004. *Language typology: A functional perspective*. (Current Issues in Linguistic Theory 253.) xiii, 690 pp. + index. Amsterdam: Benjamins. https://doi.org/10.1075/cilt.253

Catford, J.C. 1977. *Fundamental problems in phonetics*. Indiana: Indiana University Press.

Catford, J.C. 2001. *A practical introduction to phonetics*. 2nd edition. Oxford: Oxford University Press.

Chang, Moon-Soo, Ichiro Kobayashi and Michio Sugeno. 2001. A study on meaning processing of a dialogue with an example of travel consultation. *Journal of Japan Society for Fuzzy Theory and Systems* 13(1): 70–88. https://doi.org/10.3156/jfuzzy.13.1_70

Chomsky, Noam. 1957. *Syntactic structures*. The Hague: Mouton. https://doi.org/10.1515/9783112316009

Chomsky, Noam and Morris Halle. 1968. *The sound pattern of English*. New York: Harper & Row.
Christie, Fran and Beverley Derewianka. 2008. *School discourse: Learning to write across the years of schooling*. London & New York: Continuum.
Cléirigh, Chris. 1998. *A selectionist model of the genesis of phonic texture: Systemic phonology and universal Darwinism*. PhD thesis. University of Sydney.
Cloran, Carmel. 1994. *Rhetorical units and decontextualisation: An enquiry into some relations of context, meaning and grammar*. University of Nottingham: Monographs in Systemic Linguistics Number 6.
Cloran, Carmel. 2010. Rhetorical unit analysis and Bakhtin's chronotope. *Functions of Language* 17(1): 9–70. https://doi.org/10.1075/fol.17.1.02clo
Cloran, Carmel, Virginia Stuart-Smith and Lynne Young. 2007. Models of discourse. In Ruqaiya Hasan, Christian M.I.M. Matthiessen and Jonathan Webster (eds), *Continuing discourse on language: A functional perspective*. Volume 2, 645–668. London & Oakville: Equinox Publishing Ltd.
Collins, Peter. 2005. Exclamative clauses in English. *Word* 56(1): 1–17.
Comrie, Bernard and Edward L. Keenan. 1979. Noun phrase accessibility revisited. *Language* 55(3): 649–664. https://doi.org/10.2307/413321
Corballis, Michael C. 2002. *From hand to mouth: The origins of language*. Princeton, NJ: Princeton University Press. https://doi.org/10.1515/9780691221731
Costetchi, Eugeniu. 2013. A method to generate simplified systemic functional parses from dependency parses. In *Proceedings of the Second International Conference on Dependency Linguistics*. Prague, August 27–30, 2013, 68–77. Charles University in Prague. Prague: Matfyz Press.
Costetchi, Eugeniu. 2020. *Parsimonious vole: A systemic functional parser for English*. PhD thesis. University of Bremen.
Couto-Vale, Daniel. 2017. *How to make a wheelchair understand spoken commands*. PhD thesis. University of Bremen.
Cross, Marilyn. 1991. *Choice in text: A systemic approach to computer modelling of variant text production*. PhD thesis. Macquarie University.
Cross, Marilyn, Christian Matthiessen, Licheng Zeng and Ichiro Kobayashi. 1998. Building Multimodal Systems: Compromise between Theory and Practice. *AAAI Technical Report* WS-98-09. https://aaai.org/Papers/Workshops/1998/WS-98-09/WS98-09-003.pdf
Davey, Anthony. 1978. *Discourse production: A computer model of some aspects of a speaker*. Edinburgh: Edinburgh University Press.
Davidse, Kristin. 1999. *Categories of experiential grammar* (Monographs in Systemic Linguistics). Nottingham: University of Nottingham.
Delin, Judith L. and John A. Bateman. 2002. Describing and critiquing multimodal documents. *Document Design* 3(2): 140–155. https://doi.org/10.1075/dd.3.2.05del
Derewianka, Beverly. 1995. *Language development in the transition from childhood to adolescence: The role of grammatical metaphor*. PhD thesis. Macquarie University.
Derewianka, Beverley. 2003. Grammatical metaphor in the transition to adolescence. In A. Simon-Vandenbergen, Miriam Taverniers and Louise Ravelli (eds), *Grammatical metaphor: Views from systemic functional linguistics*, 185–220. Amsterdam: John Benjamins. https://doi.org/10.1075/cilt.236.11der
Djonov, Emilia. 2008. Children's website structure and navigation. In Len Unsworth (ed.), *Multimodal semiotics: Functional analysis in contexts of education*, 216–236. London: Continuum.
Doran, Yaegan, John. 2016. *Knowledge in physics through mathematics, image and language*. PhD thesis. Sydney University.
Eggins, Suzanne and Diana Slade. 1997/2005. *Analysing casual conversation*. London: Cassell.
Ellegård, Alvar. 1953. *The auxiliary 'do': The establishment and regulation of its use in English*. Stockholm: Almqvist och Wiksell.
Ellegård, Alvar. 1971. *Transformationell svensk-engelsk satslära*. Lund: Gleerup.

Elmenoufy, Afaf. 1969. *A study of the role of intonation in the grammar of English*. PhD thesis. University of London.

Ervin-Tripp, Susan M. 1969. Sociolinguistics. In L. Berkowitz (ed.), *Advances in experimental social psychology*, Volume 4, 93–165. New York & London: Academic Press. https://doi.org/10.1016/S0065-2601(08)60077-5

Fant, Gunnar. 2004. *Speech acoustics and phonetics*. Dordrecht: Kluwer.

Fawcett, Robin P. 1973. Generating a sentence in systemic functional grammar. In M.A.K. Halliday and James R. Martin (ed.), 1981, *Readings in systemic linguistics*, 146–183. London: Batsford.

Fawcett, Robin P. 1988a. What makes a 'good' system network good? In James D. Benson and William S. Greaves (eds), *Systemic functional approaches to discourse*, 1–28. Norwood, NJ: Ablex.

Fawcett, Robin P. 1988b. The English personal pronouns: An exercise in linguistic theory. In Michael J. Cummings, James D. Benson and William S. Greaves (eds), *Linguistics in a systemic perspective*, 185–220. Amsterdam: Benjamins. https://doi.org/10.1075/cilt.39.09faw

Fawcett, Robin P. 1989. Towards a systemic flowchart model for discourse analysis. In Robin P. Fawcett and David Young (eds), *New developments in systemic linguistics: theory and application*, 116–143. London: Pinter.

Fawcett, Robin P. 1994. A generationist approach to grammar reversibility in natural language processing. In Tomek Strzalkowski (ed.), *Reversible grammar in natural language generation*, 365–413. Dordrecht: Kluwer.

Fawcett, Robin P. and Gordon Tucker. 1990. Demonstration of GENESYS: A very large semantically based systemic functional grammar. *The 13th International Conference on Computational Linguistics*, 47–49. Helsinki: COLING. https://doi.org/10.3115/992507.992514

Fawcett, Robin P., Gordon H. Tucker and Y.Q. Lin. 1992. The COMMUNAL project: How to get from semantics to syntax. *Proceedings of the 14th International Conference on Computational Linguistics*. Helsinki: COLING.

Fawcett, Robin P., A. van der Mije and C. van Wissen. 1988. Towards a systemic flowchart model for discourse structure. In R.P. Fawcett and David Young (eds), *New developments in systemic linguistics, vol. 2: Theory and application*, 116–143. London: Pinter.

Fine, Jonathan. 1992. Functions of probabilities on linguistic systems. *Occasional Papers in Systemic Linguistics* 6: 9–18.

Fischer-Jørgensen, Eli. 1975. *Trends in phonological theory: A historical introduction*. København: Akademisk Forlag.

Fontaine, Lise M., Tom A.M. Bartlett and Gerard N. O'Grady (eds). 2013. *Systemic functional linguistics: Exploring choice*. Cambridge: Cambridge University Press.

Frake, Charles. 1962. The ethnographic study of cognitive systems. In T. Gladwin and W. Sturtevant (eds), *Anthropology and human behavior*. Washington: Anthropological Society of Washington.

Fung, Andy. 2015. Hasan's semantic networks revisited: A Cantonese systemic functional approach. In Wendy Bowcher and Jennifer Yang (eds), *Society in language, language in society: Essays in honour of Ruqaiya Hasan*, 115–140. Berlin: Springer. https://doi.org/10.1057/9781137402868_5

Fung Ka Chun, Andy. 2018. *Analysing Cantonese doctor-patient communication: A semantic network approach*. PhD thesis. The Hong Kong Polytechnic University.

García, Adolfo M. and Agustín Ibáñez. 2016. Processes and verbs of doing, in the brain: Theoretical implications for systemic functional linguistics. *Functions of Language* 23(3): 305–335. https://doi.org/10.1075/fol.23.3.02gar

García, Adolfo M., William Sullivan and Sarah Tsiang. 2017. *An introduction to relational network theory: History, principles, and descriptive applications*. London: Equinox Publishing Ltd.

Gazdar, Gerald, Ewan Klein, Geoffrey K. Pullum and Ivan A. Sag. 1985. *Generalized phrase structure grammar*. Cambridge, MA: Harvard University Press.

Gibbons, John. 1989. Instructional cycles. *English Teaching Forum* 27(3): 6–11.

Gibbons, John and Victoria Markwick-Smith. 1992. Exploring the use of a systemic semantic description. *International Journal of Applied Linguistics* 2(1): 36–51. https://doi.org/10.1111/j.1473-4192.1992.tb00022.x

Gleason, H.A. 1965. *Linguistics and English grammar*. New York: Holt, Rinehart & Winston.

Goodenough, Ward H. 1956. Componential analysis and the study of meaning. *Language* 32(1): 195–216. https://doi.org/10.2307/410665

Gorniak, Peter J. 2005. *The affordance-based concept*. PhD thesis. MIT.

Gorniak, Peter and Deb Roy. 2007. Situated language understanding as filtering perceived affordances. *Cognitive Science: A Multidisciplinary Journal* 31(2): 197–231.

Grace, George W. 1981. *An essay on language*. Columbia, SC: Hornbeam Press.

Greaves, William S. 2007. Intonation in systemic linguistics. In Ruqaiya Hasan, Christian M.I.M. Matthiessen and Jonathan Webster (eds), *Continuing discourse on language: A functional perspective*. Volume 2, 979–1025. London: Equinox Publishing Ltd.

Gregory, Michael J. 2002. Phasal analysis within communication linguistics: Two contrastive discourses. In Michael Cummings, Peter H. Fries and David Lockwood (eds), *Relations and functions within and around language*, 316–345. London & New York: Continuum.

Grimes, Joseph E. 1975. *The thread of discourse*. The Hague: Mouton. https://doi.org/10.1515/9783110886474

Grosz, Barbara J. and Candy L. Sidner. 1986. Attention, intentions, and the structure of discourse. *Computational Linguistics* 12(3): 175–204.

Gu, Yueguo. 2002. Towards an understanding of workplace discourse – a pilot study for compiling a spoken Chinese corpus of situated discourse. In Christopher Candlin (ed.), *Theory and practice of professional discourse*, 137–185. Hong Kong: CUHK Press.

Haiman, John. 1985a. *Natural syntax*. Cambridge: Cambridge University Press.

Haiman, John (ed.). 1985b. *Iconicity in syntax*. Amsterdam: Benjamins. https://doi.org/10.1075/tsl.6

Halliday, M.A.K. 1956a. Grammatical categories in modern Chinese. *Transactions of the Philological Society* 177–224. Reprinted in M.A.K. Halliday. 2006. *Studies in the Chinese language*. Volume 8 in the Collected Works of M.A.K. Halliday, edited by Jonathan J. Webster, 209–248. London & New York: Continuum. https://doi.org/10.1111/j.1467-968X.1956.tb00567.x

Halliday, M.A.K. 1956b. The linguistic basis of a mechanical thesaurus, and its application to English preposition classification. *Mechanical Translation* 3(3): 81–88. Reprinted in M.A.K. Halliday. 2004. *Computational and quantitative studies*. Volume 6: The Collected Works of M.A.K. Halliday, edited by Jonathan Webster, 6–19. London & New York: Continuum.

Halliday, M.A.K. 1959. *The language of the Chinese 'Secret History of the Mongols'*. Oxford: Blackwell. (Publications of the Philological Society 17.) Reprinted in M.A.K. Halliday. 2006. *Studies in the Chinese language*. Volume 8 in the Collected Works of M.A.K. Halliday, edited by Jonathan J. Webster, 3–171. London & New York: Continuum.

Halliday, M.A.K. 1961. Categories of the theory of grammar. *Word* 17(3): 242–292. Reprinted in M.A.K. Halliday. 2002. *On grammar*. Volume 1 in the Collected Works of M.A.K. Halliday, edited by Jonathan J. Webster, Chapter 2: 37–94. London & New York: Continuum.

Halliday, M.A.K. 1963a. Class in relation to the axes of chain and choice in language. *Linguistics* 2: 5–15. Reprinted in M.A.K. Halliday. 2002. *On grammar*. Volume 1 of Collected Works of M.A.K. Halliday, edited by Jonathan J. Webster, Chapter 3: 95–117. London & New York: Continuum.

Halliday, M.A.K. 1963b. The tones of English. *Archivum Linguisticum* 15(1): 1–28.

Halliday, M.A.K. 1964. Syntax and the consumer. In C.I.J.M. Stuart (ed.), *Report of the fifteenth annual (first international) round table meeting on linguistics and language*, 11–24. Washington, DC: Georgetown University Press. Reprinted in Halliday and Martin (1981), 21–28. Reprinted in M.A.K. Halliday. 2003. *On language and linguistics*. Volume 3 of Collected Works of M.A.K. Halliday, edited by Jonathan Webster, Chapter 1: 36–49. London & New York: Continuum.

Halliday, M.A.K. 1965. Types of structure. *The O.S.T.I. programme in the linguistic properties of scientific English*. In M.A.K. Halliday and James R. Martin (eds). 1981, *Readings in systemic linguistics*, 29–41. London: Batsford.

Halliday, M.A.K. 1966a. Some notes on 'deep' grammar. *Journal of Linguistics* 2(1): 57–67. Reprinted in M.A.K. Halliday. 2002. *On grammar*. Volume 1 in the Collected Works of M.A.K. Halliday, edited by Jonathan J. Webster, 106–117. London & New York: Continuum. https://doi.org/10.1017/S0022226700001328

Halliday, M.A.K. 1966b. Lexis as a linguistic level. In C.E. Bazell, J.C. Catford, M.A.K. Halliday and R.H. Robins (eds), *In memory of J.R. Firth*, 148–162. Longman. Reprinted in M.A.K. Halliday. 2002. *On grammar*. Volume 1 in the Collected Works of M.A.K. Halliday, edited by Jonathan J. Webster, 158–172. London & New York: Continuum.

Halliday, M.A.K. 1967. *Intonation and grammar in British English*. The Hague: Mouton. (Janua Linguarum Series Practica 48.) https://doi.org/10.1515/9783111357447

Halliday, M.A.K. 1967/8. Notes on transitivity and theme in English 1–3. *Journal of Linguistics* 3(1): 37–81, 3(2): 199–244, 4(2): 179–215. Reprinted in M.A.K. Halliday. 2005. *Studies in English language*. Volume 7 in the Collected Works of M.A.K. Halliday, edited by Jonathan Webster, Chapter 1: 5–54. Chapter 2: 55–109. Chapter 3: 110–153. London & New York: Continuum.

Halliday, M.A.K. 1969. Options and functions in the English clause. *Brno Studies in English* 8: 81–88. Reprinted in M.A.K. Halliday. 2005. *Studies in English language*. Volume 7 in the Collected Works of M.A.K. Halliday, edited by Jonathan Webster, Chapter 4: 154–163. London & New York: Continuum.

Halliday, M.A.K. 1970a. Functional diversity in language, as seen from a consideration of modality and mood in English. *Foundations of Language* 6: 322–361. Reprinted in M.A.K. Halliday. 2005. *Studies in English language*. Volume 7 in the Collected Works of M.A.K. Halliday, edited by Jonathan Webster, Chapter 5: 164–204. London & New York: Continuum.

Halliday, M.A.K. 1970b. Phonological (prosodic) analysis of the new Chinese syllable (modern Pekingese). In Frank R. Palmer (ed.), *Prosodic analysis*. London: Oxford University Press.

Halliday, M.A.K. 1973a. The functional basis of language. In Basil Bernstein (ed.), *Applied studies towards a sociology of language*. Volume 2, *Class, codes and control*, 343–346. London: Routledge and Keagan Paul. Reprinted in M.A.K. Halliday. 2003. *On language and linguistics*. Volume 3 of Collected Works of M.A.K. Halliday, edited by Jonathan Webster, Chapter 14: 298–322. London & New York: Continuum.

Halliday, M.A.K. 1973b. *Explorations in the functions of language*. London: Edward Arnold.

Halliday, M.A.K. 1975a. *Learning how to mean: Explorations in the development of language*. London: Edward Arnold. Reprinted in M.A.K. Halliday. 2003. *The language of early childhood*. Volume 4 of the Collected works of M.A.K. Halliday, edited by Jonathan J. Webster. London & New York: Continuum.

Halliday, M.A.K. 1975b. The context of linguistics. In Francis P. Dinneen (ed.), *Report of the twenty-fifth annual round table meeting on linguistics and language study*. (Monograph Series in Languages and Linguistics 17.) Washington, DC: Georgetown University Press. Reprinted in M.A.K. Halliday. 2003. *On language and linguistics*. Volume 3 of Collected Works of M.A.K. Halliday, edited by Jonathan J. Webster, 74–91. London & New York: Continuum.

Halliday, M.A.K. 1976. *System and function in language*, edited by Gunther Kress. London: Oxford University Press.

Halliday, M.A.K. 1977. Text as semantic choice in social contexts. In Teun van Dijk and Janos Petöfi (eds), *Grammars and descriptions*, 176–225. Berlin: Walter de Gruyter. Reprinted in M.A.K. Halliday. 2002. *Linguistic studies of text and discourse*. Volume 2 in the Collected Works of M.A.K. Halliday, edited by Jonathan J. Webster, Chapter 2: 23–81. London & New York: Continuum.

Halliday, M.A.K. 1978a. *Language as social semiotic: The social interpretation of language and meaning*. London: Edward Arnold.

Halliday, M.A.K. 1978b. *Notes on 'Talking Shop': Demands on language*. Lindfield, NSW: Australian Film Commission.

Halliday, M.A.K. 1979. Modes of meaning and modes of expression: Types of grammatical structure and their determination by different semantic functions. In David J. Allerton, Edward Carney and David Holdcroft (eds), *Function and context in linguistic analysis: A Festschrift for William Haas*, 57–79. Cambridge: Cambridge University Press. ISBN: 0521224292. Reprinted in M.A.K. Halliday. 2002. *On grammar*. Volume 1 of Collected Works of M.A.K. Halliday, edited by Jonathan J. Webster, Chapter 8: 196–218. London & New York: Continuum.

Halliday, M.A.K. 1981. Text semantics and clause grammar: Some patterns of realization. *Seventh LACUS Forum*, 31–59. Columbia: Hornbeam Press. Reprinted as Text semantics and clause grammar: how is a text like a clause? in M.A.K. Halliday. 2002. *On grammar*. Volume 1 of Collected Works of M.A.K. Halliday, edited by Jonathan Webster, Chapter 9: 219–260. London & New York: Continuum.

Halliday, M.A.K. 1984a. Language as code and language as behaviour: A systemic-functional interpretation of the nature and ontogenesis of dialogue. In M.A.K. Halliday, Robin P. Fawcett, Sydney Lamb and Adam Makkai (eds), *The semiotics of language and culture*, Volume 1: 3–35. London: Frances Pinter. Reprinted in M.A.K. Halliday. 2003. *On language and linguistics*. Volume 3 of Collected Works of M.A.K. Halliday, edited by Jonathan Webster, Chapter 10: 226–250. London & New York: Continuum.

Halliday, M.A.K. 1984b. On the ineffability of grammatical categories. In Alan Manning, Pierre Martin and Kim McCalla (eds), *Tenth LACUS Forum*, 3–18. Columbia: Hornbeam Press. Reprinted in M.A.K. Halliday. 2002. *On grammar*. Volume 1 of Collected Works of M.A.K. Halliday, edited by Jonathan J. Webster, Chapter 11: 291–322. London & New York: Continuum.

Halliday, M.A.K. 1985a. *An introduction to functional grammar*. London: Edward Arnold.

Halliday, M.A.K. 1985b. It's a fixed word order language is English. *ITL Review of Applied Linguistics* 67–68: 91–116. Reprinted in M.A.K. Halliday. 2005. *Studies in English language*, Volume 7 in the Collected Works of M.A.K. Halliday, edited by Jonathan J. Webster, 213–231. London & New York: Continuum. https://doi.org/10.1075/itl.67-68.07hal

Halliday, M.A.K. 1985c. *Spoken and written language*. Geelong, Vic.: Deakin University Press.

Halliday, M.A.K. 1988. On the language of physical science. In Mohsen Ghadessy (ed.), *Registers of written English: Situational factors and linguistic features*, 162–178. London & New York: Pinter Publishers. Reprinted in M.A.K. Halliday. 2004. *The language of science*. Volume 5 in the Collected Works of M.A.K. Halliday, edited by Jonathan J. Webster, 140–158. London & New York: Continuum.

Halliday, M.A.K. 1990. New ways of meaning: A challenge to applied linguistics. Greek Applied Linguistics Association, *Journal of Applied Linguistics* 6 (Ninth World Congress of Applied Linguistics Special Issue): 7–36. Reprinted in M.A.K. Halliday. 2003. *On Language and linguistics*. Volume 3 of Collected Works of M.A.K. Halliday, edited by Jonathan Webster, Chapter 6: 139–174. London & New York: Continuum.

Halliday, M.A.K. 1991a. Towards probabilistic interpretations. In Eija Ventola (ed.), *Trends in linguistics: Functional and systemic linguistics: Approaches and uses*. Berlin & New York: Mouton de Gruyter. Reprinted in M.A.K. Halliday. 2005. *Computational and quantitative studies*. Volume 6 in the Collected Works of M.A.K. Halliday, edited by Jonathan Webster, Chapter 3: 42–62. London & New York: Continuum.

Halliday, M.A.K. 1991b. Corpus linguistics and probabilistic grammar. In Karin Aijmer and Bengt Altenberg (eds), *English corpus linguistics: Studies in honour of Jan Svartvik*, 30–43. London: Longman. Reprinted in M.A.K. Halliday. 2005. *Computational and quantitative studies*. Volume 6 in the Collected Works of M.A.K. Halliday, edited by Jonathan Webster, Chapter 4: 63–75. London & New York: Continuum.

Halliday, M.A.K. 1992a. How do you mean? In Martin Davies and Louise Ravelli (eds), *Advances in systemic linguistics: Recent theory and practice*, 20–35. London: Pinter. Reprinted in M.A.K. Halliday. 2002. *On grammar*. Volume 1 of Collected Works of M.A.K. Halliday, edited by Jonathan Webster, Chapter 13: 352–368. London & New York: Continuum.

Halliday, M.A.K. 1992b. A systemic interpretation of Peking syllable finals. In Paul Tench (ed.), *Studies in systemic phonology*, 98–121. London: Pinter.

Halliday, M.A.K. 1992c. Some lexicogrammatical features of the Zero Population Growth text. In Sandra A. Thompson and William C. Mann (eds), *Discourse description: Diverse analyses of a fund-raising text*, 327–358. Amsterdam: Benjamins. https://doi.org/10.1075/pbns.16.13hal

Halliday, M.A.K. 1993a. Towards a language-based theory of learning. *Linguistics and Education* 5(2): 93–116. Reprinted in M.A.K. Halliday. 2004a. *The language of early childhood*. Volume 4 of Collected Works of M.A.K. Halliday, edited by Jonathan Webster, 327–352. London & New York: Continuum.

Halliday, M.A.K. 1993b. Quantitative studies and probabilities in grammar. Michael Hoey (ed.), *Data, description, discourse: Papers on the English language in honour of John McH. Sinclair*, 1–25. London: Harper Collins. Reprinted in M.A.K. Halliday. 2005. *Computational and quantitative studies*. Volume 6 in the Collected Works of M.A.K. Halliday, edited by Jonathan Webster, Chapter 7: 130–156. London & New York: Continuum.

Halliday, M.A.K. 1994. *An introduction to functional grammar*. Second Edition. London: Edward Arnold.

Halliday, M.A.K. 1996. Grammar and the construction of educational knowledge. The International Conference 'Language Analysis and Description: Applications in language teaching', Lingnan College and The Hong Kong University of Science & Technology, 26–29 June 1996.

Halliday, M.A.K. 1998a. Representing the child as a semiotic being (one who means). Paper presented to conference 'Representing the child', Monash University, 2–3 October 1998. In Halliday. 2004a. *The language of early childhood*. Volume 4 of Collected Works of M.A.K. Halliday, edited by Jonathan Webster, 6–27. London & New York: Continuum.

Halliday, M.A.K. 1998b. On the grammar of pain. *Functions of Language* 5(1): 1–32. Reprinted in M.A.K. Halliday. 2005. *Studies in English language*. Volume 7 in the Collected Works of M.A.K. Halliday, edited by Jonathan J. Webster, Chapter 12: 306–337. London & New York: Continuum.

Halliday, M.A.K. 1998c. Phonology past and present: A personal retrospective. Jacques Durand and John Goldsmith (eds). [Proceedings of Current Trends in Phonology II: Models and methods, Abbaye de Royaumont, 22–24 June 1998.] Published as: M.A.K. Halliday. 2000. Phonology past and present: A personal retrospect. *Folia Linguistica* XXXIV(1–2): 101–111. https://doi.org/10.1515/flin.2000.34.1-2.101

Halliday, M.A.K. 2002. Applied linguistics as an evolving theme. Presented at AILA 2002, Singapore. Published in M.A.K. Halliday (2007), *Language and education*. Volume 9 in the Collected Works of M.A.K. Halliday, edited by Jonathan Webster, 1–19. London & New York: Continuum.

Halliday, M.A.K. 2003. *On language and linguistics*. Volume 3 of Collected Works of M.A.K. Halliday, edited by Jonathan J. Webster. London & New York: Continuum.

Halliday, M.A.K. 2004a. *The language of early childhood*. Volume 4 of Collected Works of M.A.K. Halliday, edited by Jonathan Webster. London & New York: Continuum.

Halliday, M.A.K. 2004b. *Computational and Quantitative Studies*. Volume 6: The Collected Works of M.A.K. Halliday, edited by Jonathan Webster. London & New York: Continuum.

Halliday, M.A.K. 2005. On matter and meaning: The two realms of human experience. *Linguistics and the Human Sciences* 1(1): 59–82.

Halliday, M.A.K. 2008a. Working with meaning: Towards an appliable linguistics. In Jonathan J. Webster (ed.), *Meaning in context: Implementing intelligent applications of language studies*, 7–23. London & New York: Continuum.

Halliday, M.A.K. 2008b. *Complementarities in language.* (Halliday Centre Series in Appliable Linguistics.) Beijing: The Commercial Press.

Halliday, M.A.K. 2009. Keywords. In M.A.K. Halliday and Jonathan Webster (eds), *A companion to systemic functional linguistics*, Chapter 13: 229–253. London & New York: Continuum.

Halliday, M.A.K. 2012. Pinpointing the choice: Meaning and the search for equivalents in a translated text. Chapter 8 in M.A.K. Halliday. 2013. *Halliday in the 21st century.* Volume 11 in the Collected Works of M.A.K. Halliday, edited by Jonathan J. Webster. London: Bloomsbury Academic.

Halliday, M.A.K. 2013. Meaning as choice. In Lise M. Fontaine, Tom A.M. Bartlett and Gerard N. O'Grady (eds), *Systemic functional linguistics: Exploring choice.* Cambridge: Cambridge University Press.

Halliday, M.A.K. and William S. Greaves. 2008. *Intonation in the grammar of English.* London: Equinox Publishing Ltd.

Halliday, M.A.K. and Ruqaiya Hasan. 1976. *Cohesion in English.* London: Longman.

Halliday, M.A.K. and Ruqaiya Hasan. 1985. *Language, context and text: A social semiotic perspective.* Geelong, Vic.: Deakin University Press.

Halliday, M.A.K. and Zoe L. James. 1993. A quantitative study of polarity and primary tense in the English finite clause. John M. Sinclair, Michael Hoey and Gwyneth Fox (ed.), *Techniques of description: Spoken and written discourse* (A Festschrift for Malcolm Coulthard). London & New York: Routledge. 32–66. Reprinted in M.A.K. Halliday. 2005. *Computational and quantitative studies.* Volume 6 in the Collected Works of M.A.K. Halliday, edited by Jonathan Webster, Chapter 6: 93–129. London & New York: Continuum.

Halliday, M.A.K. and Edward McDonald. 2004. Metafunctional profile of the grammar of Chinese. In Alice Caffarel, J.R. Martin and Christian M.I.M. Matthiessen (eds), *Language typology: A functional perspective*, 305–396. Amsterdam: Benjamins. https://doi.org/10.1075/cilt.253.08hal

Halliday, M.A.K., Angus McIntosh and Peter Strevens. 1964. *The linguistic sciences and language teaching.* London: Longman.

Halliday, M.A.K. and Christian M.I.M. Matthiessen. 2006/1999. *Construing experience through meaning: A language-based approach to cognition.* London & New York: Continuum.

Halliday, M.A.K. and Christian M.I.M. Matthiessen. 2014. *Halliday's introduction to functional grammar.* 4th revised edition. London: Routledge. https://doi.org/10.4324/9780203783771

Halliday, M.A.K. and Jonathan Webster (eds). 2009. *Continuum companion to systemic functional linguistics.* London & New York: Continuum.

Harris, Zellig S. 1954. Distributional structure. *Word* 10(2/3): 146–162. https://doi.org/10.1080/00437956.1954.11659520

Harris, Zellig S. 1970. *Papers in structural and transformational linguistics.* (Formal Linguistics Series.) Dordrecht: D. Reidel. https://doi.org/10.1007/978-94-017-6059-1

Hasan, Ruqaiya. 1978. Text in the systemic-functional model. In Wolfgang Dressler (ed.), *Current trends in text linguistics*, 228–246. Berlin: de Gruyter. https://doi.org/10.1515/9783110853759.228

Hasan, Ruqaiya. 1984. The nursery tale as a genre. *Nottingham Linguistic Circular* 13. Reprinted in Ruqaiya Hasan (1996), *Ways of saying: Ways of meaning: Selected papers of Ruqaiya Hasan*, edited by Carmel Cloran, David Butt and Geoffrey Williams, 51–72. London: Cassell.

Hasan, Ruqaiya. 1985a. Lending and borrowing: from grammar to lexis. *Beiträge zur Phonetik und Linguistik* 48: 56–67.

Hasan, Ruqaiya. 1985b. Meaning, context and text: Fifty years after Malinowski. In James D. Benson and William S. Greaves (eds), *Systemic perspectives on discourse*, 16–50. Norwood, NJ: Ablex.

Hasan, Ruqaiya. 1987. Offers in the making: a systemic-functional approach. MS.

Hasan, Ruqaiya. 1989. Semantic variation and sociolinguistics. *Australian Journal of Linguistics* 9: 221–275. https://doi.org/10.1080/07268608908599422

Hasan, Ruqaiya. 1995. The conception of context in text. In Peter H. Fries and Michael Gregory (eds), *Discourse in society: Systemic functional perspectives*, 183–283. Norwood, NJ: Ablex.
Hasan, Ruqaiya. 1996. Semantic networks: A tool for the analysis of meaning. In Ruqaiya Hasan, *Ways of saying, ways of meaning*, edited by Carmel Cloran, David Butt and Geoff Williams, 104–131. London & New York: Cassell.
Hasan, Ruqaiya. 1999. Speaking with reference to context. In Mohsen Ghadessy (ed.), *Text and context in functional linguistics: Systemic perspectives*, 219–328. Amsterdam & Philadelphia: John Benjamins.
Hasan, Ruqaiya. 2009. *Semantic variation: Meaning in society and sociolinguistics*. Volume Two in the Collected Works of Ruqaiya Hasan, edited by Jonathan Webster. London: Equinox Publishing Ltd.
Hasan, Ruqaiya. 2019. *Describing language: Form and function*. Volume Five in the Collected Works of Ruqaiya Hasan, edited by Jonathan Webster and Carmel Cloran. Sheffield & Bristol: Equinox Publishing Ltd.
Hasan, Ruqaiya, Carmel Cloran, Geoff Williams and Annabelle Lukin. 2007. Semantic networks: The description of linguistic meaning in SFL. In Ruqaiya Hasan, Christian M.I.M. Matthiessen and Jonathan Webster (eds), *Continuing discourse on language*. Volume 2, 697–738. London: Equinox Publishing Ltd.
Hasan, Ruqaiya, Christian M.I.M. Matthiessen and Jonathan Webster (eds). 2005/7. *Continuing discourse on language: A functional perspective*, Volume 1 (2005) and Volume 2 (2007). London: Equinox Publishing Ltd.
Heller, Louis G. and James Macris. 1967. *Parametric linguistics*. The Hague: Mouton. https://doi.org/10.1515/9783111729657
Henrici, Alick. 1965. Notes on the systemic generation of a paradigm of the English clause. In M.A.K. Halliday and James R. Martin (eds), 1981, *Readings in systemic linguistics*, 74–98. London: Batsford.
Hinds, John. 1977. Paragraph structure and pronominalization. *Papers in Linguistics* 10: 77–99. https://doi.org/10.1080/08351819709370440
Hjelmslev, Louis. 1938. Essai d'une théorie des morphèmes. In Louis Hjelmslev (1971), *Essais linguistiques* (2nd edition), 161–173. Éditions de Minuit.
Hjelmslev, Louis. 1943. *Omkring sprogteoriens grundlæggelse*. København: Akademisk Forlag. (English version. 1961. *Prolegomena to a theory of language*. Madison, WI: University of Wisconsin Press.)
Hockett, Charles. 1954. Two models of grammatical description. *Word* 10(2): 10–34. https://doi.org/10.1080/00437956.1954.11659524
Honnibal, Matthew. 2004. *Adapting the Penn Treebank to systemic functional grammar: Design, creation and use of a metafunctionally annotated corpus*. BA Honours thesis. Macquarie University, Department of Linguistics.
Honnibal, Matthew and James R. Curran. 2005. Creating a systemic functional grammar corpus from the Penn Treebank. In *Proceedings of the 5th Workshop on Important Unresolved Matters*. 89–96.
Hori, Motoko. 2006. Pain expressions in Japanese. In Geoff Thompson and Susan Hunston (eds), *System and corpus: Exploring connections*, 206–225. London & Oakville: Equinox Publishing Ltd.
Hornby, A.S. 1954. *Guide to patterns and usage in English*. Oxford: Oxford University Press.
Huddleston, Rodney and Geoffrey K. Pullum. 2002. *The Cambridge grammar of the English Language*. Cambridge: Cambridge University Press.
Hudson, Richard A. 1971. *English complex sentences*. Amsterdam: North Holland.
Hudson, Richard A. 1976. *Arguments for a non-transformational grammar*. Chicago, IL: Chicago University Press.
Hunston, Susan and Gill Francis. 2000. *Pattern grammar: A corpus-driven approach to the lexical grammar of English*. Amsterdam: Benjamins. https://doi.org/10.1075/scl.4

Hymes, Dell. 1967. Models of the interaction of language and social setting. *Journal of Social Issues* 23(2): 8–28. https://doi.org/10.1111/j.1540-4560.1967.tb00572.x

Ito, Noriko, Taro Sugimoto and Michio Sugeno. 2004. A systemic functional approach to Japanese text understanding. In A.F. Gelbukh (ed.), *Computational linguistics and intelligent text processing*. Fifth International Conference (CICLing 2004), 26–37. Springer. https://doi.org/10.1007/978-3-540-24630-5_3

Iwasaki, Shoichi and Preeya Ingkaphirom. 2005. *A reference grammar of Thai*. Cambridge: Cambridge University Press.

Jakobson, Roman. 1949. On the identification of phonemic entities. *Travaux du Cercle Linguistique de Copenhague* V: 205–213. Reprinted in 1962, *Roman Jakobson: Selected writings I*, 418–425. The Hague: Mouton. https://doi.org/10.1080/01050206.1949.10416304

Jakobson, Roman, C. Gunnar, M. Fant and Morris Halle. 1952. *Preliminaries to speech analysis: The distinctive features and their correlates*. Cambridge, MA: MIT Press.

Jesus, Silvana Maria de and Adriana Silvina Pagano. 2006. Probabilistic grammar in translation. *Proceedings of The 33rd International Systemic Functional Congress*: 428–448.

Johnston, Trevor. 1992. The realization of the linguistic metafunctions in a sign language. *Language Sciences* 14(4): 317–355. https://doi.org/10.1016/0388-0001(92)90021-6

Kashyap, Abhishek Kumar. 2019. Language typology. In Geoff Thompson, Wendy L. Bowcher, Lise Fontaine and David Schöntal (eds), *The Cambridge handbook of systemic functional linguistics*, 767–792. Cambridge: Cambridge University Press. https://doi.org/10.1017/9781316337936.031

Kasper, Robert. 1987. *Feature structures: A logical theory with application to language analysis*. PhD thesis. University of Michigan.

Kasper, Robert. 1988a. Systemic grammar and functional unification grammar. In James D. Benson and William S. Greaves (eds), *Systemic functional approaches to discourse*, 176–199. Norwood, NJ: Ablex.

Kasper, Robert. 1988b. An experimental parser for systemic grammars. *The 12th International Conference on Computational Linguistics*, 309–312. Budapest, Hungary: COLING. https://doi.org/10.3115/991635.991698

Kittredge, Richard. 1987. The significance of sublanguage for automatic translation. In Sergei Nirenburg (ed.), *Machine translation: Theoretical and methodological issues*, 59–67. Cambridge: Cambridge University Press.

Koerner, Konrad. 1971. *Ferdinand de Saussure: Origin and development of his linguistic theory in Western studies of language. A critical evaluation of the evolution of Saussurean principles and their relevance to contemporary linguistic theories*. PhD thesis. Simon Fraser University.

König, Ekkehard and Peter Siemund. 2007. Speech act distinctions in grammar. In Timothy Shopen (ed.), *Language typology and syntactic description*, 276–324. Cambridge: Cambridge University Press. https://doi.org/10.1017/CBO9780511619427.005

Kress, Gunther and Theo van Leeuwen. 1990. *Reading images*. Geelong, Vic.: Deakin University Press.

Kress, Gunther and Theo van Leeuwen. 1996. *Reading images: The grammar of visual design*. London: Routledge.

Kress, Gunther and Theo van Leeuwen. 2006. *Reading images: The grammar of visual design*. 2nd edition. London: Routledge. https://doi.org/10.4324/9780203619728

Kuhl, Patricia K. 2010a. Brain mechanism in early language acquisition. *Neuron* 67(5): 713–727. https://doi.org/10.1016/j.neuron.2010.08.038

Kuhl, Patricia. 2010b. The linguistic genius of babies. TEDxRainier, October 2010. Available at: https://www.ted.com/talks/patricia_kuhl_the_linguistic_genius_of_babies

Labov, William. 1972. The study of language in its social context. In P.P. Giglioli (ed.), *Language and social context*, 283–307. Harmondsworth: Penguin.

Labov, William and David Fanshel. 1977. *Therapeutic discourse: Psychotherapy as conversation*. New York: Academic Press.
Ladefoged, Peter. 1971. *Preliminaries to linguistic phonetics*. Chicago, IL: Chicago University Press.
Ladefoged, Peter. 1988a. The many interfaces between phonetics and phonology. *UCLA Working Papers in Phonetics* 70: 13-23.
Ladefoged, Peter. 1988b. Hierarchical features of the International Phonetic Alphabet. *Proceedings of the Fourteenth Annual Meeting of the Berkeley Linguistics Society*, 124-141. https://doi.org/10.3765/bls.v14i0.1775
Ladefoged, Peter. 1996. David Abercrombie, 1909-1992. *Proceedings of the British Academy* 90: 239-248.
Lamb, Sydney M. 1966. *Outline of stratificational grammar*. Washington, DC: Georgetown University Press.
Lamb, Sydney M. 1999. *Pathways of the brain: The neurocognitive basis of language*. Amsterdam: Benjamins. https://doi.org/10.1075/cilt.170
Lamb, Sydney M. 2013. Systemic networks, relational networks, and choice. In Lise M. Fontaine, Tom A.M. Bartlett and Gerard N. O'Grady (eds). 2013. *Systemic functional linguistics: Exploring choice*, 137-160. Cambridge: Cambridge University Press. https://doi.org/10.1017/CBO9781139583077.010
Lane, Jonathan. 2007. *Kalam Serial Verb Constructions*. (Pacific Linguistics, 589.) Canberra: Pacific Linguistics.
Lantolf, James. 2010. Minding your hands: The function of gesture in L2 learning. In Robert Batstone (ed.), *Sociocognitive perspectives on language use and language learning*, 131-150. Oxford: Oxford University Press.
Lascaratou, Chryssoula. 2007. *The language of pain: Expression or description?* Amsterdam & Philadelphia: John Benjamins. https://doi.org/10.1075/celcr.9
Lavid, Julia. 2000. Cross-cultural variation in multilingual instructions: A study of speech act realisation patterns. In Eija Ventola (ed.), *Discourse and community: Doing functional linguistics*, 71-85. Tübingen: Günter Narr Verlag.
Layzer, David. 1990. *Cosmogenesis: The growth of order in the universe*. New York & Oxford: Oxford University Press.
Leech, Geoffrey. 1969. *Towards a semantic description of English*. London: Longman.
Leech, Geoffrey. 1974. *Semantics: the study of meaning*. 2nd edition. Harmondsworth: Penguin.
Leech, Geoffrey. 2003. Modality on the move: The English modal auxiliaries 1961–1992. In *Modality in Contemporary English*. Topics in English linguistics (44), 223-240. Berlin: Mouton de Gruyter.
Lemke, Jay L. 1985. Ideology, intertextuality and the notion of register. In James D. Benson and William S, Greaves (eds), *Systemic perspectives on discourse*, 275-294. Norwood, NJ: Ablex.
Lemke, Jay L. 1987. The topology of genre: Text structures and text types. MS.
Levin, Beth. 1993. *English verb classes and alternations: a preliminary investigation*. Chicago & London: The University of Chicago Press.
Lim, Fei Victor. 2004. Developing an integrative multi-semiotic model. In Kay O'Halloran (ed.), *Multimodal discourse analysis: Systemic functional perspectives*, 220-246. London & New York: Continuum.
Liu, Xiangdong and Wang, Bo. 2021. On the fractalization and functional variation of the language system. *Foreign Language Learning Theory and Practice* 174(02): 22-33+85. [刘向东、王博. 语言系统的分形与功能变异. 外语教学理论与实践, 2021, 174(02): 22-33+85.] https://doi.org/10.26549/jxffcxysj.v3i10.5412
Lockwood, David G. 1972. *Introduction to stratificational linguistics*. New York: Harcourt Brace Jovanovich.
Longacre, Robert E. 1970. Sentence structure as a statement calculus. *Language* 46: 783-815. https://doi.org/10.2307/412257

Longacre, Robert. 1976. *Anatomy of speech notions*. Lisse: Peter de Ridder Press. https://doi.org/10.1515/9783112329924

Longacre, Robert E. 1979. The paragraph as a grammatical unit. In Talmy Givón (ed.), *Syntax and semantics: Discourse and syntax*. Volume 12, 115–134. New York: Academic Press.

Longacre, Robert E. 1996. *The grammar of discourse*. 2nd edition. New York: Plenum. https://doi.org/10.1007/978-1-4899-0162-0

MacWhinney, Brian and William O'Grady (eds). 2015. *The handbook of language emergence*. Oxford: Wiley-Blackwell. https://doi.org/10.1002/9781118346136

McCabe, Anne. 2021. *A functional linguistic perspective on developing language*. London: Routledge. https://doi.org/10.4324/9780429462504

McCord, Michael C. 1975. On the form of a systemic grammar. *Journal of Linguistics* 11: 195–212. https://doi.org/10.1017/S0022226700004539

McEnery, Tony and Andrew Hardie. 2012. *Corpus linguistics: Method, theory and practice*. Cambridge: Cambridge University Press. https://doi.org/10.1017/CBO9780511981395

McKeown, Kathleen R. 1985. *Text generation: Using discourse strategies and focus constraints to generate natural language text*. Cambridge: Cambridge University Press.

Malcolm, Karen. 2010. *Phasal analysis: Analyzing discourse through communication Linguistics*. London: Bloomsbury.

Mandelbrot, Benoit B. 1982. *The fractal geometry of nature*. New York: W. H. Freeman and Company.

Mann, William C. 1984. A linguistic overview of the Nigel text generation grammar. *The Tenth LACUS Forum*. Columbia: Hornbeam Press. https://doi.org/10.3115/981311.981326

Mann, William C. and Christian Matthiessen. 1985. Demonstration of the Nigel Text Generation Computer Program. In James D. Benson and William S. Greaves (eds), *Systemic functional approaches to discourse*, 50–83. Norwood, NJ: Ablex.

Manning, Christopher D. and Hinrich Schütze. 1999. *Foundations of statistical natural language processing*. Cambridge, MA: MIT Press.

Martin, J.R. 1987. The meaning of features in systemic linguistics. In M.A.K. Halliday and Robin P. Fawcett (eds), *New developments in systemic linguistics*, 14–40. London: Pinter.

Martin, J.R. 1988. Grammatical conspiracies in Tagalog: Family, face and fate – with reference to Benjamin Lee Whorf. In Michael J. Cummings, William S. Greaves and James D. Benson (eds), *Linguistics in a systemic perspective*, 243–300. Amsterdam: Benjamins. https://doi.org/10.1075/cilt.39.11mar

Martin, J.R. 1992. *English Text: System and structure*. Amsterdam: Benjamins. https://doi.org/10.1075/z.59

Martin, J.R. 1993. Life as a noun. In M.A.K. Halliday and J.R. Martin. *Writing science: Literacy and discursive power*, 221–267. London: Falmer.

Martin, J.R. 1994. Macro-genres: The ecology of the page. *Network* 21: 29–52.

Martin, J.R. 1995. Text and clause: Fractal resonance. *Text* 15(1): 5–42. https://doi.org/10.1515/text.1.1995.15.1.5

Martin, J.R. 1996a. Metalinguistic diversity: The case from case. In Ruqaiya Hasan, Carmel Cloran and David Butt (eds), *Functional descriptions: Theory into practice*, 323–375. Amsterdam: Benjamins. https://doi.org/10.1075/cilt.121.12mar

Martin, J.R. 1996b. Transitivity in Tagalog: A functional interpretation of case. In Christopher Butler, Margaret Berry, Robin Fawcett and Guowen Huang (eds), *Meaning and form: Systemic functional interpretations*, 229–296. Norwood, NJ: Ablex.

Martin, J.R. 1996c. Types of structure: Deconstructing notions of constituency in clause and text. In Eduard Hovy and Donia Scott (eds), *Burning issues in discourse: A multidisciplinary perspective*, 39–66. Heidelberg: Springer. https://doi.org/10.1007/978-3-662-03293-0_2

Martin, J.R. 2003. Making history: Grammar for interpretation. In J.R. Martin and Ruth Wodak (eds), *Re/reading the past: Critical and functional perspectives on time and value*, 19–57. Amsterdam & Philadelphia: Benjamins. https://doi.org/10.1075/dapsac.8.03mar

Martin, J.R. 2013. *Systemic functional grammar: A next step into the theory - axial relations.* (Chinese translation and extensions by Wang Pin and Zhu Yongsheng.) Beijing: Higher Education Press.

Martin, J.R. and Christian M.I.M. Matthiessen. 1991. Systemic typology and topology. In Frances Christie (ed.), *Literacy in social processes: Papers from the Inaugural Australian Systemic Functional Linguistics Conference, Deakin University, January 1990*, 345–383. Darwin: Centre for Studies of Language in Education, Northern Territory University. Reprinted in J.R. Martin (2010), *SFL theory*, Volume 1 in the collected works of J.R. Martin, edited by Wang Zhenhua, 167–215. Shanghai: Shanghai Jiao Tong University Press.

Martin, J.R. and David Rose. 2008. *Genre relations: Mapping culture*. London & Oakville: Equinox Publishing Ltd.

Martin, J.R. and Peter R.R. White. 2005. *The language of evaluation: Appraisal in English*. London & New York: Palgrave Macmillan.

Martin, J.R. and Michele Zappavigna. 2019. Embodied meaning: A systemic functional perspective on paralanguage. *Functional Linguistics* 6(1): 1–33. https://doi.org/10.1186/s40554-018-0065-9

Martin, Samuel E. 1992. *A reference grammar of Korean: A complete guide to the grammar and history of the Korean language*. Rutland, VT & Tokyo: Charles E. Tuttle.

Martinec, Radan. 2001. Interpersonal resources in action. *Semiotica* 135(1/4): 117–145. https://doi.org/10.1515/semi.2001.056

Martinec, Radan. 2004. Gestures that co-occur with speech as a systematic resource: The realization of experiential meanings in indexes. *Social Semiotics* 14(2): 193–213. https://doi.org/10.1080/1035033042000238259

Martinec, Radan. 2018. Linguistic rhythm and its meaning: Rhythm waves and semantics fields. *Linguistics and the Human Sciences* 14(1–2): 70–98. https://doi.org/10.1558/lhs.38410

Martinec, Radan and Andrew Salway. 2005. A system for image-text relations in new (and old) media. *Visual Communication* 4(3): 337–371. https://doi.org/10.1177/1470357205055928

Martinet, André. 1970. *La linguistique synchronique: études et recherches*. Paris: Presses Universitaires de France.

Matthews, Peter H. 1993. *Grammatical theory in the United States from Bloomfield to Chomsky*. Cambridge: Cambridge University Press. https://doi.org/10.1017/CBO9780511620560

Matthiessen, Christian M.I.M. 1984. How to make grammatical choices in text generation. *The Tenth LACUS Forum*, 266–284. Columbia: Hornbeam Press.

Matthiessen, Christian M.I.M. 1987. Notes on the organization of the environment of a text generation grammar. In Gerard Kempen (ed.), *Natural language generation*, 253–278. Dordrecht: Martinus Nijhof. https://doi.org/10.1007/978-94-009-3645-4_17

Matthiessen, Christian M.I.M. 1988a. Representational issues in systemic functional grammar. In James D. Benson and William S. Greaves (eds), *Systemic functional perspectives on discourse*, 136–175. Norwood, NJ: Ablex.

Matthiessen, Christian M.I.M. 1988b. Semantics for a systemic grammar: The chooser and inquiry framework. In Michael J. Cummings and William S. Greaves James D. Benson (eds), *Linguistics in a systemic perspective*, 221–242. Amsterdam: Benjamins. https://doi.org/10.1075/cilt.39.10mat

Matthiessen, Christian M.I.M. 1991a. Lexico(grammatical) choice in text-generation. In Cécile Paris, William Swartout and William C. Mann (eds), *Natural language generation in artificial intelligence and computational linguistics*, 249–292. Boston: Kluwer. https://doi.org/10.1007/978-1-4757-5945-7_10

Matthiessen, Christian M.I.M. 1991b. Language on language: The grammar of semiosis. *Social Semiotics* 1(2): 69–111. https://doi.org/10.1080/10350339109360339

Matthiessen, Christian M.I.M. 1992. Interpreting the textual metafunction. In Martin Davies and Louise Ravelli (eds), *Advances in systemic linguistics: Recent theory and practice*, 37–82. London: Pinter.

Matthiessen, Christian M.I.M. 1993. Register in the round: Diversity in a unified theory of register analysis. Mohsen Ghadessy (ed.), *Register analysis: Theory and practice*, 221–292. London: Pinter.

Matthiessen, Christian M.I.M. 1995a. *Lexicogrammatical cartography: English systems*. Tokyo: International Language Sciences Publishers.

Matthiessen, Christian M.I.M. 1995b. Fuzziness construed in language: A linguistic perspective. *Proceedings of FUZZ/IEEE, Yokohama, March 1995*. Yokohama. 1871–1878.

Matthiessen, Christian M.I.M. 1995c. THEME as an enabling resource in ideational 'knowledge' construction. In Mohsen Ghadessy (ed.), *Thematic developments in English texts*, 20–55. London & New York: Pinter.

Matthiessen, Christian M.I.M. 1999. The system of TRANSITIVITY: An exploratory study of text-based profiles. *Functions of Language* 6(1): 1–51. https://doi.org/10.1075/fol.6.1.02mat

Matthiessen, Christian M.I.M. 2001. The environments of translation. In Erich Steiner and Colin Yallop (eds), *Beyond content: Exploring translation and multilingual text*, 41–124. Berlin: de Gruyter.

Matthiessen, Christian M.I.M. 2002. Lexicogrammar in discourse development: Logogenetic patterns of wording. In Guowen Huang and Zongyan Wang (eds), *Discourse and language functions*, 91–127. Shanghai: Foreign Language Teaching and Research Press.

Matthiessen, Christian M.I.M. 2004. Descriptive motifs and generalizations. In Alice Caffarel, J.R. Martin and Christian M.I.M. Matthiessen (eds), *Language typology: A functional perspective*, 537–673. Amsterdam: Benjamins. https://doi.org/10.1075/cilt.253.12mat

Matthiessen, Christian M.I.M. 2006a. Frequency profiles of some basic grammatical systems: An interim report. In Susan Hunston and Geoff Thompson (eds), *System and corpus: Exploring connections*, 103–142. London: Equinox Publishing Ltd.

Matthiessen, Christian M.I.M. 2006b. The multimodal page: A systemic functional exploration. In Terry D. Royce and Wendy L. Bowcher (eds), *New directions in the analysis of multimodal discourse*, 1–62. Hillsdale, NJ: Lawrence Erlbaum.

Matthiessen, Christian M.I.M. 2007a. Lexicogrammar in systemic functional linguistics: Descriptive and theoretical developments in the 'IFG' tradition since the 1970s. In Ruqaiya Hasan, Christian M.I.M. Matthiessen and Jonathan Webster (eds), *Continuing discourse on language*. Volume 2, 765–858. London: Equinox Publishing Ltd.

Matthiessen, Christian M.I.M. 2007b. The 'architecture' of language according to systemic functional theory: Developments since the 1970s. In Ruqaiya Hasan, Christian M.I.M. Matthiessen and Jonathan Webster (eds), *Continuing discourse on language*. Volume 2, 505–561. London: Equinox Publishing Ltd.

Matthiessen, Christian M.I.M. 2009a. Léxico-gramática y colocación léxica: Un estudio sistémico-funcional. [Translation of 'Lexicogrammar and collocation: A systemic functional exploration'.] *Revista Signos* 42(71): 333–383. https://doi.org/10.4067/S0718-09342009000300003

Matthiessen, Christian M.I.M. 2009b. Multisemiotic and context-based register typology: Registerial variation in the complementarity of semiotic systems. In Eija Ventola and Arsenio Jesús Moya Guijarro (eds), *The world shown and the world told*, 11–38. Basingstoke: Palgrave Macmillan.

Matthiessen, Christian M.I.M. 2010. Systemic functional linguistics developing. *Annual Review of Functional Linguistics* 2: 8–63.

Matthiessen, Christian M.I.M. 2014a. Appliable discourse analysis. In Fang Yan and Jonathan J. Webster (eds), *Developing systemic functional linguistics: Theory and application*, 135–205. London: Equinox Publishing Ltd.

Matthiessen, Christian M.I.M. 2014b. Extending the description of process type in delicacy: Verb classes. *Functions of Language* 21(2): 139–175. https://doi.org/10.1075/fol.21.2.01mat

Matthiessen, Christian M.I.M. 2014c. Choice in translation: Metafunctional consideration. In Kerstin Kunz, Elke Teich, Silvia Hansen-Schirra, Stella Neumann and Peggy Daut (eds), *Caught in the middle – language use and translation: A festschrift for Erich Steiner on the occasion of his 60th birthday*. Saarbrücken: Universaar, Saarland University Press. Available at: http://universaar.uni-saarland.de/monographien/volltexte/2014/122/pdf/Kunz_etal_Festschrift_Steiner.pdf

Matthiessen, Christian M.I.M. 2014d. Talking and writing about literature: Some observations based on systemic functional linguistics. *The Indian Journal of Applied Linguistics* 39(2): 5–49. Also in Barbara, Leila, Adail Sebastião Rodrigues-Júnior and Giovanna Marcella Verdessi Hoy (eds). 2017. *Estudos e pesquisas em Linguística Sistêmico Funcional* [Studies and research in Systemic Functional Linguistics], 3–37. São Paulo: Mercado de Letras.

Matthiessen, Christian M.I.M. 2015a. Register in the round: Registerial cartography. *Functional Linguistics* 2(9): 1–48. https://doi.org/10.1186/s40554-015-0015-8

Matthiessen, Christian M.I.M. 2015b. Halliday on language. In Jonathan J. Webster (ed.), *The Bloomsbury Companion to M.A.K. Halliday*, 137–202. London & New York: Bloomsbury Academic.

Matthiessen, Christian M.I.M. 2015c. Reflections on 'Researching and Teaching Chinese as a Foreign Language'. *Researching and Teaching Chinese as a Foreign Language* 1(1): 1–27. https://doi.org/10.1558/rtcfl.v1i1.27271

Matthiessen, Christian M.I.M. 2015d. Subliminal construal of world order clause by clause: Hierarchy of control in *Noah's Ark*. *Linguistics and the Human Sciences* 11(1–2): 250–283. https://doi.org/10.1558/lhs.34710

Matthiessen, Christian M.I.M. 2015e. The language of space: Semiotic resources for construing our experience of space. *Japanese Journal of Systemic Functional Linguistics* Vol. 8, May 2015.

Matthiessen, Christian M.I.M. 2015f. Halliday's conception of language as a probabilistic system. In Jonathan J. Webster (ed.), *The Bloomsbury companion to M.A.K. Halliday*, 203–241. London & New York: Bloomsbury Academic.

Matthiessen, Christian M.I.M. 2018a. The notion of a multilingual meaning potential: A systemic exploration. In Akila Baklouti and Lise Fontaine (eds), *Perspectives from systemic functional linguistics*, 90–120. London: Routledge. Version with additional figures to be available at: http://www.syflat.tn. https://doi.org/10.4324/9781315299877-6

Matthiessen, Christian M.I.M. 2018b. Transitivity in systemic functional linguistics: Achievements and challenges. In Sara Regina Scotta Cabral and Leila Barbara (eds), *Estudos de transitividade em linguística sistêmico-funcional*, Chapter 1: 14–108. [Transitivity studies in systemic functional linguistics.] Santa Maria, Rio Grande do Sul, Brasil: PROGRAMA DE PÓS-GRADUAÇÃO EM LETRAS – PPGL UFSM.

Matthiessen, Christian M.I.M. 2021. The architecture of phonology according to systemic functional linguistics. [Chapter 6 in Matthiessen (2021), Volume 1 of Collected Works, edited by Kazuhiro Teruya, Diana Slade and Wu Canzhong, 288–338. Equinox Publishing Ltd.] https://www.equinoxpub.com/home/view-chapter/?id=34628

Matthiessen, Christian M.I.M. forthcoming a. *Rhetorical system and structure theory: The semantic system of rhetorical relations. Volume 1: Foundations*. Routledge.

Matthiessen, Christian M.I.M. forthcoming b. *The architecture of language according to systemic functional linguistics*. Book MS.

Matthiessen, Christian M.I.M. in press/forthcoming. *The collected works of Christian M.I.M. Matthiessen* [working title], in 8 volumes, edited by Kazuhiro Teruya, Wu Canzhong and Diana Slade. Volume 1: *Systemic functional linguistics and the challenge of theorizing language*; https://www.equinoxpub.com/home/systemic-functional-linguistics-part-1/ [Submitted] Sheffield: Equinox Publishing Ltd.

Matthiessen, Christian M.I.M., Jorge Hita Arús and Kazuhiro Teruya. 2021. Translations of representations of moving and saying from English into Spanish. *Word*. Published online 22 July 2021. https://doi.org/10.1080/00437956.2021.1909843

Matthiessen, Christian M.I.M. and John A. Bateman. 1991. *Systemic linguistics and text generation: Experiences from Japanese and English*. London: Frances Pinter.

Matthiessen, Christian M.I.M. and M.A.K. Halliday. 2009. *Systemic functional grammar: A first step into the theory*. Bilingual edition, with introduction by Huang Guowen. Beijing: Higher Education Press.

Matthiessen, Christian M.I.M. and Abhishek Kumar Kashyap. 2014. The construal of space in different registers: An exploratory study. *Language Sciences* 45: 1–27. https://doi.org/10.1016/j.langsci.2014.04.001

Matthiessen, Christian M.I.M., Ichiro Kobayashi and Zeng Licheng. 1995. Generating multimodal presentations: Resources and processes. MS. Macquarie University.

Matthiessen, Christian M.I.M. and Christopher Nesbitt. 1996. On the idea of theory-neutral descriptions. In Ruqaiya Hasan, Carmel Cloran and David Butt (eds), *Functional descriptions: Theory in practice*, 39–85. Amsterdam: Benjamins. https://doi.org/10.1075/cilt.121.04mat

Matthiessen, Christian and Kazuhiro Teruya. 2016. Registerial hybridity: Indeterminacy among fields of activity. In Donna Miller and Paul Bayley (eds), *Permeable contexts and hybrid discourses*, 205–239. London: Equinox Publishing Ltd.

Matthiessen, Christian and Kazuhiro Teruya. 2023. *Systemic Functional Linguistics: A Complete Guide*. London: Routledge.

Matthiessen, Christian M.I.M., Kazuhiro Teruya and Wu Canzhong. 2008. Multilingual studies as a multi-dimensional space of interconnected language studies. In Jonathan Webster (ed.), *Meaning in context*, 146–221. London & New York: Continuum.

Matthiessen, Christian M.I.M., Wang Bo, Isaac Mwinlaaru and Ma Yuanyi. 2018. 'The axial rethink' – making sense of language: An interview with Christian M.I.M. Matthiessen. *Functional Linguistics* 5(8): 1–19. https://doi.org/10.1186/s40554-018-0058-8

Matthiessen, Christian M.I.M., Wang Bo, Yuanyi Ma and Isaac N. Mwinlaaru. 2022. *Systemic functional insights on language and linguistics*. Singapore: Springer.

Matthiessen, Christian M.I.M., Licheng Zeng, Marilyn Cross, Ichiro Kobayashi, Kazuhiro Teruya and Canzhong Wu. 1998. The Multex generator and its environment: Application and development. *Proceedings of the International Generation Workshop '98*, August '98, 228–237. Niagara-on-the-Lake.

Mazzaferro, Gerardo (ed.). 2018. *Translanguaging as everyday practice*. Cham: Springer. https://doi.org/10.1007/978-3-319-94851-5

Mel'čuk, Igor. 1986. Semantic bases of linguistic description (meaning-text linguistic theory). In M. Marino and L. Pérez (eds), *The Twelfth LACUS Forum, 1985*, 41–87. Lake Bluff: LACUS.

Mel'čuk, Igor. 2015. *Semantics: from meaning to text*. Volume 3, edited by David Beck and Alain Polguère. Amsterdam: Benjamins. https://doi.org/10.1075/slcs.168

Mitchell, T.F. 1957. The language of buying and selling in Cyrenaica: A situational statement. *Hesperis* 44: 31–71. Reprinted in T.F. Mitchell. 1975. *Principles of neo-Firthian linguistics*, 167–200. London: Longman.

Mohan, Bernhard A. 1986. *Language and content*. Reading, MA: Addison-Wesley.

Muntigl, Peter. 2004. Modelling multiple semiotic systems: The case of gesture and speech. In Eija Ventola, Cassily Charles and Martin Kaltenbacher (eds), *Perspectives on multimodality*, 31–50. Amsterdam: Benjamins. https://doi.org/10.1075/ddcs.6.04mun

Murcia-Bielsa, Susana. 2000. The choice of directives expressions in English and Spanish instructions: A semantic network. In Eija Ventola (ed.), *Discourse and community: Doing functional linguistics*. Language in Performance 21, 117–146. Tübingen: Gunter Narr Verlag.

Mwinlaaru, Isaac Nuokyaa-Ire. 2017. *A systemic functional description of the grammar of Dagaare*. PhD thesis. The Hong Kong Polytechnic University.

Mwinlaaru, Isaac, Christian M.I.M. Matthiessen and Ernest Akerejola. 2018. A system-based typology of MOOD in African languages. In Augustine Agwuele and Adam Bodomo (eds), *Handbook of African languages*, 93–117. London: Routledge. https://doi.org/10.4324/9781315392981-6

Mwinlaaru, Isaac N. and Winfred Wenhui Xuan. 2016. A survey of studies in systemic functional language description and typology. *Functional Linguistics* 3: 8. https://doi.org/10.1186/s40554-016-0030-4

Neale, Amy. 2002. *More delicate TRANSITIVITY: Extending the PROCESS TYPE system networks for English to include full semantic classifications*. PhD thesis. School of English, Communication and Philosophy, Cardiff University.

Neale, Amy. 2006. Matching corpus data and system networks: Using corpora to modify and extend the system networks for transitivity in English. In Susan Hunston and Geoff Thompson (eds), *System and corpus: Exploring connections*, 143–163. London & Oakville, CA: Equinox Publishing Ltd.

Nesbitt, Christopher N. and Guenter Plum. 1988. Probabilities in a systemic grammar: The clause complex in English. In Robin P. Fawcett and David Young (ed.), *New developments in systemic linguistics, vol. 2: Theory and application*, 6–39. London: Frances Pinter.

O'Donnell, Michael. 1990. A dynamic model of exchange. *Word* 41(3): 293–328. https://doi.org/10.1080/00437956.1990.11435825

O'Donnell, Michael. 1994. *Sentence analysis and generation: A systemic perspective*. PhD thesis. Sydney University.

O'Donnell, Mick. 2005. The UAM Systemic Parser. In *Proceedings of the 1st Computational Systemic Functional Grammar Conference*, 47–55. Sydney: University of Sydney.

O'Donnell, Michael. 2008. Demonstration of the UAM Corpus Tool for Text and Image Annotation. In *Proceedings of the ACL '08: HLT Demo Session*, 13–16. Columbus: Association for Computational Linguistics. https://doi.org/10.3115/1564144.1564148

O'Donnell, Michael. 2012. *UAM CorpusTool: Version 2.8 User Manual*. Available at: http://www.corpustool.com/documentation.html

O'Donnell, Mick. 2017. Interactions between natural-language processing and systemic functional linguistics. In Tom Bartlett and Gerard O'Grady (eds), *The Routledge handbook of systemic functional linguistics*, 561–574. Milton Park: Routledge.

O'Donnell, Michael. 2019. Continuing issues in SFL. In Geoff Thompson, Wendy L. Bowcher, Lise Fontaine and David Schöntal (eds), *The Cambridge handbook of systemic functional linguistics*, 204–229. Cambridge: Cambridge University Press. https://doi.org/10.1017/9781316337936.010

O'Donnell, Michael and John A. Bateman. 2005. SFL in computational contexts. In Ruqaiya Hasan, Christian M.I.M. Matthiessen and Jonathan Webster (eds), *Continuing discourse on language: A functional perspective, Volume 1*, 343–382. London: Equinox Publishing Ltd.

O'Donnell, Michael and Peter Sefton. 1995. Modelling telephonic interaction: A dynamic approach. *Journal of Applied Linguistics* 10(1): 63–78.

O'Donoghue, Tim F. 1994. Semantic interpretation in a systemic functional grammar. In Tomek Strzalkowski (ed.), *Reversible grammars in natural language processing*, 415–447. Kluwer. https://doi.org/10.1007/978-1-4615-2722-0_15

O'Grady, Gerard. 2010. *A grammar of spoken English discourse: The intonation of increments*. London: Continuum.

O'Halloran, Kay. 2003. Systemics 1.0: Software for research and teaching systemic functional linguistics. *RELC Journal* 34(2): 157–158. https://doi.org/10.1177/003368820303400203

O'Halloran, Kay. 2011. The semantic hyperspace: Accumulating mathematical knowledge across semiotic resources and modalities. In Francis Christie and Karl Maton (eds), *Disciplinarity: Functional linguistic and sociological perspectives*, 217–236. London: Continuum.

O'Halloran, Kay L., Alexey Podlasov, Alvin Chua and Marissa K.L.E. 2012. Interactive software for multimodal analysis. *Visual Communication* 11(3): 363–381. https://doi.org/10.1177/1470357212446414

O'Halloran, Kay L. and Bradley A. Smith (eds). 2011. *Multimodal studies: Exploring issues and domains.* London: Routledge.

O'Halloran, Kay L., Sabine Tan, Peter Wignell, John A. Bateman, Duc-Son Pham, Michele Grossman and Andrew Vande Moere. 2016. Interpreting text and image relations in violent extremist discourse: A mixed methods approach for big data analytics. *Terrorism and Political Violence* 31(3): 454–474. https://doi.org/10.1080/09546553.2016.1233871

O'Toole, Michael. 1994. *The language of displayed art.* London: Leicester University Press (Pinter).

O'Toole, Michael. 2010. *The language of displayed art.* London: Routledge.

Ortega, Lourdes and Heidi Byrnes (eds). 2008. *The longitudinal study of advanced L2 capacities.* New York & London: Routledge. https://doi.org/10.4324/9780203871652

Painter, Clare. 1984. *Into the mother tongue: A case study in early language development.* London: Frances Pinter.

Painter, Clare. 1999. *Learning through language in early childhood.* London: Cassell.

Painter, Clare, Beverly Derewianka and Jane Torr. 2007. From microfunctions to metaphor: Learning language and learning through language. In Ruqaiya Hasan, Christian M.I.M. Matthiessen and Jonathan J. Webster (eds), *Continuing discourse on language: A functional perspective.* Volume 2, 563–588. London: Equinox Publishing Ltd.

Painter, Clare, J.R. Martin and Len Unsworth. 2014. *Reading visual narratives: Image analysis of children's picture books.* Sheffield: Equinox Publishing Ltd.

Parodi, Giovanni (ed.). 2010. *Discourse genres in Spanish: Academic and professional connections.* Amsterdam: Benjamins. https://doi.org/10.1075/scl.40.05par

Patrick, Jon. 2008. The Scamseek Project – using systemic functional grammar for text categorization. In Jonathan J. Webster (ed.), *Meaning in context: Implementing intelligent applications of language studies*, 221–233. London & New York: Continuum.

Patten, Terry. 1988. *Systemic text generation as problem solving.* Cambridge: Cambridge University Press. https://doi.org/10.1017/CBO9780511665646

Pawley, Andrew. 1987. Encoding events in Kalam and English: Different logics for reporting experience. In Russel S. Tomlin (ed.), *Coherence and grounding in discourse*, 329–361. Amsterdam: Benjamins. https://doi.org/10.1075/tsl.11.15paw

Pawley, Andrew. 2008. On the origins of serial verb constructions in Kalam, or, What are clauses good for? For 12th Biennial Rice University Linguistics Symposium, 27–29 March 2008.

Phillips, Joy. 1986. The development of modality and hypothetical meaning: Nigel 1;7 1/2 – 2;7 1/2. University of Sydney Linguistics Department: *Working Papers* no. 3.

Pike, Kenneth L. 1967. *Language in relation to a unified theory of the structure of human behavior.* The Hague: Mouton. https://doi.org/10.1515/9783111657158

Plum, Guenter A. and Anne Cowling. 1987. Social constraints on grammatical variables: Tense choice in English. In Ross Steele and Terry Threadgold (eds), *Language topics: Essays in honour of Michael Halliday*, 281–305. Amsterdam: Benjamins. https://doi.org/10.1075/z.lt2.66plu

Prakasam, V. 1985. *The linguistic spectrum.* Patiala, India: Punjabi University.

Pribram, Karl H. 2013. *The form within: My point of view.* Westport, CT: Prospecta Press.

Pulvermüller, Friedemann. 2013. Semantic embodiment, disembodiment or misembodiment? In search of meaning in modules and neuron circuits. *Brain & Language* 127: 86–103. https://doi.org/10.1016/j.bandl.2013.05.015

Quirk, Randolph, Sidney Greenbaum, Geoffrey Leech and Jan Svartvik. 1985. *A comprehensive grammar of the English language.* London: Longman.

Renouf, A. and John Sinclair. 1991. Collocational frameworks in English. In Karin Aijmer and Bengt Altenberg (eds), *English corpus linguistics: Studies in honour of Jan Svartvik*, 128–143. London: Longman.

Robins, R.H. 1959. In defence of WP: *Transactions of the Philological Society*: 116–144. https://doi.org/10.1111/j.1467-968X.1959.tb00301.x

Robins, R.H. and Norma McLeod. 1956. Five Yurok songs: A musical and textual analysis. *Bulletin of the School of Oriental and African Studies* 18(3): 592–609. https://doi.org/10.1017/S0041977X00088078

Rose, David. 2001. *The Western Desert Code: An Australian cryptogrammar*. Canberra: Pacific Linguistics.

Rose, David and J.R. Martin. 2012. *Learning to write, reading to learn: Genre, knowledge and pedagogy in the Sydney school*. (Equinox Textbooks & Surveys in Linguistics.) London: Equinox Publishing Ltd.

Roy, Deb, Rupal Patel, Philip DeCamp, Rony Kubat, Michael Fleischman, Brandon Roy, Nikolaos Mavridis, Stefanie Tellex, Alexia Salata, Jethran Guinness, Michael Levit and Peter Gorniak. 2006. The human speechome project. The 28th Annual Conference of the Cognitive Science Society, July 2006. https://doi.org/10.1007/11880172_15

Royce, Terry. 1998. Synergy on the page: Exploring intersemiotic complementarity in page-based multimodal text. In *JASFL Occasional Papers No. 1*, 25–49. Tokyo: Japan Association of Systemic Functional Linguistics (JASFL).

Royce, Terry. 1999. *Visual-verbal intersemiotic complementarity in The Economist Magazine*. PhD dissertation. University of Reading.

Sadock, Jerry and Arnold Zwicky. 1985. Speech act distinctions in syntax. In Timothy Shopen (ed.), *Language typology and syntactic description*. Volume I: Clause Structure, 155–197. Cambridge: Cambridge University Press.

Sankoff, David and Sylvie Mainville. 1986. Code-switching of context-free grammars. *Theoretical Linguistics* 13: 75–90. https://doi.org/10.1515/thli.1986.13.1-2.75

Sankoff, David and Shana Poplack. 1981. A formal grammar for code-switching. *Paper in Linguistics* 14(1): 3–45. https://doi.org/10.1080/08351818109370523

Saussure, Ferdinand de. 1916. *Cours de linguistique générale*. Lausanne: Payot. Translation by Wade Baskin (1959), *Course in general linguistics*. New York: Philosophical Library.

Schank, Roger C. and Robert P. Abelson. 1977. *Scripts, plans, goals and understanding: An inquiry into human knowledge structures*. Hillsdale, NJ: Lawrence Erlbaum.

Schultz, Anke and Lise Fontaine. 2019. The Cardiff model of functional syntax. In Geoff Thompson, Wendy L. Bowcher, Lise Fontaine and David Schöntal (eds), *The Cambridge handbook of systemic functional linguistics*, 230–258. Cambridge: Cambridge University Press. https://doi.org/10.1017/9781316337936.011

Searle, John. 1964. What is a speech act? In Max Black (ed.), *Philosophy in America*, 221–239. London: Allen & Unwin.

Seuren, Pieter A.M. 1998. *Western linguistics: An historical introduction*. Oxford: Blackwell. https://doi.org/10.1002/9781444307467

Seuren, Pieter A.M. 2016. Saussure and his intellectual environment. *History of European Ideas* 42(6): 819–847. https://doi.org/10.1080/01916599.2016.1154398

Shannon, Claude E. and Warren Weaver. 1949. *The mathematical theory of communication*. Urbana & Chicago, IL: University of Illinois Press.

Siemund, Peter. 2015. Exclamative clauses in English and their relevance for theories of clause types. *Studies in Language* 39(3): 697–727.

Sinclair, John McH. 1966. Beginning the study of lexis. In C. Bazell et al. (ed.), *In Memory of J.R. Firth*, 410–430. London: Longman.

Sinclair, John McH. 1987. Collocation: A progress report. In Ross Steele and Terry Threadgold (eds), *Language topics: Essays in honour of Michael Halliday*, 319–332. Amsterdam: Benjamins. https://doi.org/10.1075/z.lt2.68sin

Sinclair, John M. 1991. *Corpus, concordance, collocation.* Oxford: Oxford University Press.

Sinclair, John McH. and Malcolm Coulthard. 1975. *Towards and analysis of discourse: The English used by teachers and pupils.* London: Oxford University Press.

Slade, Diana, Marie Manidis, Jeannette McGregor, Hermine Scheeres, Eloise Chandler, Jane Stein-Parbury, Roger Dunstan, Maria Herke and Christian M.I.M. Matthiessen. 2015. *Communication in hospital emergency departments.* Berlin: Springer. https://doi.org/10.1007/978-3-662-46021-4

Smidt, Sandra. 2017. *Introducing Trevarthen: A guide for practitioners and students in early years education.* London: Routledge. https://doi.org/10.4324/9781315411293

Smith, Bradley A. and William S. Greaves. 2015. Intonation. In Jonathan Webster (ed.), *The Bloomsbury companion to M.A.K. Halliday*, 291–313. London: Bloomsbury Academic.

Sohn, Ho-Min. 1999. *The Korean language.* Cambridge: Cambridge University Press.

Soon, Chun Siong, Marcel Brass, Hans-Jochen Heinze and John-Dylan Haynes. 2008. Unconscious determinants of free decisions in the human brain. *Nature Neuroscience* 11(5): 543–545. https://doi.org/10.1038/nn.2112

Steiner, Erich. 1985. Working with transitivity: System networks in semantic-grammatical descriptions. In James D. Benson and William S. Greaves (ed.), *Systemic perspectives on discourse*, 163–184. Norwood, NJ: Ablex.

Steiner, Erich. 1988. Language and music as semiotic systems: The example of a folk ballad. In James D. Benson, Michael J. Cummings and William S. Greaves (eds), *Linguistics in a systemic perspective*, 393–441. Amsterdam: Benjamins. https://doi.org/10.1075/cilt.39.14ste

Steiner, Erich. 2005. Hallidayan thinking and translation theory – enhancing the options, broadening the range, and keeping the ground. In Ruqaiya Hasan, Christian M.I.M. Matthiessen and Jonathan Webster (eds), *Continuing discourse on language: A functional perspective.* Volume 1, 481–500. London: Equinox Publishing Ltd.

Steiner, Erich. 2015. Translation. In Jonathan J. Webster (ed.), *The Bloomsbury Companion to M.A.K. Halliday*, 412–426. London: Bloomsbury Academic.

Stillar, Glenn. 1991. Discerning the discerning traveller: Phasal analysis and ideology. *Social Semiotics* 1(2): 112–122. https://doi.org/10.1080/10350339109360340

Talmy, Leonard. 1985. Lexicalisation patterns. In Timothy Shopen (ed.), *Language typology and syntactic description. Volume III. Grammatical categories and the lexicon*, 57–149. Cambridge: Cambridge University Press.

Teich, Elke. 1999a. System-oriented and text-oriented comparative linguistic research: Cross-linguistic variation in translation. *Languages in Contrast* 2(2): 187–210. https://doi.org/10.1075/lic.2.2.04tei

Teich, Elke. 1999b. *Systemic functional grammar in natural language generation: Linguistic description and computational representation.* London: Cassell.

Teich, Elke. 2009. Computational linguistics. In M.A.K. Halliday and Jonathan Webster (eds), *A companion to systemic functional linguistics*, 113–127. London & New York: Continuum.

Teich, Elke, John A. Bateman and Liesbeth Degand. 1996. Multilingual textuality: Experiences from multilingual text generation. In M. Zock and G. Adorni (eds), *Trends in natural language generation: An artificial intelligence perspective*, 331–349. Berlin & New York: Springer-Verlag.

Teich, Elke, Catherine I. Watson and Cécile Pereira. 2000. Matching a tone-based and tune-based approach to English intonation for concept-to-speech generation. *Proceedings of the 18th conference on Computational linguistics – Volume 2*, 829–835. Morristown, NJ: Association for Computational Linguistics. https://doi.org/10.3115/992730.992766

Tench, Paul. 1990. *The roles of intonation in English discourse.* Frankfurt: Peter Lang. (Forum Linguisticum 31.)

Tench, Paul (ed.). 1992. *Studies in systemic phonology*. London & New York: Pinter.
Tench, Paul. 1996. *The intonation systems of English*. London: Cassell.
Teruya, Kazuhiro. 2007. *A systemic functional grammar of Japanese*. 2 volumes. London & New York: Continuum.
Teruya, Kazuhiro, Ernest Akerejola, Thomas H. Andersen, Alice Caffarel, Julia Lavid, Christian Matthiessen, Uwe Helm Petersen, Pattama Patpong and Flemming Smedegaard. 2007. Typology of MOOD: A text-based and system-based functional view. In Ruqaiya Hasan, Christian M.I.M. Matthiessen and Jonathan J. Webster (eds), *Continuing discourse on language: A functional perspective*. Volume 2, 859–920. London: Equinox Publishing Ltd.
Teruya, Kazuhiro and Christian M.I.M. Matthiessen. 2015. Halliday in relation to language comparison and typology. In Jonathan J. Webster (ed.), *The Bloomsbury companion to M.A.K. Halliday*, 427–452. London: Bloomsbury Academic.
Tesnière, Lucien. 1959. *Éléments de syntaxe structurale*. Paris: Librairie C. Klincksieck.
Thibault, Paul J. 2004. *Brain, mind and the signifying body: An ecosocial semiotic theory*. London & New York: Continuum.
Thompson, D'Arcy Wentworth. 1917. *On growth and form*. New edition in 1942. Cambridge: Cambridge University Press.
Thompson, Geoff. 1999. Acting the part: Lexico-grammatical choices and contextual factors. In Mohsen Ghadessy (ed.), *Text and context in functional linguistics*, 101–124. Amsterdam/Philadelphia: John Benjamins. https://doi.org/10.1075/cilt.169.07tho
Thompson, Geoff, Wendy L. Bowcher, Lise Fontaine and David Schöntal (eds). 2019. *The Cambridge handbook of systemic functional linguistics*. Cambridge: Cambridge University Press.
Tomasello, Michael. 1995. Joint attention as social cognition. In Chris Moore and Philip J. Dunham (eds), *Joint attention: Its origins and role in development*, 103–130. Hillsdale, NJ: Erlbaum.
Tomasello, Michael. 1999. *The cultural origins of human cognition*. Cambridge, MA: Harvard University Press. https://doi.org/10.4159/9780674044371
Tomasello, Michael. 2008. *Origins of human communication*. Cambridge, MA: MIT Press. https://doi.org/10.7551/mitpress/7551.001.0001
Tomasello, Michael. 2019. *Becoming human: A theory of ontogeny*. Cambridge, MA: Harvard University Press. https://doi.org/10.4159/9780674988651
Torr, Jane. 1997. *From child tongue to mother tongue: A case study of language development in the first two and a half years*. University of Nottingham: Monographs in systemic linguistics, Number 9.
Torr, Jane. 2015. Language development in early childhood: Learning how to mean. In Jonathan J. Webster (ed.), *The Bloomsbury companion to M.A.K. Halliday*, 242–256. London: Bloomsbury Academic.
Toury, Gideon. 2004. Probabilistic explanations in translation studies: Welcome as they are, would they qualify as universals? In Anna Mauranen and Pekka Kujamäki (eds), *Translation universals: Do they exist?*, 15–32. Amsterdam & Philadelphia: Benjamins. https://doi.org/10.1075/btl.48.03tou
Trevarthen, Colwyn. 1974. Conversations with a two-month-old. *New Scientist* 2: 230–235.
Trevarthen, Colwyn. 1979. Communication and cooperation in early infancy: A description of primary intersubjectivity. In Margaret Bullowa (ed.), *Before speech: The beginnings of human communication*, 321–347. London: Cambridge University Press.
Trevarthen, Colwyn. 1987. Sharing making sense: Intersubjectivity and the making of an infant's meaning. In Ross Steele and Terry Threadgold (eds), *Language topics: Essays in honour of Michael Halliday*, 177–199. Amsterdam: Benjamins. https://doi.org/10.1075/z.lt1.17tre
Trevarthen, Colwyn. 2009. The intersubjective psychobiology of human meaning: Learning of culture depends on interest for co-operative practical work and affection for the joyful art of good company. *Psychoanalytic Dialogues, The International Journal of Relational Perspectives* 19(5): 507–518. https://doi.org/10.1080/10481880903231894

Trubetzkoy, N.S. 1939. *Grundzüge der Phonologie.* Travaux au Cercle Linguistique de Prague 7. Prague.
Trubetzkoy, N.S. 1969. *Principles of phonology.* Translated by Christiane A.M. Baltaxe. Berkeley & Los Angeles: University of California Press.
Tsui, Amy. 1986. *A linguistic description of utterances in conversation.* PhD thesis. University of Birmingham.
Tucker, Gordon H. 1996. Cultural classification and system networks: A systemic functional approach to lexical semantics. In Christopher Butler, Margaret Berry, Robin Fawcett and Guowen Huang (eds), *Meaning and form: systemic functional interpretations. Meaning and choice in language: Studies for Michael Halliday,* 533–566. Norwood, NJ: Ablex.
Tucker, Gordon H. 1998. *The lexicogrammar of adjectives: A systemic functional approach to lexis.* London: Cassell.
Tucker, Gordon. 2007. Between grammar and lexis: Towards a systemic functional account of phraseology. In Ruqaiya Hasan, Christian M.I.M. Matthiessen and Jonathan Webster (eds), *Continuing discourse on language: A functional perspective,* 951–977. London: Equinox Publishing Ltd.
Tucker, Gordon. 2014. Process types and their classification. In Kerstin Kunz, Elke Teich, Silvia Hansen-Schirra, Stella Neumann and Peggy Daut (eds), *Caught in the middle - language use and translation: A festschrift for Erich Steiner on the occasion of his 60th birthday,* 401–415.
Tung Yu-Wen, Christian Matthiessen and Norman Sondheimer. 1988. On Parallelism and the Penman Language Generation System. ISI/RR-88-195.
Turner, Jonathan H. 1997. *The institutional order: Economy, kinship, religion, polity, law, and education in evolutionary and comparative perspective.* New York: Longman.
Van de Walle, Jürgen. 2008. Roman Jakobson, cybernetics and information theory: A critical assessment. *Folia Linguistica Historica* 29: 87–124. https://doi.org/10.1515/FLIH.2008.87
Van de Walle, Jürgen, Dominique Williams and Klaas Willems. 2006. Structuralism. In Jan-Ola Östman and Jef Verschueren (eds), *Handbook of pragmatics.* Amsterdam: Benjamins. https://doi.org/10.1075/hop.10.str1
Veel, Robert. 1997. Learning how to mean – scientifically speaking: Apprenticeship into scientific discourse in the secondary school. In Frances Christie and J.R. Martin (eds), *Genre and institutions: Social processes in the workplace and school,* 161–195. London: Cassell.
Ventola, Eija. 1987. *The structure of social interaction: A systemic approach to the semiotics of service encounters.* London: Frances Pinter.
Ventola, Eija. 1988. The logical relations in exchange. In James D. Benson and Williams S. Greaves (eds), *Systemic functional approaches to discourse,* 51–72. Norwood, NJ: Ablex.
Walsh, John, 2002. *A linguistic perspective on the development of identity: A child language study.* Doctor of Education thesis. UTS.
Wan Yau Ni, Jenny. 2010. Call centre discourse: Graduation in relation to voice quality and attitudinal profile. In Gail Forey and Jane Lockwood (eds), *Globalization, communication and the workplace: Talking across the world,* 106–124. London: Continuum.
Wang Bo and Ma Yuanyi. 2021. *Systemic functional translation studies: Theoretical insights and new directions.* Sheffield: Equinox Publishing Ltd.
Wanner, Leo. 1997. *Exploring lexical resources for text generation in a systemic functional language model.* [Dissertation zur Erlangung des akademischen Grades eines Doktors der Philosophie der Philosophischen Fakultät der Universität des Saarlandes.] PhD thesis. Universität des Saarlandes.
Watt, David L.E. 1992. An instrumental analysis of English nuclear tones. In Tench (ed.), *Studies in systemic phonology,* 135–160. London & New York: Pinter.

Webster, Jonathan J. 1993. Text processing using the Functional Grammar Processor (FGP). In Mohsen Ghadessy (ed.), *Register analysis: Theory and practice*, 181–195. London & New York: Pinter.

Weerasinghe A. Ruvan. 1994. *Probabilistic parsing in Systemic Functional Grammar*. PhD thesis. Department of Computing Mathematics, University of Wales College of Cardiff, UK.

Wegener, Rebekah. 2011. *Parameters of context: From theory to model and application*. PhD thesis. Macquarie University.

Weinrich, Harald. 1978. Die Textpartitur als heuristische Methode. In Wolfgang Dressler (ed.), *Textlinguistik (= Wege der Forschung 427)*, 391–412. Darmstadt.

Whitelaw, Casey and Shlomo Argamon. 2004. Systemic functional features for stylistic text categorization. In *Proceedings of the AAAI 2004 Fall Symposium on Style and Meaning in Language, Art, Music, and Design*. AAAI Press.

Whitelaw, Casey, Maria Herke-Couchman and Jon Patrick. 2005. Identifying interpersonal distance using systemic features. In James G. Shanahan, Yan Qu and Janyce Wiebe (eds), *Computing attitude and affect in text*, 199–214. Springer. https://doi.org/10.1007/1-4020-4102-0_16

Whorf, Benjamin Lee. 1956. *Language, thought and reality: Selected writings of Benjamin Lee Whorf*, edited by John B. Carroll. Cambridge, MA: The MIT Press.

Wierzbicka, Anna. 1996. *Semantics: Primes and universals*. Oxford and New York: Oxford University Press.

Wignell, Peter, J.R. Martin and Suzanne Eggins. 1993. The discourse of geography: Ordering and explaining the experiential world. In M.A.K. Halliday and J.R. Martin, *Writing science: Literacy and discursive power*, 136–165. London: Falmer.

Wilkins, D.A. 1976. *Notional syllabuses: A taxonomy and its relevance to foreign language curriculum development*. Oxford: Oxford University Press.

Willats, John. 1997. *Art and representation: New principles in the analysis of pictures*. Princeton, NJ: Princeton University Press.

Willats, John. 2005. *Making sense of children's drawing*. Mahwah, NJ: Lawrence Erlbaum.

Williams, Geoff. 2019. Language development. In Geoff Thompson, Wendy L. Bowcher, Lise Fontaine and David Schöntal (eds). 2019. *The Cambridge handbook of systemic functional linguistics*, 487–511. Cambridge: Cambridge University Press. https://doi.org/10.1017/9781316337936.021

Winograd, Terry. 1968. Linguistics and the computer analysis of tonal harmony. *Journal of Music Theory* 21: 2–49. Reprinted in M.A.K. Halliday and J.R. Martin (eds). 1981. *Readings in systemic linguistics*, 257–270. London: Batsford. Reprinted in Stephan Schwanauer and David Levitt (eds). 1993. *Machine models of music*, 113–153. Cambridge, MA: MIT Press.

Winograd, Terry. 1972. *Understanding language*. Edinburgh: Edinburgh University Press.

Winograd, Terry. 1983. *Language as a cognitive process: Syntax*. Reading, MA: Addison Wesley.

Wu, Canzhong. 2000. *Modelling linguistic resources*. PhD thesis. Macquarie University.

Wu, Canzhong. 2009. Corpus-based research. In M.A.K. Halliday and Jonathan Webster (eds), *A companion to systemic functional linguistics*, 128–142. London & New York: Continuum.

Wundt, Wilhelm, 1902. *Grundriss der Psychologie. Fünfte verbesserte Auflage*. Leipzig: Verlag von Wilhelm Engelman.

Xuan Wenhui, Winfred. 2015. *A longitudinal study of Chinese high school students learning English based on systemic functional text analysis*. PhD thesis. Hong Kong Polytechnic University.

Yager, Ronald R. and Lotfi A. Zadeh (eds). 1992. *An introduction to fuzzy logic applications in intelligent systems*. New York: Springer. https://doi.org/10.1007/978-1-4615-3640-6

Zadeh, Lotfi A. 1965. Fuzzy sets. *Information and Control* 8(3): 338–353. https://doi.org/10.1016/S0019-9958(65)90241-X

Zhang, Peija, Kaela. 2018. *Public health education through posters in two world cities: A multimodal corpus-based analysis*. PhD thesis. The Hong Kong Polytechnic.

# About the Author

**Professor Christian M.I.M. Matthiessen**

Distinguished Professor
Department of Linguistics
University of International Business and Economics,
Beijing

Visiting Professor
FUNCAP research group (htttps://www.ucm.es/funcap/el-grupo)
Dep. of English Studies
Philology College
Universidad Complutense de Madrid

Christian M.I.M. Matthiessen is a Swedish-born linguist and a leading figure in the systemic functional linguistics (SFL) school, having authored or co-authored more than 160 books, refereed journal articles, and papers in refereed conference proceedings, with contributions to three television programs. He is currently Distinguished Professor in the Department of Linguistics at the University of International Business and Economics, Beijing, Distinguished Professor of Linguistics, in the School of Foreign Languages, Hunan University, Guest Professor at Beijing Science and Technology University, and Honorary Professor at the Australian National University. Before this, he was Chair Professor, Department of English, The Hong Kong Polytechnic University, and Professor in the Linguistics Department of Macquarie University. Professor Matthiessen has worked in areas as diverse as language typology, linguistics and computing, grammatical descriptions of various languages, grammar and discourse, healthcare communication studies, functional grammar for English-language teachers, text analysis and translation, multisemiotic studies, and the evolution of language. He has supervised over 40 research students.

# Index

ABSTRACTION 25, 139, 269 N5
acquisition (vs. deprivation) 85
acquisition of language 177
ACTIVITY SEQUENCE 139
adult language 17, 20–21, 24–25, 27, 29, 31, 196, 204, 210–211, 213, 215
adverb, adverbial 44, 49–50, 52, 53, 54, 82–83, 90, 178, 182
advising (field of activity) 180, 224
AFFECT (tenor) 113, 139
agnation, agnate; *see also* double agnation 3, 6, 37, 60, 61, 75, 80, 84, 91, 137, 215–218, 222–227, 230, 253, 267, 270 nn. 2 & 3, 272 nn. 16 & 19, 273 n. 25, 278 n. 6
Akan xx, 124–127, 132, 240
Akerejola, Ernest xxi, 247
Allerton, David J. 91
alternative systemic term (option) 13, 189, 209
ambiguity 225–227
ambiguity tolerant system 227
American anthropological linguistics 257
analysis, text analysis 11, 76, 96, 99, 103–104, 107–109, 111–112, 119, 124, 130, 147, 150–155, 163, 165–167, 169, 177–179, 181, 194, 198, 199, 209, 225–226, 229, 236–237, 268, 272 n. 14, 273 n. 27, 274, 278 n. 7
analysis tool 276 n. 4
annotation 167
anthropology 141, 257
antithesis (rhetorical relation) 103–104
appliable 163
Appliable Discourse Analysis (ADA) 163
appliable linguistics 163
application Chapter 5: 163–199
appraisal, APPRAISAL 69, 84, 90, 110, 136
Arabic (Modern Standard) xxi, 5, 235, 249, 272 n. 15
arbitrary 25–26, 32, 136, 197
architecture 117
architecture of language xxii, 143, 147, 166
architecture of networks 261–262

Argamon, Shlomo 165
arguing (field of activity) 224
Argyle, Michael 141
artefact 117, 154, 237, 273 n. 27
articulation (double) 21, 37
articulatory (phonology, phonetics) 4–13, 20, 22, 24, 27, 32, 120, 122–128, 130–136, 195, 197, 216, 255, 269 n. 3
Arús-Hita, Jorge 195
Asp, Elissa 118
ASPECT 5, 49–50, 223, 233–236, 246, 258
aural 139
automated analysis 165
automated choice 4, 42, 261
autosegmental phonology 255
axial order, axiality ix, xi, xxii, 9, 11, 21–23, 24, 31, 33, 81, 88, 128, 143, 144, 161, 166, 172–173, 199, 200–205, 247, 252–262, 267, 277 n. 4
axis (paradigmatic) xix, 8–9, 11, 15, 21–22, 24, 43, 57, 80–81, 88, 172, 177, 193, 200–203, 215, 225, 252, 254, 257

backchannelling 95
Bajjika xxi
Baldry, Anthony 187
Banks, David 272 n. 19
Barabási, Albert László 261
Bardi, Mohamed Ali xxi
Bartlett, Tom xxii, 107, 163, 176, 269 n. 6, 274 n. 30
Barwise, Jon 141
Bateman, John A. xxi, 59, 102, 105, 118, 149, 165, 166, 169–172, 176, 192–194, 204, 236, 242, 246, 255, 263, 275 n. 38, 277 n. 2
Bateson, M. Catherine 16
behavioural (clause, process) 67–69, 74, 75, 153, 155, 156, 216, 218, 221, 223, 230–231
behavioural (control, activity) 113, 140, 272 n. 19
Bernstein, Basil 116

Berry, Margaret 101, 110, 273 n. 28
Bickerton, Derek 27
biological system 10, 11, 15, 34, 141, 258, 259, 260, 261
bio-semiotic systems 92, 112, 114, 118
Birdwhistell, Ray L. 187
Birmingham School 88, 89, 101, 273 n. 28
bistratal (semiotic system) 27, 28
Black, Max 275 n. 37
Bloomfield, Leonard; (post-)Bloomfieldian 5, 80, 204, 253, 280 n. 1
Bloomington grammar 43–44, 275 n. 38
Bod, Rens 203, 276 n. 6
Bode, Stefan 261
bodily (resource, sound potential, space, state, system) 16, 128, 131, 135, 270 n. 4, 275 n. 6
Bohm, David 252, 256–258, 274 n. 35
Bolinger, Dwight 270 n. 4
bound (vs. free, term in system of FREEDOM) 36, 53, 54, 55, 64, 146, 153, 191, 232, 270 n. 1 (of Chapter 3), 271 nn. 6, 10, 12
boundary 60, 135, 136, 193, 216, 271 n. 14
bounding (of process) 234
Bowcher, Wendy L. 27, 130, 139
box diagram 268
Brachman, Ronald J. 173
Brazil, David 274 n. 32
Brown, Roger 116, 210, 243, 245
Brumfit, Christopher J. 177, 277 n. 6
Burton, Deidre 273 n. 28
Butt, David 115, 138, 276
Byrnes, Heidi 15, 181

Caffarel, Alice 43, 48, 51, 235, 279 n. 17
Cardiff architecture, Grammar 85, 165, 166, 273 n. 25
categorial grammar 33
categorizing, categorization 130, 140, 165, 180, 224, 273 n. 24
category xxi, xxii, 7, 37, 101, 107, 115, 117, 209, 210, 214, 221, 223, 230, 231, 257, 258, 270 n. 2, 271 n. 12, 273 n. 28, 275 n. 43
Catford, J.C. 122–125, 130–134
Chang, Moon-Soo 165
channel 113, 139, 219, 222
Cantonese 96, 177, 271 n. 7
Chinese xxi, 43, 126, 128, 154, 156, 179–180, 182, 192, 231, 233, 234, 235, 236, 245–247, 249, 275 n. 44, 276 n. 6, 277 n. 7, 279 n. 14
Chomsky, Noam 132, 199, 276 n. 6

Chomskyan (linguistics, linguists) 253
chooser-&-inquiry framework 170–171
chord 122, 150, 153, 188, 254
Christie, Fran 29
chronicling 222, 224
circumstance 44, 49, 51, 52, 58, 59, 62, 64, 66, 71, 75–76, 82, 86, 189, 190, 194, 195, 219, 249, 272 n. 19, 273 n. 24
circumstance (rhetorical relation) 103
clause 12, 34–37, 39, 41–42, 44–50, 51–95, 100–101, 105–106, 109, 121, 144–146, 148, 150–157, 160–161, 167–169, 173–174, 178–179, 183, 185–186, 195, 199, 206–208, 215–219, 223, 225–227, 229–232, 237, 240–242, 245–246, 249, 255, 265, 268, 270 nn. 1 & 2, 271 nn. 6, 9 & 12, 272 nn. 15 & 19, 273 nn. 23, 24 & 26, 274 n. 31, 275 n. 42, 278 nn. 5, 6, 8 & 9, 279 n. 17
clause complex 76, 79, 83, 92, 100, 105–106, 278 n. 5
chunking (of clause into information units) 60
Cléirigh, Chris 259
cline (continuum) 11, 221, 251
cline of delicacy 81–83, 88, 89, 204, 247
cline of instantiation 11, 13, 20, 88, 89, 111–114, 137, 142, 144, 154, 157, 158–161, 163, 167, 194, 236, 258, 260, 274 n. 30, 276 n. 49
clinical linguistic studies 164
Cloran, Carmen 107–108, 274 n. 30
codal variation 20, 117, 251
code 242
code-mixing, -switching 242, 243
coding tree 254
cognitive (term in TYPE OF SENSING) 231, 232, 242, 278 n. 6
COHESION 49, 89, 198
cohesive (analysis, clause sequence, conjunction) 49, 63, 79, 82, 83, 106
collaborating (field of activity) 224
collective 259
Collins, Peter 270 Chapter 3 n. 2
commonsense knowledge 28, 204
Comrie, Bernard 249
complementarity xx, 29, 67, 88, 96, 118, 135, 137, 199, 215 (Section 6.4), 217, 223, 224, 233–237, 251, 272 n. 18
complementary (activities, descriptions, insights, lines of research, models, opportunities, perspectives, representations, roles,

systems, types, views) 13, 34, 74, 95, 109, 111, 130, 181, 198, 201, 222, 224, 233, 234, 235, 246, 259
complex adaptive systems 178, 205, 259
complex entry condition 206, 208
componential analysis 86, 255
composition 91, 105–109, 111, 120, 258, 274 nn. 31, 32, 33
composition (gesture) 196
composition (pictorial) 187, 198
composition (register: essay) 177–180
compositional (hierarchy, scale) 92, 108, 109, 111, 120, 260, 274 n. 32
compositionality 27
comprehensive (account, description, map) xxiii, 43, 44, 48, 76, 84, 85, 111, 118, 162, 175, 198, 204, 209
computational (application, linguistics, modelling, representation) xix, xx, xxi, 86, 105, 119, 134, 140, 145, 149, 163, 164–176, 186, 188, 191, 199, 204, 209, 231, 236, 240, 242, 251, 255, 271 n. 12, 274 nn. 30 & 32, 276 nn. 48 & 5, 277 n. 3
conation 83
concordance, concordancer, concordancing tool 164
configuration 3, 44, 46, 51, 66, 67, 70, 86, 89, 139, 185, 201, 273 n. 24
conflate, conflation 57, 193
conjunction (of systemic terms) 17, 206, 257
conjunction (textual system, class) 47, 49, 50, 52, 58, 63, 79, 82, 83, 110
connotation 49, 82, 83, 90, 227, 269 n. 5
connotative semiotic (system) 43, 186
construction (pattern) 81, 88
construction (construal) 118
Construction Grammar 88, 255
construal (of experience) 3, 25, 44, 67–70, 74, 76, 91, 118, 131, 192, 195, 218, 221, 222, 223, 230, 231, 233, 234, 237, 272 n. 19
construal (of higher stratum by lower one) 115, 137
construe (meaning into system) 17, 19–20
content (plane, strata) 4, 6, 16, 20–22, 27, 31, 32–33, 37–39, 43, 91, 106, 112, 114, 119–120, 136, 191, 194, 196, 217, 224, 237, 260, 270 Chapter 2 nn. 1 & 3, Chapter 3 nn. 2 & 4, 273 n. 25
context (of language, as connotative semiotic) xxii, 1, 3, 4, 6, 12, 16, 17, 20, 25, 27, 28, 31, 33, 41, 43, 51, 88, 96, 104, 105, 111–119, 135, 136, 137–142, 149, 151–152, 157, 175, 176, 180–186, 194, 199, 200, 203, 210, 214, 217, 218, 219, 220, 222, 224, 226, 227, 243, 258, 267, 270 n. 3, 274 nn. 33 & 35, 275 n. 36, 276 nn. 48, 49 & 50, 277 Chapter 1 n. 1
(context of) culture 42–43, 111, 115–116, 137, 149, 270 Chapter 2 n. 2
(context of) situation 51, 111, 115–116, 139, 149, 164, 182, 275 n. 36
contextual parameter (field, tenor and mode) 114, 116, 137–139, 219, 222, 243
contextual structure 104, 138, 140–141, 184, 276 nn. 49 & 50
contextual system 42, 43, 137–141, 267
continuative 58
conventional (arbitrary) 25–26, 32, 37, 91, 136, 197, 275 n. 41
conventions (graphic, marking, systemic) 12, 17–18, 34, 53, 56–57, 74, 125, 134, 172, 200, 240–242, 263–268
conversation 42, 95, 157
Corballis, Michael C. 259
corpus 41, 88, 89, 109, 154, 158, 160, 164, 176, 194, 209, 226, 233, 276 n. 6, 278 n. 9
corpus-based (studies) 89, 278 n. 9
corpus linguistics 164
corpus tool 165, 276 n. 4
cosmogenesis 259–260
Costetchi, Eugeniu 165, 176
Coulthard, Michael 81, 101, 273 n. 28
Couper-Kuhlen, Elizabeth 274 n. 32
Couto-Vale, Daniel 165
Cross, Marilyn xix, xxi, 86, 237
cross-coupling 135
cross-referencing (terms in systems) 65
crypto (grammar, type) 257–258
culture 29, 42–43, 111, 115–116, 137, 149, 270 Chapter 2 n. 2

Dagaare (language) xxi
Davey, Anthony 165, 166
Davidse, Kristin 234, 258
Debashish, Meena 27
delicacy xx, 17–18, 23, 27, 34–36, 39, 42, 44, 48, 53, 55, 57, 80–89, 95, 135, 139, 140, 144–147, 158, 164, 177, 194, 204–208, 216–217, 220, 229–232, 240, 243–248, 264, 279 n. 14
delicate 20, 35, 42, 55, 74, 81, 88–89, 139, 143, 149, 167–168, 177, 185, 214, 216, 231, 240,

244-245, 248-249, 271 n. 7, 273 n. 24, 279 n. 17
Delin, Judith L. 194
denotation 49, 90
denotative semiotic (system) 33, 43, 92, 114, 117-118, 136, 137-138, 141-142, 194, 224
dependency (parser, structure) 176, 274 n. 29, 278 n. 7
Derewianka, Beverly 15, 29
description (of particular language, systemic ~) xx, xxi, xxiii, 32-33, 37, 42, 43-44, 51, 60, 63, 65, 75-76, 80, 82, 84-92, 95-96, 98, 101, 105, 110-115, 117-128, 132-142, 145-149, 172, 175-177, 180, 181, 186-191, 193-199, 201, 203-206, 209-210, 215, 216-220, 222, 230-232, 234, 240-249, 251, 255, 258, 261, 267, 271 n. 11, 272 nn. 15, 18 & 19, 273 nn. 24, 25, 26, & 28, 274 n. 31, 275 n. 35, 276 nn. 48, 49, & 50, 277 Chapter 6 n. 2, 278 n. 3
descriptive (alternative, aspect, category, challenge, data, decision, detail, division of labour, exploration, fragment, generalization, gloss, interpretation, issue, label, linguistics, project, resource, stage, stepping stone, use, variation, work) xxi, xxiii, 33, 36, 59, 65, 76, 85, 86, 89, 91, 112, 118, 126, 142, 176, 203, 215, 220, 243, 247, 265, 271 nn. 12 & 13, 272 n. 19, 273 n. 20, 277 Chapter 6 n. 2, 278 n. 9
development (of language; ontogenesis) Chapter 2, 29, 202, 270 Chapter 2 n. 3
diagnostic tool 177, 181, 199
dialect 119, 214, 251
dialectic relationship 20, 115, 176, 251
dialogue 26, 28, 34-35, 40, 41, 51, 52, 53, 94-105, 111, 135, 165, 191, 246, 249, 268, 270 Chapter 3 n. 1, 271 n. 7, 273 nn. 27 & 28
dictionary (view of lexis) 80
dimension (semiotic ~) xxii, 6, 15-17, 21-24, 31, 54, 88, 139, 143, 221, 259, 271 n. 6, 275 n. 43
DIRECTION (of identification) 47
direction (of motion) 86-87
direction (of pitch movement) 195
direction (interstratal: activation / construal) 115
direction (instantiation: generation / analysis) 167
direction (giving ~) 138
directing (field of activity: doing: ~) 224
discontinuity 217

discourse analysis 103, 163, 194, 199
distinctive feature 126, 132, 203, 253-255
division of (grammatical, phonological, semiotic) labour 46, 120, 126, 237, 274 n. 31
division (of morphemes into phonemes) 254
Djonov, Emilia 187
doing (as opposed to saying, thinking) 7, 25, 139
doing (field of activity) 220, 224
DOING (TYPE OF ~) 47, 50, 68
doing-&-happening (clauses, verbs of ~) 68, 83, 103, 118, 230, 231
Doran, Yaegan, John 194
double agnation 37-43, 91, 137, 217, 270 Chapter 3 nn. 2 & 3, 273 n. 25
double analysis 229
double articulation 21, 37, 195
drama 2, 154, 220
drama (clause as ~) 66
dramatizing (field of activity) 224

ecological 105
ecologism 205
eco-social environment 10, 135
educational applications (implications) 176-181, 194, 199
educational contexts 54, 176
educational linguistic studies 180
educational linguistics 140, 240, 276 n. 48
educational knowledge 28
ELAN 165
element (of function structure) 35, 36, 53-59, 61-66, 68-69, 76, 140, 187, 190, 191, 214, 233, 245, 253-254, 271 n. 6
element (as member of set) 221
element (type of phenomenon in ideational semantics) 105, 110
elemental (interrogative, question) 12, 41, 94, 99, 247-249
elicitation 249, 279 n. 17
Eggins, Suzanne 48, 88, 110, 138
Ellegård, Alvar xix, 160-161
Elmenoufy, Afaf 27
embedded (downranked) 54, 146, 270 Chapter 3 n. 1
emergence 15-23, 30, 31, 91, 161, 259-261, 270 Chapter 1 n. 1
enabling (field of activity) 113, 114, 138, 157, 220, 224
enabling (textual metafunction as ~) 25

enacting (interpersonal mode of meaning) 22, 32, 82, 114, 117, 273 n. 27
entry condition 11, 12, 17–19, 35, 42, 54, 56, 62, 65, 67, 73, 74, 84, 126–127, 131, 143, 145, 167, 170–172, 206, 208, 211, 214, 240, 244, 245, 255, 263–264, 267, 271 n. 10, 278 n. 9
ergative (model [of transitivity] vs. transitive model) 67, 68, 74, 223, 234, 272 n. 17, 273 n. 20, 278 n. 8
Ervin-Tripp, Susan M. 117, 209–215, 278 n. 3
event (phenomenon of experience; flow of ~) 16, 44, 51, 52, 66–67, 92, 122, 195, 218, 222, 234
Event (verbal group function) 84, 90, 225, 226, 273 n. 24
event potential 260, 261
EVENT TYPE 49, 50, 68, 70, 82, 88, 198
eventive (clause) 231
evolution 84, 115, 131, 161, 205, 216, 260, 278 n. 4
exchange (of attention, meaning, proposition) 18, 21, 26, 40, 42, 51, 52, 53, 54, 82, 94–105, 111, 139, 194, 220, 247, 271 n. 9, 274 nn. 28 & 29, 278 n. 6
existential (term in PROCESS TYPE; ~ clause, process) 65, 67, 70, 74, 75, 153, 155, 156, 216, 218, 219
exosomatic semiotic system 29
expand (realization operator) 191, 266
expansion (vs. projection) 70, 73, 75–80, 82, 99, 100, 168, 169, 171, 227
EXPANSION TYPE 47, 50, 168
experiential (metafunction) 2, 3, 16, 44–52, 58, 59, 62, 64, 65, 66–76, 78, 79, 82–84, 89–91, 92–93, 108, 110, 111, 115, 145, 150, 153, 154, 167, 195, 196, 208, 218, 234, 258, 271 n. 9, 272 nn. 18 & 19, 273 n. 20
experiential mode (of construing experience, of composition) xx, 105, 233
experimental (studies) 118
expertise (degrees of ~) 48, 88
explaining (field of activity) 140, 224
exploring (field of activity) 219, 220, 222, 224
exponence 115
expounding (field of activity) 138, 140, 157, 220, 224
expression 15, 17, 21, 26, 27, 32, 36, 42, 91, 92, 118, 136, 164, 187, 193, 195, 196, 197, 204, 205, 209, 231, 237, 248, 255, 259, 260, 270 Chapter 2 n. 1, 279 nn. 15 & 17

expression plane, strata 4, 6, 16, 20–22, 24, 27, 29, 31, 33, 119, 128, 136, 187, 191, 194–196, 270 Chapter 2 n. 3, 275 n. 41
expression substance 42, 128, 135
expressive (modality, resource) 27, 29, 30, 195, 196, 270 Chapter 2 n. 1, Chapter 3 n. 4

familiarity (tenor) 113, 114, 117, 215
Fant, Gunnar 132, 254
Fawcett, Robin P. 61, 85, 105, 165, 166, 171, 215, 240, 243, 263, 265, 267, 277
field (context) 105, 113, 114–115, 137–140
field (lexical ~) xix, 3, 84, 88
field of activity 113, 114, 138, 140, 180, 217, 219–220, 222, 224, 276 n. 49
field of experience 113, 131
field (observation, work) 141
film 117, 273 n. 27
Fine, Jonathan 276 n. 6
Finnish 249
first language development Chapter 2 (15–29)
Firth, John R. 8, 9, 10, 42, 43, 61, 88, 124, 130, 137, 154–155, 200, 201, 202, 253, 255, 257
Firthian (linguistics, notion, phonology, prosodic analysis, system-structure theory, tradition) xx, 115, 119, 126, 130, 140, 202, 276 n. 50, 277 n. 9
Fischer-Jørgensen, Eli 280 n. 1
flow of discourse, text 25, 92
flow of events, experience 44, 52, 58, 67, 92, 195, 218, 234
flow of exchange 52
flow of information 51, 52, 58
flow-&-return (syllable) 127
flow chart 55, 162, 169, 194, 209–215, 240, 251
folk (knowledge, linguistics, model, taxonomy) 7, 28, 80, 86, 204
Fontaine, Lise xxii, 85, 269 n. 6
forensic linguistics 199
form (vs. substance) 32, 92, 119–121, 135–137, 141, 195, 196
formal (approaches to meaning, grammar, linguistics, representation, semantics, structure, theory) 7, 13, 24, 26, 42, 166, 205
formalism 205
FORMALITY (interpersonal system) 244, 249
fractal, fractal (pattern, principle, system, types) Chapter 3 (31–142), 199, 204, 256, 257, 266, 272 n. 19, 273 nn. 21 & 23, 276 n. 51
Frake, Charles 86

frame-based (inheritance network) xx, 162, 173, 176, 240, 255
French xxi, 9, 84, 117, 118, 235, 237, 245, 249, 279 n. 11
FREEDOM (free vs. bound) 47, 50, 53, 208, 270 n. 1, 271 n. 10, 278 n. 9
frequency (relative of ~combination, of instantiation, of selection) 71, 83, 88, 154–158, 160–161, 179, 218, 278 n. 9
FREQUENCY, Frequency (circumstantial system, function) 70, 73
function (*see also* metafunction, macrofunction, microfunction; [systemic] functional linguistics; speech function; functional; element) xix, xx, xxi, xxii, xxiii, 7, 57, 60, 61, 63, 64, 89, 102, 139, 164, 193, 198, 201, 209, 225, 246, 247, 257, 265, 266, 278 n. 4
function structure xix, 51, 57, 58, 89, 124, 143, 145, 171, 201, 225, 226, 227, 257, 265, 268
function-rank matrix 48, 49, 50, 81, 109–110, 120, 145, 148, 149, 198, 265
function word 81
functional component 115
functional grammar 271 n. 9
functional diversification 16, 115
functional load 160
functional slot 274 n. 28
Functional Sentence Perspective (FSP) 254
functional variety, variation in context 112
Fung Ka Chun, Andy 96, 136
fuzzy (logic, theory) 217–222

gap (descriptive, theoretical) 167
gap (systemic, in paradigm) 37, 241
García, Adolfo M. 34, 118, 143
Gazdar, Gerald 200
geographic spread (of types of realization) 248
General System(s) Theory (GST) 10
general theory of language 203, 274 n. 31
Generalized Phrase Structure Grammar (GPSG) 200
Generalized Upper Model 118, 119
generative linguistics 80, 86, 200, 253, 255, 273 n. 21, 276 n. 6
Generic Structure Potential (GSP) 140
genesis Chapter 2 (15–30), 31, 158, 159, 161, 167
genre 107, 139, 140, 194, 217
German 117, 118, 182–186, 245, 247, 249, 277 n. 8, 278 n. 6, 279 n. 11

gesture 20–22, 26, 27, 29, 138, 186, 187, 191, 194–198, 236, 270 Chapter 2 n. 3
gesture (articulatory, phonological) 126, 129
Gibbons, John 177–180, 277 n. 6
Gleason, H.A. 6
Glossematics 33
Goodenough, Ward H. 86
Gorniak, Peter J. 27, 141
Grace, George W. 246
grammar (*see also* lexicogrammar, systemic functional grammar) xx, xxi, 1, 7, 22–23, 37, 44, 55, 60, 63, 76, 79, 80, 81, 82, 85, 88, 114, 118, 135, 145, 146, 149, 151, 152, 154, 165, 173, 185, 195, 199–205, 217, 231, 232, 233, 234, 241, 242, 243, 245, 246, 248, 249, 250, 255, 257, 258, 268, 271 n. 11, 272 n. 19, 273 n. 25, 274 n. 31, 278 n. 9, 279 n. 17
grammatical metaphor 28, 29, 39, 80, 91–92, 137, 176, 273 n. 25
grammaticalization 84, 205, 279 n. 14
grammatics 154
graphetics 29, 41
graphology 29, 41, 88, 92, 187, 274 n. 31
Greaves, William S. 27, 59, 121, 130, 187, 196, 203, 275 n. 42
Gregory, Michael J. 108, 274 n. 30
Grimes, Joseph E. 103
Grosz, Barbara J. 274 n. 32
growth 22, 28
Gu Yueguo 41
Guinness, Alec 91

Haiman, John 26
Halle, Morris 132, 254
Halliday, M.A.K. xix, xx, xxi, xxii, xxiii, 6, 8, 9, 10, 11, 15, 16, 17, 18, 19, 20, 21, 22, 23, 24, 25, 26, 27, 28, 29, 33, 27, 39, 41–49, 51, 56, 59, 61, 76, 78–84, 86, 88–89, 91, 95–96, 101, 105, 106, 107, 109, 11, 112, 117–122, 126–130, 135–137, 139, 140, 141, 146, 149, 154, 156–161, 163–166, 172, 173, 174, 176, 176–178, 182, 186–187, 189, 194, 195, 196, 198, 200–206, 209, 216, 218, 219, 221, 222–228, 230–234, 236, 240, 245, 246, 255, 256, 257, 258, 259, 260, 263, 265, 268, 269 n. 4, 270 Chapter 2 nn. 1 & 2, Chapter 3 nn. 2 & 3, 271 nn. 5, 6, 7, 9, 12 & 13, 272 nn. 14, 15, 18 & 19, 273 nn. 21, 25, 26 & 28, 274 nn. 30, 31 & 32, 275 nn. 36, 38, 42, 44 & 48, 276 nn. 49 & 6, 278 n. 8, 279 nn. 14, 15 & 17

Hallidayan (version) 273 n. 23
handbook xxii, xxiii
Harris, Zellig S. 253
Hasan, Ruqaiya xxii, 37, 83, 84, 85, 89, 91, 95, 96, 105, 107, 110, 115, 117, 136, 137–141, 163, 176, 216, 253, 255, 271, 274, 276, 277
healthcare 163, 199
Heller, Louis G. 203
Henrici, Alick 165, 171, 172
Herke, Maria 165
hierarchy 21, 31, 32, 51, 88, 92, 105, 109, 111, 120, 175, 195, 221, 245, 246, 249–250
hierarchy of features (Ladefoged's ~) 133–134
hierarchy of stratification 21, 31, 32, 88
higher-order (content plane, semiotic system) 114, 116, 143, 196, 259, 260
Hinds, John 274 n. 32
Hiippala, Tuomo 194
Hjelmslev, Louis 7, 9, 10, 33, 114, 135, 136, 160, 201, 203, 257, 269 n. 5
Hjelmslevian 275 n. 41
Hockett, Charles 5, 203
holistic (approach, orientation, theory) 33, 76, 175, 176, 205, 258
Honnibal, Matthew 176
Hori, Motoko 233
Hornby, A.S. 177
Huddleston, Rodney 278 n. 9
Hudson, Richard A. 166, 173
Hunston, Susan 88
Hymes, Dell 210
hypotactic, hypotaxis 76–79, 82–83, 168–169, 247

ideational (metafunction, resource, semantics, system) xx, 16, 25, 28, 32, 44, 46, 48, 50, 76, 79, 109, 110, 118, 192, 198, 222, 233, 236–237, 273 n. 23
ideational: logical 16, 50
ideology, ideological 7
IFG xxiii, 50, 79, 86, 146, 149, 177, 216, 218, 231, 234, 273 n. 26, 274 n. 31
image 117
image (of language) 6, 7, 13, 138, 187–191, 194, 198, 236
immaterial system 11, 260
immediate constituency (IC) analysis 255
individual (learner, meaner) 15, 24, 29, 157, 181, 259, 260, 261
Indonesian 243–244, 277 n. 7, 279 n. 11

induction 182
information (COMMODITY TYPE: vs. goods-&-services) 12, 36, 37, 53, 54, 91, 94–103, 151–152, 223, 270 Chapter 3 n. 2
INFORMATION (textual system) 36, 49, 51, 52, 58–60, 76, 92, 161, 185, 217, 222, 234
information focus 161
information theory 276 n. 6
information unit 59–60, 271 n. 14, 275 n. 42
Ingkaphirom, Preeya 279 n. 11
initiator power 123–124
insert (realization operator) 191, 193, 265–266
instance (pole, of cline of instantiation) 10, 11, 15–17, 19–20, 24, 27, 56, 96, 111–112, 115, 144, 146, 149, 153–158, 166, 167, 205, 214, 226–227, 232, 258, 260
instance type 137
instantial (character, gloss, pattern, pole) 11, 27, 138, 144, 154, 157, 194, 236
instantiation (cline of, frequency of ~) xxiii, 10, 11, 16, 20, 81, 88, 89, 111–112, 114, 115, 137, 142, 144, 147–149, 154, 157–159, 163, 167, 172, 185, 194, 205, 236, 258–260, 274 n. 30, 276 nn. 49 & 50
institution 6, 13, 29, 111, 139, 163, 199
institutional role 113
instructing (field of activity) 224
intensive (clause) 69, 75, 76, 77, 89–90, 226–227, 258
interaction base 110
interactional (microfunction) 17, 18, 20, 23–25, 27, 186
interface (metafunctional) 63–64
interface (stratal) 26, 32–33, 92, 111, 112, 114, 118, 119, 128, 130, 131, 135, 136
interlevel 92, 112, 135, 275 n. 36
interpersonal 1, 3, 16, 25, 32, 34–42, 45, 46, 47, 48, 49, 50, 51, 52, 53–58, 59, 60, 61, 62, 63, 64, 65, 69, 76, 79, 80, 82, 83, 84, 90, 92, 93, 94–95, 100–105, 109, 110, 111, 115, 116–117, 121, 145, 146, 148, 150, 153, 154, 160, 167, 195, 197, 198, 206, 208, 210, 218, 222, 227, 232, 240, 243, 245–249, 271 n. 7, 273 nn. 23, 26 & 27, 274 n. 30, 279 n. 17
interpersonal metaphor 246
interpersonal realization 246
interpersonal system 3, 36, 53, 69, 82, 101, 117, 150, 167, 206, 227, 246, 247
interpersonal Theme 52, 58, 59, 62, 63, 65
inter-rank realization 126

inter-stratal realization 33, 36, 92, 143, 144
intonation 27, 37, 119, 122, 124, 130, 187, 195, 196, 203, 205, 271 n. 7, 279 n. 17
inventorying 224
ITERATION 139
Ito, Noriko 165
Iwasaki, Shoichi 279 n. 11

Jakobson, Roman 132, 203, 254–255, 276 n. 6
Japanese xxi, 233, 242, 249
Jesus, Silvana Maria de 276 n. 6
Johnston, Trevor 270 Chapter 2 n. 3

Kashyap, Abhishek Kumar 43, 51, 86, 209
Kasper, Robert 165, 171, 172, 176, 255
Kay, Martin 147
Kittredge, Richard 186
knower 246 101
Kobayashi, Ichiro 165, 192–193
Koerner, Konrad 269 n. 5
König, Ekkehard 248
Korean 245–247, 249, 279 n. 14
Kress, Gunther 187–191, 198
Kuhl, Patricia K. 158

Labov, William 101, 274 n. 28
Ladefoged, Peter 130–134, 275 n. 47
Lamb, Sydney M. 33–34, 202, 204
Lane, Jonathan 246
language as (complex adaptive system, meaning potential, probabilistic system, resource, system of choice) 6, 7, 8, 13, 57, 112, 155, 199, 205, 206, 221, 252, 276 n. 6
language as rule 7
language development (*see also* ontogenesis) 13, 15
language evolution 26
language (functioning) in context 1, 31, 176, 199, 200, 203, 218, 227, 258, 276 n. 48
language teaching 279 n. 10
*langue* xix, 8, 9, 159
Lantolf, James 29, 195
Lascaratou, Chryssoula 234
Lavid, Julia 185–186
Layzer, David 259
learning how to mean 15, 25–29, 200, 202, 259
Leech, Geoffrey 86, 181
Lemke, Jay L. 37, 217, 270 Chapter 3 n. 3
lens 203

level (of organization) 16, 24–26, 42, 92, 112–116, 119, 134, 135, 136, 172–173, 175–176, 225, 251, 256, 273 n. 25, 274 n. 31, 275 nn. 36 & 41
level tone 35, 121
Levin, Beth 85–87
LexCart 126 146
Lexical Functional Grammar (LFG) 33, 255
lexical cohesion 49
lexical collocation 82
lexical field xix
lexical delicacy 80
lexical inventory 234
lexical metaphor 89, 90, 91, 135, 273 n. 25
lexical profile
lexical item, verb 3, 81, 83, 84, 120, 123, 225
lexical semantics 255
lexical set 84, 89, 90
lexical system 88
lexical zone 48, 279 n. 11
lexicalism 80
lexicogrammar xx, 12, 16, 22, 24, 26–28, 31–49, 51, 55, 63, 73, 76, 79–81, 84, 88, 89, 91–93, 101, 105–106, 109, 115, 117, 119–121, 135–137, 141, 144–151, 187, 195, 203, 204, 217, 233–234, 243, 258, 270 n. 2, 273 n. 25, 279 n. 11
lexicogrammatical function-rank matrix 49
lexicogrammatical metaphor 80, 91, 176
Lim, Fei Victor 187
Liu Xiangdong 79
Lockwood, David G. 34
logical xx, 16, 44, 46, 48, 49, 50, 76, 78–79, 82, 83, 104, 105, 108–110, 102, 220, 221, 233–236, 272 nn. 18 & 19
logical mode 48, 105, 109, 272 n. 18
LOGICO-SEMANTIC TYPE xxii, 70, 76, 77, 78, 79, 82, 99, 103–109, 110, 111, 140, 168, 204, 237, 272 n. 19, 274 n. 32
Longacre, Robert E. 103, 274 nn. 31 & 32
longitudinal (case) study, sample 15, 29, 181, 270 Chapter 2 n. 2
logogenesis 167, 274 n. 30
logogenetic (emergence, pattern, unfolding, view) 39, 108, 153, 274 n. 30

MacWhinney, Brian 274 n. 30
McCabe, Anne 15, 29
McCord, Michael C 165, 166, 173
McDonald, Daniel (282)

McDonald, Edward 156, 231, 233–234, 245, 275 n. 8
McEnery, Tony 209
McKeown, Kathleen R. 141
Ma Yuanyi xxii, 182
Macris, James 203
macro-function 16, 25, 28
macro-genre 107
macro-phenomenal 230
macro text 107
macro-Theme 110
Malcolm, Karen 108, 274 n. 30
Malinowski, Bronislaw 7, 116, 141
Mandarin (Chinese) 119, 120, 128, 129, 246, 275 n. 44, 278 n. 8
Mandelbrot, Benoit B. 273 n. 21
manipulate 253
Mann, William C. xxii, 99, 165, 166
Manning, Christopher D. 276 n. 6
manual (coding ~) 95
manual analysis 155, 165
maps (of resources, SFL) 145, 179
Martin, J.R. xxii, 43, 51, 76, 84, 88, 89, 90, 101–102, 110, 135–140, 176, 187, 194, 217, 219–220, 231, 243, 257, 258, 263, 272 nn. 18 & 19, 2973 n. 28, 278 n. 8, 279 n. 15
Martin, S.E. 245–246
Martinec, Radan 187, 191, 194–197, 236, 274 n. 32
Martinet, André 21, 37
Marxism, Marxist 163
Mason, James 61
MATERIAL ACTION 139
material clause 52, 64, 67–69, 74, 75, 77, 78, 85–87, 150, 153, 155–157, 167, 195, 216, 218, 221, 223, 225, 226, 227, 230–231, 247, 272 n. 19, 278 n. 8
material system 11, 15–17, 18, 21, 25–26, 27, 161, 162, 260, 270 Chapter 2 n. 1
materialization, phonic material 128, 130
matrix, matrices 48–51, 81, 109–110, 120, 145, 147–149, 162, 198, 265
Matthews, Peter H. 253
Matthiessen, Christian M.I.M. xx, xxi, xxii, xxiii, 11, 25, 39, 43, 44, 46, 47, 48, 49, 51, 59, 71, 74, 75, 76, 78, 79, 80, 82, 83, 84, 85, 86, 88, 89, 90, 95, 96, 99, 110, 118, 120, 125, 135, 140, 143, 145, 146, 149, 153, 155, 159, 163, 165, 166, 169, 170, 171, 172, 176, 178, 180, 182, 185, 187, 192, 193, 194, 195, 202, 203, 204, 209, 216, 217, 219, 222, 223, 224, 228, 230, 234, 236, 237, 242, 246, 247, 251, 254, 255, 258, 263, 265, 270 Chapter 3 n. 3, 271, nn. 5, 6, 7, 9, 11 & 12, 272 nn. 14, 15, 18 & 19, 273 nn. 21 & 24, 274 nn. 30 & 31, 275 nn. 38 & 42, 276 n. 6, 277 nn. 7 & 10, 279 nn. 10, 12, 14, 15 & 17
Mazzaferro, Gerardo 242
meaner 15, 157–158, 242, 260
meaning xx, xxii, 4, 6, 7, 10, 13, 15–23, 24–32, 34–37, 42–43, 53–54, 57, 72, 80, 82, 92, 109–119, 131, 135, 137, 138, 139, 142, 149, 157–158, 161, 163–164, 182–186, 187, 189, 192, 194, 202, 203, 204, 205, 206, 209, 217, 219, 220, 222, 223, 226, 230, 231, 235, 236–237, 242–246, 252, 257–261, 271 n. 7, 273 n. 27
meaning group 15, 31, 204, 260
meanings at risk 25, 111, 157
Meaning Text Model 89
medical consultation 96
medium (contextual parameter) 113, 139
medium (of expression) 279 n. 17
medium (term in system of FALL RANGE) 12, 36
Medium (ergative participant role) 52, 57, 67–70, 73–75, 78, 86, 89, 230, 272 n. 19, 273 n. 24, 278 n. 8
Mel'čuk, Igor 89
mental (clause, process) 50, 67–68, 71, 74–75, 77m 80, 91, 113, 150, 153, 155–156, 167, 168, 185, 189, 191, 216–218, 221, 223, 225, 230–231, 242, 278 n. 6
message (quantum of information) 1, 51, 52, 58–59, 92–94, 271 n. 12
message semantics 105, 106, 110, 271 n. 9, 273 n. 26, 274 n. 34
metafunction 25, 46, 48, 49, 59, 64, 79, 83, 120, 146, 236, 279 n. 17
metafunctional (environment, guise, mode, organization, perspective, role, strand, theory, use of gesture) 15, 25, 28, 44, 48, 58, 59, 92–93, 105, 109, 110, 111, 161, 195, 205, 259, 260, 270 Chapter 2 n. 3, 271 n. 9
metalanguage 34, 172–173, 175–176, 251
metalinguistic (level, meaning potential, stratum, translation) 161, 172, 204, 251, 256, 271 n. 12
metaphor 28, 29, 32, 33, 39, 41, 76, 79–80, 90–92, 135, 137, 160, 176, 200, 226, 234, 246, 271 n. 12, 273 nn. 22 & 25

metaredundancy 270 Chapter 3 n. 3
microfunction 17, 20, 22, 25, 27, 28, 260
Mitchell, T.F. 140, 276 n. 50
modal (term in system of DEICTICITY, vs. temporal; related to modality) 40, 53, 180, 230
modal adverb 53, 83, 182
modal analysis 179, 182
MODAL ASSESSMENT 47, 49, 50, 52, 54, 82, 83, 240
modal function 53, 60, 61, 63, 64
modal operator 2, 37, 83, 181, 223, 225, 226, 228–229, 277 n. 8
modal particle 187, 279 n. 17
modal structure 52, 58
modal verb 177, 178, 179
MODALITY 1, 2, 10, 40, 47, 49, 50, 53, 54, 80, 82, 83, 146, 177–181, 181–183, 223, 225, 227–229, 233, 234, 277 n. 8
modality (expression of semiotic system); *see also* multimodality 117, 198
mode (contextual parameter) 28, 113–115, 137–139
mode (verbal) 5, 258, 277 n. 8
mode of composition 105, 107, 109
mode of construal (logical vs. experiential) 48, 233
mode of cosmogenesis 260
mode of expounding knowledge 140, 224
mode of expression 92, 120, 121, 193, 205, 248, 279 nn. 15 & 17
mode of meaning 15, 25, 92, 205, 236, 260
mode of realization 187
MODE OF RELATION 47, 50, 69, 70
mode of representation xxi, 136, 199
mode of visualization 240
model (of experience; ergative / transitive [transitivity] ~) 43, 46, 67–68, 70, 74, 223, 224, 234, 236–238, 271 n. 17, 273 n. 20, 278 n. 8
model (of language) 7, 8, 11, 33, 80, 89, 103, 140, 149, 172, 192, 194, 195, 204, 206, 209, 234, 271 nn. 12 & 13
model (of semantic composition, semantics) 111, 114, 118–119, 135, 177, 275 n. 38, 275 n. 50
model (of systemic functional metalanguage) 173, 176, 251
modelling (context, language [as system / structure], meaning, multilingualism, paradigmatic potential, resource, speech, speaking, text generation) xix, xx, 10, 13, 33, 86, 115, 122, 128, 134, 141, 143, 155, 163–170, 172, 186, 199–200, 204, 205, 234, 255, 256, 260–261, 271 n. 12, 274 nn. 29 & 30, 276 n. 5
module 204, 275 n. 39
Mohan, Bernhard A. 138, 194, 215
MOOD (interpersonal clause system, including MOOD TYPE, MOOD TAGGING and other subsidiary systems) xxi, 12, 22, 25, 34, 35–38, 41–43, 45–50, 52–58, 60–62, 64, 65, 83, 92–96, 101, 143–146, 148–153, 158, 160, 167, 185–186, 187, 206, 208, 216, 218, 225, 241–242, 245–249, 265, 270 Chapter 3 n. 2, 270 nn. 7 & 10, 278 n. 9, 279 n. 14
Mood element 35–36, 54, 55, 56, 191, 245, 266, 271 n. 6
morphology xix, 5, 33, 200, 203, 204
mother tongue 15, 24–28, 31, 177
multilingual meaning potential 242–246
multilingual studies 277 n. 7
multilingual system network xxi, 161, 204–205, 235, 242–247, 252, 265, 279 nn. 11 & 12
multimodal xxi, xxii, 27, 163–165, 187, 188, 204
Multimodal Analysis Lab 277 n. 1
Multimodal Discourse Analysis (MDA) 199
multimodal (multisemiotic) studies 186–199
multimodal text generation 191–194
multimodality xxii
multiple Theme 59
multisemiotic 118, 186–199
multi-semiotic system 192, 236
multi-stratal 277 n. 4
Muntigl, Peter 194
Murcia-Bielsa, Susana 185
Mwinlaaru, Isaac Nuokyaa-Ire xxi, xxii, 51, 209, 247

narrating (field of activity) 222, 224
narrative 86, 138, 157, 187, 189, 191, 198, 219
natural (discourse, example, occurrence, text) 1, 13, 25, 41, 249
natural (vs. conventional, arbitrary) 25, 26, 31, 32, 37, 91, 118–121, 136, 197, 275 n. 41
natural kind 221
NLP (Natural Language Processing) 166
navigational tool 48, Chapter 4 (143–162), 163
Neale, Amy 82, 84, 85–86, 88, 273 n. 24
NEGOTIATION, negotiation 2, 39, 54–55, 92–105, 110, 222, 273 n. 23
Negotiator 246, 247
Nesbitt, Christopher N. 80, 255, 276 n. 6

network science 162, 261
neurosemiotics 118, 119
non-transformational 200
non-verbal (action, behaviour) 56, 100, 190
nursery tale 140

object (material) 25, 27, 116, 175, 270 Chapter 2 n. 1
object (in cartographic system) 193
object-oriented programming 175
objective (vs. subjective) 10, 53, 80, 178, 179, 222
O'Donnell, Michael 105, 165, 166, 169, 171, 176, 255, 274 n. 30, 276 n. 4
O'Donoghue, Tim F. 277 n. 4
O'Grady, Gerard xxii, 27, 163, 176, 269 n. 6, 274 n. 32
O'Grady, William 274 n. 30
O'Halloran, Kay 165, 199, 277 n. 1
O'Toole, Michael 117, 194, 198–199
Oko xxi
ontogenesis 15, 24–31, 158, 161, 176, 200, 204, 259, 274 n. 30, 275 n. 41
ontogenetic (semogenesis, time frame) 25–30, 39, 270 n. 2
order (realization operator) 191, 193, 265, 266
order (of semiotic system) 114, 116, 143, 149, 196
order (axial ~) 143, 161, 172, 199, 200, 204, 252–261
order (implicate vs. explicate ~) 256–261, 274 n. 35
order (paradigmatic ~) 57, 201, 247, 252
order (syntagmatic ~: sequence) 54, 55, 139, 191, 252
ORDER OF SAYING 47, 50, 69
ordered in delicacy 17, 23, 249, 250, 264
ordered in frequency 155
ordered in rank 33, 44, 48, 105
ordered typology of systems 13, 15, 43, 118, 141, 176, 252, 259
Ortega, Lourdes 15

Pagano, Adriana 276 n. 6
Painter, Clare 15, 27, 187
paradigm 5, 39–40, 62, 65–66, 70, 74–75, 147, 165, 177, 201, 203, 233–234, 241–242, 249, 267–268
paradigm shift (in Kuhnian sense) 166

paradigmatic (axis, environment, grammatics, organization, order, orientation, pattern, principle, representation, *valeur*) xix, xx, 8–11, 13, 17, 21, 22, 24, 36, 37, 43, 51, 57, 80–82, 84, 88–89, 109, 126–127, 138, 141, 143, 149, 154, 164, 172–173, 175–176, 187, 190, 193, 199, 200–205, 215–217, 240, 247, 249, 251, 252–257, 260, 269 n. 5, 272 n. 19, 273 n. 25, 280 n. 1
paralanguage 135, 194
parameter 16, 122–123, 132, 134, 244, 270 Chapter 3 n. 2
parameter (contextual ~) 114, 116, 137–139, 219, 222, 247
paraphone 274 n. 32
parataxis, paratactic 76, 77–79, 82, 169, 247
Parodi, Giovanni 29
participant 3, 13, 44, 51, 52, 57–71, 75, 78, 139, 189–191, 217, 218, 231, 249, 269 n. 4, 272 n. 19
*parole* xix, 8, 9, 159
parser 176, 255, 278 n. 7
patient 96
Patrick, Jon 165
Patten, Terry 112, 165
Pattern Grammar 88
Pawley, Andrew 246
person (social individual, aggregate of personae) 22, 29, 43, 113, 158, 214, 260, 270 Chapter 2 n. 1, 279 n. 13
PERSON (including MOOD PERSON, SUBJECT PERSON) 5, 40, 47, 49, 50, 54, 55, 57, 227, 243–245, 269 n. 4
person-oriented (vs. object-oriented) 27
personae 260
personal identity 42
personal (microfunction) 16, 17, 20, 21, 25, 186
personality 7
phasal analysis 274 n. 30
phenomenal order 11, 13, 15, 43, 118, 141
phenomenal realm 11, 259, 260
Phillips, Joy 161
phoneme 120, 123–128, 203, 240, 253–254, 275 n. 43
phonetic yoga 4–6, 13, 275 n. 46
phonetics 4, 16, 31–33, 41–42, 119–121, 128–137, 195, 224, 275 nn. 41, 46 & 47
phonology xx, 4, 12, 16, 26, 31–37, 41, 49, 88, 91, 92, 114, 119–137, 141, 144, 150–152, 187, 200, 203, 250, 253–255, 259, 260, 271 n. 7, 274 n. 32, 275 n. 41, 276 n. 6

phrasal verb 87
phraseology 88, 89, 91, 273 n. 25
phylogenesis, phylogenetic 39, 84, 274 n. 30
physical system 256, 259-261, 274 n. 35
Pike, Kenneth L. 274 n. 32
Placement (in context of traditional narration) 140, 219
Plum, Guenter A. 276 n. 6
polysemous (item) 225
post-infancy 20, 25, 27, 29-31, 196, 204
potential (systemic; culture, meaning, wording, sounding ~; action, behaviour, cartographic, event ~;~ pole) xix, 10, 11, 13, 16, 17, 20-29, 54, 55, 59, 73, 80, 86, 109, 111-116, 119-120, 128, 130, 135, 137, 141-142, 144, 145, 149, 153, 154, 158, 161, 164, 185, 186, 189, 192-195, 205, 206, 209, 230, 235, 242-246, 250, 260-261, 275 n. 46, 276 n. 49
potential for application 199
potentiality (modality, readiness: potentiality / inclination) 39, 56, 178-180, 183, 223, 225, 227, 229, 240
power (status) role (tenor parameter) 114, 116-117, 215, 247
Praat 130
pragmatic (macrofunction) 16, 25
Prague School 254
Prakasam, V. 203
pre-language 130
preposition 69, 82, 83
prepositional phrase 44, 49, 52
preselect, preselection 82, 95, 124, 125, 171, 193, 216, 266
pre-systemic xx, 101, 130, 134, 221, 249, 273 nn. 24 & 28
Pribram, Karl H. 256
Priestley, J.B. 61
primary semiotic system 18, 31, 196, 220, 259
probabilistic (interpretation, nature of language, system) 56, 154-161, 186, 199, 203, 276 n. 6, 278 n. 9
probabilistic linguistics 203, 276 n. 6
probe 226, 230, 240, 272 n. 19, 278 n. 9
procedural (commitment, knowledge) 58, 171, 172, 173, 175, 206, 215
procedural recount 224
Process, process 3, 43, 44, 51, 52, 54, 58, 59, 61-64, 66-80, 83, 85-87, 89-91, 113, 118, 189, 191, 195, 217, 226-227, 235, 239, 266, 273 n. 24, 278 n. 8

PROCESS TYPE 3, 47, 49, 50, 52, 66-75, 79, 82-87, 150, 153, 155-158, 167, 189, 194, 208, 216-219, 221, 223, 225, 230-232, 234, 272 nn. 18 & 19, 273 n. 24, 278 n. 8
programming language 172, 175-176, 277 n. 3
PROJECTION, projection 47, 50, 70, 71, 73, 75-78, 86, 169, 230, 239
projection (context: mode) 139
projection system (pictorial) xxiii, 29, 162
promoting (field of activity) 224
proportionality 75-76, 215
prosodic (expression, feature, nature, pattern, system) 4, 22, 27, 37, 109, 120, 123-127, 248, 255, 279 n. 17
prosodic analysis 119, 124
prosodic phonology xx, 37, 121-122, 203, 274 n. 32
prosody xxi, 22, 27, 122, 197, 247
protolanguage 6, 15-27, 30, 31, 186-187, 196, 204
public health 199
Pullum, Geoffrey 278 n. 9
Pulvermüller, Friedemann 118

quadristratal (model of language, system) 28, 196
qualitative (epithesis, outcome) 44, 47, 50
qualitative (vs. quantitative) 153, 156
quantitative (evidence, pattern, preference, studies, systemic picture, tendency) 71, 144, 154-158, 203
Quirk, Randolph 278 n. 9

Range (participant function, in ergative model) 67-70, 73, 75, 78, 89, 90, 230, 273 n. 24
ranged (vs. non-ranged) 52, 67-70, 74, 75
RANGING 47, 50, 67-70
rank (scale) xvii, 33, 44-50, 51, 54, 55, 78, 79, 81, 88, 91, 92, 101-103, 105-111, 120-128, 145-149, 162, 171, 195, 198, 215, 225, 255, 260, 261, 265, 267, 270 n. 1, 271 n. 9, 273 nn. 21 & 24, 274 n. 31, 275 n. 42, 276 n. 51
rank (Jespersen's notion) 273 n. 21
*rapport* (French) 8, 9, 269
reactance xxi, 219, 231, 257, 258
realization (operand, operator, statement) xix, xxi, 12, 13, 20, 22, 26, 32-53, 55-59, 65, 79, 80, 84, 85, 89, 92-96, 102, 112, 114, 115, 119, 120, 124, 126, 137, 138, 140-141, 143-144,

145, 149, 150, 170–173, 177, 180, 185–186, 187, 189–197, 200, 201, 202, 205, 210, 214, 216, 219, 231, 240, 242, 244–248, 255, 256, 257, 263–267, 270 Chapter 2 n. 1
re-analysis (of functional organization) 25
recommending (field of activity) 138, 180
recreating (field of activity) 157, 219, 220, 222, 224
recreation of meaning (translation) 182
register (functional variety) xxi, 20, 28, 48, 74, 86, 92, 105, 109, 112, 114, 117, 154, 155, 157, 158, 159, 161, 175, 180, 181, 185, 186, 192, 193, 194, 205, 216, 217, 236, 237, 251, 260, 274 n. 33, 275 n. 25, 277 n. 40
register variation 88, 105
registerial repertoire 28–29
regulating (field of activity) 114, 191, 224
regulatory (micro-function, semantics) 16, 17, 25, 112, 113, 114, 116, 181, 187
relational (clause, process) 62, 67, 69, 70, 74, 75, 77, 78, 79, 80, 89, 90, 150, 153, 155, 156, 167, 216, 218, 226, 227, 237, 247
relational (network) 33–34, 143, 145
relational (rhetorical-relational) 104, 107, 108
relational (role network) 260
Renouf, A. 89
replicate 27
reporting (hypotactic projection) 77
reporting (field of activity) 157, 219, 220, 222, 224
representational (enhancement, issue, justice, phenomenon, power, resource, strategy, system) 327 xix, xxi, 34, 43, 191, 209, 217, 240, 242, 251, 277 n. 10
representational (function, vs. modal, compositional) 198
RESONANCE (phonological system) 4, 5, 6, 124, 126, 128
resonance 115
resource (articulatory, declarative, descriptive, enabling, experiential, expressive, graphic, ideational, interpersonal, language-specific, lexical, lexicogrammatical, logical, phonetic, phonological, pictorial, representational, semiotic, somatic, systemic, systemic functional reference, unified ~; capable of supporting, for construing, for exchanging meaning, for initiating, for interactants, for making meaning, for negotiating, for realizing content as sound, for tasks, for transducing wording as sounding, of clause, of lexicogrammar, of grammatical metaphor, of meaning, of modality, of negotiation, of semantics, of wording; language as ~) xxi, 4, 6–7, 13, 17, 25, 27, 29, 34, 36, 39, 44, 46, 48, 51, 53, 54, 57, 58, 62, 65, 66, 76, 80–82, 85, 94, 96, 100, 101, 102, 109, 111, 112, 117, 119, 121, 128, 131, 134–136, 141, 143, 145, 147, 162, 163, 171, 172, 176, 177, 179, 181, 188, 189, 195, 196, 199, 200–208, 211, 215–217, 221, 234, 237, 252, 259, 270 Chapter 2 n. 1, 272 n. 30, 279 nn. 10 & 11
reviewing (field of activity) 234
rhetorical mode 139
Rhetorical Structure Theory (RST) 99, 107, 108
rhetorical unit 107, 108, 111
risk (meanings at ~) 111, 157
Robins, R.H. 5, 277 n. 9
role relationship (tenor) 115, 116, 185
role structure 108 139
Rose, David 110, 140, 176, 217, 258
Roy, Deb 27
Royce, Terry 236

Sadock, Jerry 248
Salway, Andrew 236
Sankoff, David 243
Saussure, Ferdinand de xix, 8–10, 32, 159, 203, 257, 269 n. 5, 275 n. 41
scale-&-category (theory) 101, 231
Schank, Roger C. 141
schema 141
Schultz, Anke 85
scientific (activity, challenge, discourse, English, register, research, theory) 10, 11, 157, 161, 162, 259, 261
Searle, John 41, 116, 275 n. 37
second/foreign language(s) 15, 28, 164, 177, 242, 279 n. 10
second-order parsing 165
secondary (actor, data, knower, participant, pattern, reality, school, verb class) 7, 13, 28, 29, 69, 86, 101, 177, 189, 219
secondary tense (future, present, past) 226, 232, 246
Sefton, Peter 105
selection expression 52, 127, 169, 171, 225, 226, 227, 268
semantic component (in componential analysis) 86, 255

semantic networks xx, 12, 31, 33, 34, 36–39, 42–43, 91–102, 111–112, 116, 118–119, 136–138, 144, 176, 177, 192–193, 251, 267, 273 n. 25
semantic rank scale 91, 101–102, 105–109, 271 n. 9
semantic structure 99, 101–104, 106–109, 184, 274 nn. 28 & 32
semiotic phase 16
semiotic power 16
semogenesis 13, Chapter 2 (18–30), 25, 29, 159, 205
semogenic vector 16, 21
sensorimotor 114, 118, 136
sentence 7
sequence (of structural functions) 35, 266, 279 n. 17
sequence (cohesive ~, of clauses) 79
sequence (of moves, exchanges) 101–103
sequence (of phonemes) 125, 254
sequence (medium of expression) 187, 257, 279 n. 17
sequence (semantic unit) 105–108, 110, 192
sequential (algorithm, processing) xv, 169–170
sequential complex (*Simultankomplex*) 254, 254
sequential explanation (field of activity) 140
sequential relationship (between structural functions) 35, 266, 279 n. 17
serial verb construction xx
service encounter 103–104, 151–155, 268, 276 n. 50
setting (institutional ~) 29, 163
setting (of parametric values; probabilistic ~), re-~ 105, 114, 116, 117, 158, 186, 273 n. 27
setting (circumstance in pictorial semiotics) 189, 191
Seuren, Pieter A.M. xix
SFG 85
shadow versions 3
Shannon, Claude E. 276 n. 6
sharing (field of activity; of experiences, of opinions, of values) 96, 99, 157, 180, 219, 220, 222, 224, 205, 214, 227
shunting 88, 147
Siemund, Peter 248
signification 91, 121, 216, 271 n. 12
Sinclair, John McH 89, 101, 273 n. 28
situation (immediate, social ~; context of ~), situational 22, 42, 51, 111, 115, 138, 139, 141, 149, 164, 182, 275 n. 36

situation (material ~) 27
situation type(s) 28, 111, 112, 114, 116, 137, 138, 140, 276 n. 49
Slade, Diana 96, 110
Smidt, Sandra 27
Smith, Bradley 121, 130, 199, 203
social (action, activity, behaviour) 115, 138, 139, 220, 261
social distance 185
social psychology 141
social role 185
social value 43
sociological semantics (sociosemantics) 119
sociology 141
Sohn, Ho-Min 245
somatic (semiotic system) vs. exo-somatic 29
song 277 n. 10
Soon, Chun Siong 261
sounding potential 119, 120, 142
Spanish 195, 235, 245, 249, 277 n. 7, 278 n. 11
specimen 154, 226
spectrum (of [meta-]functions) 92, 120, 176, 198
speech act theory 41, 116
speech community, fellowship 20
SPEECH FUNCTION 34, 36–40, 43, 54, 55, 80, 92, 94–99, 101, 103, 110, 111, 112, 117, 144–145, 150–152, 185, 211, 216, 245, 248, 270 Chapter 3 n: 2, 279 n. 14
speech level 245–246, 249
speech role 34, 40, 55, 94–99, 113, 116, 139
SPHERE OF ACTION 139
stage (contextual, generic ~) 104, 151–152, 179
stage (developmental phase) 23–27
STATUS (major / minor) 36, 47, 50, 53, 249
status (textual ~) 1, 58–66, 217, 271 n. 12
status role (power role) 113, 117, 139, 214–215, 243–246, 250, 279 n. 13
Steiner, Erich 91, 182, 187
stratal (allocation, ascent, boundary, descent, domain, environment, hierarchy, interface, location, neighbour, organization, plane, resource, slice, subsystem, system, system network) (*see also* bistratal, quadristratal, interstratal, intrastratal) 13, 16, 20, 31–37, 41, 44, 92, 111, 117, 119, 128, 130, 135, 136, 137, 143, 162, 175, 261, 274 n. 32
stratification xix, xii, xxiii, 15, 16, 21–22, 24–25, 31–34, 88, 143, 147, 149, 173, 175, 202, 217, 259, 260, 270 Chapter 3 n. 3

stratification-instantiation matrix 147, 149
Stratificational Linguistics xix, 33, 34, 143, 202
stratified (into content and expression, into stratal planes, into semantics and lexicogrammar; ~ model, system) 16, 28, 31, 115, 172, 173, 178, 251
stratum, strata 12, 16, 22, 26, 28, 31–39, 41–43, 49, 80, 84, 91–92, 101, 105, 111, 119, 120, 121, 128, 130, 135–137, 141–144, 145, 162, 171, 172, 173, 182, 183, 200, 225, 235, 236, 251, 255, 260, 270 n. 2, 273 n. 25, 274 nn. 30 & 33, 275 n. 41
stratum of computational representation 172–176
stratum of systemic functional theory 172–176
stratum of theoretical representation 172–176
Steiner, Erich 91, 182, 187
stretched verb construction 91
structural (analysis, background, combination, element, fragment, function, interpretation, organization, pattern, place, presence, realization, setting, theory) 42, 52, 53, 67, 89, 95, 105, 106, 141, 145, 146, 187, 247, 253, 255, 266, 268
structural Theme 62
structural vs. cohesive 49, 58, 63, 82, 83
structuralist (American) 5, 80, 201, 252
structuralist (European) xix, 9, 159, 200, 201, 202, 275 n. 41
structure xix, 7–10, 13, 19, 24, 27, 35, 42, 45, 51–53, 57–58, 63, 65, 76, 80, 81, 82, 88, 89, 99, 101–104, 106, 108–109, 114, 115, 116, 118, 124, 126, 134, 138–141
structuring (principles) 109
Stuart-Smith, Virginia 107–108, 274 n. 30
Subject 35–40, 52–58, 60–66, 143–145, 187, 191, 245, 247–248, 266, 27 nn. 5 & 6, 272 n. 14, 279 n. 17
subject matter 139
SUBJECT PERSON – see PERSON see PERSON
subpotential 158
substance (stratum; vs. form)
 32–33, 42, 114, 120, 128, 130, 132, 135–137, 260
Sugeno, Michio xix, 165, 221
surveying (field of activity) 224
SWAT analysis 251
Swedish 12, 255, 275 nn. 40 & 41, 279 n. 11
syllable 119–128, 240, 271 n. 7, 275 nn. 40 & 43
symbolic organization 115, 139

syndrome 161
syntagm (arrangement of classes in sequence) 201, 225
syntax xix, 26, 33, 200, 204, 243, 253, 275 n. 48
SysFan 147, 165
system (distinct but related senses) 8–12, 259–260
system (of choice, of [systemic] terms, in a system network) xx, xxi, xxii, xxiii, 1–3, 4–8, 8–12, 13–14, 17–18, 22–23, 25, 34–36, 37–38, 40–43, 43–50, 52–237, 241–246, 247, 248–251, 257, 258, 263–265, 267, 269 nn. 4 & 7, 270 Chapter 3 nn. 1 & 2, 271 nn. 6, 7, 10, 11, 12 & 13, 273 nn. 18 & 19, 273 nn. 20 & 24, 275 n. 41, 277 n. 8, 278 nn. 8 & 9
system of systems; see also content system, expression system; lexicogrammatical system, semantic system; phonological system, phonetic system; stratal system; system network 24, 28, 32, 251, 273 n. 19
system (potential, vs. instance); see also (cline of) instantiation 15–16, 20, 27
system as fractal principle Chapter 3
system in semogenesis Chapter 2
system-&-process 10, 164, 206
system-based (theory, typology) xxi, 1, 229
system network xix, xx, xxi, xxii, 10, 12, 18, 20, 28–29, 31–39, 42–48, 50, 51, 54–59, 62–66, 73–74, 81–82, 84–95, 111, 116, 119–131, 134–150, 153–154, 157, 161–164, 166–181, 182, 186–221, 226–229, 233, 235, 240–241, 242–249, 251, 255–257, 261–262, 263–268, 271 n. 10, 273 nn. 24 & 25, 274 n. 28, 276 n. 5, 277 n. 10, 277 n. 9, 279 nn. 11, 12 & 13
system-structure theory 43, 126, 200, 253, 255
systemic functional grammar (SFG) 85
systemic functional linguistics (SFL) xxi, xxii, xxiii, 1, 6, 8, 10, 11, 33, 34, 43, 81, 86, 88, 91, 101, 111, 118, 119, 120, 130, 134, 136, 141, 142, 163, 165, 166, 167, 173, 175, 176, 182, 188, 193, 195, 199, 200, 202, 215, 217, 240, 243, 251, 252, 256, 257, 266, 271 n. 9, 273 n. 25, 274 nn. 30 & 32, 276 n. 4, 277 nn. 2, 7 & 9, 278 n. 7
systemic functional metalanguage 173–176, 251
systemic functional theory 33, 255
systemic organization 15, 20, 33, 51, 55, 63, 73, 81, 91, 92, 177, 205

systemic template 46, 141
systemic term 12, 20, 34, 35, 40, 55–53, 73, 84–85, 92, 102, 121, 125, 121, 134, 138, 140, 143, 144–148, 149, 153–158, 167–172, 189–191, 194, 206, 209, 216, 221, 228–229, 240, 244, 255–257, 261, 265–267, 276 n. 5, 279 n. 13
systemic text analysis 150, 167
systemic tradition 273 n. 24
systemic turn 81, 200, 203
systems thinking 76, 176, 204, 205, 252, 258, 261

tabular (analysis, paradigm) 150, 222, 267
tactic (paratactic / hypotactic) 76, 78, 82, 106, 114, 247
tactic (vs. strategic) 248, 257
Tagalog 235, 242, 249, 272 n. 18, 278 n. 8
tagged / untagged (terms in MOOD TAGGING) 12, 52, 53, 56, 95, 143, 144, 167, 168
Tagmemic Linguistics, Tagmemics 274 nn. 31 & 32
Talmy, Leonard 195
TAXIS 49, 50, 76–79, 82–83, 168–169
teaching language 164, 279 n. 10
Teich, Elke 135, 165, 166, 172, 185
Tench, Paul xx, 27
tenor 39, 41, 105, 113–117, 137–139, 210, 215, 243, 245–246–250, 273 n. 27, 279 nn. 11 & 14
TENSE 5, 10, 15, 45, 47, 49, 50, 53, 82, 83, 86, 155, 178, 201, 223, 225, 229, 230, 233, 234–236, 246, 258
Teruya, Kazuhiro xxi, xxii, xxiii, 43, 51, 163, 185, 187, 195, 209, 217, 219, 222, 224, 242, 258, 277
Tesnière, Lucien 66
text 10, 13, 51, 58–59, 74, 80, 92, 93, 96, 98, 101, 104, 105–112, 117, 122, 139, 144–160, 163, 165, 167, 172, 177, 181, 182, 184, 185, 199, 205, 218, 219, 226, 227, 228, 233, 236–239, 265, 268, 271 nn. 11 & 12, 273 n. 21, 274 nn. 30 & 32
text analysis ([appliable] discourse analysis) 76, 149–158, 163, 165, 166, 167, 169, 199, 268, 272 n. 14
text as (artefact, [semantic] choice, logico-semantic complex, prosodic patterns, specimen) 105, 107, 109, 112, 122, 149, 153, 154, 167, 205, 274 n. 30

text generation xix, xxi, 165–170, 188, 191–194, 199, 231, 241, 242, 255, 275 n. 38
text in context 111
text score 167, 181
text typology (see register)
text understanding 255
Textpartitur 153 (see also text score)
textual (metafunction; agnation, choice, pattern) 1, 3, 25, 32, 36, 37, 45–52, 58–66, 76, 79, 82–83, 92–93, 105, 109, 110, 115, 121, 140, 150, 153, 154, 164, 167, 198, 208, 217, 218, 222, 271 nn. 9 & 12, 272 n. 14, 273 n. 23
textual Theme 59, 61, 62, 63, 208, 235, 249, 279 n. 11
Thai xxi
thematic (analysis, principle, status, structure) 52, 58–66, 76, 204, 271 n. 13, 272 n. 16
Theme (^ Rheme) 1, 46, 52, 58–66, 110, 185, 245, 271 nn. 11, 12, & 13
THEME (SELECTION) 3, 45, 46, 47, 48, 49, 52, 57, 58–66, 82, 93, 150, 167, 206, 208, 218, 234, 271 nn. 13 & 14
theoretical (account, aspect, conception, consideration, interpretation, linguistics, method, model, notion, power, representation, value, vision) xix, 7, 11, 13, 33, 81, 105, 115, 118, 137, 164, 166, 172–173, 175–176, 203, 216, 226, 243, 251, 253, 256, 273 n. 1
theory (association, holistic, information, linguistic, network, metafunctional, music, paradigmatic, physical, Relational Network, Rhetorical Structure, [crisp, fuzzy] set, speech act, scale-&-category, structural, syntagmatic, system-structure, systemic theory, X-bar) xix, xxii, 1, 8–10, 26, 33, 34, 41, 43, 44, 76, 99, 101, 108, 115, 116, 117, 126, 136, 137, 141, 143, 149, 154, 162, 164, 173, 175–176, 188, 199, 201, 202, 203, 205, 217, 218, 221, 224, 251, 253, 255, 269 n. 5, 273 n. 21, 274 n. 31, 275 n. 35, 276 nn. 51 & 6
thesaurus (in machine translation) 166, 182
Thibault, Paul J. 29, 118, 187
3rd-order system: social systems 11, 15, 116, 258, 259–261
Thompson, D'Arcy Wentworth 206
Thompson, Geoff xxii, 96, 163, 176
Tomasello, Michael 27, 270 Chapter 2 n. 2
tool (analytic, cartographic, computational, diagnostic, [mind] mapping, mathematical, navigational) (for thought) 48, 81, 130, 142,

Chapter 4, 147, 161-162, 163-166, 177, 181, 199, 211, 251, 262, 276 n. 21
tonal harmony 165, 187-188
TONALITY 120
TONE, tone (tone 1, tone 2 ...) 12, 20, 34, 35-36, 37, 41, 42, 49, 55, 92, 95, 119-122, 124, 125, 128, 144, 145, 150-152, 187, 195, 197, 216, 247, 248, 270 n. 4, 271 nn. 7 & 8, 279 n. 17
tone group xxi, 34, 35, 36, 49, 120, 121-122, 124, 271 nn. 7 & 8, 274 n. 32, 275 n. 44
TONE SEQUENCE 49
TONICITY 49, 120, 121
tool for meaning 161
topical Theme 58-65, 150, 271 nn. 13 & 14
topology 33, 74, 215-222
Torr, Jane 15, 27
Toury, Gideon 182
traditional grammar 55, 67
transactional (pictorial system) 190
transduction 121
transferred (vs. direct negative polarity) 179
translanguaging 242
translation 182-186
transformational (grammar, rule) 200, 255
translation (machine, inter-semiotic) xii, 80, 117, 147, 163-166, 182-186, 195, 199, 242, 277 n. 7, 278 n. 6, 280 n. 1
translation of system networks (re-representation) 208-215, 240
translation equivalence 182
translation studies xxii, 182-186
TRANSMISSION 139
transition (semogenic) 15, 16, 24-28, 31, 204
transition (articulatory) 123
transition network 140, 255
transitive (model) 67, 68, 74, 223, 234, 272 n. 17, 273 n. 20, 278 n. 8
TRANSITIVITY (system, transitivity structure) xxi, 25, 43-50, 52, 58, 63-64, 66-76, 82, 85, 93, 145, 156, 189, 194, 206, 217-219, 223, 231, 234, 258, 269 n. 4, 272 nn. 17 & 18, 273 nn. 20 & 24, 278 n. 8
tree bank 176
Trevarthen, Colwyn 27
trinocular (vision) xxiii, 74, 88, 105, 121, 218, 221, 231, 252-255, 256, 272 n. 19
Trubetzkoy, N.S. 254
Tsui, Amy 273 n. 28
Tucker, Gordon H. 82, 84, 85, 88, 91, 165, 166, 273 n. 25

Tung Yu-Wen 169
turn 28, 34, 36, 94, 97, 98, 102
turn-taking 28
Turner, Jonathan H. 141
typological (characteristics, database, literature, studies, variation) xxi, 43, 48, 209, 247, 249, 279 n. 11
typological (vs. topological) 135, 217-220, 229

UAM Corpus tool(s) 165, 276 n. 4
undulating pattern 109
unification ([-based] grammar) 93, 165, 173
unified system networks (in multilingual system network) 242-243
univariate (structure) 76, 106

*valeur see* value (systemic order, *valeur*)
validity (of proposition, proposal) 48, 54, 55, 234, 249, 271 n. 6
value (tenor, in a culture) 43, 82, 137, 149, 177, 190, 219, 222, 224, 273
value, VALUE (modal degree) 10, 47, 50, 53, 76, 178-183, 225, 227-229, 240
value (systemic value, *valeur*) 8, 12, 41, 86, 105, 113, 116, 121, 122, 123, 155, 203, 233, 242, 254
value (social order) 260
Value (participant) 70, 231, 237, 239
Van de Walle, Jürgen 276 n. 6
van Leeuwen, Theo 187-191, 194, 198
variation (codal, dialectal, registerial) 25, 48, 74, 88, 92, 105, 117, 157, 251, 274 n. 33
variation (typological) 120, 245-248, 271 n. 11, 272 n. 18, 279 n. 11
vector (pictorial, semogenic) 16, 21, 189, 190, 191, 249
Veel, Robert 140
Venn diagram 162
Ventola, Eija 100, 105, 110, 215
VERBAL ACTION, verbal action 139
verbal clause, process 69, 191
verb (auxiliary, lexical, modal), verbally ('as verb') xxi, 3, 5, 7, 39, 83, 84, 87, 118, 177, 179, 209, 225-226, 229, 233, 247, 249, 257, 258, 273 n. 24
verb class 86-87
verbal (PROCESS TYPE) 67, 68-69, 71, 75, 77, 153, 155, 156, 157, 167, 189, 191, 216, 218, 231, 272 n. 19
VERBAL ACTION 139

verbal group (complex) 44, 49, 50, 52, 74, 82, 83, 229, 245, 266, 273 n. 24
verbal operator 10
verbal response / non-verbal response 56, 100
verbal suffix 246
verbal system 277 n. 8
verbal text 237–239
VERBIAGE, Verbiage 47, 50, 77, 272 n. 19
Vietnamese xxi, 235, 271 n. 7, 277 n. 7
VISUAL, visual XIX, 27, 117, 139, 189, 206, 270 Chapter 2 n. 3
visualization, visualized 122, 124, 158, 206, 208, 211, 217, 218, 222, 229, 240, 241, 251, 267
vocabulary 179
Vocative 55
VOICE, voice 47, 49, 50, 52, 57, 59, 64, 83, 218, 234, 258
voice (reporter's voice) 157
voice auxiliary 83
VOICE QUALITY, voice quality 6, 29, 135, 136, 231
voiced / voiceless 123
VOICING 6

Walsh, John 15
Wan Yau Ni, Jenny 135
Wang Bo xxii, 79, 182
Wanner, Leo 88
Watt, David L.E. 130
wave (of information, textual mode of expression) 51, 105, 109, 127, 222, 272 n. 14
Webster, Jonathan J. xxii, 163, 165, 176
Weerasinghe A. Ruvan 165, 276 n. 6
Wegener, Rebekah xxii, 138, 141
Weinrich, Harald 153
West-Coast (Functionalism, Functionalists) 4, 74–75 26

White, Peter 69, 84, 90, 110, 136
Whitelaw, Casey 165
whole texts 208 108, 167
Whorf, Benjamin Lees 7, 257–258
Wierzbicka, Anna 86
Wignell, Peter 48, 88, 138
Wilkins, D.A. 177, 277 n. 6
Willats, John 29
Williams, Geoff 15
Winograd, Terry 165, 166, 175, 187–188
word 7, 9, 22, 44, 46, 48, 49, 79, 81, 82, 88, 91, 93, 105, 122–124, 128, 204, 225, 257, 270 Chapter 3 n. 1, 274 n. 31, 275 n. 45
word grammar (morphology) 203
word-&-paradigm (WP) 203
wording 26, 31–32, 36, 37, 51, 80, 89, 115, 120, 121, 142, 145, 233, 272 n. 19, 273 n. 22
wording potential 142
WordSmith 165
written language 110, 233
written medium (writing) 28, 110, 139, 157, 177, 179–180, 224, 233, 236
writing system 29
Wu Canzhong 147, 165, 185, 277
Wundt, Wilhelm 269 n. 5

Xuan Wenhui, Winfred 51, 179–181, 209

Yager, Ronald R. 221
Yoruba 247, 248
Young, Lynne 107–108, 274 n. 30

Zadeh, Lotfi A. 221
Zappavigna, Michele 194
Zeng Licheng 192–193, 204, 242
Zhang, Peija, Kaela 199
Zock, Michael 166